Praise from Students Who Have
Fallen Through the Tree...

My world exploded... If you know the thirst and haven't yet partaken, please throw yourself in the deep end. Jane Meredith will not disappoint. You can thank me later.   *Deb Gutteridge*

An embodied, enlivening, awakening magical mystery that touches every aspect of your being in both subtle and profound ways. The magic of it is still alive in every cell of my body sixteen months later.   *Rose Weaver*

Jane Meredith's Experiential Kabbalah class changed my life and my spirituality. I think about the Kabbalah and feel it often, as it relates to so much of my practice and life.   *Charlie*

This course is still working in me... a powerful teaching like a magical and mysterious key opening a marvelous variety of doors.   *Pistil*

Jane's guided journey through the spheres of the Tree of Life has introduced me to a most powerful model to understand the universe and set me on a path of lifelong exploration and practice.   *Bee*

I never had the patience or the will to read and understand Kabbalah before. The way you teach helped me to see the foundations and helped me to look at the books!   *Lilo Assenci*

An embodied experience that cracks you open to the wonder of self and the mystery of what lies without as reflected within.   *Sue Dunwoody*

I experienced vivid, somatic, ecstatic receptions of mystical truth. Jane's style of immersive facilitation enabled me to understand the Tree of Life emotionally and be able to intimately dance with the Infinite. Wondrous.   *Fio Gede Parma*

I'd read about the Tree of Life, but there's nothing like standing in each sephira and experiencing it fully. I remember being in Kether, looking down at the rest of the Tree and shaking with excitement.   *Cait Duggan*

Jane created and held a cauldron in which the energy of creation could be explored... thus making it available to gloriously enhance my daily life and magical practice.   *Kathleen*

Climbing the Tree of Life gives you ways to see the world around you and the world within you. I feel richer for having done so and am grateful to have had Jane as my guide. *Laura Moverin*

Working with the Kabbalah in a holistic way ... opened the doors to a more comprehensive and experiential understanding of the traditional Jewish teaching. *Aurelia*

The process of embodying the Kabbalah connected me to a deeper level of myself, accepting myself more completely so that I can be fully engaged with life. *Rae*

My previous attempts at understanding Kabbalah using various books were frustrating, uninspiring, and didn't take me very far. It wasn't until I learned to journey through the sephirot in a deep and grounded way that my understanding shifted—and a vibrant, living wisdom slowly began to unfold. *Kia LaFey*

I had read a lot about the Kabbalah before I joined Jane's study, but I had limited in-depth understanding. It was a journey of being active within each aspect of the Tree, which taught me so much more than just reading about it. It engaged all of my senses. *Diana Craig (Astarte)*

I loved the expression of art and magic in decorating the sephirot. To have a large-scale Tree of Life to engage with was so visceral. All this made studying the Kabbalah go deeper then ever before for me. *Jane Pawson*

Descending the lightning flash into the Kabbalah and exploring each sephirot for a month gave me a new sacred tree, a new way of connecting to spirit and to life. Thank you, Jane Meredith, for steeping me in the Tree of Life. *Mignon Rook*

Not only does Jane have a terrific knowledge and experience of the Kabbalah, she is able to guide students through this complex mystical system with ease and finesse. Her course was a fantastic introduction to the Kabbalah in theory and ideas as well as feeling into the Tree of Life and experiencing it through the body. *Simon Clay*

Mysticism, of its nature, is a multisensory experience. Jane Meredith's work brings Kabbalah out of the realm of musty dark libraries and into our lives in vibrant, personal, and deeply sensed ways I had not even dreamed of. As a Jewish woman (and magical practitioner of many decades), I found Jane Meredith's approach a beautiful exploration of this ancient mystical tradition. *Dawn Isidora*

My time spent with Jane and the lived experience of the sephirot was deeply meaningful. I found synchronicities illuminated and profound understandings integrated. The sensations and the turnings within my own self are something I have gained and an awareness that has stayed with me long after the class ended. *Ash-lee Jeanne*

[Jane's course is] a magical container to explore every depth of life and death … Journeying through the tree, I have had many an *aha* moment when experience and spiritual insight tessellate into place. *Susie Andrew*

Working with Jane Meredeth's experiential approach to the Kabbalah has provided me with a rich landscape [and] enriched my understanding of world philosophy and magic. *SusanneRae*

Your course helped me relate to the Tree in a very loving and embodied way— rather than just intellectual. It made exploring the Tree—and Kabbalah in general—more approachable and practical. *Ariadne Weaver*

Studying Kabbalah with Jane Meredith has helped me become more aware of how I perceive and move within and outside of the binary state of consciousness. Her class also helped me develop the tools to begin to metabolize opposites into a new third thing in an embodied way. *Madge Minnow Whaley*

Jane's Kabbalah course was a fascinating and well-facilitated doorway into the world of this enormous mystery … I would have never gotten started with this study without her guidance as it seemed too enormous to do by myself. Grateful ❤ *Sari Tolvanen*

Praise for
Falling Through the Tree of Life

This book offers a take on the Kabbalah that is experiential, poetic, artistic, and individual. Unlike anything you have read! For beginners and more experienced Kabbalists alike.

   Deborah Lipp, author of *Magical Power for Beginners*

A beautiful integration of Kabbalah and body/mind/spirit practices. Jane Meredith invites us to create an intimate relationship with the divine through breath, movement, and writing. The text is grounded in the author's experience as a spiritual teacher and practitioner, and she offers many insights on how to make the teachings of Kabbalah practical for contemporary seekers.

   Mat Auryn, bestselling author of *Psychic Witch* and *Mastering Magick*

A gushing love letter to Kabbalah, full of wonder and joy, *Falling Through the Tree of Life* invites the reader into a full-body, full-sensory, ecstatic experience of living in, around, and through the Tree. Jane Meredith meets the reader not as a lecturer but as a guide, pointing out signposts while inviting the reader to chart their own unique embodied understanding of the Tree through art, ritual, and trance ... I'll be returning to this book again and again as I deepen my work with the Tree.

   Enfys J. Book, author of *Queer Qabala*

What Jane Meredith has done with *Falling Through the Tree of Life* is to show an embodied way to connect with the Kabbalah. She outlines a way to take the wisdom of the system into myself, allowing for a visceral understanding. Jane shares exercises and deeply profound personal experiences that will help anyone to have a deep relationship with the Kabbalah.

   Phoenix LeFae, author of *Witches, Heretics, and Warrior Women*

Falling Through the Tree of Life is a living, breathing document. Reading it is an initiatory experience in itself. The work is flexible and accessible while still being complex and highly intellectual.

Lasara Firefox Allen, author of *Jailbreaking the Goddess*

There is never any question in *Falling Through the Tree of Life* that what you are reading can be put to use in your personal life and your path ... It truly is a book to both plant the image and the presence of the Tree of Life in your psyche and discover the tree of your life within.

Ivo Dominguez Jr., author of *Four Elements of the Wise*

I learned more about the Kabbalah in the first chapter of Jane Meredith's book than I have done previously from several other entire books and courses ... This book is a must-have for anyone who is interested in the Kabbalah or, like myself, anyone who has previously tried to delve into it and failed. Jane's book has been an inspiration; I cannot recommend it highly enough.

Rachel Patterson, author of *Curative Magic*

Practical, powerful, and profoundly inspirational, Meredith's guide to the wonder of Kabbalah and the enigmatic Tree of Life is a breathtaking love story to a mystery that was old when the world was new ... Meredith takes the reader by the hand and unpacks the magic of Kabbalah in a manner that is accessible without once detracting from its profundity.

Kristoffer Hughes, Chief of the Anglesey Druid Order,
author of *Cerridwen* and designer of *Celtic Tarot*

In this daring, poetic, and committed book, Jane Meredith gives us a Tree of Life that is truly alive: not a diagram or a set of doctrines but a vibrant and ever-growing Tree based in nature as well as ancient wisdom. This is a Tree that we experience by both surrendering to it and working with it at the same time.

Rachel Pollack, author of *Seventy-Eight Degrees of Wisdom*

Falling Through
the
Tree of Life

Jane Meredith is an Australian writer and ritualist. Her books include *Magic of the Iron Pentacle*, *Elements of Magic*, *Rituals of Celebration*, *Journey to the Dark Goddess*, and *Aspecting the Goddess*. Jane is passionate about myths and magic, co-created ritual, trees, rivers, and dark chocolate. The Kabbalistic Tree of Life is one of her special loves. She teaches internationally and is a teacher within the Reclaiming Tradition. Visit her online at janemeredith.com.

© Luke Brohman

JANE MEREDITH

Falling Through the
Tree of Life

Embodied Kabbalah

Llewellyn Publications | Woodbury, Minnesota

FIRST EDITION
First Printing, 2022

Cover design by Kevin R. Brown
Illustrations by Llewellyn Art Department
Interior book design by Rebecca Zins

Llewellyn is a registered trademark of Llewellyn Worldwide Ltd.

Library of Congress Cataloging-in-Publication Data
Names: Meredith, Jane, author.
Title: Falling through the tree of life : embodied kabbalah / Jane Meredith.
Description: First edition | Woodbury, Minnesota : Llewellyn Worldwide,
    Ltd, [2022] | "Interior book design by Rebecca Zins"—Title page verso.
    | Includes bibliographical references. | Summary: "A radical departure
    from traditional Kabbalah books, the rituals, meditations, memoirs, and
    hands-on activities in *Falling Through the Tree of Life* immerse the
    reader in living, breathing magic, transforming the Tree of Life from a
    complex topic into an embodied dance of love and learning"—Provided by
    publisher.
Identifiers: LCCN 2022010141 (print) | LCCN 2022010142 (ebook) | ISBN
    9780738768694 (paperback) | ISBN 9780738769202 (ebook)
Subjects: LCSH: Cabala—Introductions. | Magic. | Tree of life.
Classification: LCC BM525 .M466 2022 (print) | LCC BM525 (ebook) | DDC
    296.1/6—dc23/eng/20220504
LC record available at https://lccn.loc.gov/2022010141
LC ebook record available at https://lccn.loc.gov/2022010142

Llewellyn Worldwide Ltd. does not participate in, endorse, or have any authority or responsibility concerning private business transactions between our authors and the public.

All mail addressed to the author is forwarded but the publisher cannot, unless specifically instructed by the author, give out an address or phone number.

Any internet references contained in this work are current at publication time, but the publisher cannot guarantee that a specific location will continue to be maintained. Please refer to the publisher's website for links to authors' websites and other sources.

Llewellyn Publications
A Division of Llewellyn Worldwide Ltd.
2143 Wooddale Drive
Woodbury MN 55125–2989

WWW.LLEWELLYN.COM

Printed in the United States of America

Land Acknowledgment

This manuscript was researched, written, and lived on sacred lands, including those of the Parisi, a Celtic tribe who first settled on a few small islands in the middle of a river that came to be called the Seine in a city named after that tribe, and those of the Bundjalung and Arakwal people, also known as Northern New South Wales in Australia.

All land is sacred land. Living and working on it, breathing its airs, drinking its waters, and eating its food, it becomes part of us as we are part of it. We recognize it as the source and sustainer of life.

I offer my respect to the Indigenous guardians and custodians of these lands and their elders past, present, and emerging.

Kabbalist Acknowledgment

So many came before me. I am one speck, one fleck—and you another—in the great river of Kabbalists, mystics, alchemists, scientists, dreamers, visionaries, creators, and those in service to the divine, whatever names or titles they have held. So many libraries of wisdom, so many lifetimes of experience and learning, and all of it from the stars, from the original point of singularity, however far we've come, journeying through dark vast waves of space to this point of time and place.

Still we remember.

The Kabbalists. Those who received. They who sought knowledge to understand the world and their part in it, to define and glory in the Tree of Life. Those who dared, who studied and taught, who experimented, who argued with God, who risked their lives for it. Those whose lives were given to it or taken by it; those who were celebrated, well-loved, whose names were lost; those who were too radical or too obscure. To those whose words or thoughts have survived and those whose haven't, I offer honor and respect and gratitude. May my words find a way to describe what you also knew as sacred.

Sitting or walking by a river in afternoon sunlight, the light dances off the drops of water, sparkling briefly but meeting and changing the eye that sees it. Let this book be one of those dancing flecks of light on the great river that feeds the roots of the Tree of Life.

To the Jewish lineage I claim through one side of my ancestry: to the survivors, to the slain, to the mixing of race, religion, and heritage, I offer blood, acknowledgment, and gratitude.

contents

THE ABYSS

contents

invitation to the reader

Falling Through the Tree of Life is a radical retake on the powerful mystery of the Kabbalah.

The Kabbalah is a living, breathing magical system that invites us to remember our intrinsic belonging to the universe in every moment. We are one with the divine and all that is. The Tree of Life reveals, step-by-step, the unfolding pattern of becoming—the journey of spirit into matter and the great expansive arc from the Big Bang through to the outer stretches of the universe. It explains the place of living matter and individual consciousness that we inhabit. Here we weep, breathe, sigh, laugh, and delight in the layered push and tumble of mysteries, knowing our own bodies are temples and every moment is a gateway to the divine.

Perhaps you're following a Pagan, Wiccan, or other earth-based spiritual path and are seeking a doorway into this foundational mystery of the Kabbalist Tree of Life. Or perhaps you're a feminist, a Goddess worshipper, or a radical magician looking for work that speaks to you, that makes this topic accessible, relevant, alive. *Falling Through the Tree of Life* is written for you. Perhaps you already have a background in Kabbalah or have visited or explored it in other ways; this book invites you to taste, to dance, to breathe and live the magic of the Tree. Perhaps you have Jewish heritage or simply are called to the mystery; this book is for you. These pages offer an intimate engagement with the Tree of Life—one that is rich, gorgeous, and accessible.

This is an invitation to step inside the realms of Kabbalah. Previously you may have gazed at technical diagrams of circles and paths that seem to have no relation to embodied human life. *Falling Through the Tree of Life* makes sense of those diagrams because we learn how to inhabit them not just with our minds but with our bodies, emotions, and lived experience. The Tree of Life is not purely an abstract concept but a dynamic magical force. Working this way can open the doors to further Kabbalah study, reading, or magic.

The Kabbalah has often been presented as obscure, inaccessible, and dense, especially in books. Partly this is because it is an oral tradition, meant to come to life between teacher and students and the direct relationship between participants and the mysteries. Embodied Kabbalah asks us to recognize that we are alive! The Tree is alive! We are in direct communion with the mysteries, and our teacher is the divinity we were born from—and, on death, return to. Right now our living bodies are within the Tree of Life, and in discovering the wonders of the Tree, we discover ourselves. The Tree unfurls branch by branch as we inhabit, dance, and make love with this living magic. We fall in love at each step of the journey, meeting the world and pieces of ourselves in an unfolding map of the universe.

I've been actively working within the Tree of Life for more than ten years, though I don't think I've gotten to the end of it yet. This book offers my own experience and doorways into this life-changing knowledge. For over twenty-five years, I've taught magic and ritual, mythology and personal development, and published seven other books. Yet in this work I find myself trembling at the edges of the starscape, witnessing the universe unfold.

By blood I'm half Jewish, although not at all by custom, culture, or observance. Yet this magic had always called to me. I had heard whispers of it—extraordinary claims, hints, in all sorts of corners and circumstances. Perhaps you are similarly drawn to it. I brought everything that I am to the Tree: my feminism and Paganism, my writer's mind, my questions and yearning, and I found not just the Tree but myself, reflected back and then balanced, healed, changed. I understood my part in the universe—not intellectually, although that too, but viscerally, in my guts. I learned my part in the song of all things.

The Tree of Life has taken me and reshaped me and gave birth to me in the first place. I've seen the resonances in my dreams, how it's wrenched my magic about and forged it with starlight and rooted it in the body and left it spinning maps and stories in my head. It's freed me from everything and given me to everything and left me believing I understand something. Writing this book, I thought—if I can put this on the page, if I can offer this in digestible form, then all of my life makes sense. Perhaps I'm not qualified in the usual ways of Kabbalah. I'm qualified instead by sap and bud, by adventure and magic and love. It's a code, a force, a language made of sparks of fire so impossible it was written by the gods—except that it wrote the gods.

As a child I desperately wanted to understand: *Explain it to me.* The universe, life and death: *Why am I here? How can I live with this?* I got hints, and I always thought the answer lay in dreams, in forests and rivers and fairy tales, in geometry, and in sex: those things specifically. Now—almost unbelievably—I think I have it. Dreams, forests, rivers, sex, fairy tales, and geometry come together in the Tree. That understanding I wanted so fiercely—the Kabbalah gave it to me, opened the door, and I went through. It's impossible to write down, of course, or really explain it to anyone else. But maybe I can describe the door? Or, at least, the pathway toward the door?

I've been delaying starting this book for eighteen months. I wouldn't call it writer's block, exactly, more struck with awe. Observing my ideas has been like watching two octopuses wrestling and trying to trace the tentacles, but they're in movement all the time and as soon as I think I've seen the origin of one, it's tangled up with two or three others or has slipped out of my line of sight and is replaced by different suckering, twisting, grappling ideas. Suddenly all I've got is the distance between atoms or stars—and I'm falling through that space, almost without a thought in my head but understanding—something—if only I knew what that was. Oh yes, space, and the universe expanding all the time, like the sephirot being so far away from each other, exactly like atoms and stars—has anyone ever said that, that exact thing before? How can I research that?

The only way I was able to learn about Kabbalah—after years of trying to make headway through books that seemed written almost in another language—was to draw out a Tree of Life in chalk on a large wooden floor, move into it, and start creating magic there. From the first moment I walked onto that map, the Tree began to resonate through my body. I felt things. Saw things, understood things; concepts came into my mind and words came out of my mouth. I felt the living Tree moving and speaking within me, and I was within it.

This book invites you to do just that: to create your own map of the Tree of Life and immerse yourself in each of the *sephirot*, the ten different emanations of the divine, the singular of which is *sephira*. To learn bodily by not just reading and thinking but by inhabiting each of the sephirot in turn. The structure of this book follows the structure of the Tree. There are ten main sections, each devoted to one of the sephirot. Within each section are five different access points to learning.

Firstly, there is the theory behind this particular sephira—its nature and its role in the unfolding process of the divine toward embodiment, which is the whole journey of the Tree. Each section also has a piece on the mechanics of the Tree. We learn about the sephirot themselves; later we learn about pairs, triads, pillars, and paths in the Tree. Then there are processes: rituals, spells, trances, exercises; these offer immersion into each of the sephirot and build our relationship with each one. Another thread through this book is creative: the invitation to create a visual representation of the Tree in the form of ten decorated cardboard disks, which are then used in ritual and other processes. In this way, you can stand or sit in the Tree of Life, feel it stretching around you, and let it begin to whisper its secrets to you. At the end of each section are instructions on how to make these disks.

Finally, there is my own journey in the form of a memoir piece in each section. Memoir brings a living, breathing aspect to this work. Yes, one can read and learn about the sephirot and the Tree. One can understand the dynamics of how the Tree works. Processes, rituals, and creative expression are wonderful invitations, but unless we can see and feel what it's like to be immersed in the magic of the Tree—to inhabit it not just as an exercise but within the flow of life—it remains theoretical. At its most abstract, it's the diagram you can find on page 10. At the other end—the embodied end—it's how it plays out in someone's life, the immersive magic.

Memoir is intimate writing. Each time I've traveled through the Tree in the way outlined in this book—eight times and still counting—I've had a focus, an intention. One time I had leadership as my focus; another time I worked to bring magic more fully into my life. For this book I chose to record a journey of isolation to intimacy. By intimacy, I don't mean a significant relationship. I mean blasting my heart open with the forces of the universe to become a living, breathing vibration of love in the world, emanating through the dynamics of the Tree. These ten memoir pieces contain writing that is intimate, emotional, and sometimes sexually explicit. It might be confronting, surprising, or shocking. It's writing that's as close to the bone as I can manage—the raw, revealed self of me on the page. This is one of my experiences of the Tree of Life, falling in love with the world.

It's been suggested that it's unusual to equate sex and the Kabbalah so closely, though I think it's obvious. We're talking about the Tree of Life—and how does life arise? By sex, of one sort and another. Sex is the raw emanation of the life force. Maybe it's the sex of sunlight into sea water, maybe it's pollen on the breeze, and maybe it's two human animals scenting, tasting, touching, and merging. The whole of the Tree of Life is about sex. The bursting complexity of atom-building, the vast throbbing expanse of space, the irresistible seduction of a black hole, the layered delights of the world. And the Tree and trees themselves: roots into soil, branches to the sky. Birds nesting, insects burrowing, small animals living in, on, and within its trunk, branches, and roots. Caterpillars eating leaves, forming chrysalises, transforming themselves, bound to the twigs and emerging as butterflies, ephemeral symbols of the beauty of life.

Each student of Kabbalah has their own Kabbalah. Mine is the Kabbalah of Broken Butterflies, the briefest and brightest. Humans—all living creatures of this earth—are bright and beautiful. And compared to the Tree, to the divine, to the universe, we are impossibly brief, almost impossible—but then, miraculously, possible. Existing anyway in spite of our brevity. What could we understand in these few moments of universal time granted to us? Hardly anything. And yet—something. Caterpillars eat the leaves of the Tree on their way to becoming butterflies. They bind themselves to a tree in their process of transformation, trusting it to hold them as they dissolve their bodies and allow the wondrously named imaginal cells to re-create them in the butterfly form that will be birthed, open its wings—and fly—through the Tree.

How much can a butterfly know of a tree? It is fed, sheltered, birthed by the tree. Like the butterfly we stretch our metaphoric wings and flutter through its leaves and branches. The Tree formed us and so we belong to it, but we only know a tiny part, and that imperfectly from our butterfly or human experience. Rather than understand it, it would be more true to say we *are* it—the butterfly is the tree in butterfly form. I am the Tree of Life in human form. And in living, I'm breaking—breaking open from the chrysalis, breaking my heart with this life, breaking free from old selves, breaking down my form as I fall through life's journey from birth to death.

I think of us as shards, sparks of life flung out from the beginning of the universe, falling into this momentary form as human just as the Tree breaks apart into its many selves, its ten sephirot. They're always still part of the one, the All, just as we are. Merged together we are unbroken, and the very atoms of our cells remember that. But as individual selves we're always broken—broken off from the divine, though striving to remember and return with every heartbeat, every lover, every mystical quest and heart-stopping ritual. Breaking. It's not a bad thing but an opening, a remembering of who we really are. Like a butterfly, the tiny color-drenched feathers on their wings brushing off here, there, parts of them crumpling and tearing, each one of their lives a song to the glory of life. Like us. Flying and falling, intrinsically a part of All and yet just separate enough to hold the reflection.

Flying but falling. In the Tree of Life, we fall from the very top of the diagram—Kether, the divine, where all things are one—to the very bottom, Malkuth. It's like gravity: the only thing to do is fall. Malkuth is the living world we are part of, where we live and die and create love. Born through another human's body, we fall into this life, and at the end we fall out of it through the gateway of death. Alive, we fall in love—with ideas, with other humans, with land, with magic, and, if we are lucky, with life itself. Falling is surrendering, letting gravity take us, toppling from the divine to the human. It mirrors the biblical descent from Paradise to Earth and the fall of the angels. Falling is about separation and union—we fall away from the other, the beloved, the All, but we fall into the embrace of the lover, the dark earth, and fleshy incarnation. It's all about falling.

I'm writing this book to dare the dark stretch of the universe, to attempt to capture the bright sparks that whispered the gods into being, to redeem meaning. I'm a butterfly perched or falling through a tree so impossibly beautiful, the structure of the universe etched in its branches, the poetry of its leaves and buds. I ate of this tree; the cells of my body were formed by this tree as I lay bound in a cocoon to a twig of this tree in the imaginal realms, unknowing of what could emerge or how brief and bright my life would be, transformed and falling, so delicate and pigment-drenched with life force, and dying in each moment. I fell in love. In love with the breath of the Tree and each breath of mine shared with/from/through the Tree. The tree wrote me, the tree sees me, breathes me, holds me, forms and unforms me. My body, the tiny scraps of breaking wings, will nourish the earth-drenched roots, but in the moment I fly, flutter through the spaces cut out in space by this tree, and celebrate, dance, glory in what I am reflecting and born from and born for: this moment of Treeness called butterfly.

I'll write as the butterfly flies, falling on its brief and terrible journey, catching a wing and tearing those delicate feathers of color, time eating it up faster than it can fly, falling. I'll write for the butterfly and for love and impossibility.

background on the tree of life

The Kabbalah is a love poem that connects us to the pulse of all life—that same pulse that began the universe.

Kabbalah means "to receive." In opening up to all that we receive—this life, each breath, the beautiful world we live in and are a part of—we catch glimpses of the Kabbalah's breadth. While the Kabbalah's philosophies and abstract intellectualism may appear detached from nature, its key image is that of a tree, the Tree of Life. Diving into the depths, we discover Kabbalah addresses this very thing: our history of separation from the living world, something we can never truly be separate from. We could call what we are receiving the breath of the divine. In the Way of Kabbalah, a course taught by Rabbi David Ingber through the Shift Network, the rabbi suggested that the name of God cannot be spoken not because it is forbidden, which is what is commonly assumed, but because it is the sound of a breath. It is breath itself; perhaps it is every breath and therefore the very essence of life.

When we use the term *the Kabbalah*, we are discussing a body of occult knowledge that is received—either directly from God, Source, or the infinite, or through engagement with Kabbalistic practices, teachers, study, contemplation, and magic. Teaching, argument, and discussion can help to unpack this knowledge; one does not receive passively but actively. It is our own reception of this material, these raw experiences and our understanding of them, that makes us students of Kabbalah.

The Kabbalah is Jewish. Non-Judaic mystery schools, including Christian and occult schools, have versions of the Kabbalah, often written as Qabala or Cabala (or other variants), but these are based on, and build from, Judaic sources and writings. In other times and places, access to this material has been strictly regulated as to who is and is

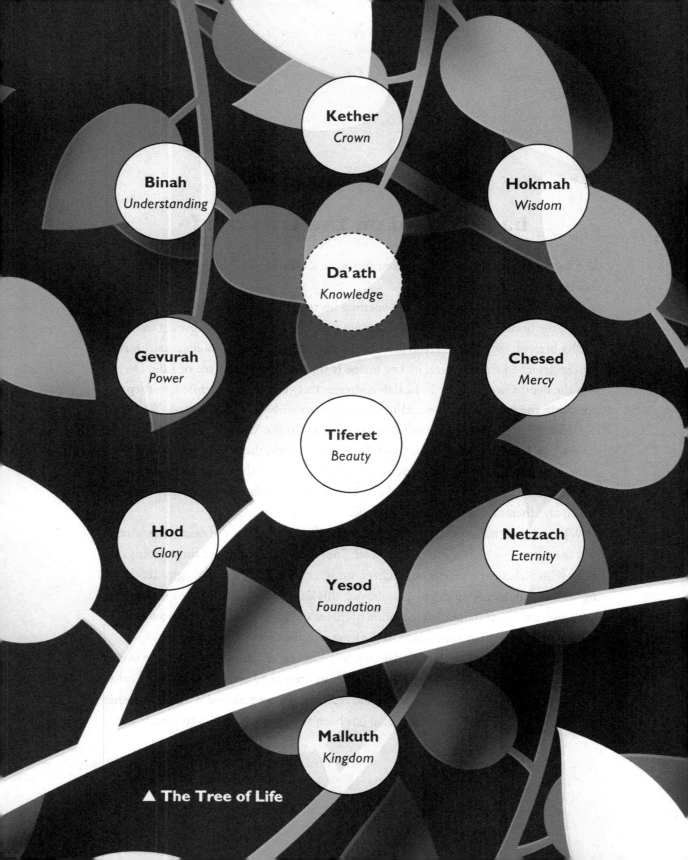

Kether
Crown

Binah
Understanding

Hokmah
Wisdom

Da'ath
Knowledge

Gevurah
Power

Chesed
Mercy

Tiferet
Beauty

Hod
Glory

Netzach
Eternity

Yesod
Foundation

Malkuth
Kingdom

▲ The Tree of Life

not able to become a Kabbalistic scholar. Contemporary schools and traditions may still place limits on participants according to their lineage, gender, age, or other qualifications, but it is also widely accepted that much of the more general material and practices are available to anyone who seeks them. This is not to say we will all have the same experience in, or even access to, learning Kabbalah, or that we can take for granted the privilege of studying it.

While there are sacred texts and teachings within Kabbalah, the essence of the Kabbalistic path is not fixed or linear but many-branched, revelatory, and experienced uniquely by each individual. Rather than learning by rote, inquiry and study are actively undertaken by the student. This exploration of the relationship of the divine to all things, and particularly to us human inquirers, takes place through ritual and study, practices and contemplation, discussion, dream, and examining sacred texts on many levels, the mystical and allegorical as well as the literal. The layers within Kabbalah are many, the field of material enormous, and the complexity and nuance seemingly endless. Its history is similarly layered.

Way back in the beginnings of the story, maybe during the Middle Ages—

oh before then, surely—

let's go back as far as the first Jewish sages, before the Old Testament was written down ... but of course Kabbalah's always been around. Always, people of faith have received the mysteries, one way or another. Human societies, even the smallest groupings of them, have always participated in this thing we now call faith, though surely for most of the history of humankind it was inseparable from living, from life. To have a separate concept—*faith* or *religion* or *spirituality*—shows how far away from belonging to the All we have journeyed.

There have always been ways to understand our intrinsic connection to everything: stories and myths, patterns in nature and human lives, movements of the stars across the skies, dreams and inner gnosis, rituals and ceremony. Poets, artists, mystics of all traditions, diviners, and oracles have dedicated their lives to discovering ways to access the mysteries. To the extent that the patterns of existence can be found within all things, scientists—from astrophysicists to biologists to geologists—as well as teachers, philosophers, architects, gardeners, therapists, and so many others offer us ways to understand these patterns.

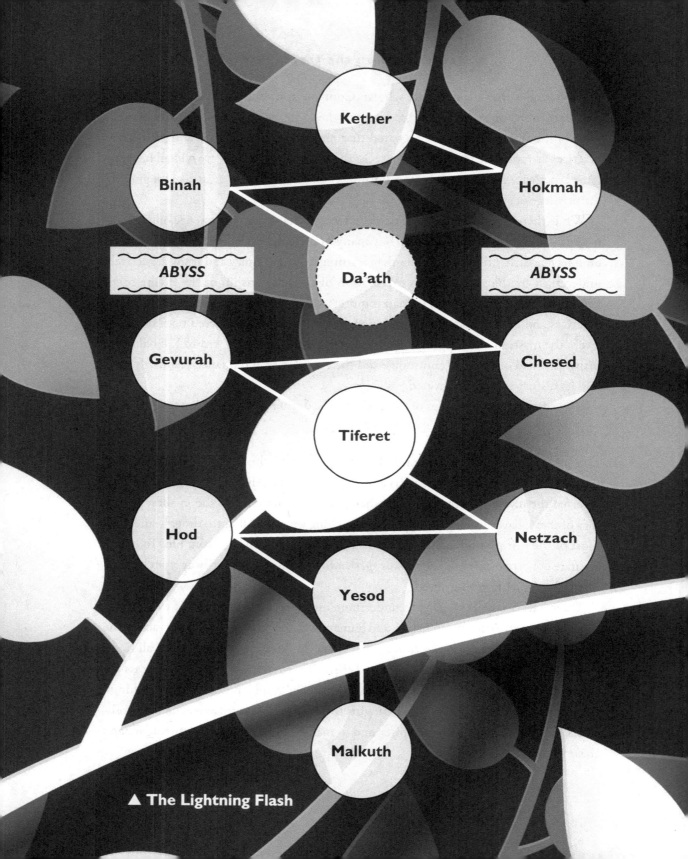

Kether

Binah

Hokmah

ABYSS

Da'ath

ABYSS

Gevurah

Chesed

Tiferet

Hod

Netzach

Yesod

Malkuth

▲ The Lightning Flash

To return to the Jewish Kabbalistic path, key periods in the development of what we now consider to be Kabbalah occurred at various points in history. Medieval Kabbalah was established during the twelfth and thirteenth centuries in Spain and parts of France. This period includes the writing of the Zohar, the key written text of the Kabbalah. Another crucial period of development occurred with Lurianic Kabbalah during the 1500s, named for the teacher Isaac Luria. He taught in Safed in Israel, then in Ottoman Syria. Luria established a form of Kabbalah and developed many concepts still worked with today, such as the shattering of the vessels. There's also modern Kabbalah, developed in the last hundred years or so, which includes non-Jewish schools of Kabbalah (Qabala, Cabala) and the work of the Golden Dawn, a tiny but very influential Western magic society that—by wildly appropriating everything they resonated with—combined many diverse systems, such as Egyptian mysteries, Western astrology, tarot, and the Kabbalistic Tree of Life.

It's often said that Kabbalah is a spoken tradition—a tradition of debate and discussion and shared exploration—and that any written material comes only third, after inner gnosis or experience, and after the spoken dialogue between Kabbalist students and teachers. Unlike the first two iterations of Kabbalah, written Kabbalah is static, fixed, can't respond or develop. The Jewish tradition of debate appears to include a rigorous argument with God, and this is considered an integral part of engaging with the mysteries.

Throughout much of the Kabbalah's history, there have been different schools or branches divided by purpose. I recognize these as a scholastic branch—those who studied Kabbalah for the sake of learning and knowledge; a devotional branch—those who studied Kabbalah to come closer to the divine; and a magical branch—those who studied Kabbalah to influence and change themselves and the world. These distinctions are not as relevant within contemporary Kabbalah, as most works and courses of study overlap several of these areas.

The Tree of Life is one of the central concepts in what we now regard as the Kabbalah. While we receive wisdom both passed down to us and imbibed directly from our experiences with the Tree, there's no belief within Kabbalah that what we have or know now is final or complete. Other versions of the Tree have existed prior to the current widely circulated one, and Kabbalah continues before, outside, and beyond the Tree.

The Tree of Life is a metaphor for the whole of existence. Usually shown as a glyph, it's considered an explanation of the formation of the universe, as well as of the relationships between all things, most immediately the relationship between ourselves and the divine.

This Tree of Life diagram consists of ten circles, spheres, or disks in a strict arrangement with each other. The circles are known collectively as sephirot, the singular of which is a sephira. They come in three pillars or columns, the center one longer than those to the sides. There is the dotted outline of an eleventh disk partway down the middle pillar. Each sephira is understood as an emanation from the divine evolving along the lightning flash (see page 12). The sephirot have Hebrew names. Translated to English, there can be some variation on their spelling and translation between sources and traditions. The names used in this book are Kether (Crown), Hokmah (Wisdom), Binah (Understanding), Chesed (Mercy), Gevurah (Power or Justice), Tiferet (Beauty), Netzach (Eternity), Hod (Glory), Yesod (Foundation), and Malkuth (Kingdom). The dotted outline is called Da'ath (Knowledge). The top triad of sephirot—Kether, Hokmah, and Binah—is separated from the rest of the Tree, also known as the lower Tree, by the Abyss, where Da'ath hovers.

The map of the Tree of Life operates as a blueprint of the universe, and its exploration forms the content of this book. The Tree can be used as philosophy, as a spiritual guide, and for practical purposes. We might work with it as an inspiration toward communion with the divine or for plotting the stages of a project or for healing and balance. It is a theology, an explanation of the relationship of the divine to the human and all other things. A concept known as Adam Kadmon plots a human body over that of the Tree, with the sephirot relating to different body parts, and in this way our connection to the divine becomes even clearer: we carry a map of it in our own bodies; as we map the divine, or all things, onto a tree, and that tree onto a human form. Amongst other things, the Adam Kadmon can be used as a way of working with distinct energies within ourselves.

Two powerful and apparently contradictory imperatives run through individual lives and within societies and cultures: to individuate and to surrender into union. Each person, each group and place in history finds different ways and a different balance to meet these imperatives. Within the Kabbalah these opposite-seeming demands, longings, or drives are reconciled. The Tree of Life elucidates this. In one direction—heading down the Tree—we become increasingly defined, separate, and finite. In the other direction—heading up the Tree—we become increasingly indefinable, merged, and infinite. Within the Tree these movements occur simultaneously. They are of equal importance and inseparable from each other. Kether exists as much to create Malkuth as for any other reason, while Malkuth exists to fully express Kether. The more individuated we become, the more fully we can, individually and collectively, express the totality of existence. The union we seek—whether with another; a philosophy, creed, or group; the divine; or through an artistic, intellectual, or political expression—returns all our differences to belonging.

The Kabbalah answers questions about the purpose and meaning of individual lives. As with the seeds of a tree scattered on the ground, we can see that the fate of any individual one of them matters not at all—it's chance, random, there's so many of them—and also that what happens to every single one of them matters totally. We can apply this directly to our own lives, seeing that both answers are simultaneously true. Within the breadth of life we are minuscule, microscopic, so it really doesn't matter much what any one of us does, yet at the same time it matters completely: every seed has the potential to become an entire tree. Within the Tree of Life metaphor, those seeds of ourselves are sparks from Kether scattered onto the ground of Malkuth. Our dance of union and differentiation echoes the fate of the worlds.

The Kabbalah has an immensely long and complex history, and these scraps of explanations are just the barest reference points. Many books exist on the history of the Kabbalah, different Kabbalistic schools, the development of Kabbalistic concepts, and the great teachers of the tradition. This book is not one of them, being both experimental and experiential. But however immense the Kabbalah might be—and since it describes everything, we can assume its immensity matches that of the universe—it's worth keeping in mind that really its origins are the same as our origins: stardust explosions and the beginning of something out of nothing. At its heart the Kabbalah is an offering from the divine that pours into us. And it's an offering in the other direction as well; like all the best love stories and spells, it's also an offering from the receivers back to the source.

how to use this book
practical guidelines

The Kabbalah is a vast, impossible, unwieldy topic.

Even taking one specific part of it, the Tree of Life, and addressing solely that part in its simplest rendition is still like navigating an immense, multidimensional, and shifting landscape with a compass, a piece of string, and good intentions. Comprehension of the whole is mainly gained piece-by-piece as we journey on foot over acres of terrain. It's hard to understand the mountains, the ravines, and the rivers that twist among them when one is on the plains or at the ocean. Egypt, New Zealand, and Hong Kong are one thing on paper, watching a documentary, or listening to someone's tales but another thing entirely when we are standing on that land, hearing its voices, experiencing its weather, digesting its food, and drinking its water. Until we have those experiences, it's impossible to really understand what it's like to be old or in a deeply loving relationship or to hear the words of the gods.

Experience of one sort or another is key to comprehension, and when we set out on an excursion as ambitious as this one, into the very Tree of Life itself, we want to gather as much experience as possible. Therefore, this book is based on experiences. This is unusual for Kabbalistic literature. As a Pagan version of the Kabbalah, it's responsive to the people undertaking it, their surroundings and relationship to the world and the earth. It places humans *within* the web of life (or the Tree of Life), not as the center, especially elevated or chosen by any god. As Pagans we work with embodiment, even while studying ritual and magic, even in deep trance, and certainly while exploring our relationship to the divine. My own experience has shaped every word, inclusion, and exclusion on these pages. The exercises that I love most are here. My own thoughts and understandings form the basis of the writings on the sephirot. And my lived experience, as I danced and swam and wept through this Tree of Life, is in the memoir sections.

The idea of this book is that it doesn't stop at my experiences but that it becomes the basis for your experiences as you explore the Kabbalah. *Falling Through the Tree of Life* invites strong intentions around creating experience for yourself. There's a process to create a personal intention for this journey into the Tree of Life in the process section on "Setting Your Intention" on page 51. There are exercises, practices, trances, and rituals throughout the book, structured to create experience and learning—for example, exercises on the pillars of the Tree in chapter 4. Yet another set of experiences is to create your own version of the Tree of Life with ten disks that represent your experience of the sephirot. How to do this is outlined at the end of each chapter.

But the most important, central—crucial—experience this book offers is to inhabit the Tree of Life and each of its sephirot in turn. To experience this magic not from the sidelines but from within. To be a reader who throws yourself into this waterfall of Kabbalah, one who is embraced by the Tree, speaks with it, lets it dance through your mind and alter your vision and open doorways, both within and also in the external world; imbibing this experience as you would a piece of fruit plucked from the Tree itself and offered to you by a serpent. Oh yes, we are right back there in Paradise—curious, tempted, trembling on the verge of revolution in the walled garden—*Will you eat?* Having eaten—when we have tasted, chewed, swallowed, with juices on our mouths and fingers—ingestion will occur ... and with it, knowledge.

That's the poetic form; there's also a practical form that accompanies it. That is, to inhabit and work intimately with each of the sephirot as you read and travel through this book.

What You Will Find in This Book

Each section of the book begins with an in-depth piece on one of the sephirot, outlining its nature and different perspectives on how to understand and relate to it. The first section is about Kether, the first sephira, and they continue on down the Tree in order, following the lightning flash. Starting with Kether is a mixed blessing; because Kether is the Mystery of Mysteries, it's almost impossible to explain, yet having a sense of Kether is essential for understanding the Tree of Life. The further down the Tree we get—and the further into the book—the more the concepts we are considering become recognizable and even mundane. So we examine ineffable mystery with Kether and move to division and union with Hokmah and the potential of creation with Binah; by the time we get near the bottom of the Tree, we are discussing gardens and libraries. Finishing at Malkuth we contemplate our own lives and deaths.

After each of these studies on an individual sephira is a piece on the mechanics of the Tree—how it actually works. These develop sequentially and build on each other, beginning with unpacking sephirot themselves and moving on to pairs, triads, pillars, and so on. Each section also contains three processes—a mix of rituals, trance, and other experiences. There is also a memoir piece of my own embodied journey with the Tree of Life. These are emotional, sometimes erotic, and some contain explicit sexual description. Each one is my rendition of what it means to be falling in love with that particular sephira, to be a living, breathing, embodied human creating fierce Kabbalah magic to invoke intimacy and deep connection.

The final piece in each section is an invitation to create a Kabbalah disk—a decorated piece of cardboard—to represent your journey with, and understanding of, that particular sephira. These disks are used throughout the book for ritual, contemplation, and creative exploration of the Tree. They are a crucial part of this journey, as they capture our own experiences and make these tangible; they become magical artifacts with which we can create powerful, life-changing magic and ritual. When internal work, revelation, and transformation move into the material world in this way, we receive their power as a reflection of our own and can dynamically move among them, weaving changes that affect all the worlds.

At the very end of the book is a piece on Da'ath, the missing or hidden sephira (or non-sephira), as well as the ritual skills appendix. There's also the resources I've found most helpful, a glossary, and references.

How to Approach This Book

There are several ways you can approach this book. You may choose simply to read it from start to finish. You might choose to read through, doing some or most of the exercises and rituals as you progress. Or you might read the whole book first and then go back to the beginning, this time inhabiting the sephirot one by one and doing the accompanying rituals and processes. You can also skip around, reading all of the pieces on the sephirot or all of the memoirs or whatever pieces speak to you. If you are already familiar with the Tree of Life, you might begin with reading about, or doing the processes for, a particular sephira or a group of them. You might want to learn firstly about pillars, triads, and paths before going back to other sections of the book.

There's no single way to do it. If this is your very first meeting with Kabbalistic material, it makes sense to move through the book as written, from start to finish, doing the exercises as you go. You can read and work alone or with another person or with a group. There's more details about how to undertake this work with a group at the end of this section.

Essential Skills

The rituals and processes in this book take several magical skills for granted—including grounding, entering and leaving trance, and acknowledging sacred space—and refer to them only briefly. At the end of the book, the appendix explains these ritual techniques. You may also wish to refer to other sources and teachers for more in-depth instruction.

Learning as You Go

This is not a stand-alone book. The material written on the Kabbalah is vast, possibly endless, and could doubtless fill many libraries. As this is not a traditional, historic, or occult book, I encourage you to read widely within your interests as you travel these paths. There is a constrained list of resources that I have found useful or inspiring at the end of this book. What has often inspired me, Kabbalistically speaking, has not been traditional Kabbalah books but rather writing in the realms of nature and science, decolonization and sociology, and speculative fiction. Some contemporary Kabbalah books stand out to me—first and foremost, Rachel Pollack's brilliant, incisive, and user-friendly *The Kabbalah Tree*, written around Hermann Haindl's artwork of the same name. Sadly out of print, this book is available secondhand and digitally.

Falling Through the Tree of Life is a journey as we inhabit each sephira in turn, in the order of the lightning flash, heading downward. At Malkuth we zap up to Kether in one movement. This has a deep, unfolding logic—a progressive system in the direction of embodiment as we drop through all the levels between divine and earthly—although within the Kabbalah, Kether is just as embodied as Malkuth, and Malkuth exactly as divine as Kether.

How to Inhabit a Sephira

When we inhabit one of the sephirot, we dedicate ourselves to it, usually for a fixed period of time. During this time we focus our curiosity, our study, meditation, trance, and personal inquiry upon this particular sephira and its attributes. For example, if we are spending a month with Gevurah, as well as reading about and researching that sephira, we might also focus on its attributes of power and justice, learning about them within the political world we inhabit, in magic and mythology, and in our own lives. How do we show up for personal power and shared power within groups or communities? How do we meet the persistent power-over our society offers as the main model of power? What are our powers—magical, personal, interpersonal? Where do we stand with justice? We might choose to relate to red deities—the Red Goddess, the Red God, Mars, Kali, fire spirits, and others we associate with this color. We might deepen into menstrual and fertility journeys and magic. We can also lean further into concepts of boundaries, severity, and restrictions—where do these impact us and where do these support us? What learnings can we undertake to become more skilled in those things?

In our trances or meditations, we will focus on Gevurah's red color or its warrior aspect; we might perform rituals of release and ending, we might work fire or flame magic, we might study consent and learn about boundaries. Many of us will notice that boundaries and power are huge themes in our lives, with people and situations seeking to push or step over them constantly. To inhabit Gevurah we will have to be willing to learn its lessons in action, not just by reading or thinking about them.

Gevurah is a whole world—or a whole way of interpreting and being with the world. If we work with it for a month, by the end of that time we will have some understanding of this sephira. Then—probably having felt that we are only just beginning to know it, that the doorway is now open—we'll leave Gevurah to travel into the next sephira, Tiferet. Our new month will begin as we open to beauty—all the ways we are and are not living a life of beauty, all the ways we do and do not see beauty reflected back to us in the world, Tiferet's place in the Tree…After a month of this, we will move on, yet again, to Netzach.

Two Paths Through the Tree

There are two different paths you can take through this book, inhabiting each of the sephirot in turn. These are the linear path, beginning with inhabiting the sephira of Kether, and an alternate path, which begins with inhabiting whichever sephira you are most drawn to.

Both paths follow the lightning flash—which means that each time we move to a different sephira, we move one space down the Tree in a zigzag motion (see diagram on page 12). The sole exception to this is that after we have spent time with Malkuth, the lowest sephira, we move all the way up the Tree—again via the lightning flash, but in the opposite direction—to Kether. Theoretically it would be possible to move upward stage by stage and then downward all in one go, but I have chosen this direction to emphasize the progression of the divine toward embodiment and singularity into complexity.

The Linear Path

With the linear path you follow the book through from beginning to end.

Begin by inhabiting Kether, the first sephira. During your time in Kether, read about and relate to Kether, as well as cover the content of section 1, which is about the ten individual sephirot. Do the processes in section 1. At the end of your time in Kether, make your Kether disk and move, via the lightning flash, to Hokmah, the second sephira. Once there, you work with Hokmah and the content and exercises in section 2, which is about pairs in the Tree of Life. After making your Hokmah disk, you travel the lightning flash again to arrive in Binah and the third section of the book, which is about triads.

I have taken this path several times. If you have little or no experience in magic, Kabbalah, or self-guided study, you might choose this path through the book as being simpler. Or perhaps you want to follow the outline of the book and the progressive logic of the lightning flash. But there are also good reasons to choose an alternate path through the Tree.

The Alternate Path

An alternate way to work through this book is to start the journey in a sephira that isn't Kether—any of the other sephirot. This is the path I have almost always taken through the Tree, and there are several reasons for choosing it.

If you are working with a group (see more information on this below), it is most optimal to have everyone in a different sephira so that the whole Tree is inhabited, so to speak. If you had a group of ten people, this means only one person will begin in Kether—the nine others will all begin elsewhere.

Another reason you might choose an alternate path is if you have a strong affinity—or curiosity or impulse—toward one of the sephirot that isn't Kether. Given the magnitude of the journey through ten sephirot, the vastness of the material, and the relative obscurity of Kether, beginning somewhere we feel at home can bring us more gently into this study, creating a path individually tailored to where we are in our lives. The sephirot we successively move into after the first one will be those heading down the Tree (unless we began in Malkuth, in which case we first have to head upward), which will develop on the themes we were drawn to with our starting place.

To follow this path through the Tree of Life, begin with the trance exercise "Meeting the Ten Sephirot" on page 54 to find your starting place. If you are working with a group, do this exercise together and decide collectively who will begin in which sephira.

Each section of the book is linked both to a sephira and also to a structural aspect of the Tree. For example, section 1 contains the material both on Kether and on the sephirot themselves. Section 2 contains both Hokmah and the material on pairs in the Tree. Section 3 addresses Binah and also triads. Section 4 holds Chesed as well as the pillars of the Tree.

Following the alternate path through the book means you separate these pieces out within each of the sections.

Let's say you start your journey in Tiferet. If you were spending a month with each sephira, during your first month you would read "Tiferet: Heart of the Tree" in section 6. But because it is your first month, the rest of the material you would work with would come from section 1—"The Ten Sephirot of the Tree of Life" and the exercises in section 1: "Setting an Intention," "Meeting the Ten Sephirot," and "Journey with a

Sephira." Section 1 also includes a memoir piece, "Alone," as well the initial instructions for creating disks. Following these instructions, you would create your first disk, which would be for Tiferet. While you are in section 1, you might also choose, for curiosity or context, to read "Kether: In the Beginning."

When you are complete in your time with Tiferet, you would travel the lightning flash downward to the next sephira, Netzach. Then you would read the piece on Netzach, "Netzach: The Garden," in section 7. Because it is your second sephira and your second month, you would read section 2's piece on the structure of the Tree: "Pairs in the Tree of Life," and do the exercises and rituals from section 2.

Each sephira will have perspectives on every structural element of the Tree; thus, it is just as useful to learn about the sephirot or about pillars or polarity whether you are with the sephira linked in the book to that structural content or another sephira altogether.

The book is laid out in a way that you can easily follow this alternate path, skipping around to read about the sephira you are currently with but otherwise following the order of the book. The table of contents at the beginning will assist you.

Working Solo or with Others

This journey through the Tree can be undertaken solo; the book is written to facilitate that. However, it can also be done with a group of people—from two to ten or, indeed, twenty or any number. I have traveled this journey both with a group and solo, and found both rich and magical. Your decision to work solo or with a group may be purely practical or a preference. Either way, the Tree of Life—with all its sephirot, pillars, paths, and magic—is waiting for you.

Working Solo

Many of us choose to do magical work and ritual alone. Working solo you get to set your own pace and are free to explore and journey exactly as you wish. You can have deep, magical, and ecstatic experiences and be completely in relationship with the Tree of Life. This may suit you or be your only option. Going through this journey solo, it can seem as if the Tree is filled with ghosts, or aspects of former selves. Holding my place in Tiferet, I turn and look through the Tree and remember my experiences in Gevurah, Binah, Kether as if looking at mirrors of myself through time. Maybe you will choose to work through the Tree solo to begin with and later find others to share the journey.

Working with Others

Working with a group in the Tree of life is rich, rewarding, and really my favorite way. You can inhabit the Tree together, work some of the rituals, trances, and exercises with each other, and have discussions. The dialogue, the spark, and the degrees of difference—and therefore insight—are just so much more than can occur alone. The complexity of the Tree comes to life with human beings, as well as facets of the universe to interact with—or when the facets of the universe we're interacting with look and behave like human beings. It's true that, working solo, one can debate with books, have intense mystical, trance, or magical experiences, and even argue with God, so to speak. But there's nothing quite like having a human or a group of humans to discover the Tree with and play in it together.

It is possible to have everyone start at the same sephira and continue all together through the Tree, but a much more dynamic and powerful arrangement is to have people holding different sephirot, and this is how I have always done it. You may have less than ten people, in which case not all sephirot will be filled at any one time; exactly ten people, meaning one person for each sephira; or more than ten people, meaning some people double up within sephirot. I have done it successfully all these ways. It doesn't matter if you have less people than sephirot—the Tree holds itself, regardless, and will be entirely magically present whether people are inhabiting every position or not. The emphasis is on the Tree and the sephirot—the people are the additions, moving around the Tree like birds or butterflies.

You can create shared disks. For a group, I use much larger cardboard disks, and each person adds a piece of decoration to each one as they spend time with it, resulting in shared composite creations. I've also done this work with groups at a distance from each other, meeting regularly on virtual platforms, both for live calls and keeping in touch via social media, each with our own disks but following the program together and talking and discussing as we go. One lovely thing about working with a group is hearing everyone's version, over time, of Hokmah, Tiferet, Yesod, and all of the sephirot. Hearing the different reflections and discerning repeated themes feels to me like hearing directly from the sephira itself.

With the processes, exercises, and rituals, it's great to have one or two people run them for the group—different people each time. You may prefer to design your own work and rituals inspired by what's in this book or what you find elsewhere. With a group of people, you will have a whole array of resources at your disposal; you may have an artist, a drummer, a scientist, someone who knows about permaculture, another who's studied breathwork, and another who practices yoga and meditation. People's magical and ritual backgrounds may vary widely so that each person brings a variety of skills, points of view, and previous experience into the group. Or you might do this work with a group who already work ritual and magic together. You can choose to each read different Kabbalah books or sources and pool information.

If you are working with a group, it's great to have some guidelines. For example:

- ▶ What is the group's purpose?
- ▶ How often do you meet and where and for how long?
- ▶ How many meetings are there in total?
- ▶ What will happen during the meetings?
- ▶ How can someone leave the group or join the group?
- ▶ What roles exist within the group, and how can each person contribute?
- ▶ What avenues exist for feedback, conflict resolution, and support?

Timelines

A realistic timeline to read and actively work through this whole book would be ten months or ten moons, one for each of the main sections and therefore one moon or month for each of the ten sephirot. This would allow time to do the reading, fully engage with each of the practices and exercises, do the journaling, create a disk, and learn—for a little while at least—to see the world through the lens of that sephira. A very concentrated journey could take ten weeks. An alternative is to simply move through the book at your own pace, however long that takes, so some sections might take a month and others a fortnight or several months. It can be harder to complete a process that has no fixed timeline or endpoint, and the time spent in each sephira will be unequal, but it may suit you or just be what happens.

Kabbalah Warning

The Kabbalah and its glyph of the Tree of Life is a system that will embed itself into your thinking and forever afterward change the way you experience magic, see the world, and think about yourself.

The Kabbalah is a mass of contradictions. Everything moves down—and up—the Tree at the same time. It's the blueprint of the universe in a map that can't be properly seen due to the blinding light. The sephirot, the precious vessels of the divine, have shattered, and we are working amongst the shards, although they continue to function as the vessels known as sephirot on the Tree. We work with concurrent truths, dissecting each thing to examine it this way, then that way, then the other way, while saying all are true and none are true. The Kabbalah turns itself—and us—inside out.

Each time I do it, working through the Tree of Life is like updating the software of my brain. The download occurs; everything reorganizes itself and looks … different. I understand more and, having understood, can't return to my previous ways of thinking or being in the world. The Kabbalah rewrote me and is still rewriting. I'm a work in progress. This is a warning as well as a temptation. For me, this magic contains a comprehension of the world, of the divine, and the purpose of my life that I never thought to achieve. Its magic is so potent I'm often afraid of it—not in a malignant way, but more in the way of having to trust throwing my body off the edge of the planet into the slipstream of the Milky Way. If you do this work, I'm pretty certain you won't be the same afterward.

The Kabbalah will eat you. This is not a bad thing. I've lost count of the people who've told me of the ways their thinking has been challenged, has changed; of the deep personal healing they've received or significant rewrites of their understanding of themselves and their lives—not by doing intentional magic but simply by inhabiting the Tree and showing up to its learnings. Maybe it's not that the Kabbalah will eat you exactly, but more—as we eat of the Tree of Life, we remember that we belong.

We rediscover our intrinsic belonging to life, the universe, and the divine; it's inescapable. There's nowhere else to go. We are already deeply part of this system, and finding ourselves there (already there, always having been there), something shifts within us—doubt, fear, distress, disorder—and we are reconnected.

Think of these pages like leaves of the Tree held within your hands or fluttering before your eyes or unfolding, word by word, into your ears. Turn the pages and step within—

pick up the apple and bite into it.

We catch a glimpse of the universe—the stars at night crowning our world, gazing into someone's eyes, or realizing a deep truth of our heart—it's a breath, a moment, a heartbeat, a stab of light in the darkness, and we are free—in free fall through life and death; for a moment our questions cease, embraced in the moment and released—and we fall

Tumbling, dancing through the distances of our lives, we exist as a flash of wisdom, an echo of the great and impossible whole; laughter and tears are the same, and we have no expectation of arriving, only the falling, we are already there, we never left and only by imagining we left, briefly, can we see feel know touch this stream of infinity we are bound within, our very bodies, every atom, true to that above all

Here we are, surfacing, plunging again into deeper realms of understanding, maybe it's a dream or a vision or a still true moment in time, we are sundered from the collective and falling, surrendered, feeling the dense pull of atoms— those same ones that were there at the beginning of the universe the start of time and always retain that memory no matter how far they travel

Take a breath and dive, free fall into the becoming as time streams past and we breathe the primal nothingness and then—tumbling tumbling the great fall as we know bone deep each particle exploding with knowledge and the aeons wash through us, birthing and dying with stars, the impossible, light falls, the leaning toward becoming tips and we, still falling

Time is part of us endlessly as we
turn and plummet downward,
always like rivers like waterfalls in
waves like streams of blood or stars
or words the mercy of the world, of
worlds still being born with each
word and breath and thought, each
one endless the great outward flow,
the force of it the grace

Tumbling further, into polarity
now time has started, feel its
power pulsing though each particle
defined, separate, each moment,
each form, created before dissolving
again and the yearning toward
life life life the fierce cradle of it,
the beat of it, the crucible the rigor
formed and unformed endlessly
and we're falling, tumbling through
form after form bound and
unbound

Into brightness, beauty the sheer
shining light the heart of mysteries
as we fall and fall our hearts burst
open the way they were always
meant to, radiating light, or love,
and we surrendered joined forever
to all that is if we ever lost our way

or forgot every heartbreak takes us
there again

And again into the birthplace
the garden, eternity that walled
paradise with no walls, it's the flow
of ceaseless creation, we are created
and creator living a thousand lives,
a thousand thousand of the wind
and bees, the goannas and ferns,
every rock and wind and us born,
falling, naked free and bound in the
flow of becoming, endless becoming

Known, through and through
each chemical each calibration
each vibration in the glory of it
all of starbursts infinity the vast
boundaries of the universe as
above so below and still falling, a
butterfly pinned in time knowing
everything, everything a butterfly
could, a vast library of taste and
breeze and nectar, sex and death
and tumbling into the world

Through dreams through layers of
becoming the foundation of all that
is or might be, we are nearly born,
nearly fixed swimming in the ocean
of all that is, the realms layering

. . .

themselves through us and over
us and into us until we crack and
complete in the same moment and
falling

Falling falling forever into a
moment and the moment's here
this form takes a breath, opens
its eyes, welcomed to the kingdom
flesh and form, grief and pleasure,
to the place where spirit is matter
and it all matters, always forever
each action thought choice ... Falling
into life, a form of light a butterfly,
breaking in the tides of becoming
and unbecoming and it's all here all
real all now

A whole life as part of this earth,
an expression of star, from the first
to the last breath and maybe, on
the final outbreath, light is born
again from us as we return to
where we never left, one with the
infinite all this time and flaring,
impossibly bright, too bright to see
to understand

Here is the apple. Some call it the
fruit of the knowledge of good and
evil, others say it is eternal life,

others still that to eat this fruit is
to partake in all the forms of the
universe, and others that it is to be
released from slavery. Take it. Eat
of it, for that is what humans do.
Smell the perfume, feel the weight
of it, and bite—delicately in a rush
as if there were no choice as if every
choice existed as if we were every
choice ourselves, each one of us,
sensually, pragmatically, longingly,
fearful, hesitant eager delighted
laughing weeping bleeding dying

oh

eat.

On an outbreath, maybe the first
ever outbreath, watch as Kether is
born from the mind of the Nothing
as all possibility. Flaring impossibly
bright—too bright to see, to know

I

Sephirot in the Tree

AIN

AIN SOPH

AIN SOPH AUR

Kether
Crown

The Tree of Life begins with a single sephira—an emanation, an existence—that emerges from the great Ain Soph, which is both nothing, no-thing, and also endless light. The Ain Soph is sometimes divided into three segments, generally called Ain, Ain Soph, and Ain Soph Aur, all of which are degrees or aspects of nothingness, of increasing potential or density. The sephira that emerges contains everything, in contrast to the nothing. It is the arrival of the point of singularity into the map of becoming. It holds all potential.

There was nothing, then there was everything. Perhaps, unspoken, is the idea that at some stage there will be nothing again. Meanwhile, we have this single sephira, one that contains all. This fundamental essence that comes out of the nothing is known as Kether, Crown.

This moment of becoming at the first sephira—which at this stage is the entirety of existence—can be seen as having happened already or as still in the process of happening. In the same way as the echoes or ripples of the Big Bang are still occurring, the birth of Kether is still vibrating through the Tree, through everything. It has both happened and is still occurring, in the same way as our own lives have happened—we've come into existence and are still happening. The sephirot, and therefore the Tree or the seed of the Tree, are born in the form of Kether. This creates the beginning of the pattern of what will become the Tree of Life. The great story of Kabbalah has begun.

Kether: *In the Beginning*

Kether is the first, and at this stage the only, sephira.

I Am That I Am is a phrase commonly associated with Kether, showing it is both irreducible and at the same time encompasses all possibilities. We can unpack this string of words to learn a little more about this most distant and essential sephira. In Pagan circles these words are used to illustrate the oneness of all things, showing our intrinsic belonging to everything. In the Old Testament "I am that I am" is the Name of God told to Moses. These English words are an inexact translation, as the English *am* is only inferred in Hebrew, so it could be translated as *I that I*. Other interpretations include *I will be what I will be* or *I will create whatever I create*, but most commonly it is understood as *I am that I am*.

It is difficult to describe Kether for many reasons, one being that the notation *I* is already all of it. So any extra words at all, such as these words or those that follow, cannot be more purely Kether than that single mark on the page. Extra words seek to explain and court the totality of that concept. Then we pack all the words up and return to the beginning, to I. Now we might be able to accept the concept more deeply, letting go of the complexity of explanation to allow the pure *yes* of existence, the *I Am* to strike us, own us fully, allowing the cells of our body to receive and reverberate with the ripples that this *I* creates, like the lightning flash itself, throughout time and space from the very beginnings to the very end of the universe, with us caught in that string of happening, vibrating.

I describes Kether in its absolute fullness. Everything is only ever, and can only ever be, experienced through the medium of an I, a viewpoint, an existence. Kether's viewpoint and existence is the original singular one and so, in effect, the only one. Entire unto itself. This is not so much an omnipotent God—there is nothing to be omnipotent of except itself—but a singularity. Because this *I* exists so powerfully and entirely as the beginning of everything, by necessity all future *I*'s refer back to that original *I*, as if they borrowed a little scrap of that concept and operate as a fragment of it. We can imagine a prism, endlessly faceted and of which we are each a facet, but the facets are only able to exist at all as faces of the prism, the original *I*. Each of us small *I*'s is a unique lens viewing the universe.

In holograms each pixel contains the whole image in miniature, but they need to be added together for the viewer to actually see anything. Following this analogy, perhaps we cannot even see ourselves without the other pixels or facets, the other *I*'s that, like ourselves, also each reflect the original *I*. Each of us projects into the world slightly differently, just as each pixel appears at a different place in the hologram, and thus has the ability to have a different experience. When the hologram or prism is consciousness itself, or the everything of Kether, these mini lenses or ways of experiencing the world feed back information and experience to the whole. This hologram is not static but endlessly becoming—and since there is nothing apart from itself, it is endlessly becoming itself. The *I* does not have a full stop after it but is the first word in a sentence, inferring that it is evolving or in process.

To elaborate on this wonder a little, we add another word—*Am*—so that the explanation of Kether becomes *I Am*, while understanding that any additional attempt at clarification actually muddies and detracts from the meaning because the *I* is already everything. Kether is all things, as represented by the *I*. However, the *Am* shows that the *I* exists—I *am*—if that wasn't clear before. Perhaps it helps us to define this *I* more completely. The *I* is in current time. It is not *I was* or *I will be*, it is *I am*. This *I* is everything that is existing currently. Although because Kether is everything, this naturally includes the *was* and the *will be*, but all of it is present, existing now, within the *I*—so *I Am* in the present tense contains also the past and future.

In an attempt to clarify this even further, we add a third word, *That*, so the descriptor becomes *I Am That*. Each additional word is distancing us—both along the page and conceptually—from the actual thing that is Kether, the I. However, by now we might understand that this I, which exists, is *that*—that is, all things, each thing. So the *I* exists and it is all, both within itself and including everything that is temporarily not itself or perceived as being outside itself. *That* could be the universe, a sunrise, a poem, a crying child, a drop of dew, a rotting corpse. *That* is each thing. Each thing belongs to the *I*, is part of the *I*, and in this way things are not separate, but all one thing—*That*, which is *I*.

In the ways of poetry and philosophy, we then add yet another word, a further *I*. The description is now *I Am That I*. This clarifies that the *I* is itself. The whole phrase has become circular, reductive, and even more mystical than the brevity and obscurity of the first three words on their own. Each time we add a word to refine and clarify meaning, we are also stretching further and further away from the actual meaning. Perhaps this second *I* attempts to return us to the beginning, circling the phrase upon itself. With this addition the *I* is in existence, is everything that is and is not immediately itself, and it is also consciously aware of itself: *I am that I*. In English we could play around with that further: *I am that Eye, Eye am that Eye, Eye am that I*.

Curiouser and curiouser! we might say along with Alice as we fall down the impossible rabbit hole past pieces of our old life that we cannot hold onto or witness the stars exploding into being at the beginning of things or as the mythic shards of the vessels of sephirot shatter and spill through the universe. With each layer—of another word to this description, of meaning or interpretation that we add—it's important to hold onto all previous layers as well, to allow the layers to complement each other and add nuances rather than obscure or overlay each other. Thus Alice's new world always remained a commentary on her original world rather than a replacement; that was the power of it and the source of its mystery. All of the becoming of the universe—of which story we are a part—never changes or takes away from that initial happening. Although so many things exist, including all the sephirot beyond Kether, these are all still expressions of Kether. Through obscuring and elaborating things in impossible ways, the original becomes clearer. So we hope with the Kabbalah.

There is one word yet to add to our essential explanation of Kether, and this repeated word *Am* continues the circular motion of the sentence *I Am That I Am*. By now we are not expecting this descriptor to make sense in the ways we are used to definitions making sense of a complex concept. We have surrendered into the rhythm of it, the cadence and deductive logic; we have accepted the facts conveyed so briefly: that Kether is, exists, is everything, is aware, and in this second *Am* is completed. To understand even more fully, we will temporarily insert another word so that it reads *I Am [everything] That I Am*. As the explanation gets lengthier, it becomes less exact, so that while *I am everything that I am* elucidates the obscurity of the structural concept, it also reduces it in an unfortunate way. After all, each thing we can think of could be described that way: a chair is everything that it is; a flower, book, or breeze is exactly everything that it is. So this sentence ends up not distinguishing Kether in any way from any other thing. But this is also the point of this explanation—because Kether, in being itself, *is* every other thing, includes every (other) thing within itself. I am that I am.

In English the word *I*, that single stroke on the page, replicates and is almost indistinguishable—in handwriting it may be indistinguishable—from 1 (one) in the international mathematical language. I and 1. I = 1, 1 = I. The value of one, both mathematically and linguistically, is that it is other than nothing, more than nothing; therefore, it is also the opposite of nothing. Every other whole number comes from adding ones together, thus one contains all whole numbers. Kether, emerging out of Ain Soph, that great infinity of nothingness, is the sole thing that exists, and thus it is everything. Every other thing that is and is yet to be will come from Kether. Therefore, it is 1 as well as I. From Ain Sof came the I. From nothing came the everything. From zero came the one. They are bound together as two parts of a single mystery, for really it is never exactly explained how anything at all could come out of nothing. We can say that it happens, but not how or why it happens.

This is apparently how the universe began, some estimated 13.8 billion Earth years ago. The theory of cosmic expansion explains that prior to the Big Bang, all energy that would later become matter and radiation belonged to the space-time fabric, so it was there ... sort of. Stephen Hawking's no-boundary proposal suggests that as we follow the arrow of time backward, past the Big Bang, the singularity gets smaller and smaller but never entirely doesn't exist, although time and space as we know them cease to exist. According to astrophysics, the start for our universe was a singularity, a single point of density with everything-that-is in the same place, contracted into an almost impossibly tiny point. At this point everything could have collapsed into a black hole (returned to nothingness), but it didn't. Instead, everything rapidly expanded and cooled—and is still in the process of expanding and cooling. Thus one could say the Big Bang, or the Great Becoming, is still in the process of occurring.

Kabbalistically speaking, we are trying to peer back at the Ain Soph in an infinity of no-thing-ness, which is also all the light that ever was or will be. From this emerges the concentrated point of singularity, the beginning of everything—or Kether, the I Am, and all that is. These stories parallel each other, and we see echoes of them in the great creation stories of mythology. *The waters came into being and the earth rose up from them ... In the beginning was the Word ... The sky separated from the earth and between them all beings came to life ... A vast egg hovered on the infinite waters waiting to crack open ... The rainbow serpent dreamed its way across the lands and in its wake the landscape was born.*

Why did this even happen? The Kabbalah might answer because there is an inclination toward becoming. Because the potential was there—the potential of Kether all the way through to Malkuth—and in that potentiality, that focus, room was made for existence to begin. *Tzimtzum* is a Kabbalistic concept explaining what happened in the moment before there were moments, before time and the universe came into being. How do things progress from the Great Nothingness into anything at all? Tzimtzum posits that a contraction occurred, squeezing the nothing together so that there would be space left over for something to come into being—a space for creation, and into that space, or out of that concentration, emerged Kether and therefore all of the Tree of Life.

It's a lot more complicated than that, and perhaps there's really no separation between what we call a singularity and what we know as the Big Bang; they are all part of the same event. Perhaps our singularity was a sort of bubble universe, being born from within a much vaster, already existent universe. Or it's a circular event, proceeding through births and deaths on a universal scale, so this was not the first or only time this occurred, and the end of one universe triggers or arrives into the beginning of the next. But it seems clear to me that the Tree of Life and the birth of Kether out of the Ain Soph are as much a blueprint for the beginning of the world as the variants on the Big Bang theory. I would even posit that they are the same theory expressed differently.

The beginning of the Tree of Life with Kether is the beginning of everything, since prior to that was only nothing, although perhaps not in the ways we are used to thinking about nothingness. This process—to move from nothing to everything, from zero to one—looks like a balancing act. They balance each other out: on the one hand nothing and on the other everything. Perhaps we get a sense of it if, clear-eyed, we try to remember back to before we were born—nothing—or after we are dead—nothing, again, forever—and contrast that with being alive, any of it, including this moment, writing or reading these words. Oh this is everything, especially compared with that. But—everything. Every experience, thought, sensation I have ever had is bound into this life. It's my everything. Taken on a grand universal scale, this is Kether.

An alternative to the linear view of "first there was nothing and then everything" is that the two are not sequential but instead are dualistic states—opposite sides of the coin, so to speak. One does not follow on from zero; instead, it is utterly other. The universe is not so much born out of nothingness as the opposite side to a (perhaps still continuing) nothingness. After all, our universe contains black holes, dark matter, and dark energy; we are very far from being able to define or understand the mechanics of these things or what parts they play in the production and continued existence of the universe or, indeed, any other universes. Ain Soph is continuous and still present above the Tree, as well as the non-sephira of Da'ath within the Tree, as if to make room for all these unknowns.

To explore this concept of dualistic states, let's look briefly at computer code, which is a series of zeros and ones, 0 and 1. There is the nothing, zero, and the something, one. These binaries correlate with off and on, which is how they work in computer code. This one is, by default, everything, since the only other thing that exists is zero. Between them, one and zero, they describe everything, which is the all and the nothing. The every-thing and the no-thing. We could also say the yes and the no(thing). Kether is this great *yes* to life, just as the 1s in the computer code are the yeses ... until they appear, it's all nothing. But it's not just that the 1s make things happen, although they do; it's that they wouldn't be possible, they couldn't be effective or have meaning, unless there were also the 0s. It is circular, deciding which came first, 1s or 0s, chickens or eggs, somethings or nothing, because certainly they tail each other, follow and swallow each other, bounce off each other, complement and deny and adore each other. This adds some strength to the lack of linearity idea—they coexist as opposite states, between them describing ... everything.

Ain Soph is both nothingness and endless light. The singularity point, if it existed, certainly contained light, as it contained everything. When this light first contracted or came into being, then to expand throughout Kether and the other nine sephirot, or through the expansion of the universe, it stretched the universe out or spilled from sephira to sephira through the Tree. *Light in Extension* is an occult maxim with various or clouded sources. Perhaps the Golden Dawn, that tiny but very influential occult society in the early 1900s, made it up or were divinely inspired; it's been linked to ancient Greek or Egyptian temple, or initiatory, rites. It has an alternative, equally attractive rendition of light rushing out in a single ray. Both seem to describe this event—the Big Bang, or point of singularity and rapid expansion into a hot, dense mass that became our universe—and this birth of Kether from Ain Soph. I think the notion behind this—that light extends itself, is its own reason for extension—speaks to both the spilling out of the light from Kether into what becomes the rest of the Tree and also that phase of universal explosion—the Bang part—as well as many other phases of this transition through our universe's journey, or the journey of working with the Tree of Life.

Light is intrinsic to our stories about the beginning of things. But there's a deep mystery underlying the concept of light. Although humans can perceive light either as waves or particles, according to Marcus Chown in his book *Quantum Theory Cannot Hurt You*, this concept is more of an explanation of observed behavior rather than a statement about what light actually is. He says it's like explaining two sides of the coin—the two sides in this case being particles and waves—without explaining the coin. A bit like our zeros and ones earlier, we can say that they are opposing states and that both exist but not how that could be so. According to Chown, we still don't know what light actually is and have no way to explain how or why it appears either as waves and particles, and thus—as far as we can tell—it is either both waves and particles simultaneously or something else entirely. "What light actually is is as unknowable as the color blue is to a blind [person]" (Chown 2007, 19).

What light actually is, is … unknowable. This seems irrefutably relevant to Kether and the Kabbalah mysteries. The Ain Soph, all of the sephirot, and most particularly Kether are associated over and over again with light. A light so bright it cannot be looked at. A light so strong that it splits open the great nothingness and becomes itself. A light which is everything that can ever be, exploding into existence. Ten emanations of light. The light of flaming, living words spoken into the nothing, which becomes the beginning of the universe, of time and existence; becomes Kether, the genesis of the Tree and, therefore, everything we know or can imagine or understand, including things we don't understand: Ain Soph, how something arose from nothing, the movement of zeros into ones, and what light actually is.

With the teaching of light in extension, we see that the light is not passive, merely existing, but that it is in some kind of action, it is happening. Specifically, it is extending. It is not just particles, but also waves. It is light (a particle or many particles) in extension (in a wave). This fits well with what we know of the Tree—that light extends from Kether down through all of the Tree, spilling or flowing or creating as it goes.

The particles and waves of the Tree of Life are concurrent. This light is not just literal, such as daylight or starlight, but the holistic concept of light, including the ability to perceive and thus the potential to understand. It also concurs with what we know of the universe: that it is expanding, extending outward into the beyond, presumably into nothingness or creating somethingness where before there was not. When we acknowledge we can only describe some of light's (apparently contradictory) behaviors—*Oh we have this vital thing, crucial to everything, that does this and that, but we don't actually know what it is*—that sounds the very essence of Kabbalah. And Kether is the repository of it, the starting place, the place where this light is held, birthed, realized, becomes—and then it extends from there. Perfect.

There is one further concept I want to explore in this unpacking of Kether: the concept of entangled particles. Entangled particles is a definition applied to subatomic particles of matter that have become close to each other and intermingled in some way. What's most interesting about this is how, from that point on, they continue reacting as if they were connected, even if they are vastly separated from each other. Chown says "they lose their individuality and in many ways behave as a single entity" (Chown 2007, 167). The example often given is that if one particle were on earth and the other of the entangled pair on the far side of the moon, when we flipped the one on earth, instantaneously its partner on the moon would also flip.

At the time of the Big Bang or just before it, absolutely everything was squished together into a beyond-imaginable tiny space. This is a Kether moment: all is one. But it means that all the particles were entangled, not just one with one other but collectively. This is absolutely what we know of Kether, that all things are this one thing. Then these same particles were flung out through all the creation of the universe as *light in extension*. But once a particle has been entangled with another particle, it never forgets. I think this means that every particle in existence remembers every other particle, and Chown agrees: "All particles in the Universe are to some extent entangled with each other" (Chown 2007, 59). Therefore, to some extent, they must continue to respond to each other and react as one.

Where did the universe begin? Where did the Big Bang happen? Right here, because all heres were squashed together in the same place and only since then have spread out far away from each other. So it happened in my study, so to speak, and everywhere else, too. Where is Kether? Right here in the components of my computer, in the breeze outside my door, in the white cockatoo that swooped low and fast past my window just moments ago, in the future moment of you reading these words, in the cup of tea you might make or the chair you sit upon. Kether is everything, is all, is everywhere because it was the only thing, it was everything packed up tight, so now it is everything expanded out, and the very cells of our bodies are part of its composition.

All of the ten sephirot emerge from Kether—they are each a reflection of or a part of Kether. In some ways they all are Kether, just looked at through successive layers of darkness, less light. We unpack the Tree into its ten sephirot much as we unpack scientific theories, or the I Am That I Am, in order to be able to put it back together again with greater understanding. Each of the sephira emerges from Kether—or from all the sephirot that come before it, all of which came from Kether—and each one is a way of understanding Kether. It's not so much that Kether split into ten pieces; Kether remains entire and complete. It's more that with each different sephira we are offered a different way to view Kether, thus elucidating, somewhat, the vast complexity of the everything. The sephirot are like us, each a lens through which the divine, or the All, becomes itself.

Here we have the whole universe separated out into millions beyond millions of bits and pieces so that at the subatomic level one would imagine they are impossibly diverse, distant, and irredeemably lost to each other, and yet they all remember each other, they have all been part of one thing, entangled, and to some extent they must continue to operate as one. Kether. Kether before there was anything, and Kether when the whole Tree exists, and Kether as the spark of the universe even as the universe expands endlessly outward, further and further away in time and space from that Big Bang moment. Yet it turns out that time and space are mutable, and the one constant in the known universe is light. Chown again: "The constant thing in our universe isn't space or the flow of time but the speed of light" (Chown 2007, 93). Light—this thing that appears as both wave and particle and therefore places itself beyond being knowable to us—is the constant. Light in extension: the speed of light. Quantum physics and the Kabbalah seem united in this study of the unknowable nature of Kether.

We are particles of light within the wave of light; they exist simultaneously but can only be viewed, or maybe experienced, separately. Thus we, in this moment, are having the particle experience of being separate. The Tree also has its particle experience of being ten sephirot. But that is only one way to understand it. The other way is as a wave, where everything is part of one thing; the whole Tree belongs to Kether and is described by Kether, and all the particles of this and every other world are actually in wave form. We can understand the wave experience a little by realizing our existence as profoundly part of the whole, whether that whole is our lines of ancestry, our belonging to the human species, the intrinsic expression of this planet that describes each of our lives, or our belonging to the universe and the divine.

This first sephira in the Tree of Life, Kether, is everything; Kether encompasses past, present, and future and is in some way self-aware, as well as contains all oppositions and being the beginning of time and the explosion of light. It is the All.

The Ten Sephirot of the Tree of Life

The circles, or disks, on the Tree of Life glyph are known as sephira (singular) or sephirot (plural). Various other spellings exist, including sefira, sefirot, sephiroth. The word *sephira* refers to an emanation or attribute of the divine, the All. It also refers to the disk we see on the map of the Tree of Life (see page 10) and the realms we associate with that particular sphere. Each sephira has a name—usually written as an English version of the Hebrew word, and thus often with several possible spellings—and a word (or sometimes several variations) in English that is accepted as a workable translation of the name. In contemporary Kabbalah studies, each one also has a color associated with it. To go further into occult and Kabbalistic magic, there are correspondences with Names of God, angels, and many other things, but these are beyond the scope of this book and are easily sourced elsewhere.

There are ten sephirot. But there is also Da'ath, the non-sephira. So there are ten—but sometimes eleven—sephirot, or one becoming-sephira, or a place allowed for a potential eleventh sephira, which might only be the shadow of something that isn't there. Each of the ten sephirot holds a distinct place on the map currently agreed upon as the Tree of Life; even Da'ath is always in the same place. Although this has existed in different formations through previous centuries, no contemporary author that I've read disputes that this map, this Tree, is the one we are working from; it is the most useful one we currently have.

The sephirot are distinct from each other, but this distinction is more of a gateway into understanding than a profound separation between them. They all remain essentially part of Kether. At the same time, they are completely different from each other. Each one has a name and a location. The sephirot do not blend, or drift, one to the next. They are utterly themselves; you cannot describe one by starting with another and then add or subtract something. They do not overlap but are more like ten oppositions. They spill, one from another. As each new one emerges, they balance and polarize each other in an endless dance. But they don't merge at the edges. Instead, there are distinct paths that lead from one to another.

The Tree itself is one whole thing. But our minds work best in dissecting information, breaking down complexities, and attempting to understand discrete parts, only later allowing them to add back together into the truth they always were. So we examine the sephirot individually, remembering all the while that they are not ten different things. They are not even ten different aspects of the same thing. Rather, they are ten different ways of viewing the same thing: Kether.

We might think of holding up a pair of colored glasses to the scenery of our lives: with pink glasses, everything is pink, or pinkened, although actual pink things are no longer so noticeable. When we hold up green or blue or yellow glasses to look through, those same scenes or objects become green or blue or yellow; we are still looking at the same scene, but things are noticeable in different ways, and different things are noticeable. The sephirot can be worked with as lenses, and each will bring attention to a different set of actions, understandings, and patterns.

Another way to explain the sephirot being all different but essentially one thing is to say that the first sephira, Kether, is unveiled. Because it is so bright, it is unseeable and completely unknowable. The second sephira, Hokmah, is the same thing but with a veil placed over it. Because the veil dims the light a little, we might catch an after-impression of something—probably of the veil. So we can both see more because of the veil, but paradoxically we also see less because it is veiled. At the next sephira, Binah, a second veil is placed over what we are looking at and thus we are now looking through two veils. We begin to see the veils a little more clearly because what we are trying to look at is dimmed, although also obscured. This process continues through all of the sephirot until we get to Malkuth, the final of the ten, where we are looking at ten veils and can finally see something more clearly, although of course we can't really see it at all because of the veils.

The sephirot offer ten different entry points to understanding aspects of the Tree of Life. Before we can put them together as one Tree or begin to explore the structure of the Tree's pillars, pairs, triads, and paths, we need to examine the sephirot individually. At the same time we try to remember that these are aspects of the All that are not truly separate.

Kether

Kether, pronounced *ket-er* and translated as Crown, is at the top of the Tree of Life. It is the first sephira and is bright white, brilliant light. It's what we might think of as the Big Bang, that impossible searing flash still rippling out to the edges of the universe. It's the moment where everything became possible but nothing yet quite existed. It's the heart of stars, the place where hydrogen compresses and compresses until it starts creating other atoms. Kether is a furnace that both contains the possibilities of all future shapes yet has no shape itself, and no shapes can exist within it. It is ever-becoming, and from this all things come. It is the All before anything else. It is almost impossible since it came from nothing, and yet it has created all possibilities just by existing. Kether is the One, the whole undivided, complete and entire unto itself.

Hokmah

Hokmah (sometimes written as Chokmah) is pronounced *hok-ma* and translated as Wisdom. It is the second sephira, born out of Kether and usually colored gray. It is below and diagonally to the right of Kether. Hokmah is the moment past that first moment. Everything was packed entirely within Kether, and then separation occurred. If we think of the beginnings of the universe as we currently understand it, there's everything compacted into one thing (Kether) and then, less than microseconds later, it explodes or expands. This is Hokmah coming into existence, with separation and otherness. In many creation stories the creation of the world is associated with longing or love. *The Star Goddess reached out into the curved mirror of dark space...* Hokmah is the curved mirror. It reflects back, endlessly, all that has been, and yet it is distinct from Kether. Hokmah means division and difference exist.

Binah

Binah is the third sephira. Translated as Understanding and pronounced *bean-ah,* it completes a triad with Kether and Hokmah, directly across from Hokmah, on the left. Its color is black. Binah is the place where birth and creation become possible. At the beginning of the universe, following the discrete actions we believe to have occurred, there's the All (Kether), a splitting apart (Hokmah), and a becoming of pieces of the universe as atoms rapidly expand away from each other. That movement is Binah. In the myth of the Star Goddess, we might see Binah as Miria, the beloved who is reflected in the Star Goddess's mirror and drawn forth to begin the dance. From this, all of creation will be born.

Da'ath and the Abyss

The non-sephira of Da'ath (pronounced *dah-t*; some people say *dah-th*), Knowledge, hovers in the realm of the Abyss, which is a space or gap that separates the upper and lower parts of the Tree of Life. Da'ath is lightly marked into the glyph of the Tree with a dotted outline or sometimes left off entirely. It has no color. We can imagine the Abyss as the pause between the All and the creation that emerges or between the Big Bang and what follows, as the rapid expansion slows toward the rate we are familiar with today, allowing stars (and therefore all other things) to be born. The Abyss is rarely specifically marked in on the map of the Tree.

Chesed

Chesed (sometimes written Hesed) is the fourth sephira, pronounced *hess-ed* and in English called Mercy or Loving-Kindness. It is positioned underneath Hokmah in the right-hand pillar and diagonally across the Abyss from Binah. Its color is sky blue. Chesed is considered the top, or the first, of the lower Tree, which is composed of the bottom seven sephirot. Each sephira has aspects of flowing forth, but in Chesed this is particularly strong. The essence of the top triad must move through Chesed into the lower Tree, where it will manifest, unfold, and resolve. As the universe comes into being, there are masses of matter expanding outward, endlessly spilling forth from that first set of actions. Chesed seems the place where we begin to experience love as caring or compassion, rather than Kether's piercing, radiant light of existence, Hokmah's separation and loss, or Binah's chthonic birth and becoming, all of which we could also understand as love. Chesed's love is the kind that reaches us when we are lost, that we can feel as a cloak of warmth and support.

Gevurah

Gevurah, pronounced *gev-you-ra* and translated variously as Power, Justice, and Strength, is the fifth sephira, across from Chesed and directly below Binah in the left-hand pillar. Its color is red. It is a place of balance and boundaries, where all that has flowed through from Chesed, and indeed all that is flowing downward from Binah, is measured and contained. In the story of the universe becoming, that endless flow from Chesed starts to form dense masses where galaxies will be birthed. Gevurah is a place of limits—not limits as we commonly think of them, where something is made less of, but limits where what is precious or vital is contained; we might regard Earth's atmosphere as a limit. Without that limit, that boundary, the planet's life could not exist. Gevurah is the honed ferocity of perfection, where only what is just survives.

Tiferet

Tiferet, pronounced *tiff-er-et* and translated as Beauty or sometimes Truth, is the sixth sephira. Its place is in the middle pillar directly below Kether, although the non-sephira of Da'ath lies between them. It is a golden, sunny yellow. Tiferet is the heart of the Tree. If you fold a diagram of the Tree lengthwise and top to bottom, the fold lines will meet in a cross in Tiferet. It also carries many heart-related qualities such as openness, compassion, and joy. Tiferet represents our sun sparking into being, thus beginning our solar system, a local version of Kether. Tiferet forms a triad with Chesed and Gevurah and offers an integration between those two powerful, opposing energies. Holding and balancing so much, the tenderness of beauty reminds us again of the heart. This is Kether brought into the lower Tree through all those temperings of the previous sephirot.

Netzach

Netzach is pronounced *net-zark* and in English is usually translated as Eternity. Netzach is the seventh sephira, underneath Chesed and holding the bottom of the right-hand pillar. It is green. It is where all the potentials, the idea-forms of the things we know and love, come into being. Possibilities of ferns, forests, seas, clouds, butterflies ... all exist in Netzach. If existence is having thoughts toward creations, here are the sketches. Netzach is strongly resonant of the Garden of Eden, perhaps because of the green color and also the mythos with the Tree of Knowledge. All green divinities belong here—those who dwell in, embody, and protect forests and wild places. Netzach combines Hokmah's original separation and the pouring forth of Chesed.

Hod

Hod, pronounced simply as it's written, *hod*, with the translation into English being Glory, is the eighth sephira, across from Netzach and holding the bottom of the left-hand pillar, directly under Gevurah. It is colored orange. I think of Hod as the place of systems: the periodic table of elements, the biological classification system, as well as natural and human laws. If the idea of a fern comes into existence in Netzach, in Hod all of its requirements are understood and categorized so that such a thing as a fern could actually exist. Netzach is the concept of a piece of clothing or a house or a book or a solar system; Hod is the mathematical laws, materials, and structures that are required to bring it toward existence. These two are said to be more closely tied together than any other pair. Hod draws on the birthing power of Binah and the precision of Gevurah to make form a possibility.

Yesod

Yesod, pronounced *yess-odd* and translated as Foundation, is the ninth of the sephirot. Yesod is purple. It is on the middle pillar, underneath Tiferet, and forms a triad with Netzach and Hod. Yesod gathers what have until now been three streams of the Tree—the left-hand, right-hand, and middle pillars—and funnels them together. This blending of such distinct differences creates many layers and nuances and a dizzy feeling of rush and chaos. Yesod is linked with the subconscious and Jung's collective unconscious, a realm where the archetypes are formed, live, and emerge from. It is the sephira most directly and obviously accessible to us from Malkuth through to the rest of the Tree. Access points such as dream, trance, and myth are the territory of Yesod. In Yesod whatever has been made possible, conceived, divined, and delineated all through the rest of the Tree is on the cusp of becoming.

Malkuth

Malkuth, pronounced *mal-coot*, is the tenth and final sephira, named Kingdom in English and considered to contain this earth and all that we know and experience. It is directly under Yesod in the middle pillar and is the point on which the entire Tree rests. Our whole lives, from birth through death, exist within Malkuth. Often it is shown as divided into four quarters, colored citrine, olive, russet, and black, perhaps referencing the four elements. I usually choose brown for earth and as the combination of all previous colors. Here all that has been explored or made possible within the Tree comes into manifestation. Here is the stardust from the formation of the universe. Here is separation, birth, endless outpouring of potential, death, and strict limitation; joy in the expression of life force and the touch of spirit; the endless possibility of force and the precision and law of form. This is the realm where the collective and individual dreams of Yesod unfold in beauty and terror, all of life. What began in Kether is completed in Malkuth; Malkuth is considered the perfect expression of Kether.

process | Setting Your Intention

Setting an intention enhances our work within the Tree, giving direction to our magic and learning. The Tree is so vast—its sephirot manyfold and complex, its paths and learnings labyrinthine—that it's easy to feel swamped, directionless, uncertain. An intention will remind us where we're headed and direct us to tasks and areas of relevance along the way. Sometimes people have a layered intention or several intentions; everyone doing this work seeks to learn more about the Kabbalah and the Tree of Life. But what's your deepest intention in life right now? How would it be to carry that intention through this magical Tree that describes the universe and offers a potent, visceral magic?

Intentions guide much of our magical work and are considered a magic in their own right. When we set an intention, our focus sharpens and refines, our thoughts keep returning to it, and we are much more likely to direct our actions toward it. When offered a choice or an opportunity—perhaps in the outside world, perhaps in inner work—if it reflects our intention, perhaps we will take the risk to change, to try something new, or to break a pattern. It's like marking out our destination on the map: we've chosen it, now we need to find a pathway there and continue making choices that help direct our journey. Sometimes this becomes simpler the closer we get, as it's more or less right in front of us, but other times we experience powerful internal patterns or external fixtures in our lives like roadblocks, and we may have to stop and reassess—both how deeply we are committed to that destination and how to go around or dismantle the roadblock.

Something often quoted around magical intentions is be careful what you ask for—the implication being you will surely get it, and it may not be in the way you expected or wished; therefore, care and clarity of intentions are highly recommended. If the intention is a powerful life-changing one, be willing to let go of, or change, everything that is currently in your life to achieve it. Being careful around magic is never a bad thing; however, risks are involved if we want change. So we set an intention to find love and realize along the way we have to let go of many old relationships and self-destructive habits to learn a whole new way of being within intimate relationships. Or we set an intention to pursue our career, only to find we have to move cities, postpone having a family, and so on.

Working through this book and the Tree of Life, we may set a straightforward intention such as *To learn about the Kabbalah* or *To connect with my Jewish heritage*. We may set a more specific intention such as *To develop my magical skills and understanding* or *To follow this course of study for a year*. Or our intention may be very personal: *To find the essence of myself* or *To learn to live in truth and love*. There are set-and-forget intentions, where an intention is created within deep layers of magic and then released to work its own way, and these can be very effective. To some extent, once we are deep in the work, any intention does its own thing. But we will largely be working with consciously made, and held, intentions.

The type of intentions I like best for this work are focused on one issue or theme that is strong in my life and that I don't yet know how to meet. One year I worked the Tree of Life with an intention around developing my leadership; another time it was to deepen into the relationships I truly yearned for. This exercise will guide you to set an intention that's right for you. Throughout your journey with the Tree of Life, you can return to this intention and watch its unfolding.

How to Find and Set an Intention

TIME: 30 minutes

YOU WILL NEED: Your journal and a pen

I recommend having a journal dedicated to your work in the Tree of Life. I prefer hardcover, unlined blank books so I can draw diagrams and pictures more easily.

Before beginning, you might like to cast a circle, sit before an altar, clear your space, meditate, or dance.

Leave the first few pages of your journal blank for a title page and a diagram of the Tree of Life.

Ask yourself *Why am I studying the Tree of Life?* Write the answers down in list form.

Then ask *What changes am I seeking in my life?* Again, record your answers as a list.

Thirdly, ask *What do I seek to learn magically, energetically, or in my life?* Write down the answers.

Place the pen down and allow your eyes to close fully or partly. Breathe deeply, letting yourself sink below the level of thought and words. You can place a hand on your heart if you wish. What are you feeling? Breathe with these feelings, whatever they are, and allow them to develop.

Let yourself sink even further, into your intuition, your gut feeling. What is most real for you? What do you feel tugged toward or repelled from? What is the strength of your desires? What is your truth?

Allow your eyes to open and read through what you wrote. Perhaps you will circle some things, underline or cross things out, or add some new words. Find what is calling you most strongly that your head, heart, and intuition can agree on. Perhaps you will refine one of your intentions or combine several of them so that thought, feeling, and instinct are all met.

Work on the wording of your intention, aiming for simplicity, clarity, and a resonance through your whole being.

When you have a clear intention for your journey through the Tree of Life, write it on a page all by itself. Decorate the page if you like.

trance | Meeting the Ten Sephirot

This is the process you can use to determine which of the ten sephirot to begin your own personal journey through the Tree of Life with. Reading a book, even many books, can inform and guide but never substitute for embodied experience. Working with—almost within—each sephira is a crucial part of embodied Kabbalah, which forms the entry to Kabbalist magic.

It is entirely possible to begin with inhabiting Kether in this first section of the book and move to Hokmah for the second section, Binah in the third, and so on, down the Tree and through the book. But a much more exciting and personalized way is to begin with a sephira you feel a resonance with and then continue onward from that point. So if you emerge from this trance feeling the most resonance with Tiferet, you can begin there, inhabiting and working with Tiferet for the first section of this book, then moving down the lightning flash to Netzach for the second section and Hod for the third section and so on. This process is described on page 23.

For more information on how to inhabit or work with a sephira, see page 21 as well as the practice on page 65, "Journey with a Sephira."

If you are working with other people, do this trance together and at the end assign a sephira for each person. If you have more than ten people, some double up. If you have ten or less than ten people, space yourselves through the Tree, as the whole journey is much more powerful when each of the sephirot has a person within it. For more on working with groups, see the relevant section in "How to Use This Book."

TIME: 45–60 minutes

YOU WILL NEED: A blank map of the Tree—an outline of the ten circles of the Tree of Life drawn up (usually by hand as a rough sketch) on a piece of paper or a page in your journal, including the names of the sephirot written in the appropriate circles; see page 10 for a template. Also a pen or pencil and a journal.

Preparing for the Trance

The purpose of this trance is to provide a personal experience of the Tree and the individual sephirot. It is ideal to first read the description of the sephirot in "The Ten Sephirot of the Tree of Life" on page 45 or reread it immediately before this trance journey. It doesn't matter if you can't hold the ten sephirot distinct in your mind yet. That information is a guide and framework so that within the trance, as we meet each sephira, a few words (listed below) can remind you of its essence. The trance includes references to both the Ain Soph (above Kether) and the Abyss that lies between the top triad and the lower Tree, but the focus is the ten sephirot.

I often scribble a few words on my blank map as I go through a trance like this—ten different impressions or experiences are a lot to remember if the writing or recording is done only afterward. These words then unlock my memory of that experience, enabling me to record the whole thing in more detail after I've finished.

This trance can be done numerous times and with many variations. One variant is simply to redo the trance, spending five minutes or longer with each of the sephirot. Other variations exist in this book, and you may research, invent, or stumble across more. This version is its most essential form, where for a few minutes we simply visit each of the ten sephirot in order, gather some impressions, and record them. It's written descending the Tree, from Kether through to Malkuth, but can equally be run in the other direction, Malkuth up to Kether. It's a good practice, over time, to run it in each of those directions.

I am using the term *trance* to describe a deepened or sensitized state of awareness, where we remain open to guidance, sensations, and experiences. For some of us, these will come in visual form all or some of the time. Others may experience mainly body sensations or emotional states or hear sounds or words. Your experience may not fit neatly into one of these categories—for example, you may have sensations of heat and coolness, experience some vivid flashes of color or sound, and access some memories. Within a trance we accept whatever information we receive, although we can also sometimes push our boundaries a little, asking questions of ourselves such as *If I were to see something, what image comes to mind? I wonder if any words accompany this vision? What am I feeling in my body now?* In this way we can build our skills within trance, opening to richer, more complex and layered experiences.

There are some further notes on trance and trance states in the appendix at the back of this book.

Prepare by settling yourself comfortably, either seated or standing. Lying down is not recommended unless you are wishing for a much dreamier, more extended trance or you have great discipline on focusing within. Have your pen, map, and journal to hand. You might be at an altar, in your study or living room, or even outside. Perhaps you will cast a circle, call on the elements, drum, dance, or meditate before the trance.

Begin the trance by settling into your body, relaxing, and focusing on your breath. You might even imagine yourself as a tree, your upright spine the trunk, with roots into the ground and branches overhead. Take some conscious breaths to continue relaxing your body and preparing your mind to travel into the realms of trance. You can imagine that each breath is carrying you a little further into this realm, helping relax you and attune your senses.

You can run the trance from memory, half gazing at your blank map of the Tree, or you can refer to the prompts below for each sephira.

The Trance

Let yourself become aware of deep space, the night sky, a vast emptiness that stretches in all directions. You might say *Ain Soph* quietly to yourself or just take a few breaths into this experience.

Then lead yourself to each of the sephirot in turn, starting with Kether. You might imagine that each of the sephirot appears to you as a glowing disk, a whole realm, or a doorway, or just discover what happens. At each sephira allow yourself two to three minutes to receive impressions, images, or sensations, jotting down a few words on your blank map of the Tree as you go. You might speak the prompts aloud or find other words or phrases to speak. You might whisper them or say them silently. You can space them out; for example: *Chesed* [breath, pause]...*Blue* [breath, pause]...*Mercy* [breath, pause] or you can speak the whole prompt as you arrive and then wait to see what happens. Each time you do this trance, you can use different prompts or techniques.

You can acknowledge the Abyss with just a breath when you come to it, or you may choose to remain for a few breaths.

- Kether—White. The beginning. Crown. Everything from nothing. The top of the middle pillar. All.
- Hokmah—Gray. Division. Wisdom. The reflection of the everything. The top of the right-hand pillar. The mirror.
- Binah—Black. Completing the triad. Understanding. The possibility of becoming. The top of the left-hand pillar. Cosmic womb.
- The Abyss—space
- Chesed—Blue. Mercy. The center of the right-hand pillar. Everything flows into this point and is dispersed out and downward.
- Gevurah—Red. Justice or power. The center of the left-hand pillar. Limits and boundaries exist.
- Tiferet—Yellow. Beauty. The center of the middle pillar. The heart of the Tree.
- Netzach—Green. Eternity. The bottom of the right-hand pillar. The garden of possibilities.
- Hod—Orange. Glory. The bottom of the left-hand pillar. The library of detail.
- Yesod—Purple. Foundation. In the middle pillar. The collective unconscious.
- Malkuth—Brown. Kingdom. The bottom of the middle pillar. Where everything becomes.

Once you have completed all ten sephirot, take several breaths in quietness before returning from the trance. To leave a trance, we reverse the steps we took to enter it, so in this case become aware again of deep space, the night sky, the universe, then bring your focus to the breath as it enters and leaves the body, then return to your waking awareness. At this point we often like to stretch, yawn, have a few mouthfuls of water, and sometimes pat along the edges of our body, particularly our arms and legs.

Make notes, preferably straightaway, either directly onto your blank map or in your journal. Another way to record images and feelings is by drawing onto or coloring the map, maybe adding just a few words.

Now choose the sephira you will begin your journey through the Tree of Life with. If you are working solo, you can either begin with Kether or choose the sephira you are most immediately drawn to, regardless of where it is in the Tree. This will help create a strong beginning for your relationship with the Tree. If you are working with a group, some negotiation may be needed as it's best to spread yourselves through the Tree, but try to ensure everyone is assigned a sephira they feel at least some resonance with.

Inhabiting a Sephira

Each time you move into a new sephira, aim to do these things.

As soon as possible:

- ▶ Record your very first impressions on arriving there.
- ▶ Undertake the practice "Journey with a Sephira" on page 65 or some version of this.

At some stage during your time with the sephira:

- ▶ Read what you can about the sephira in this and other books or online.
- ▶ Work through the three exercises in whichever section of the book you are up to.
- ▶ Contemplate and journal about your responses to the gifts and challenges of this sephira.
- ▶ Deepen into your connection with the name of the sephira, its color, and its position within the Tree.
- ▶ Talk with others about the arising themes; for example, mercy if you are in Chesed or power if you are in Gevurah. You may also choose to read or research within these fields.

Toward the end of your time with the sephira:

- ▶ Create a disk to sum up your experience with the sephira as described in "Creating the First Disk" on page 69.
- ▶ Reflect on what this sephira offers toward your intention.

At any stage you may also wish or find it helpful to:

▸ Create a piece of art reflecting the sephira.

▸ Create an altar for the sephira.

▸ Create a ritual to deepen into your connection with the sephira.

▸ Host an event themed to the sephira—a discussion, party, ritual, bushwalk…

Memoir: *Alone*

I am alone. So alone and I've been this way not just for days and months, but years—it feels like aeons. I live alone, I work alone, I sleep alone. Since I turned forty, let alone fifty, it's been hard to find lovers. I keep living in the country and then traveling all the time—either of those might be difficult but both together mean I am fractured in my social connections. There's a sense of a vast amount of time surrounding me and awaiting me; my life of continuing to get older stretches out, and it's dark space—I can't feel any warmth or see how to get to a different place. I struggle. I sleep with my cat but it's years since a lover shared my bed. I adore physical love, sex, and affection, and this loneliness carves deeply into my sense of belonging to the world. I'm falling—there's a great falling distance placing itself between me and everyone else; the beginning of the fall.

I can hardly understand—how can this be? How do people go about their lives, walk the streets, sit in meetings, attend social events with this screaming inside them—for connection and touch, to be held, to gaze into the eyes of a lover—and my horror that perhaps they don't have this longing, it is only me. I go out to cafés and music events, gatherings and parties and workshops, and all the time, every minute, it seems my skin is tearing off me in the effort to be polite and interested and present, to stay calm, remain calm, and not break down, not start screaming or sobbing, not reach out more than I should to these other humans carrying on with their own lives. I choke it down until I am home, alone, and then it bursts out of me as I scream into pillows and sob in horror, grief, fear, and the desperation of it. I think no one really notices. I come across as engaged and a little remote or warm and clever but anyway self-contained. I am containing myself, this self that is so uncontainable, so volatile, so rent with yearning.

Since I was a teenager, I've heard women in their fifties and even late forties saying what a relief it is to be over being driven by sex and desire, how calm and happy they feel on their own or how little interested they are, now, in making love with their partners, and I always swore—or perhaps I just knew myself—*I won't be like that*. I am not like that. I am the opposite of that, but I do see that there's a choice—this is so impossible, so monumentally difficult to sustain—the ferocity of longing within complete absence, over years—I see how I could turn it off. Give it up. Put that piece of my life aside, focus on other things, close down a little, and in return not be in this flayed-alive, raw state. It doesn't tempt me, but I don't know how to live with this. It feels like I'm dying by degrees, by lack of touch and affection and no prospect of anything but aging, still moving through the world on my own and gazing out of these eyes at a human realm I can't quite join.

There's the nonhuman world and I give myself to the waves, the sun, the turn of the moon, the forest and cliffs, the white cockatoos; I vibrate all through with pleasure at having them as my beloveds. I have baths, beautiful clothes to wear, I taste delicious food or a glass of wine and it's something of delight to be sweet to myself, but it's not like having a lover, not really. I've always said I don't mind being lonely, and that's true to an extent. I wouldn't sacrifice much to fit in with someone else's needs: not my sense of self and not my work or living in a beautiful place or traveling. I hate making myself small to suit someone else, living in conflict, or dealing with addiction, jealousy, or control. I choose loneliness over any of that.

But how much loneliness can I stand? Because if I start to close my heart, shut down to the calling of love and connection, I can see—I know—I won't have a hope. Not of finding what I want, not of becoming lover and beloved in a human way. Or I'd have the chance of randomness; for some people it falls into their lives when they're not looking/have given up/got on with other things, but not many, I think. Not most. And I'm not willing to take those odds. So I choose to stay open, truly open, rendering each moment vivid and filled with life and connection and—absence. All the choices I make for connection and intimacy that aren't returned.

I think I will die of it. Or that I will spend thirty years dying slowly, each moment of yearning breaking me, and this is the only way I can do it. I can't live with it; it isn't bearable to be this open and this unmet so continually over such length of time, but I can die with it. Dying, if I say I'm dying, it's killing me but I'm doing it anyway, staying open and offering love and softness to myself and the world and those I meet. I believe that changes my chances. That it's not just random anymore; it might or might not happen, but if I don't die first, it will happen. Switching my consciousness from living with this to dying with it makes the change for me; somehow it's not shouldering an impossible burden but surrendering to inevitability, and it allows me grace within this vast and consuming unmet distress of passion.

I make the choice. I'll stay open though it's killing me and choose dying with it rather than living comfortably by closing down this longing for touch and intimacy. I am so keenly attuned, so aware of this each moment, that everything around me purifies and I live in a great ferocity of receptivity. I know I can't walk around the world in this depth of need and desperation, so to not have it running me as a shadow in every interaction, I have to feel every particle of it, let it all rush through me and be expressed in my writing and ritual and tears and on my own, each day and night alone, so that when I come into contact with people it's not there as an undertow, calling out for help like a drowning woman.

I am dying in moments, wide open, and I look at and glory in each human that crosses my path. I gaze at people in the street, in cafés, at events I attend, wondering. I am soft in it, yearning and open and alive with my own gifts; I offer into each interaction whatever I can. I let each word or glance or touch feed me, and so in the moment I am not looking for more but am only present with what is. At home alone I weep, gut-wrenching need and grief and terror, sob convulsively in the morning or at night, most nights or mornings, and it's all confused, anyway, with the deaths of my mother and my friend so that I hardly know who I am, but I want to feel it all, every moment of it. I let it drown me, like dark matter tearing through, in between the atoms of matter—this enormity of isolation and constant desperate longing so that I can continue with it month after month.

A few friends know I am in this state and give what they can—deep conversation, shared ritual, physical affection. One young man, whom I don't see that often because we live far apart, but when I do see him, it's often for a few days in a row, holds me. Not a hug, not a cuddle, but hours and hours of holding, sometimes four hours of holding, so that we fall asleep together, frequently two hours, one hour. He puts his arm around my shoulder, he holds my hand when we walk along the street, and we lie or sit cuddling for hours, sometimes day after day. This stitches me together. I have been in the severest of droughts, and it waters me. I have been starving and he brings me food—delicate, beautifully prepared food—and serves it to me with grace and kindness. I weep with gratitude.

I think about how if you arrived at your friend's house hungry, they'd make you a meal. If you turned up crying on the doorstep, they'd take you in and put their arms around you, make you tea, and listen to your crisis, whatever it was. If you needed a rain jacket, tarot deck, spare pen, red dress, they'd lend you one or find one for you. If you needed twenty dollars or even a hundred, they'd give it to you. But if what you need is the sensual and erotic, intimacy and sex, they say *Oh well, good luck with that* and hope that perhaps you'll meet a stranger who will fulfill this longing.

How is it that we require strangers, not friends, for the most intimate of needs? How has this situation come about? How do we subscribe to it, allow it? My friends can happily meet all of my more incidental needs, but when it comes to the depths, the truth of me, I have to outsource it and rely on the random intervention of strangers. This is deeply peculiar and fascinating—or it would be, if it wasn't killing me. Each of my friends, maybe twenty or thirty of them over a year or two—I'd make love with them. It's part of my great opening to the world, and obviously they have no similar desire; even to discuss it is painful because it requires that they take themselves to a place where their answer to that question, for one reason or another, is *no*, and I can see they don't like to do that.

Yes, I'm fifty, and all the fifty-year-olds I meet are settled in themselves or with partners, concerned with matters of work, money, and their growing or grown children, and it's not that I don't care about those things, but compared to intimacy they're nothing. I'm so alive I'm burning up—too fierce, perhaps, frightening in my intensity—but attractive, intelligent, independent, sensual, open to so much and so many, and I can't find anyone interested. If they're my age, they're obsessed with their diet or can't stay up past 8 p.m. or drive on the highway at night or bear to try yet another relationship, and if they're younger, they've got their own demanding lives and lovers or families.

I gaze at men in the street and wonder *Would you make love with me? Would you, or you?* Hundreds of them, surely some of them might answer *yes*. How do I find this? Is there any way but to become it myself, the all of it, the lover and the beloved? Each single kiss or caress that I receive, often spaced many months apart, feels carved into me, like a river running again after drought and bursting into life for a moment or an hour on the strength of a memory. I am so fiercely present in receptivity that it feels like each second is diamonds, clear and fierce and utterly precious. I collect these jewels, try to string them together enough to convince myself that somehow I might survive this utter dearth of affection and physical contact, let alone sensual or sexual, as it stretches on week after dreary week into yet more months and years. Each spark is a whole universe of depth and belonging, and I give myself entirely into each one of them.

There's a thread of fierce glory in it that I can live this way, and I feel myself burning through old patterns as I learn to meet each being with wonder and reverence, expecting nothing. I am starlight glittering as I burn through my fuel, my days of life. There's a man I meet in a Parisian bakery and shyly exchange a few words with ... that barista I've always liked ... this dear friend ... and I hope, oh I hope they know the delight it gives me, how each of those moments is a whole world and I would go anywhere with them, give myself entirely, this is the core of my existence and it's shimmering there, alive and yearning. This process is so engrossing, this dying-wide-open; it's like a star consuming itself, and surely I blaze with it. I'm on the edge of it—singular but all that is. Both.

In Paris I visit an exhibition of immersive art within a repurposed power station, l'Atelier des Lumières. It's art transcribed to the walls and floor; viewers wander though a shifting world of color and form. The enormity, the explosion of it, how it's held within the building but is all the wonder of life unfolding, living, dying—this is the interior. Of the heart of a star, how it feels to be all alone but yearning for the other, of the dare and risk of each breath, shimmering at the edge of self and then falling. I can almost feel the colors as they run over my fingertips, how it flows out of me, the dance of life, and that I am alone is incidental; the stars form through me. That I am alone is crucial; it's the beginning. All of existence is here with me, forming me and receiving me, and if I choose to meet it with love, then how much better for me. If it tears me in two with impossibility, then I surrender like the stars do, like butterflies, at inevitability, paying the price for these living breaths of consciousness.

This is it—I'm watching the stars forming, seeing each brushstroke, movement, moment; they cascade onto the walls in all directions and I am immersed, seeing their light on water, dancing, shimmering. I am in the water of it, it ripples and drips around me, undulating like blood beating; I am one with it, pulsing the in and out, the breath and pause of it. I am the ripples on the floor, the star exploding in the flower created petal by brushstroke by petal and the sun itself—a flower, a star, the birth of a universe in orange yellow citron, vermilion and white—white—white—the silver effervescence collapsing to purple and blue and gold in every fleck and shimmer of it. This is Kether.

The juice of this, the liquid gold, the light and pattern into and out of infinity, take me again, wash me through with your gold and silver that pierces, moonlight and stardust on water, drink me, rock me on waves unending, death this is, and life—all of it together the moment drawn out forever and ending endlessly. I am in stripes now, sedimentary layers of becoming; I am rippled, opened, divided through line and dance and leaf and flower. I am in this bud and branch and orchestra of it—the sap, the cliffs and fields, oceanic, the fall of seasons, of stars and rivers the ever becoming and the light—the blue of it, gold, red, carmine—the patterns, grain of wheat the sunburst, feathers on the wings of birds and I am that and that and that all through into the becoming I am thread and weave and disarray out into the night, the nothing/all—

I am here at the birth—the beginning. It's all wave and breath and pulse—no form, a thread, an edge of light—effervescence violet, purple, cobalt spark explosion becoming—I bring the dark, I flood, explode into light, fragment and form, rivers of stars that are fountains, waterfalls. Cascading light light it is all light, blossoms, billowing rippling unending folded space/time the nothing is here, backdrop to becoming, giving birth that is all I want forever, I am fragmented by it, this is why I am, how I came to have these eyes, this blood-beating-heart consciousness to be here on the edge at the birth of the universe—brilliance upon brilliance in time in ecstasy waterfalling out from every moment like kisses, wine, waves of blessings—

cascading collapsing—desire—the becoming of desire and sheer explosion of it

the strokes of sunlight

I am so singular I become not just one but a reflection of All, so clear, so unmuddied with intimacies and overlaps with other humans, I can ring one true note: my own. If that justifies these years of aloneness, this despair, then I'm pleased; I see why abstinence can be considered holy; the bell of me is clear to ring out into the farthest reaches of the universe. This vast loneliness—each star is everything in itself. But also I am filled—torn—by the most ferocious yearning, so extreme I would rip myself in half to achieve it. I could collapse back on myself and become secret, a dark universe, and perhaps that will happen but not while I have a choice. I choose to burn stellar, to feel the atoms of me collide and collide and collide, making love alchemically blazing with life, light, in love with each moment, each dying second, and I'll give everything, burn each piece of me, in this determination to live, yearning even if unmet, dancing light into the cosmos, one tiny fleck, a spark, a ferocious blossoming pulsing life, giving everything, dying and not knowing—

I am an exploding star of a woman, born to burn up every atom and give everything in each heartbeat, not knowing but flinging myself out toward the edges of the universe in pure desire.

practice | Journey with a Sephira

There are many ways to learn about the individual sephirot.

Reading and researching some of the great quantity of material that's available is an obvious entry point, as we discover what other Kabbalists have thought or experienced about each sephira. It can also open our mind to the array of possibilities and meaning that lie within the different parts of the Tree of Life. Each sephira is a vast realm about which whole books could be written. Instead, most books give a chapter, at most, to each of the sephira. One way to study Kabbalah is to have several of these books and, whenever we move to a new sephira, read the relevant section within each book. That way we can focus on that sephira, comparing sources and adding our own experience, instead of trying to hold all ten sephirot in our minds at the same time or being halfway through a single book and therefore reading about a completely different sephira than the one we're inhabiting currently.

I consider our own experience to be a primary source of information about the sephirot. There are several ways to create these experiences. One is to dedicate a period of time—a day, a week, a month—to learn, think about, lean into, and see through the eyes of one sephira. This is my favorite way of investigating magical systems. I like to spend a month with each of the sephirot in turn, letting my thinking and dreaming be shaped by its influence, drawing impressions and creating a felt relationship. It's an embodied style of learning that leaves me with individual relationships with each sephira and also a comprehension of the system as a whole.

Another (briefer) way to gather information and begin creating active relationship with a sephira is to make a specific journey into it. This can be done, particularly usefully, while also spending a week or month with that sephira, but it can also be done as an individual exercise unrelated to the embodied inhabiting of the sephira over an extended period of time. There are many ways to do this, and I have detailed some below. It is not meant to be an exhaustive list. Perhaps you are a musician and will craft a song for each sephira you work with or perhaps you'll blend a tea or an incense after consulting with plant allies or perhaps you'll create a dance or a painting. It can be great to use several different methods to journey into a sephira because each way can show us different things—or perhaps they'll be showing us the same things in different ways.

Trance Journey

TIME: 30–45 minutes

YOU WILL NEED: Journal and pen

The basics of how to undertake a trance journey are outlined in the previous exercise, "Journey with a Sephira," with more in-depth instructions on trance in the appendix. This time you will be trancing into a single sephira rather than all ten.

Choose which sephira you will explore, then prepare yourself for the trance. You might want to begin with grounding, lighting a candle, casting a circle, or otherwise invoking or recognizing sacred space. You might begin with some gentle movement or a prayer or song to the Tree of Life.

Here are some potential entry points to the trance:

- ▶ Imagine yourself seated or kneeling at the edge of a round pool. It might be a pool of water or light or energy. Allow the color of your sephira to suffuse through the pool. You can begin by gazing into this pool or dipping in a hand to feel it. Perhaps you will drink from it, bathe yourself, or step within it as a portal and pass through into a realm of the sephira.

- ▶ Imagine the Tree of Life as a towering giant above you. When you focus on any part of it, you can bring it closer to you. After breathing a little with this Tree, find the place where your sephira resides and allow your attention to deepen. Let your breath take you closer and closer until you can move into the sephira.

- ▶ Approach your sephira as if it were a door or gateway. Perhaps it will carry certain insignia or signs. Notice your reactions, feelings, and perceptions; information that may be visual, aural, sensory, or emotional. When you are ready, open the door or gate, or allow it to open for you, and step through.

- ▶ Prepare some food or drink, either in trance or the material world, that is the relevant color of your sephira. When you are ready, consume it and let the energy and information of that sephira begin to unfold within you.

Once you are inside the trance, you can ask yourself or the sephira questions. Make sure you leave some time just to be within the experience, however it unfolds. Samples of questions are:

- ▶ How does it feel within this sephira?
- ▶ What is the place, or the function, of this sephira within the Tree?
- ▶ What are its relationships to the nearby sephirot?
- ▶ What part of my life or my personality does this sephira resonate with?
- ▶ What does this sephira have to teach me?

Make a record of your trance afterward in your journal.

Journey Through Terrain

TIME: 30–60 minutes

YOU WILL NEED: Journal and pen; coloring things optional

Choose a physical location to have an adventure with your chosen sephira. It might just be wherever you happen to be or can get to—in your house, a local park, around your suburb—or you might go on a special excursion, especially to somewhere you feel is relevant to the sephira. Possible locations include a forest, beach, river, lake, outside under a full moon, cemetery, hilltop, orchard, ancient well, stone circle, temple, or cave.

Prepare yourself to enter ritual space, knowing that when you leave this place or complete the ritual you will return to your own ways of experiencing the world. Imagine taking yourself literally within the sephira and experiencing everything as part of, or a commentary on, the sephira.

Perhaps you will go for a walk from the perspective of the sephira you are working with or spend some time stationary but experiencing the world around you through the lens of that sephira.

When you are complete, record your experience in your journal. You might want to create a map or drawing as well.

Automatic Writing Journey

TIME: 10–15 minutes

YOU WILL NEED: Journal and pen, timer

Set aside a predetermined length of time for this exercise, such as five or ten minutes.

The idea of automatic writing is that you keep writing for a set period of time, even if this means you are repeating the same words or phrases. Aim to get into a flow of thoughts and ideas without judging or editing. Allow yourself to tap into words or ideas that are intuitive, below the surface of our usual ways of thinking. To assist this process, there is usually a prompt or a series of prompts. Each time we hesitate, we return to these prompts, starting the next sentence with one of them, then allowing our pen, words, and thoughts to continue on past that beginning.

Prompts for this exercise are:

▸ [Name of sephira] is ...

▸ [Name of sephira] reminds me ...

▸ [Name of sephira] says ...

So, for example, if the sephira we were working with was Tiferet, the prompts would be: *Tiferet is ..., Tiferet reminds me ...,* and *Tiferet says ...*

Start your timer and write for the set amount of time. When the time ends, finish the sentence you are writing.

Lay your pen down and reread through what you've written. Perhaps the writing will inspire questions you want to research, insights into the nature of this sephira, or aha moments about your connection to the sephira. You might wish to go back and circle or underline particular sentences or phrases, or rewrite clearly the pieces that have the most meaning for you.

activity | Creating the First Disk

At the completion of working with one sephira—whether you have taken a week, a month, or however long it took you to work through this section of the book—take some time to record your learnings. The Tree is vast, and our experiences within it so rich and sometimes mystifying and obscure, that unless we find ways to record where we've been, we can't possibly remember it all. Later on, in our journey with a different sephira, we'll probably want to refer back to it or pursue that reference we came across or recall exactly what it felt like to be there.

Journaling in some way is vital. Some of us record our impressions and learnings onto our computers, others have a hard-copy journal, some use voice notes or combinations of those. As well as journaling, in this process of experiential Kabbalah we create a physical representation of each sephira at the conclusion of our time with it. This is done in the form of a disk—a round piece of colored cardstock about the size of a dinner plate, of the appropriate color and decorated in some way that represents your learnings and experience of that sephira. I buy colored cardboard from a craft or office supplies shop and cut my disks out. Other methods I've seen are using recycled cardboard and painting on the background colors (thanks Rose), making fabric disks (thanks Pistil), and fused glass art (thanks Caithness Gael).

The disks are not just a record of our experiences and understandings during our time with a particular sephira; they are also a way of physically representing the Tree when we lay them out on the floor in the Tree of Life arrangement. We do this whether they are decorated or not—that is, many or most of them may still be colored disks of cardboard with only their name written on them, while the sephirot we have already inhabited are written/drawn/collaged/painted. This ratio gradually changes as we move farther along our journey with the Tree. Laying out the disks enables us to move amongst them and sit within our representation of the Tree to meditate, trance, or conduct ritual, to create a whole embodied experience entering the magic where we experience ourselves as part of the Tree.

At the end of each section of this book will be a short piece reminding you to create your disk. The disks may all be quite similar or they may come out very differently to each other—one may be covered in poetry, another have a single symbol drawn in black, another have a collage of photos, another have a painted or drawn scene on it. Any way that you feel like creating your disk will be perfect. If you possibly can, make the disk while you are still working with that sephira, before you move to the next one. The Tree of Life is a powerful system. When we give ourselves to it, each sephira shapes our dreaming, our seeing, and our experiencing of the world, and once we shift to another one it's nearly impossible to get back those exact feelings and thoughts.

Creating a Disk for a Sephira

TIME: Allow 60 minutes, although it may not take that long. Alternatively, you could do it over a week or a month, doing little pieces in different moments.

YOU WILL NEED: 11 cardboard disks about the size of a dinner plate, of these colors: brown, purple, orange, green, yellow, red, blue, black, gray, white, and silver. (I chose silver for Da'ath, but you might choose something different; it should be utterly different than the others and, of them all, will not need to be drawn on or marked in any way.)

CRAFT MATERIALS AND TOOLS: Scissors, glue, colored pens/pencils/pastels or paint, magazines or photos for collage. Optionally, stickers, glitter, and other things you might wish to incorporate.

Write the name of each disk onto it with a marker pen. You can include the name in English or, if your first language is not English, you may prefer to use a word from your own language.

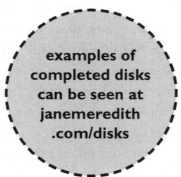

examples of completed disks can be seen at janemeredith .com/disks

Select the relevant color for the sephira you have been working with.

Sephira	English Name	Disk Color
Malkuth	Kingdom	Brown
Yesod	Foundation	Purple
Hod	Glory	Orange
Netzach	Eternity	Green
Tiferet	Beauty	Yellow
Gevurah	Power (or Justice)	Red
Chesed	Mercy	Blue
Binah	Understanding	Black
Hokmah	Wisdom	Gray
Kether	Crown	White

Before you begin decorating your disk, ask yourself what have been your strongest experiences, key learnings, and overall impressions of this sephira. You might like to jot down a few notes or make a quick sketch.

You can decorate your disk as a ritual or as part of a larger ritual, after a trance into the disk, or in some other way that feels good to you.

Decide how you want to decorate the disk and gather your materials. Ask yourself *What will convey my lived experience in this sephira?* and be guided by that. Possibilities include writing or drawing on the disk, painting it, using collage, or any combination of these. It may be very simple or very detailed.

Create your disk, allowing yourself to follow your intuition.

Once you are done, you can place it down on the floor within the whole arrangement of the eleven disks. Some people choose to keep their disks on a wall or the back of a door so they can be seen. Alternatively, you might keep your current disk on your altar.

there's no beginning and no end but this
piece tears itself away from all-self and
tumbles outward into endless dark space,
a bright shard falling, falling, the sheer
impossibility of it, the dream, the reflection
born from yearning, oh desire, pulsing
through like a heartbeat, like blood like the
very beginning of all things but beginning
now again and falling away, into separation,
grief already at the tearing vastness as
light separates, entangled particles are
flung apart from each other eternally
remembering and now separated—the utter
experiment of the universe, falling—

a butterfly shimmers into being—a fragment
of an impossible dream, a dream of a
dream—its wings unfold, and it falls…

2
Pairs in the Tree

73

After a time which is all time or no time, or even before time existed, the single sephira of Kether divides itself and becomes two. They are now plural, sephirot, yet each also remains singular. What is utterly new with this second sephira is duality. Difference. Opposition. Reflection. The other. The existence of Hokmah creates the first pair, as the diagram of the Tree transforms from a single point into two points with a line between them. As well as an entire world being within each sephira, there are also dynamics between them.

This concept of two, of *other*, had never been before. There had been the nothing and then the everything, but they were states of such utter difference they could not exactly be in relationship. Or, their relationship was and remains shrouded in mystery. But this splitting of the one into two is a concept we can understand. These two must know each other utterly since they were the same thing. Yet in that moment of splitting, their experiences were different—because one split itself and the other was split away— so their journeys past that point became increasingly different. Between them they are all that is, so they continue in intrinsic relation to each other, endlessly reflecting and commenting on the other.

Hokmah, the reflection of Kether, is called Wisdom. With Hokmah relationship, balance, and duality have come into the Tree.

Hokmah: *Lover and Beloved*

Hokmah arises because Kether divides itself. This coming-into-existence is not as completely inexplicable as the birth of Kether, when something arises out of nothing, but it is still a happening of great moment and mystery. If Kether is everything, and then something else comes into being, clearly this is because part of Kether has separated itself from Kether and is now not-Kether. Does the coming into existence of Hokmah reduce Kether in any way or make it less? If we follow the Feri and Reclaiming Traditions' story of the Star Goddess, who is all alone until She reaches out to the mirror of curved space to see Herself reflected there, the answer may be no, Kether is not made less by the existence of Hokmah. If we think of it more conventionally, Kether is all of matter, and part of matter divides off to become Hokmah—or something like the Big Bang occurs, and matter expands out from a single point very rapidly; potentially this makes Kether less than it was, unless Hokmah remains forever part of Kether, even if further away.

If Hokmah is indeed the mirror, the reflection, of Kether, then Kether loses nothing by Hokmah's existence—and it could be argued that potentiality is doubled by Hokmah, even if the amount of actual matter remains constant. The creation of Hokmah is reminiscent of myths where gods, hungry for sensation, create humans, whose experience they feed on vicariously. Underlying this theme of splitting is the concept that one, even if that one is All, is not enough—or in universes where it is enough, we never get to know about it. In this universe the All had to, or chose to, or just did this splitting—which means I can be sitting here writing this at a table in Huonbrook in October of 2019 and you can be elsewhere but participating in another part of this same activity. Otherness exists. In some ways we are split apart, though it can always be argued that ultimately there is no split, or only a brief, partial, or illusory split.

Splitting, even momentarily, creates space. Space where Hokmah—although it came into existence as a reflection of, or part of, Kether—differentiates. Within space and time they become inevitably, increasingly differentiated from each other, even if all their difference arises purely from that single original difference: Kether split into two, or created a reflection of itself, while Hokmah was split off from, or was the mirror or reflection. Because they are from one source, there's always an inference that they remain parts of the same thing, that even in their increasing difference and two-ness, they are still one. This deep mystery is part of the terms of our existence. When we are born, we emerge from—separate and yet created by—another: by our mother, by both parents, by all of our ancestors until this time, by molecules and atoms and stars exploding, and we never escape this. When we die this state of separation dissolves and we return back into the oneness, which, it could be argued, we never truly left.

This great story of separation and return plays through not just each human life, but every life and every thing. Stars come into existence—great masses of gasses and other elements drawn together into a body that we name *star*; at the end of their lives, their mass has dispersed again, back into the fabric of the universe. The building blocks that created them have been changed by their existence in the star and then returned into the All. Every breath we take could be seen this way: breathing in, we separate that air from the All to become part of ourselves, and then, in breathing out, that air merges back into the All. We do this ourselves with our first and last breaths—at our first breath we enter into life as a separate living being, and at our last outbreath we die, so returning to the great, essentially indivisible whole. Each breath, while it is within us, we transform, so each breath is part of changing the dynamic whole. Our own lives that we live change the All. So Hokmah, by changing within itself, changes Kether.

The concept of distance or separation creating an other, even if both were originally and in some ways continue to be part of the same thing, is the essence of Hokmah's story. Hokmah is other than Kether, and so the experience of Other is born. Before, when only Kether had emerged from the Ain Soph, there was no other. The I Am is all that is. Hokmah creates a different state; although Kether is drawn into this different state, the main experience of it is held by Hokmah since it is the entirety of Hokmah's existence. Differentiation has come second to Kether, after the original state of being whole/All/one, whereas for Hokmah the first thing is separation. This is their intrinsic difference. Kether's story is about being whole unto oneself. Hokmah's story is about separation, otherness, and being in relationship.

These two were mirror images, but one was the beginning and the other, the mirror. How is it to be this mirror? It is to be the reflection, the other. It is to hold the beginning of the infinite story of splitting, which is the story of differentiation, which is also the story of yearning for union. Before this split there was only one. The fact of separation creates the possibility of union. We can see this splitting as cells divide, we can see it as a baby is born from its mother or as a seed sprouts or an egg hatches. We practice splitting in our nations, languages, wars, class and caste systems, and the attempted separation between human and nature. Union we experience in sexual intimacy, magic, and in the great return of death. We can see it within families, cultures, political and spiritual movements, ecosystems, and in spiritual ecstasy.

So many things are impossible when there is only one, especially when the one is All. Hokmah has brought separation and union into the world, although at this stage all there is to be separate from is Kether and all there is to experience union with is Kether. So this is a love story. At Hokmah comes love, for love is expressed toward, about, or with another. Kether may *be* love, as it is everything, but it cannot *experience* love by itself. Even self-love arises within the context and consciousness of love that is taught interactively with another. So the other is beloved and the great forces of love and union have become possible. For us this beloved may be a tree, an animal, the river, another human, the divine, and all things in between.

It's not just love that has come into existence or potentiality: loss is right there with it. That essential division, that separation, carries enormous loss. When we go on to posit the possibility of union, of rejoining that from which we arose, there is also, hand in hand, the possibility or the experience of renewed loss. The beloved is, in some ways, already lost to us forever because we are essentially separate. In a human body, this can mean that one of us will die first. Often it means that our love will not just carry a thousand losses and separations along the way, but is quite likely to culminate in a definite ending, where the beloved is gone from us. By that point in a human story we may not be experiencing them as our beloved at all, but in the timelessness of Kether and Hokmah's story, they are always the beloved and always lost.

This division, the falling away from the beloved, is one thing in a story where things stay static, but that is not the universe we live in. Our universe has been expanding ever since the Big Bang, or Great Expansion, and it is still expanding, with everything getting farther and farther away from everything else, as a general rule, although in various localities that's not the case at certain points in time. Star systems may still be drawn toward or into each other, as is happening with our own Milky Way and the galaxy next door, the Andromeda system. Cloud nebulas are still birthing stars in great explosions of heat and gas that are compressed into new forms, and lovers are still drawn to each other on our little planet. But these local instances of getting closer to things is not the great story of the universe. Universally, everything's getting farther apart, and this seems indicative of the relationship between Kether and Hokmah, or indeed of Kether and everything else.

I think Hokmah speaks of grief. The grief of separation from the beloved—whether that separation is through death, a relationship ending, or the expansion of the universe. Hokmah's color is gray, and even though that's not a traditional color for mourning—

white and black are that—the unsubstantiality of it, the not quite one thing or the other of gray, the mistiness, the fog of it, hold an emotional tone that represents this grief. Our human grief around loss or death can be exacerbated by the realization that as we go on living, time moves us further and further away from the beloved. We can essentially never return to them or the part of our lives when we were with them, and, altered by this loss, we become increasingly different from the self we were then.

Cosmic drift. Mourning. The human emotions of sadness and grief as we contemplate death, separation, loss, and the existential nature of the pull of the universe out toward the edges of things. The opposite to a happy ending, it all just gets farther and farther apart, perhaps infinitely so. This great first division will never be reversed, but its impact continues on and on, resonating, rippling out to the edges of space-time, which ... just keeps going. All of this is what Hokmah is holding, what Hokmah's very existence is creating. Yes, the mirror at the edge of curved space, and then this mirror distances the other and continues to do so as things fall away, as the other continues to define themselves, either in relation to us or in relation to anything else. The more clearly we see the face of the beloved, the more we understand that they are different than ourselves, and increasingly so. The more we contemplate and react to the separation, the more separate we become.

Yet still at the heart of this mystery remains the fact that Hokmah was, firstly, a way of seeing Kether or of Kether seeing itself or Kether manifesting itself. Hokmah is the result of the *I Am* becoming; it is the *Am* to Kether's *I*. Hokmah *is* the light extending or the start of that. In this reflection of the All, Hokmah—however veiled, however in love, however grief-stricken—contains wisdom. It is not the beloved one who holds this wisdom, but the lover. Think of the great poets—Rumi and Sappho, Keats and Dickinson, and whoever else you can name—they do not write about what it is to be loved, but what it is to love. They examine love from the place of the lover. The beloved is the other, not oneself. This is where wisdom comes from—not by being loved, but by loving. Of course we might learn how to love by receiving love—from the stars and earth, hopefully from our parents and those around us—but wisdom begins when we fall into the deep wells of what it means to love another, whether that other is human, a piece of land, an animal, a community, the divine.

Then we learn what it is to give ourselves to another. We learn what it is to yearn, to desire, to risk, to lose. We learn the joy in meeting the beloved and reach transcendence in devotion, sexual ecstasy, nurturing, artistic expression, deep communion. All of this comes into being in Hokmah, for how could Kether have held this as a single entity, even so vast? Hokmah is still the mirror, and so Kether receives this wisdom, this experience, back into its holding; now we see how division and separation can create more than was there before, or more deeply realized, or experienced, than was previously possible. This also is the union between them.

I associate Hokmah with Sophia, the goddess whose name is Wisdom, the beloved of God. Her devotion is absolute, her existence dedicated to reflecting and knowing the other, the All. In their universe of two, there is only self and other; nothing else has yet come into being. Thus when we hold our face—our soul—up to the goddess, to Wisdom, we see ourselves as reflected in her eyes. She sees both the best of us and the truth of us. Dare to gaze into a mirror, seeing your reflection as the beloved of the divine, and you will see what I mean. There's a quiver in this of the break, the memory of the break; in this moment Hokmah is whole, complete, and Kether is the one that was broken to create Hokmah. Hokmah sees that wound and reflects back love—love which, now that they both exist, we can say was the impulse that led to this splitting in the first place. The desire for love, for the other, for reflection, for the beloved to exist. The break that enables love.

As we gaze at or think of or make love to the beloved, our desire is to adore them, to know them utterly, even to become them or consume them. This beloved may be our lover, our art, a deity, our child. These acts and thoughts of love are only possible with the separation that exists between us. In moments of union we might experience ourselves as *becoming* love, rather than loving, just as we can worship the divine while we are living but after our life or before our life, when we are inextricably one with the All, we cannot worship or love. Hokmah is still the light, but the light is having a different experience, an experience of division, extension, separation, and reflection. The light reflecting back on itself has created space for love.

Past this moment when just the pair of Kether and Hokmah exist, this gaze of love and reflection can be turned anywhere; it will be turned everywhere. Binah will be next.

The pair of Kether and Binah will startle with extremes—black and white—and the pure potential of Kether will be reflected by the potent possibility of Binah. Hokmah and Binah will be as twins; Wisdom and Understanding holding hands across the void, each with their own domain but strongest when paired together. Then will come more and more pairings: Kether and Chesed will reflect each other's responsibility, Kether for the upper Tree and Chesed for the lower, each of them the first in that part of the whole system.

The existence of Hokmah brings pairing into possibility, but Hokmah itself is far more nebulous than Kether, which, even though it is ultimately unknowable, we can still categorize with the Kether-is-all-that-is type of statement. Hokmah is not *exactly* all that is. Hokmah might be a reflection of all that is, but we know that's not the same. Reflections are tricky things. What is the substance creating the reflection? Is the reflection just the face of this substance or the truth of it? Maybe something of both, in this case. But Hokmah is not only the reflection of Kether. Hokmah has brought separation and union into existence, and in the human realm surely all of us experience grief and love.

The wisdom of Hokmah is available to all. We are all separate—separated from our mothers at birth, from the All or oneness throughout our lifetimes, from everything we know at death. Many, many times we experience separation from what we love and feel belonging with: from beloveds, places we are connected to, roles and jobs we have held, relationships we were part of. How we react to, understand, and develop under these circumstances can lay the basis for our own personal wisdom, as well as potentially allowing us to connect with Wisdom, so reflecting the divine, as Hokmah does. We all can learn to love through the separations imposed on us by the facts of being alive, embodied, and finite. Each of us gets a particular and unique set of circumstances in which to do this: our own lifetimes, with all that they contain.

Perhaps this wisdom is what creates Hokmah, that clear or mirrored surface that can then reflect Kether. Although the wisdom must come from Kether, like love it is not realized until Hokmah holds it and reflects it back. How does this wisdom come to be realized? It must be from this experience of separation, which results in both the longing for (memory of) union and the fear of (experience of) loss. Each of us has this experience unendingly written into us. Perhaps in some way our very cells remember that they are stardust and know how far they have come from being at the heart of a star. Surely our bodies carry an imprint of having lived in our mothers' wombs for nine months and the absolute schism of birth in that foundational separation. All through our lives we have nights of sleep, of merging again with the everything, both within oblivion and in dream states. And most of us actively seek union—in love, sex, family, community, ritual, and with nature. Our passions inspire us to seek out these immersions with and reflections of the other through sexual passion, political passion, artistic passion, and spiritual passion.

Less glamorously, addiction can also be understood as this seeking of union, and even an extreme intolerance of states of non-union, of separation. This becomes more sinister as we recall that, for humans, the ultimate state of union is death, where once again we become indivisible from all that is, the great I Am. If addiction has become our experience of union, we see how great is the threat of its removal. It would surely be only by replacing that particular union with other unions that withdrawal would be possible. If Hokmah were cut loose from Kether, there would be nothing to reflect, no process of wisdom, and only utterly unending loss for both of them because Hokmah is a part of Kether; Kether would be made less by losing Hokmah. Perhaps this makes clear the dynamic between the divine and those so far removed from that as ourselves; as the Greek myths always showed, the gods cannot bear their existence without our notice.

Where addiction can be seen as a dependence upon the state of union, depression is its opposite: the state of being without that experience of union. Naturally, they can come together within one individual (or one society) and each can feed the other in a particularly vicious circle. Treatments for depression not involving medication (which can be viewed as another addiction) include simple acts of seeking union: meditation, socializing, self-reflection, therapy, walking, connecting to nature, or even simply being outside. In all of these activities we meet the other. We are reminded of reflection, longing, the possibility of union, and also loss. Within a depressed state loss may be the all-pervasive experience, but not loss in a dynamic form, such as in a meditation or on a walk where we may briefly connect with the oneness of all things and then lose it again, or a social encounter that begins, contains moments or possibilities of union, and then finishes. Weathering these small losses, coupled with these smaller longings or moments of union, is what builds our capacity to be with great losses.

Anomie—the state of existential angst, of separation from all that is—describes the state of Hokmah if it were divided completely from Kether, unable to reflect back. I think we all carry an awareness of this, as well as its absolute terror, just as we all carry an experience of complete union. Addiction and depression can be interpreted as ways of fighting back against this threat of anomie. One feeds the threat with endless experience of union and one starves it of that experience, but both come very close to an actual state of anomie because both are disconnected from the fundamental cycle of connection and separation, of union and reflection, a cycle so intrinsically a part of us as the beating of our heart, constricting and expanding, or the breath that continuously moves in and out of us. Addiction seeks to consume and depression to deny the other, whereas the dynamic between Kether and Hokmah shows the endless dance of connection and separation.

Just as Hokmah (or Kether or any of them) can form a pair with any other sephira within the Tree, so can we, maybe just momentarily, form a pair with any other thing. Perhaps we will spend a moment paired with a tree, standing next to or leaning against it, finding how we are similar and how different. Perhaps we will pair with a mountain, a kookaburra, an emotion, a death, a god, a lover, a child, or an ancestor. In each of these pairings we can find a connection, some sort of reflection, and a separation. In these separations, reflections, and connections, we learn more about ourselves. Perhaps we also learn more about the nature of connection, reflection, and separation. If we are paying a lot of attention, we learn about the other as well, and this whole concept of Other.

Where Kether is the great story within itself, Hokmah is the great story of the other and of all the stories that this opens up: the story of the stranger, the lover, the source, death, love, union, separation. In some ways each of us is a Hokmah separated from the divine and involved intrinsically in reflecting that divine back to itself. Everything we do does this. Constructive or destructive, selfish or in service, seeking wisdom or turning away from it, all things must be a part of this reflection because Kether has no divisions in itself and each of its divided-off pieces must reflect it. We barely remember or glimpse the oneness of Kether, and so we provide difference. We are the other, split away but still belonging to and reflecting the All. Each of our differences, from

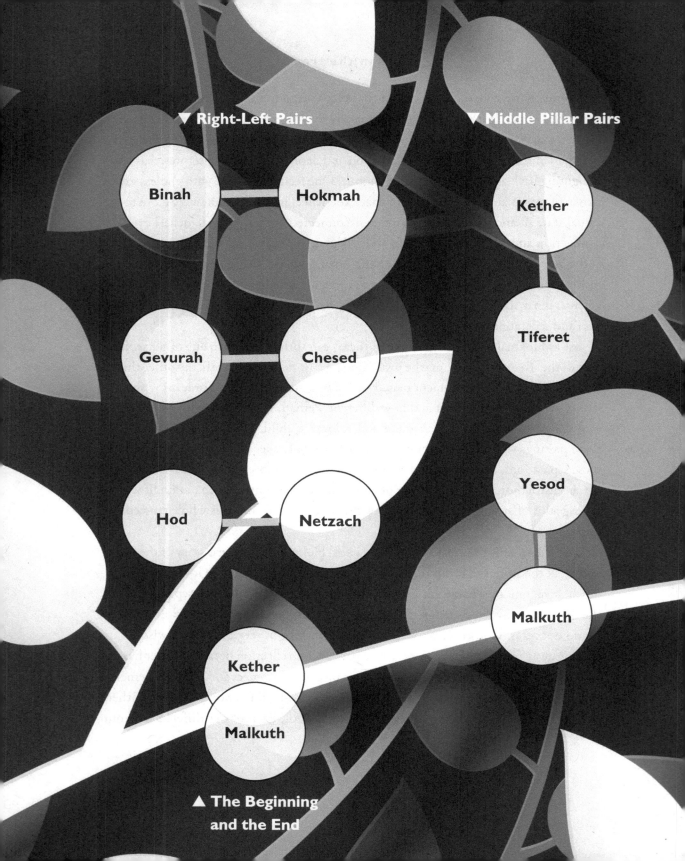

▼ Right-Left Pairs

Binah

Hokmah

Gevurah

Chesed

Hod

Netzach

▲

Kether

Malkuth

▼ Middle Pillar Pairs

Kether

Tiferet

Yesod

Malkuth

▲ The Beginning
and the End

each other and each other thing, add to the richness of this reflection. The fracturing or splintering of experience that is begun in Hokmah carries onward through the rest of the Tree and all existence.

Pairs in the Tree of Life

One of the dynamics—even the original dynamic—that occurs in the Tree of Life is that of pairs. Across the Tree, from right to left, the sephirot form pairs. At the top of the Tree is the pair of Hokmah and Binah. Below the Abyss and in the middle of the Tree is the pair of Chesed and Gevurah, and in the lower Tree there is another horizontal pair, Netzach and Hod. Pairs are also formed along the middle pillar, the most obvious pairings being Kether with Tiferet, and Yesod with Malkuth. But other possibilities are hinted at by the arrangement of the middle pillar, such as Kether and Da'ath, and Tiferet with Yesod; a system which leaves Malkuth as a single, receiving all and joining together all oppositions. Yet another pairing is the top of the Tree with the bottom of it, Crown and Kingdom—that is, Kether and Malkuth—leaving Tiferet and Yesod as the remaining pair in the middle pillar.

The Kether-Malkuth pair seems so obvious that, as soon as we have seen it, other pairings also spring to life. There is Kether and Hokmah as the first pair to come into existence; indeed, the creation of pairs rests with them. Binah and Malkuth have often been cited as a pair, linked together as the path into manifestation. Once we get this far, it becomes clear that every sephira could in some way pair with every other of them, thus creating forty-five possible pairs—and this is while we are ignoring the possibility of including Da'ath in pairings.

A pair is not just a dynamic or a push-pull or the reflection of an opposite. A pair also works within the Tree, often in crucial ways. Across the Tree they balance each other, so we could say that Chesed can be more and more utterly itself—more of the entire, endless essence of Chesed—only because this extreme is met and counterbalanced by Gevurah. Gevurah, on its own, might collapse entirely into itself, but its partner Chesed continually stretches and expands. Either of those forces, unbalanced, could obliterate the whole Tree. If they didn't have each other, and the Tree were to continue existing, they would have to be muted rather than the full force and depth that they can represent, entire unto themselves, because of their pairing. We can see this as an echo of the formation of our universe: if everything was spread evenly apart, there would be (almost) nothing, or if everything was crunched back together, again there would also be (almost) nothing. Because both dynamics exist and interact, we have everything.

Looking at pairs in the Tree, we can reflect on pairings we are familiar with such as parent and child, two lovers, best friends, siblings, boss and worker, or, more mythically, king and queen, regent and subject, or teacher and student. Some pairings have equal power, or a power balance, while others are hierarchical. This is reflected in the Tree according to whether the pairing is running across the Tree, where the pairs fundamentally balance each other out with equal strength, or whether they are down or up the Tree from each other, where there seems to be more of a power dynamic with one sephira above the other. Our feelings around some of these pairings may be reflected as we experience the relationship of the sephirot to each other. We may come to experience our own relationships differently as we learn more about how pairs operate within the Tree, as well as learn how different aspects of ourselves can balance each other out, potentially leading to a more complete expression of the whole.

Horizontal Pairs in the Tree

HOKMAH AND BINAH

Looking at the Tree from the top down, this is the first of the classic pairings, although it was Kether with Hokmah that created the possibility of pairs existing. Hokmah brought this possibility into the Tree, so it makes sense that Hokmah then forms the first of the most commonly worked pairs with Binah. Each of them is the head, or top, of a pillar. Sitting on the rung of the Tree below Kether, both Binah and Hokmah are very far away from us and almost as unknowable as Kether itself. Hokmah is veiled, gray, while Binah is hidden, black. Both of these non-colors are a commentary on the blinding white of Kether.

The relationship of these sephirot with each other is one of the things that helps make them accessible. If Hokmah is the initial division or explosion, Binah is the place where some things, at least, coalesce—clusters of gasses that become star systems, for instance, or the possibility of material existence or a child forming in the womb. I think of these two sephirot as expressions of two aspects of Goddess—Hokmah as veiled Wisdom, Sophia, the goddess in her majesty and power, and Binah as the Dark Mother, she who gives birth to all things. Hokmah and Binah are sisters in the Tree and, as Judith Laura points out in *Goddess Spirituality for the 21st Century,* both their names are feminine in Hebrew (Laura 2011, 124). They offer two different expressions of the manifestation of light. Where Hokmah veils her light, Binah lives in darkness, where light can be revealed. If Hokmah holds only mind and essence, the progression to Binah brings the possibility of body.

Working with this pair, we could examine our spiritual practice, seeing that both Binah and Hokmah hold gateways to Kether. We might ask if our mind-based practices are in balance with our body-based practices. Do we care for the temple as well as the flame within it? Is our body as sacred to us and as honored as our spirit? We could look at our soul journey through life so far (Hokmah) as well as our embodied journey through life (Binah). Which one needs our attention? Do we meet the needs of both as fully as we can? What practices might bring us more into fullness with each of these aspects of divinity? Hokmah and Binah are different parts of the same thing, and like all the horizontal pairings in the Tree, the ideal is that they work together.

There is no point in wisdom without understanding; that would be like a library full of the greatest literature, science, and philosophy, but the only person in the library cannot read. Understanding is a lovely quality, but intrinsically it must be applied to something. If I find myself in a foreign country, for example, I can be as understanding as I like, but without some wisdom about what I am experiencing, understanding on its own will not help me much. Hokmah and Binah are more different than any other pair, and yet the progression in the Tree from Hokmah to Binah (if we move from the top downward) or Binah to Hokmah (if we are ascending the Tree) comes at the crucial point: immediately after, or before, the transition from or to Kether. As access points to Kether, Hokmah carries the forms of the ritual and teachings, while Binah carries lived experience. Both are required to open the gateway to transformation.

CHESED AND GEVURAH

Chesed and Gevurah are the most iconic of pairs and often cited as the example when discussing pairs in the Tree. They are in the middle of their respective right- and left-hand pillars and in the middle section of the Tree. They seem extremely different—utter opposites. Where Chesed is ever-unfolding expansion, Gevurah is all about boundaries, limits, and contractions. Their colors are the cool blue of water contrasted with the hot red of flame. I think of the spreading nature of water and the concentrating power of fire. Yet they do not cancel each other out or contradict each other; they work together.

If we consider breath as an example of expansion and contraction, we can immediately understand that one cannot continue to breathe out; a breath in is needed as well. Similarly, we cannot just breathe in; outbreaths are also required. The in and out breaths are not limiting each other; they are enabling and supporting each other. Gevurah and Chesed operate in this way, not so much as alternates but as two oppositions that, in concert, create viability. The stuff our planet is made from was formed in the hearts of stars, and the planet itself went through a volcanic period while forming; whereas now Earth is thought of as the blue planet, with all life based around our waters, which cover two-thirds of the planet's surface. Life formed in the oceans' interaction with sunlight. Both of these elements were required even though, in different amounts, fire evaporates water and water quenches fire.

Gevurah's strict boundaries interact with Chesed's expansion. We use a vessel to contain our drink, a page to hold our words, a language to express our ideas. Expansion is given a form—turned into a drink, a book, or the communication of an abstract concept—because of the boundaries placed around it: the cup, the pages, the words and grammatical structure. Boundaries can make us feel safe, even adventurous; in the absence of boundaries we might be more hesitant. Think of stepping out onto a glass floor. Even though it is merely the illusion of not having the usual boundary of a floor, our bodies and minds have nothing like the confidence they do when walking forward over a wooden, concrete, or carpeted floor, where the boundaries are strongly apparent. Boundaries can also serve creativity. A piece of canvas is a particular size, the boundaries of a project such as a poem, landscape photography, or a clay vessel help shape the result. Without those boundaries we hardly know how to create anything, yet as soon as we pick up the oil pastel, consider a piece of clothing, or think into the brief for an artwork, our imaginations are unleashed.

Compassion and justice. Mercy and force. Loving-kindness and power. All of these are interpretations of Chesed and Gevurah's names. Any one set of these qualities, unchecked, leads either to complete free-form or to dictatorships of one kind or another. There is a tempering that happens when they are placed together; they each allow the best qualities of the other to shine. Looking at our relationships with others—whether a child, friend, or lover—if we only practice compassion, mercy, and loving-kindness, we will not even know when and where to turn up, let alone be able to discuss or make agreements, or be sure that each person's needs are being met. If we only practice justice, rigor, and power, it seems likely to be a very unpleasant relationship, yet without those qualities in the mix, the more expansive qualities cannot be fully realized.

NETZACH AND HOD

Netzach and Hod are the final, or bottom, horizontal pairing on the Tree. This is considered the most enmeshed pair in that they are even less able to operate without each other than the other pairings. Such a concern is abstract; they don't have to exist without the other, but this observation can help discern some of the subtleties of their relationship. They each hold the bottom position in their pillar, to some extent buttressing it or providing as much grounded reality as that pillar will get, remembering that the middle pillar still has two sephirot that are lower than Netzach and Hod.

I envision Netzach as a garden and Hod as a library. Not just any garden and any library: the most iconic, all-encompassing possibility of these. Garden—and all that is meant by garden, including the Garden of Eden, the garden of life that forms and grows and dies, the garden of imagination, the garden of the endless possibilities of creation. Library—the sum of all knowledge, and not just human knowledge, the possibilities of wisdom lying in wait to be read. The periodic table of elements, the system of biological taxonomy, the Akashic Records, and all the great libraries of history and literature.

Netzach and Hod dance together, one supplying vision and one the manifest of how that vision can become form. In Netzach we have concept—of a fern, a relationship, a scientific hypothesis, a house. In Hod we find out what laws govern the existence and particulars of a fern, how to build and sustain the relationship; we create experiments to test the hypothesis, we draw a blueprint for the house. Or, looking at it from the other direction, Hod to Netzach: when we know what it takes to build a house, to investigate scientifically, to relate with others, or to examine particular objects in our world, we can learn the skills and apply them.

As this is the horizontal pair closest to our world, perhaps we can understand their operations with each other more clearly. Or maybe the closer things get to manifestation, the tighter the arrangements have to be. Perhaps these endeavors of Netzach and Hod have matched the focus of Western cultures over the last thousand or so years. Our awareness of the eternity of unfolding existence and possibility is contrasted with the glory of underlying laws and the particularities of how each part functions. We can walk through a forest consumed by beauty (Netzach), we can walk through that same forest noticing species, habitat, ecosystems, and a thousand other details (Hod), or, like most of us most of the time, we exist in a blend of the two, appreciating the grandeur of Forest and the particularities of this iteration.

Vertical Pairs in the Tree

KETHER AND TIFERET

Kether and Tiferet are what we might term a distant pairing. Not only are they a vertical pair, running up and down the Tree rather than across, but they are separated by the Abyss and the space for Da'ath. Nonetheless, they do operate as a pair, although not so much in the way of horizontal pairings, which bring opposite forces into balance. A vertical pairing, within a pillar, allows us to examine a progression in either direction. So Tiferet can be seen as a certain rendition of Kether, or Kether can be understood as in some ways an elevation of Tiferet. Their colors are closely related—the brilliant, unseeable white light of Kether and the softer, more visible yellow light of Tiferet.

Tiferet is known as the Kether of the lower Tree—below the Abyss, it is the highest sephira on the middle pillar and so transmits some of the qualities of Kether into the bottom seven sephirot. It is associated with the sun, the center of our solar system. As our local star, the sun is the closest manifestation of those distant brilliances we see in the night sky, whose existence shimmering there can remind us in each second of the beginnings of the universe and the Big Bang still rippling out in tides through every thing and scrap of matter. In this way Tiferet is holding a place for Kether, our local piece of the infinite. By studying the sun we learn more about stars, even though they are separated from us by such distance. By inference, in studying Tiferet we learn more about Kether, even though Kether lies across the Abyss and is unknowable.

Kether is the source of all things, the One behind all ideas of gods and the divine. Tiferet can be accessed through mythic figures such as Zeus, Jesus, Odin, Isis, and

Buddha, as well as spiritual leaders such as Gandhi, Joan of Arc, the Dalai Lama, Mother Theresa, and many others throughout history. They can be seen as channels for the divine, and their teachings or sometimes even their presence can offer us a gateway to access the divine within ourselves.

The crown of Kether is ineffable and inaccessible, but the beauty of Tiferet can bring us closer to it, can open our hearts. The heart—and Tiferet is considered both to be *in* the heart of the Tree and to *be* its heart—is the most direct access that we have to the divine. When our hearts are closed, we cannot feel the divine. Then a moment of grace—a dawn ray—can reach us even while we are experiencing what feels like an endless dark night of the soul. This opens our hearts and returns us to the world. Saved. Reminded by Tiferet that Kether exists.

Yesod and Malkuth

Like Kether and Tiferet, the pairing of Yesod and Malkuth is vertical, continuing down the middle pillar. At Malkuth we reach the depths of the Tree, although, as Yesod is the channel, we pass through some strange territory. Yesod has been associated with the subconscious, with Jung's collective unconscious, and the mythic realm, while Malkuth is everything we see, touch, hear, feel, and taste—all that is part of the earth. This pair holds almost opposite and certainly complementary energies. What would life be like without access to imagination and dreams and a felt sense of the connectedness of all things? Yet those things appear a direct contradiction to how we spend most of our lives: in the pragmatic business of making a living, caring for those we love or who are dependent on us, and focused on existing in the world.

Both Yesod and Malkuth contain *all things*—Yesod in the realms of the imaginal and Malkuth in the material. If Yesod is the cocoon wherein the caterpillar is dissolving its own body and calling upon those mythic-sounding imaginal cells, Malkuth is the place where the butterfly is born, to briefly live in this kingdom. Yesod is the one that channels the nine previous sephirot directly into Malkuth, whereas Malkuth returns the great experiment of life and existence back up the Tree to Yesod. Their interaction is an act—continual acts—of transformation. Yesod is the foundation of the kingdom, even in its insubstantial and intangible nature. It is the dream that dreams reality. Yesod makes it possible for us, as part of Malkuth, to imagine what we do not yet know—to reach beyond our own reality.

Malkuth is entirely dependent on Yesod to receive the visions or understandings conceived higher up in the Tree or from the divine, and this does explain why visions and dreams can be so powerful. If we think of callings that many of us receive—a voice or vision telling us of our soul purpose, our ability or potential—those dreamlike, resonant qualities of such an experience contain this power. Malkuth is the only sephira where all that has existed in the Tree can come into what we know as existence. It's as if they are shells for each other—each containing and within the other—rather than merely a pair on the middle pillar. This is another way to understand the Tree: as progressive rings encompassing each other. Because this is Kabbalah, the rings work in both directions, with Kether as either the central or the outermost ring, and the same for Malkuth. In this model Malkuth and Yesod enclose each other.

Our lives—all human lives—are lived within Malkuth and Yesod. They are as intrinsic to each other as our material and immaterial worlds. If we consider a concept such as love—or hate or fear or joy—we have physical, bodily responses to these. But we also carry a broad understanding of how these forces operate in ourselves and in social settings. These are embodied experiences within a collective archetype. We can feel the power of the archetypal when we are within a group, especially a large group. Think of the infectious, joyous atmosphere of a wedding, the escalated fear of a street riot, the love emanating in a room with a great spiritual leader, the power of propaganda in a war. Yesod can magnify the many similar individual responses into an enormous wave of feeling so that even those not contributing much individually can experience more than a single share of the emotion.

Other Pairs in the Tree
KETHER AND MALKUTH

This is the most obvious pairing in the Tree that is not covered by the conventional horizontal and vertical pairings. Malkuth is sometimes described as *the bride in the mud* or *the bride with mud on her dress*. But whose bride? Malkuth is the bride of Kether. They are both All—all that is. Malkuth is all that has come into manifestation. Kether is the One; without Kether, there would be nothing. All of Malkuth is an expression of [all of] Kether.

In the story of the shattering of the vessels, when Kether pours its light down the Tree, Malkuth is the only vessel in the lower Tree that does not shatter. This great cascading tragedy is rescued by Malkuth. This pair is as far apart as you can get in the Tree, yet they are utterly dependent on each other within its structure and logic. They are the top and bottom of our map, yet when we curl the map into a cylinder or fold it in half across the middle, they meet, merge, and possibly their lovemaking is the source of all that arises. Spirit is infused into each blue wren, possibly each feather of each blue wren, each vane of each feather, each molecule and atom. Spirit and matter are not divided but are one. Malkuth is Kether. Between them, they hold the whole Tree.

BINAH AND MALKUTH

Binah and Malkuth are said to have a special relationship, linked together by manifestation or birth. Binah is the first point on the Tree when manifestation becomes a possibility. Malkuth realizes that potential and gives birth to the world. These are very goddess-like concepts and imagery, the womb of the dark mother in Binah and the bright rain of beings born into existence on earth, each of us one of those. Malkuth could not exist without the progression through each of the sephirot, including those that come before Binah, as a baby could not be born without its parents first having been born, or their parents, and without nine months of sheltering and nurture in the womb, and yet—that moment of conception and that moment of birth are linked intrinsically as tremendous change points in the state of being. The pairing of Binah and Malkuth resonates with this reminder.

KETHER AND DA'ATH

This is a less common idea, to pair Kether with Da'ath rather than Tiferet, because of course Da'ath isn't actually there, even in the liminal way we are talking about the other sephirot being there—where is *there*?—oh, the delights of Kabbalah. But if we accept the diagram of the Tree as a model of philosophical and religious concepts, discussing a piece of it that doesn't quite appear on that map—if we get past that, we can see some reasons why this could be a logical pairing.

For a start, they are right next to each other—there's a massive gap between Kether and Tiferet, and they literally have to span worlds to reach across it. Da'ath's place on the Tree is right below Kether, and now that we look at it this way, we might wonder how

Tiferet ever came to be paired with Kether, with this shadowy third player in between them. But, most convincingly, where Kether is all that is, Da'ath doesn't even exist; so they meet and fill each other. If Da'ath is a black hole, and the entire universe poured down into it, wouldn't it finish everything utterly neatly? Kether and Da'ath have a similar weightiness to them—the All of the Tree and complete absence. In spite of this logic, because Da'ath is not actually one of the sephirot, most systems do not include it as a possible pair for anything. It hovers alone, offering glimpses of alternate universes that may cancel themselves out in an instant.

TIFERET AND YESOD

If Kether and Da'ath are a pair, or in the moments that we consider them a pair, that leaves Tiferet and Yesod to pair—unless Tiferet were to be left single in the center of the Tree and Yesod to remain in its original pairing with Malkuth. But Tiferet and Yesod are worth considering as a pair. We could say it's through our imagination and our opening to the collective consciousness that we are able to love another, whether it is another human, a place, or the divine. When we are in love or when we allow our hearts to be touched, we find ourselves in a liminal place where possibilities open up. The concept of the human heart, so much greater than the physical organ of the heart and the human imagination, so difficult to explain, even when studying the brain in intricate detail, are to a certain measure inexplicable while also being immediately understood by all. Yesod is linked with the genitals and sexuality, so the close connection with the heart makes sense. Making love, not just with our genitals but with our hearts, we span this middle pillar, drawing down the divine and at the same time entirely in our bodies. The pairing of Tiferet with Yesod encapsulates this.

ENDLESS PAIRINGS

Now that we've come this far with pairings, what's to stop us going through the entire Tree? Why shouldn't Kether be paired with Binah, with Chesed, Gevurah, Netzach? What about Netzach with Yesod, Netzach with Malkuth, Netzach with Hokmah? There could be every possible variation of pairing throughout the Tree, and they would all make a certain sort of sense. This is the Kabbalah, after all, so we could just keep going and going. I'll leave this for your imagination...

practice | Traveling the Lightning Flash

The lightning flash is an instrumental part of experiential Kabbalah work in the Tree of Life. It's an informal but well used path that runs quickly through the whole Tree in either direction, upward or downward. Although most of its sections run along actual numbered or named paths that connect the sephirot to each other, part of it runs diagonally through the center of the Abyss, which none of the formal paths do. The lightning flash reminds me of those public rights-of-way in England where you cut across a field, go down a bit of laneway, along someone's drive, and then onto a forest track. It's point-to-point. Eventful. Exciting.

There are two basic ways in which to work, or run, the lightning flash, and two directions: from Kether to Malkuth and from Malkuth to Kether. The two styles are either an express all-the-way-in-one-direction or a stopping-at-all-stations, where we jump onto the lightning flash to travel from one sephira to the next. Traveling the lightning flash, we are not paying an enormous amount of attention to the paths we happen to be on, which is a whole area of study in itself (see section 6), but rather riding the lightning flash as a method of transport between sephirot.

You can do this exercise entirely in your mind or on a paper map of the Tree, but I like best to do it physically. You can mark the Tree out on the floor with chalk, on the beach in sand, or on the ground in some way. Even better, use your colored sephirot disks, decorated or not. You can run the lightning flash with a group or by yourself. There are some notes about the special dynamics of working this with a group at the end of the practice.

We travel via lightning flash from one sephira to another to transition from a month of working with Hod, for example, to a month of working with Yesod. Or a week, a few hours, or whatever time period we are spending within each sephira. We also use it to travel the entire length of the Tree, either because we are leaving Malkuth and the next sephira we are going to inhabit is Kether or as a study or ritual in itself. A diagram of the lightning flash is on page 12.

Traveling the Lightning Flash

TIME: 10–15 minutes

YOU WILL NEED: 11 sephirot disks, decorated or not (or at various stages), journal and pen. Alternatively, the map of the Tree drawn out on a floor, the ground, or on a piece of paper.

Lay out your disks in a map of the Tree or draw the map out on the floor, ground, or paper.

The lightning flash runs in straight lines from Kether to Hokmah, Hokmah to Binah, Binah to Chesed (over the top of/through Da'ath; it doesn't stop there), Chesed to Gevurah, Gevurah to Tiferet, Tiferet to Netzach, Netzach to Hod, Hod to Yesod, Yesod to Malkuth. When I am drawing it or using a ribbon or tape to mark it out, I stop the lines at the edges of the sephirot (or run the ribbon underneath the disks), but I run it across/over the top of Da'ath. This is at least partly because Da'ath is only a location (or, more accurately, a potential location) within the Abyss. It's quite possible to pass through the Abyss without having to interact with Da'ath. You can draw or mark the lightning flash out or just know where it is.

If you are using the lightning flash to transition from one sephira to the next, stand or sit on or nearby the related disk. If you are working the lightning flash as a whole thing, separate from making any transition, stand or sit to one side of the Tree or the top or the foot of it (depending on which direction you intend to travel). You can also do this in trance, meditation, or focusing on a drawn map of the Tree.

TRANSITIONING FROM ONE SEPHIRA TO THE NEXT

If you have spent time with one sephira and are about to transition to working with another, ground and center yourself. Then take a few moments to honor this sephira and thank it for all it has shared with you. Allow yourself to sink fully into how that experience has been, and acknowledge it from this place of connection. Then release it.

See or feel yourself as hovering near the Tree and nearby or over that sephira. Feel how it is to be connected, traveling, not yet immersed in a new sephira or on the lightning bolt path. Share some breaths with the Tree.

Begin slowly moving from the sephira you are leaving along the line of the lightning flash to the next sephira. When you arrive, stop and open all your awareness. What does it feel like to arrive here? You may have visual images, body sensations, emotions, hear words or sounds or anything else, including a sense of the unknown, blankness, or uncertainty. Take some time to arrive fully; stand or sit here, on or next to this new sephira. Look at the Tree all around you and notice how it seems from this position. Spend five minutes recording your immediate impressions.

RUNNING THE WHOLE LIGHTNING FLASH

If you are running the whole lightning flash, begin at the top or bottom of the Tree. Ground and center yourself, then move to either Kether or Malkuth. Pause and take a few breaths there, noticing any impressions you receive before moving to the next (Hokmah or Yesod, depending on where you started). Take several breaths and again open yourself to impressions—sensations, thoughts, visions, or anything else—before continuing to move, sephira by sephira, up or down the whole Tree.

Stop when you reach your destination. Step out of the Tree, turning to look at the Tree from this perspective. Take some time to record your impressions of the journey.

There is another way to travel the entire lightning flash, which is within a deeper level of ritual. Spend some time beforehand thinking and feeling into this. What would symbolize this journey for you? I have seen it done many ways. One person lit a tealight for each sephira and placed it there as they passed through. One person danced through the Tree. One person stripped off their clothes and dragged themselves over the floor, like a marine creature crawling onto land. One person sang a brief prayer into each sephira. What is the magic waiting for you?

RUNNING THE LIGHTNING FLASH IN A GROUP

This process assumes that each person in the group is holding different sephirot and that all are transitioning at the same time through the Tree and to their next sephira.

Stand or sit near or on your sephira. Look around at the Tree and its people. Then begin the process of grounding, acknowledging, and honoring the sephira you have been working with. Have someone guide the process or have an agreed-upon amount of time for this, usually a few minutes. Then, all together, step out from those sephirot to one side.

The person in Kether moves slowly down the lightning flash until they reach Hokmah. When this happens, the person in Hokmah begins their journey across to Binah.

As they reach Binah, the person there begins to travel along the lightning flash across the Abyss until they reach Chesed. This continues on until the person who's been in Yesod arrives at Malkuth. Everyone except the person who was in Malkuth before the lightning flash began takes a step to the side to make room. The person transitioning from Malkuth to Kether then runs the whole lightning flash, bottom to top, either by simply walking it or in a more ritualized manner, as described above.

When that person reaches Kether, everyone else steps back into their sephira. Look at the Tree again, with this arrangement of people, then sit down to contemplate and record in a journal your first impressions of the new sephira. It's lovely to have a round where everyone shares their impressions, either very briefly or at greater length.

If there is more than one person in a sephira, allow each to have their own journey. If there are gaps in your Tree where there's no one holding a sephira, when it's the time for that part of the lightning flash to be run, allow the appropriate amount of time to elapse as if someone was physically moving that distance.

trance | The Orchard of Ten Trees

We usually see the sephirot as all a part of one tree, the Tree of Life, but there are many other ways to view this map. As Kabbalists we often need to deconstruct the map as we focus on one particular detail. Then we put it all back together again, the experience having added to our understanding, not unlike the original splitting of Hokmah away from Kether and the entire journey of the Tree and of everything. Thus in these exercises we are often taking things apart, doing something with them while they are separate, and then putting them back together again.

The orchard trance imagines that the Tree is not one but ten trees. In this version they compose an orchard, where trees are set apart from each other, but in another version they could be a forest, where trees are close and interdependent. The orchard is a human-built concern, catering to our needs rather than the desires, inclinations, or requirements of trees.

TIME: 30 minutes to an hour

YOU WILL NEED: A comfortable place to trance, journal and pen, coloring things optional

Trances come in many forms and different ways to each person. You may be someone who experiences strong visual imagery or not. You may find instead that what comes to you within trance states are bodily feelings (such as sensations of hot, cold, tingling, numbness, tension, relaxation) or emotions (such as tiredness, excitement, anxiety, pleasure) or memories or words or sounds. You may have different experiences each time you trance.

Within any single trance you can learn to develop your receptivity or awareness. For example, if you do receive mainly visual images, you can ask yourself *What emotion do I associate with this? What is my body feeling right now?* If you mainly feel and remember things during a trance, you might ask yourself *What might I hear if I listen closely? Is there a visual image I associate with this memory or feeling?* We can learn to wake up our senses during trance, just as we might do while recalling a dream or while wide awake, walking around in and interacting with the external world.

Unless you have an excellent memory, it's best to emerge briefly from this trance at the ten points to record whatever you have experienced. We move back and forth between these two worlds of inner trance and outer world. You might need some practice to do this confidently or perhaps you will find it easy. There is more written on trance, grounding, and sacred space in the appendix.

Settle yourself for a trance journey, perhaps beginning with a simple grounding and some quiet, regular breathing. Have your journal or a pen and paper nearby.

Begin with an induction to the trance state, either one you are familiar with and comfortable using or a version of the following.

With your eyes either closed or in soft focus and breathing gently, conjure up an awareness of the room or space around you. Let yourself feel its dimensions, the texture and temperature of the air, the placement of the walls or whatever surrounds you, the position of your body within the space. Continue to breathe a little more deeply and slowly, now bringing your awareness to your body and making any adjustments for comfort that you need. Let your awareness briefly visit your different body parts, noticing how your breaths in and out affect them. Now focus on the breath, allowing it to soften. In particular, follow the inbreaths, feeling the space expanding within you as they enter your body. Let your awareness dwell on that space, that expansion...keep feeding it with the breath, and imagine the vastness that resides within you.

Imagine that you are facing a gate. It could be any sort of a gate or stile or even a gap within a hedge or a stream of water to cross. On the other side of this gate lies the orchard you have come to discover. Continue breathing deeply and slowly. When you are ready, open the gate, cross over the boundary, and enter the orchard.

You will notice a tree nearby. Perhaps it is one of many; perhaps it is by itself. Move toward it, noticing what type of tree it is. It might be a fruit tree, a nut tree, a tree native to your region, a tree you are familiar with, or a tree you have never seen before. You might be able to name it but still have it be completely different than how this type of tree appears in the external world. It might be a sapling, a mature tree, or ancient. It may be a tree from fairy tale or myth.

This first tree in the orchard represents Malkuth. Notice what you feel, see, and experience as you approach it. You might want to place your hand on its trunk, lean against it, sit at its base for a moment, or reach out and touch its leaves, branches, flowers, or fruit. Spend a few moments simply being with this tree, noticing your thoughts, what you receive through your senses, and your impressions.

Before you move on, record this tree. For example, I might write: *Malkuth—golden oak. Vast.*

Leave this tree behind and move on, deeper into the orchard. You notice or are drawn to a second tree. Perhaps it is quite close to the first one or perhaps far apart. This second tree in the orchard of your mind represents Yesod.

Again, notice your sensations and impressions as you approach it. It might be completely different than the Malkuth tree or quite similar. Spend a few minutes with this tree, feeling into its particular nature. Imagine yourself touching, smelling, looking at, listening to, and possibly even tasting this tree. What type of tree is it? How do you feel beside it? What impressions do you receive?

Before you move on, again briefly record this tree. For example: *Yesod—pear tree, in fruit. Tall.*

Journey on toward a third tree, which represents Hod. As before, spend some time with this tree, gathering sensations, thoughts, impressions. Again, record the type of tree that has appeared for Hod. For example: *Hod—hazelnut. Abundant.*

The fourth tree will represent Netzach. You may notice that your journey is taking you in a straight line or that you are wandering around this orchard, spiraling, or maybe following the map of the Tree of Life. Spend some time with your Netzach tree and get to know it a little. Before you move on, record it as you have the others. For example: *Netzach—flowering pink eucalypt.*

The fifth tree is Tiferet. As well as taking in the particulars of this tree, we might pause here. Tiferet is halfway through our journey. What have we noticed about the trance, the orchard, and ourselves so far? Then record this information; for example: *Tiferet—wattle, full bloom. Feeling deeper within the orchard.*

The sixth tree will be Gevurah. Spend a few moments noticing how this tree—as each one—is different from all the others. Record it before moving on; for example: *Gevurah—flame tree. Alight.*

The seventh tree is Chesed. We are a long way up the map by now, or a long way into the orchard. Perhaps the air or ground is becoming different, perhaps we feel differently within ourselves. After spending a couple of minutes with this tree, record it; for example: *Chesed—huge white flowers, low branches.*

Between trees seven and eight lies the Abyss. Perhaps this will be represented by a mist you pass through, a bridge or stream you cross over, or some other experience.

On the other side of the Abyss is the eighth tree, Binah's tree. Again, spend a few moments with this tree, noticing the impressions you receive and writing a brief note for yourself before moving on. For example: *Binah—copper beech.*

The ninth tree represents Hokmah. Perhaps you have noticed a change in the qualities of the trance, your immersion in it, or the appearance or impressions of the orchard itself since crossing the Abyss. Spend a few moments with this tree before recording your impressions and moving on. For example: *Hokmah—mountain ash. Very tall.*

The tenth and final tree we visit represents Kether. Perhaps it is the world tree itself that you see, or the biblical Tree of the Knowledge of Good and Evil. Perhaps it is a young sapling or an ancient giant. Allow just as much time as you spent with each of the other trees before gathering your impressions and jotting down a few words. For example: *Kether—silver icicle tree. Fairy tale.*

Move away from the tenth tree and let your attention be drawn toward the end of the orchard. In some way we have journeyed through a complete circle and find ourselves back at the gate we originally entered. Know that on the other side of this gate is the end of the trance and your journey back into the external world.

Cross back through the gate, letting your awareness return fully to your own breath. This time focus on the outbreaths, how they leave your body and enter into the space around you. Allow this direction of the outbreaths to take you up, out of the trance state, and into an awareness of your body patiently waiting for your full return. Let your attention be drawn to the space around you, the location you are in, and take a little time to open your eyes, move your head and shoulders, stretch your legs, and maybe change position entirely.

Now that you have finished the trance, it is the ideal time to record it. You might do this by writing all or parts of it down, using the notes you made as memory prompts. You might draw either a map of the orchard with its ten trees or one or more of the trees themselves. You might write down questions or try relating what you experienced to your knowledge of the different sephirot. Take some time to reflect on what you learned by experiencing each of the sephirot as a tree.

You can return another time to explore the orchard more deeply, perhaps spending an extended time with one particular tree or visiting the orchard at nighttime or within ritual.

Memoir: *The Beloved*

I walk into the café and he is sitting at the very last table, his back to the wall, facing the door. His face lights up when he sees me. He is wearing a purple silk shirt, loose; it's extravagant in the setting of an early afternoon country town. He has long, tangled dark hair with a few threads of silver. He's clean shaven, has slightly darkened skin, and when he stands I see he has a rangy, looming sort of body. We kiss cheeks in greeting and go to the counter to order; I'm impressed that he has found a café with fresh ground decaffeinated coffee. He pays for my drink although every single thing about him and everything he says shows he has far less money than me. Somehow I already know that he likes an extravagant gesture.

When we sit he begins talking. I look at his hands on the table between us and relief washes over me. I think that here is a man who will at least make love to me. At last. He has a warmth, an immediacy, and an energy, but it's really his hands—why do I think, gazing at them, that these are hands that will be willing to—will want to, even—make love? All those so careful, so removed, polite, cautious men I have met or been friends with, wrapped up in their discretion as if a kiss, let alone actual sex, would undo them completely and they haven't wanted to be undone at all. They've been unavailable by choice, prior commitments, sexual preferences, pure caution, ingrained aloofness, but his hands on the table between us—I think these are hands that want to hold, caress, explore. These are hands reaching out to life and, across the table, even to me.

This changes how I am, how I feel, and how I behave. Believing I have found a man who might actually be into sex—extraordinary that they've been so rare in my life lately, but anyway—I blossom with possibility. I can feel I am, in this meeting, a slightly more extravagant version of myself; magnanimous, delighted by life. We talk for an hour or so. He tells me stories of tragedy and love and horror—that is, various parts of his life—and occasionally he asks about me, but mostly not. He does say that I am gorgeous. I think he might be nervous and so driven to entertain instead of be deeply present. The scale of his stories is extreme. Car crashes and death threats, hospitals, despair and breakups. Perhaps I ignore that because I have already decided what is possible between us.

When we leave the café he places the palm of his hand against my lower back as we go to cross the road and there's a car coming; I want to weep with relief. *Oh yes— hands, body, please touch me.* The physical touch, skin to skin through my shirt, the warmth of someone caring for me as we do this so mundane thing of crossing the road in a shopping block in a country town. He is anxious, saying goodbye to me, he says several times that it's up to me, and he'll wait to hear if I want to see him again, and I almost laugh standing there in the street by my car. I promise him *Definitely I will contact you, yes I will see you again.*

Driving home I remember a conversation I had with a friend. *Sure*, my friend said— *meet him for a coffee—why not? It's just a coffee.* Oh, nothing is just a coffee. This is a whole landscape, a whole play. There's something a little unsettling about how familiar he feels to me, as if we already had a relationship rather than that we were at the beginning of something. Because we are at the beginning of something, I can tell. There was an undertow between us and although undertows are usually dangerous, I have given myself to this one. Does one really even have a choice when it's like this? There's a part of me standing on the shore, watching. Thinking, as the other part of me vanishes out to sea, *Oh she's gone on this one. She's in the tide of it. Goodbye.*

The familiarities, the patterns, keep unwinding. He has the same name as an ex-lover of mine—not just a casual ex, some sort of fling or light and beautiful thing, but a heavy name resonant in my personal history. I almost don't want to call him by it, so I couple his first name with his last name and I always call him by this double name. It grants him a certain stature in my personal landscape since I do that for my own name. Plus, his names are beautiful. They could be the conjuring of magical space, sacred landscape, wild nature—they are mythic. Just to say these names is an invocation of sorts. He's a musician. Of course. My past is littered with musicians, most especially guitarists—I've always often chosen musicians. Far more of my ex-lovers are musicians than any other thing, way out of proportion to their numbers in the general population. Whenever I have a lover who isn't a musician, I'm a little surprised by it—not that I'm even a musician myself but I've just come to expect *Oh, of course, a musician. A magician.*

He has a massive pain problem from multiple injuries and then surgeries. Chronic pain. I know the enormity with which it can rule a life, a mind, a psyche. The grip and thrust of it, the fierce walls and private terrors of it, the isolation, the desperation. I remember. The way it's astounding that anything else gets done at all, apart from simply existing—to leave the house, to connect with someone, achieve practical things such as shopping or cooking—I remember how impossible they all are. The body as prison, as torturer, as captive. Yet I also know that without those temptations, without the call of coffee with a beautiful stranger, a drive down the coast, a meal to prepare and eat, the pain has won already. I know what it means to take those risks, the cost of them, and the necessity.

He hasn't been in a relationship for three years. Neither have I. Three years: the exact same length of time, to the month. He's my age. He knows the Wheel of the Year, he can discuss ritual and magic, he knows what they mean. He looks like a Celtic king from long ago. He calls himself a warrior, believes in fighting for what he loves, but really I see him as broken and more of a lover than a warrior. Although they can be the same thing, I suppose. He has been broken by life. He doesn't have much will to live and he knows it's a problem, he's fighting it desperately. He's more or less homeless when I meet him, staying with a friend and then another friend, looking all the time for somewhere to live but so inflexible and rude and contrary it doesn't surprise me, the difficulty he's having. He believes that to soften, to compromise, is to lose utterly, to go under, and so he won't.

He's the opposite of me. It's as if at some crucial point each of us had a choice and I chose one way and it's led me to a life of optimism, of believing the best, being gentle with myself and others, finding joy, and he chose something different. Or maybe it wasn't a choice, and it's class or money or advantage or luck, but he's struggling, doing the best he can against overwhelming circumstances, but with nearly everything we encounter we have opposite reactions. He is fierce and hurting, lashes out, he twists in bitterness, hates the world, he's gratified when he gets to take his anger out on someone or something. It horrifies me. Once we know each other a little better, I say that I see how unhappy he is, but I am not unhappy and do not wish to become that way. If being with him is going to require my unhappiness, I will not choose it, and he agrees.

He's the same as me. Once he is talking about some woman's looks, maybe one of his past lovers, and I ask what he thinks of me, physically, and he says *Look at you—you're the fucking image of me in a female form*. When we hold hands or I rest my head against his there is a merging—it feels almost a physical melting, as if our bodies already blended and it is mere confirmation that we touch now. We talk about this, we wonder at it, and it's as if we are two sides of one thing. I say that he will have to be the one who makes almost all the changes to be with me because my life is good and his is terrible, and he says he knows that.

I meet him at the beach. It's overcast and slightly windy. We walk on the beach, talking as if we have known each other for years. We sit down, slightly sheltered by coastal scrub trees, cross-legged and facing each other. We take each other's hands. He asks when he can kiss me and I say *You'll know when it's time*. We gaze into each other's eyes and there's a falling, there's a joining, there's recognition. He says *Will we be able to come back to this place, this moment?* and I say *No, this is the only time we will ever have this moment* and we are playing a game; he says *What if we come back here to this exact place, can we have it again?* and I say *No, in all the worlds this is the only iteration of this moment.* I sit between his legs and he has his arms around me and his face against my hair and I feel held by the world and luminous, aflame, and I think we are blazing through the worlds and time has come to rest here, in this moment.

He tells me his last relationship was broken up by text—she sent him a text message to tell him it was off. The level of his vehemence and hurt three years later—he rails against her, against the pain of it and the shallowness of the action and the avoidance of confrontation…I get it, yet I do take note. It is running so strong in him, I think that he'll do it. He'll break up with me over text. I guess I can take it. But largely I am not thinking we will break up, even though we are not actually in a relationship yet. This is the second time we have met.

We stand on the little wooden platform overlooking the beach and sea. He stands behind me—even though he is much larger than me, he is soft in it, so I don't feel over-awed by him physically but sheltered and connected. He has his arms around me and it's a seduction that doesn't need to seduce because I'm already there. Gently he lifts my hair off the left side of my neck and bends down and places a kiss against my skin, slowly. It's incredibly sexy. I shiver and laugh with a sort of delight and half turn to him and we kiss oh so slowly, soft soft lips finally I've found his softness and our hair gets mixed up in the kiss, we have the same sort of hair, long, the same length and curly, the same sort of curl so it doesn't lie flat or smooth but blows about and catches in everything and tangles and gets in the way all the time and we both like it and that is incidental because this kiss, this thing with lips and mouths and breath, is taking all my attention.

He kisses the same way I kiss. It's not a way men usually kiss. Soft, so soft and just hovering there, letting kisses arise of themselves and melt across to the other, merge into the mouth and breath and I am wrapped up in him now, wrapped up in his arms and this minute and the wind and ocean and the warmth of another body and the belonging here and there's an intent within the softness, of meeting and showing up and being seen and abandoning everything just for this kiss. It's cold, he's in pain, and I let him go, confident—oh so confident—that this is the beginning of a large journey, unfolding. My mouth cannot stop smiling because of the kisses.

He comes to visit me bringing flowers and food and his guitar. The food he chose was the same food I chose, so we have two sets of smoked salmon, salad, bread, dark chocolate. He plays the guitar, long, complicated classical pieces and also a little song he makes up about me. I offer to untangle his hair and he sits patiently while I comb through it with my fingers, unpicking the knots one by one. We eat food, we have long—hours long—conversations about desires and our histories and what we are feeling. Eventually it gets late. We have spent most of the day and evening together, and he says he should leave. I think about asking him to stay, but I am operating in the belief that there's lots of time and I don't feel any need to rush. So I don't. I am still a little frightened of him, of the magnitude of what seems to be between us.

We arrange to see each other in a few days but he postpones it, day by day for over a week because he is exhausted, sick, has too much on, isn't coping. He says maybe he will give up living in this area and go back to the place he grew up that he hates but at least he can stay there. I can't tell if he's serious or just angry at the world and punishing himself. I'm about to go away for ten days and finally he agrees to see me the afternoon before I go.

He's in a terrible state when I arrive and I spend the first few hours just soothing, massaging, listening, and cutting through some of the spiraling self-talk. We lie together on the bed and he falls asleep, an arm around me. I cry a little, it seems so slender. Perhaps there is not room for me in this life. Later we go out for food—I drive but I am horrified by the way he talks to other drivers and pedestrians on the road—they are all idiots, deserve to be shot, according to him, are a waste of space. We buy food and eat in the park, an uneasy alliance between the potential there's been and now these distances sweeping in—all the things that will take us apart. He feels ill again so I drive him home and then drive home myself.

While I am away, he calls me every night and talks for an hour. Once or twice he remembers to ask how I am. His talk is bitter and endless and circular and I alternate between listening supportively and deconstructing his narrative. Neither seems to make much difference. The day before I come home, I send him a text saying that I am seeking delight and softness and joy and maybe he doesn't really have space for that. I realize why his last partner may have sent him a text to break up. Text is the only way I feel I can get some words in, break through the tide of his story and claim some space. I am not breaking it off, but I am offering him an out. Even though I would have said we are two halves of one possibility, we belong together, I think that perhaps he cannot do it or does not even want to or doesn't want to enough. But he texts back immediately, in capital letters, *BRING IT ON!!* and so I smile and believe a little longer.

When I get home he cannot see me. Each day there is another reason: he is tired, busy, in pain, elsewhere, overwhelmed. One morning he sends a text saying he's leaving the area immediately, tomorrow, and will not be pursuing any relationship. I text back *Can we talk about this?*—but we never do. He breaks up with me by text. Not that we were ever actually together. I am shocked—winded by it, I double over with the suddenness and ferocity of it. This whole—thing, love affair, person, potential relationship— has just vanished. The kind of connection I have only in dreams, and I met it in real life and—it's gone. He doesn't choose it. I see him caught in a rip of the universe and pulled away by pain and circumstance and poverty, bad luck and bitterness.

We never made love. I can hardly believe that—the promise in his hands, vanished. I can't reconcile it. I have almost never, maybe never at all had a premonition that strong that didn't come to be. Did I somehow fail to tell him that that was what I wanted? It's as if I've lost a piece of myself. What actually has happened? This person, who I saw as being so like myself, only they made different choices all along the way—he made a different choice here, as well. Maybe it's that simple. Where I experience power, agency, choice, and seek out love, expansion, connection, he—perhaps—experiences powerlessness, persecution, and hopelessness and so he retreats, gives up, shuts down. We are opposites, and the tide of this takes us in opposite directions, like a double spiral that's come in so close together and now the two pieces are sweeping out to the opposite edges of the universe.

But couldn't you have made love to me first?

I had a lover—almost. I had the idea of a beloved, a mirror; one so close they knew the bones of me, one I longed to make love with, not just once but many times, uncountable times. Maybe it would have been worse if we'd been lovers—certainly it would have been worse, but at least I would have had that. I am left with grief and longing and separation.

ritual | Mirror of the Gods

This exercise was inspired by David Cooper's exercise "Through God's Eyes" in God Is a Verb.

Mirrors have often been used to critique, correct, or find fault with ourselves, but they can also be a powerful gateway for magic and self-reflection. In the moment of Kether splitting apart, Hokmah becomes the mirror for the All. Working with a mirror, we can glimpse a piece of this mystery.

TIME: 30–45 minutes

YOU WILL NEED: A mirror you can sit in front of, a veil or scarf to cover the mirror, journal and pen; optional: a candle, sacred objects

Arrange the mirror so you can see yourself, then cover it with the veil or scarf. If you are using a hand mirror, find some way to prop it up so you don't need to hold onto it. Have your journal and pen to hand.

Take some time to ground and center yourself. Light the candle if you are using one. If you have sacred or special objects, you can place them at the base of the mirror or nearby. You might wish to cast a circle. You can choose to do this ritual nude.

Gaze at the mirror. What can you see through the veil? Perhaps a dim shape, an outline, or maybe you can only see the veil. Can you find the place inside yourself where you know that everything—including you, the mirror, and the veil—are all unendingly a part of Kether, the divine?

When you are ready to look upon that mystery, remove the veil. Try to simply notice what you see without getting involved in any story about it. Breathe deeply a few times and watch what happens to your reflection. Look at every part of yourself that you can see in the mirror, but especially your face.

Spend some time gazing into the eyes of this reflected self. If you were meeting this being for the first time, what feelings, thoughts, and reactions might you have?

Take some slow breaths and feel yourself dropping deeply within, through time and space and back as far as the time of the singularity—when all of time, space, and matter was concentrated into one point. Allow yourself to consider this point as Kether, the All. Perhaps you can even feel within your body or hold the thought of how each atom of you was there at that time, and in some way it still recalls that reality.

Breathe with this for a while. Notice what arises—maybe you have body sensations, emotions, visions, or understandings. You might want to take some notes or even sketch a picture.

Then let yourself remember the moment of splitting, where the All split into two. Breathe with that moment—as part of the All falls away into the universe. You are that part. Gaze at your image. Breathe with it.

Look at the particularities of this fragment that has been divided away from the whole. What do you see? What emotions arise as you gaze at this being? How does this fragment look to you? When you look closely, maybe you can see some of the challenges and gifts that this piece of the All is experiencing or has experienced in their life. Maybe you feel compassion, joy, grief, love, or fear as you gaze at them.

Look deeply into their eyes. What message would you give this being? Can you see how they are the beloved? If you tell them *You are my beloved*, what happens to their body, face, and in their eyes as they receive this message?

Breathe with this experience for a few minutes or longer if that feels right to you. Veil the mirror again. Spend some time recording your experience in your journal.

When you are complete, make sure to ground yourself fully. You can thank the universe or any other being or spirits that seem relevant to you in this moment. Blow out the candle if you had one and pack away the mirror, veil, and other objects.

activity | Creating the Second Disk

As you complete the work of this section, make sure to create a disk to represent the sephira you've been focusing on. Perhaps you spent the first section concentrated on Kether and this section with Hokmah; in that case, it will be the gray Hokmah disk you are working with. Perhaps you began somewhere else in the Tree and so the disk you are making now is for Gevurah, Netzach, Yesod, or another sephira.

TIME: 30–60 minutes

YOU WILL NEED: The appropriate colored disk (see page 69, "Creating the First Disk") and whatever art materials you wish to work with, such as colored pens and markers, paint, oil pastels, collage materials and glue, stickers

Begin by remembering the time you have spent in this sephira, including looking through your journal, recalling any Kabbalah exercises, processes, or rituals you did, especially how these related to this particular sephira, as well as the general mood and events in your life during this time.

Allow images, words, feelings, and ideas to arise. You can hold these in your head, immediately begin work on your disk, or jot down notes or sketch.

You might begin by marking the name of the sephira—I use both its name and the English translation—onto the disk. If your primary language is not English, I encourage using your own language. I use a black marker (and gold, silver, or white for the Binah disk, which is already black) or you might want to use gold or silver for all of them.

Then decorate your disk. You might use poetry—your own or someone else's. You can use shape and color or draw or paint a scene, symbols, or patterns that make sense to you. You can cover the whole or part of the disk with collage, cutting or tearing pictures from magazines and wrapping paper. You can cut shapes out of colored foil and glue them on. You can use words as concrete poetry, letting the words themselves form shapes and symbols. You can stick other things onto your disks: leaves, dried flowers or petals, glitter, ribbon, or other things.

Your disk might be complete within itself or it might reference other sephirot that are close by or in the same pillar. It might contain a sense of the paths that connect it with other sephirot, an image of the Tree itself, or a reference to this sephira's position within the Tree. Often I have one theme, such as butterflies or shards of light, running through all my disks. I usually create a strong edge around the disk with paint or oil pastel, often a darker shade of the same color as the disk, so a darker blue around the edge of the blue Chesed disk.

You might complete your work in one session or come back later to add details or another layer; for example, to use gold or silver pen over the top of a collage.

examples of completed disks can be seen at janemeredith .com/disks

*light shatters and breaks again, already
broken, fragments of light fall through the
branches, the edges of the universe reflecting
back to the center and breaking, falling, the
endless question unending reflection oh the
beloved, the dream, union and past all that,
because of that—I dream of your face and a
door opens within it and through the door I
see the universe the countless stars sparkling
all that is, infinity—all dimensions—we are
given, free, released, adored—you are the
gateway the gate and each breath I enter*

*...falling, the wings of the butterfly open,
once, and color flashes through the universe,
a saturated wave of becoming, and it's
caught in the gusts of the winds of time and
stellar explosions so it falls, is swept down
and away—*

3

Triads in
the Tree

There is one, the All. The one splits and then two exist. Between them they are all that is and a single action, the splitting, has created all their differences. So they are mirrors but opposites; one that created the other, and one that was created by the other. There is the All of Kether. Then there is its opposite and reflection, Hokmah. They reflect and comment endlessly on each other. From this dynamic a third point on the diagram arises: Binah.

The progression goes from the first to the second, from the second to the third—but from the instant the third arrives, it is intimately connected not just to the second, but also to the first. Suddenly, what was a single line between two becomes three lines, connecting three: a triangle.

In the Tree of Life Binah, Understanding, is the third sephira. Single sephirot exist; each of Kether, Hokmah, and Binah is single. Pairs exist: Kether and Hokmah were the first pair, though now Binah and Hokmah look to be the more obvious pair. With Binah triads are brought into the Tree. This pattern is begun here, with the top triad of Kether-Hokmah-Binah, and will be repeated twice within the lower Tree. Structurally a triangle is the strongest shape, and interplay within a triad is very dynamic.

With Binah structural solidity and triangularity have come into the Tree.

Binah: *The Dark Womb*

The arising of a third sephira within the Tree of Life seems as mysterious as the arrival of the first or the advent of the second. How do these new sephirot keep being born? The first sephira was already All, the great I Am That I Am. The second sephira reflected it and so seemed a product of parthenogenesis, purely from Kether. But the progression of the Tree does not stop there. Hokmah's disruption of Kether's singularity spells great changes, and the immediate result of these changes is Binah, the third sephira. One exists—is duplicated—and from this arises a third. Like the very first living cell that split itself in two, from there it seems inevitable that the process will continue: this great leaning into existence, the inclination toward becoming that we struggle to explain but witness and partake of in our small human lives. Binah's arrival into the Tree is the product of evolution. It points to the potential for life.

The whole conundrum of the individuation of sephirot and yet their essential oneness is distilled in this top triad of the Tree. It demonstrates both the splitting apart and also the underlying union of different pieces of the whole. The triad that Binah completes is not just made of three separate sephirot as different from each other as it's possible to be, but also these three add together to express one concept: a triple divinity, three faces of the divine, three aspects of the forces that create the potential of life. Not only life as we are accustomed to thinking about it, but the life of the universe, atoms gaining increasing complexity, the births and deaths of star systems. The three stages of this triad could be summarized as existence, replication, and evolution.

In the previous section on Hokmah, we examined what it means to be the replication, or mirror, of all of existence. Now, one step further into the Tree, we study how this evolves. Binah is distinctly different from both Kether and Hokmah, although everything remains always a part of Kether. Binah's difference is a commentary on the evolving complexity both of the Tree and of the unfolding of Kether itself. Kether's Crown was the All, complete unto itself. Its reflection is Hokmah's Wisdom. Wisdom was a quality contained within the All, but it could not be fully realized until it was separated from it. From this point Binah, Understanding, arises.

The triplicate that we are discussing at the top of the Tree is the nature of God, divinity, all the gods. The progression of these three sephirot is what allows or even demands the existence of everything, of which we are a small part. And Binah is the dark womb where future manifestation gestates. If we were to examine this triplicate in human terms, we might see them as the soul, the mind, and the body. The soul is the crown or the spark of the divine within each individual. The mind is the individuation. The body is the living manifestation of this being. Three parts distinct yet indivisible in practical terms.

Kabbalistic thinking is not linear, just as the Tree isn't linear. We don't receive a single explanation for something and imagine that's the end of it. On the contrary, in Kabbalah we layer images, models, and thought experiments over each other. This does two things. It reveals that all these ways of examining what we're looking at are metaphors rather than any finite truth. And it creates a dynamic soup of ideas from which we can perhaps taste or glimpse or have a felt sense of something beyond words. When we accept the paradox of explaining something via different, possibly even contradictory models, using one set of images and explanation followed immediately by a different set while saying that neither of these is exactly true, it creates room for inspiration, interpretation, and debate. What follows is a series of thought experiments into the nature of Binah.

There's a point at the beginning of space-time, with everything concentrated into a tiny space, the All, the singularity—and still within this same moment, or non-moment, there's an explosion or division and then rapid expansion. These more or less come all together or are part of the same thing, but we separate them out into these three aspects to try to make sense of it. If Kether represents the singularity at the beginning of space-time and Hokmah is the division or explosion, then Binah is that very rapid expansion. In this model Binah is the unfolding of the universe—perhaps Kether conceived it, and Hokmah was the splitting open—but the expansion, the coming-forth-into-existence part, belongs to Binah.

In the Feri and Reclaiming creation story, the Star Goddess who is All gazes into the curved mirror of dark space and sees the image of Herself, which She names Miria, the beloved. In their lovemaking Miria is flung away to the edge of the universe, there to tumble through shifting god-forms of blue, green, and red, before finally returning, as everything must, to the embrace of the beloved and the completion of all things. We can hear the echoes in this story of the top triad of the Tree of Life, as well as the beginnings of the universe. The Star Goddess aligns with Kether and the singularity point at the beginning of space-time. The mirror is Hokmah—the explosion or division within the singularity. Miria, drawn forth from the mirror to join with the Star Goddess in the dance of all creation, is Binah, which is the point at which the very rapid expansion takes place. Space-time unfolds, Miria is flung away to the edges of the universe, and in the Tree of Life the first three sephirot become separated from the rest of the Tree by the Abyss that lies below them.

Perhaps the Kabbalistic translation for the Big Bang is "light in extension." If we assign these three words to the top triad, Kether carries light, Hokmah the transition word "in," expressing the relationship between other words (or sephirot), and Binah the event, the extension. With this perspective we can comprehend how Binah, the finishing and extending piece of that three-in-one action, creates space for existence in the way we comprehend it. Binah is the extension of the light in extension out to the edges of space, the seeding of stars, and even across the Abyss, thus creating the possibility of life.

Binah is distinctly different than anything that has occurred so far. Until now we have been only concerned with light—the brilliant, explosive light of Kether and the reflected light of Hokmah. Binah heralds the extension of light but is the edges of the universe where no stars yet exist. Binah is night and the darkness pre-birth. This sephira is colored black. Immediately in darkness we are confused and confronted because we can't see anything, and even though we may be used to not being able to see the sephira we're examining because the light is too fierce (Kether) or the sephira appears veiled (Hokmah), we're still used to being able to see *something*, even if it is just reflections or rays of light beaming outward. In Binah we cannot see.

Binah and Hokmah offer different, some might say opposing, ways to access the divine. This triad sets up what will become the three pillars, with Hokmah at the head of the right-hand pillar, Kether crowning the middle pillar, and Binah at the top of the left-hand pillar. Hokmah and Binah, representing the right- and left-hand pillars, anticipate two different approaches to magic and the divine. Hokmah's right-hand path is study, wisdom, and application; Binah's left-hand path is the gnosis of understanding—mysteries revealed not philosophically but bodily, through intimate experience.

With Binah we enter into the mysteries; this is the surrender. Everything is in darkness, so it has to be experienced. We can read about what the stages of an initiation process are, but only when we are in it ourselves do we have any way of truly understanding. Each person has to fall in love for the first time to understand what falling in love is. Before that we may sympathize with it, have observed its effects, analyzed it in literature or from the point of view of chemistry, psychology, sociology, or even theology, but the raw effects of experiencing it cannot be duplicated by any other method. Binah demands embodied experience.

The mysteries have always contained both birth and death; it's the Dark Goddess who holds the powers of both. The places of womb and tomb, their essential similarities, and the idea that a soul is born into this world and exits by the same gateway. On either side of our lives, before and afterward, we have the same lack of knowing, the same absence of individuality, the same disembodied status. We are, in effect, part of the All, indistinguishable from it, and although things we have done and memories others have of us remain in this world of individuals and individual histories, we ourselves have left it. Binah, while containing all of that mystery, depth, and darkness, still is the gateway into the state of becoming. In effect, Binah is the gateway from the divine through—eventually—the manifest.

The blood mysteries, the birth mysteries, the death mysteries—I keep wanting to write that word *mysteries*. Places and times of deep transformation when we are remade, turned over to the requirements of the life force, and issued forth anew and perhaps unrecognizable. These profound states of life-into-nonlife and nonlife-into-life are essentially unknowable to us and thus surrounded with rituals and mystique, fear and reverence. Initiations—into magical, occult, or mystery traditions, into religions or stages of life—mimic parts of this birth-death-rebirth cycle, a cycle with which we are all intimately familiar. Stepping into these initiation events, surrender is a requirement, just as when we are giving birth, assisting someone's death, or being born or dying ourselves. Our abilities to control and order, to choose, and even to conceptualize do not count for much. Our abilities to be present, to let go, receive, and offer from the deepest parts of ourselves are essential if we wish to stay aware and participate in what's happening.

Darkness, surrender, transformation, and the powers of birth and death are all shunned in the Western, capitalist world. Those of us raised in this paradigm are not trained in how to be present with them or how to navigate these territories, and we are not even used to viewing them as essential, describing maybe half of life, just as darkness prescribes half of any length of time on earth. We are underprepared when difficult or testing times hit us or those we love; we do not know the language, the customs, the territory, and perhaps we don't even trust the guidebooks. Stillness, acceptance, and surrender are not values prized in modern life; rather, the emphasis is on continual motion, struggle, and achievement. Yet truly, as many of us know to the detriment of our health and well-being, life cannot always be upward and onward. We need time to rest, to recharge, drop deep within and reassess what is important to us, and we need to be able to cull, to release the old, the undesirable—whether that's emotional patterns, obligations, relationships, ways of living, values, or beliefs—to make room for the new to arise.

Binah corresponds with the rapid inflation of the universe, which makes possible the formation of stars, galaxies, planets, and—eventually—life on earth. This is a vast thing. To view the whole universe as the dark womb that gives life … to extend this metaphor down to the micro level, so that each pregnant mother-to-be is carrying a universe within her, with each child the universe is born anew. Each one carries all the potential of those top three sephirot—the memory or original state of oneness, the separation, and the birth into form. This must not just be the case for human children, but also for each animal, bird, insect, plant … and if that, why not for each river, mountain, wind? The different forms that these molecules, born in the hearts of stars, now take—surely each is a reflection of the divine or the All from which they have emerged?

If we take as a premise that initiations—whether biological initiations such as birth and death, or ritualized initiations—do echo this movement from the embodied into the divine and back again, we can understand why they are so powerful. In particular, we get a glimpse into what ritualized initiations hope to simulate and how they can prompt a complete re-writing of our life. This is their revelatory aspect—that we are returned to the All within their form. Through the initiation experience we are granted direct access to the mystery and almost, one could say, reigniting our own body knowledge of this state of becoming-out-of-the-nothing, as well as a premonition or fore-experience of what death may be like, the great unbecoming. All of us have the experience of being born, and the experience of living a life that will end with a death. Some of us choose, are able to, or maybe are required to tread those pathways consciously during our lifetimes, as well—to investigate these realms of life-and-death, of initiation, and understanding within the mysteries.

Timothy Freke and Peter Gandy explain in *Jesus and the Goddess: The Secret Teachings of the Original Christians* that the Gnostics believed in three fundamental states of existence, which are echoed in theology, forms of consciousness, and daily human life.

These three states can be summed up as being at one with God, being in communion with God, and being separate from God. The states are identified with Spirit (which is All), the soul (which is where individuation occurs, with parts of Spirit split off into separate identities but still connected to source), and the body (where souls identify as separate bodies). In our daily cycles, these aspects of identity exist in our three different states of consciousness: asleep, dreaming, and awake.

In Gnostic understanding, when we are deeply asleep, unconscious, we are indivisible from the All, or Spirit. When we are dreaming, we are in communion with the All; as we are still within separate consciousnesses, we are not entirely subsumed within it. For the Gnostics, this dreaming state represents the state of the individual soul. Awake, we experience separation and individuation within a single body. The great conundrum, elucidated by the Gnostics in their search for understanding, is that it is when we are alive, awake, and conscious that we are within death, if death is separation from the divine. When we are actually dead, we are alive with everything-that-is. Like a miracle, a great exemption, we have been granted an in-between state where we can access both these realities at the same time, the state of dream. But to put into effect any of the understandings we may gain from that dream realm, we have to be in our living, embodied, and thus separated states.

The further away we get from God, or the All, or we might say Kether, the more individual we are, the more directors of our own will, the more yearning for union, for belonging, for meaning. In fact, our daily state of consciousness is ironically when we are least conscious—least aware of our connection with that to which we intrinsically belong. Perhaps we can see why the Gnostics were persecuted by the Christian church—their theory posits that we are least connected with God while awake. Thus it is not attendance at church, obedience to scripture, or listening to priests that brings the living individual to the divine but our own states of dream, revelation, and surrender.

As Kabbalists—or witches, magicians, ritualists, priestexes—we might lean further into this, asking about ecstatic states, trance, meditation. Surely these are times when, while still entirely conscious of our individual body-state (and thus held firmly into the unconsciousness of separation), we enter a dreamlike state and experience ourselves in communion with All. The edgewalking of magic workers is thus perhaps not just between different levels of awareness, but also between different levels of conscious belonging to divinity. We might even cast the view of this in another direction to posit that pre-birth, or after death, we are one with the All. Throughout our lifetimes we experience the separation of individuation. Throughout life we have countless opportunities—and some of us court them, and train or specialize in these skills—to enter states of communion with the All, even while separated from it; these states include dream, trance, meditation, prayer, sex, and magic.

What is the special role of Binah within this? To be separate allows, even creates, the possibility of union, as we learned with Hokmah. But that is still a separation between only two. Binah is a further separation from the source, where the two become many. Binah is the mother of all the possibilities that can come forth from this union, this separation, this ongoing creation. This imagery is echoed in the beginnings of our universe as the very rapid expansion. We all emerge from this dark womb of creation/deep space that stars exist within—stars whose material literally makes up our bodies and our world.

When we are most separate—that is, as individual living humans—we most fully experience and thus most understand. Not only can we understand individual experience, since that is our state, but intriguingly we can also understand union and the All from this perspective of our individual existence. The more separate we are—or the more awake we are—the more we have the opportunity to grasp what oneness is, or belonging to complete unconsciousness, to the All that has no divisions within it. Fully awake we can conceptualize the state of deep sleep. In deep sleep, however, we cannot comprehend any state. The mediator is the dream, the realms between, the mirror of the Star Goddess, the division of that first cell, the self that yearns to merge.

We cannot understand the place of separation from within the place of oneness. Pre-birth, or pre-conception, we have no way to imagine being born or being alive, yet it still happens. Perhaps a cell cannot anticipate dividing until it divides. This is the mystery at the heart of cosmology, and the top triad of the Tree is devoted to stages of this mystery. Light, at Kether, though we don't know what it is apart from that the speed of light is the one constant in our universe. At Hokmah, a division that we don't know how it could occur, though we can clearly say, see, and know that such divisions do occur. And an entry into life, or possible life, with Binah. Once again, we don't exactly know how or why this occurs, and we even have a lot of trouble explaining or understanding the difference between living and non-living things. Nonetheless, this awareness exists, and this categorization is one we use constantly.

It is life that introduces death into the whole scheme, so the place where life begins—whether it is in the rock pools of planet Earth approximately 3.5 billion years ago, in our mother's womb, or in Binah as the third sephira on the Tree of Life—is also the place where death begins. In the great scheme of things, Binah holds a place for death as well as life. It's noteworthy that after this sephira comes the Abyss, as if Binah has completed that first great movement and now everything must change. Binah is the dark mother of the universe wherein the mysteries become apparent, translated into the living forms we walk around in but also translated into the great gassy clouds ranged throughout the universe that give birth to stars.

Recalling those single-celled organisms that began the history of life on earth, we might remember that originally they replicated purely by splitting, thus duplicating themselves. This type of reproduction is considered an asexual process. Then at some point, only a little over a billion years ago, sexual reproduction began. This process involved two individuals combining their DNA to produce offspring that contained genetic material from each of their parents: sexual reproduction. When we see this as the third stage in the process—the first being a singular living organism and the second stage being the splitting of that organism into two—we once again see how Binah, as the third sephira on the Tree of Life, has introduced almost unlimited possibility within its combinations of life, death, and sex. This is evolution as we are used to thinking about it, evolution through sexual reproduction. Unlike asexual reproduction, where the death of an individual entity does not result in a death of that particular form (for its exact replicates still exist), with sexual reproduction each individual is unique. When an individual dies, that exact form is gone forever.

Binah is a holder of the mysteries, but these are mysteries we participate in bodily by being born, by reproducing, by dying. Being part of the mysteries does not mean we necessarily understand them, but our participation can lead to understanding or at least toward understanding. In Kabbalistic terms we layer these patterns over each

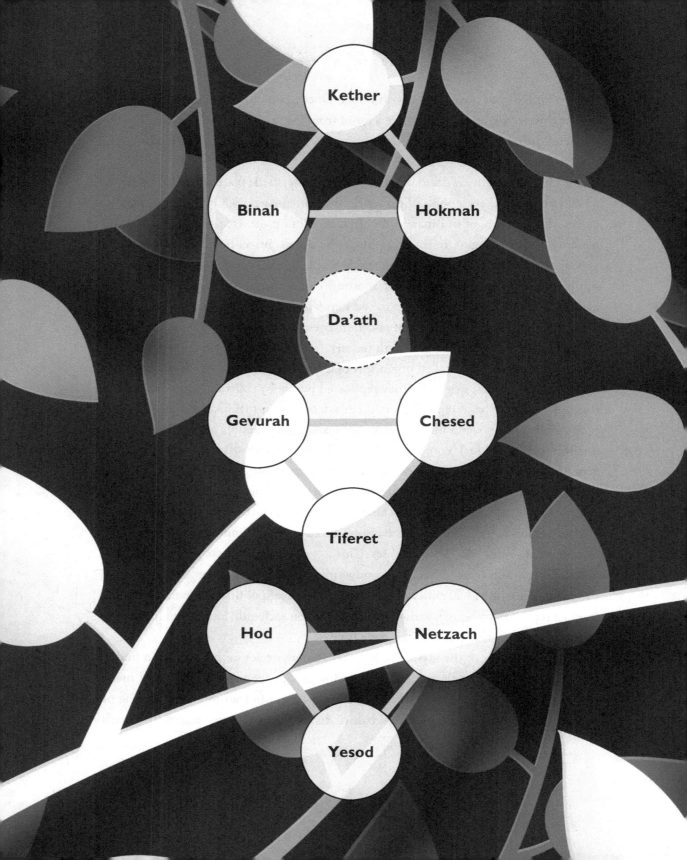

other; the Great Expansion piece of the Big Bang, the separation of Miria from the Star Goddess, initiation mysteries, the state of consciousness that separation allows, and the mechanics of sexual reproduction and therefore individual birth and death. Considering Hokmah, we reflected on how Kether must have always contained the Wisdom that Hokmah is, but until it was separated out, it couldn't be fully realized. With Binah there is a similar commentary; the All must contain Binah's darkness, but we usually experience that All as light, even a piercing light. Any darkness is lost in there. When it is separated within its own sephira, we can recognize its qualities, surrendering to this process of life and death, separation and the promise of union.

In death we belong to the All. A dream arises that dreams us into consciousness. Alive, we realize our separation and long to return. Or the other way—we spend our lives striving for meaning, for connection, for achievement. Occasionally we glimpse, as through a veil, our oneness, belonging, the Mind of God, the great I Am. In dying we achieve that union. We participate bodily and with our whole lives in this mystery. As agents of Binah, we give birth to others to participate in it. We may also voluntarily surrender to the mysteries, experiencing death-within-life through ritual initiation. In trance, ritual, dream, and initiation, we are offered entry to the mysteries, and within them understanding beckons.

Triads in the Tree of Life

Once we have considered sephirot and pairs within the Tree of Life, triads are the next construct to examine. Like the pairs, triads work with the dynamic of difference—each of the three components brings substantially different qualities into the triad. As soon as the first triad is in place, the whole top of the Tree looks stable. The Tree's structure and what it will become is made possible by this triangle that can be seen as three aspects of divinity, or three eternal essences in collaboration with each other.

Triads are made from a horizontal pair added to a sephira from the middle pillar, which brings balance and synthesis. This means each triad contains sephirot from all three pillars. Those who formed the pair do not carry more weight than the previously single sephira; it is a system of equals. Because each triad is at a different level of the Tree, they each operate as separate strata. Each triad holds a part of the Tree: the top triad of Kether-Hokmah-Binah, the middle triad of Chesed-Gevurah-Tiferet, and the lower triad of Netzach-Hod-Yesod.

Only Malkuth, the tenth and final sephira, is left out of the triads. It stands alone at the bottom of the Tree, meeting the downward point of the lowest triad, Yesod. The other two triads are balanced on top of that, unless we follow David Cooper's suggestion in *God Is a Verb* that Hokmah and Binah form a triad with Da'ath, leaving Kether alone at the top of the Tree just as Malkuth is left alone at the bottom (Cooper 1998, 89). This creates three downward-pointing triangles instead of an upward-pointing triangle on top of two downward-pointing ones. It's an unusual suggestion with interesting possibilities and a certain visual appeal, but as Da'ath is not really considered a sephira, this version is not as solid as the more accustomed modeling of triads.

Triads form a set of cross-sections within the Tree, although pillars, pairs, and paths all receive more attention. Perhaps it's the sealed-off nature of a triangular structure that means they attract relatively little attention, whereas the straight lines of pairs, pillars, and paths appear open-ended.

Triads in the Tree
KETHER-HOKMAH-BINAH

This first triad of Kether, Hokmah, and Binah is known as the supernal triad. This is the triad that creates triads. The other two triads are modeled on this one, although it could be argued that the later ones develop the pattern more fully. Each of the three sephirot in the top triad represents states of totality. They are depicted as the stark grayscale shades of white, gray, and black. They hold the top of the Tree as its pinnacle of expression and originators of the rest of the Tree. This triad is removed from the other sephirot by the Abyss, as if a line is drawn under these three and then the attempt at explanation starts again underneath, although the triads below the Abyss are flipped over, pointing down instead of up.

The supernal triad is vastly removed from our knowing, our experience, and our ability to explain anything very much. However, I believe it is not utterly apart from our experience. Each of us has experiences that are very hard to put words to or define absolutely. We have moments in ritual, prayer, meditation, lovemaking, dreams, visions, in nature, in art, in illness, witnessing death or birth where vastness surrounds us, meets us, we are within it and part of it, and we belong. Celestial. Larger than life. Transcendental. Inspirational. These are experiences I associate with the top triad. We don't necessarily understand what has happened to us or why it happened then or at all, and these experiences may not fit in with the rest of our life. Sometimes we receive them as blessings, gifts; other times we change our lives to pursue them or the vision they offered. These are incredibly personal experiences, yet they still fit a pattern. We expect each human life to contain them, not that they come to order or when we wish and only sometimes when we need them.

Kether. Hokmah. Binah. Faces of God, of Goddess. One obliterated with light, one veiled, one concealed in darkness. Faces that are not faces at all, though we might experience the form of a face. A triple godhead. The divine split into three aspects. The brilliant, unknowable All. The veiled, compassionate, and wise lover. The dark, hidden, and potent giver of life. All are literally unseeable. Three ways to know the divine—to be blasted with light, to reflect the essentially unknowable, or to enter the mysteries of darkness. Three entry points to our own spiritual nature or three states of sublime bliss or three sets of challenges. This triad is also setting up what will become the remainder of the Tree, the lower Tree, both in their pattern of a triad and also in that they will each become the head of one of the pillars.

We can choose to view the triad in a progressive order—one, two, three (or three, two, one)—as descending from or ascending to the most entirely divine, inaccessible state. We can also see them as a single with a pair; Kether above and then—supporting, explaining, and elucidating Kether—Hokmah and Binah. We can see the right-hand and the left-hand paths of magic twining together up the Tree, their heads in Hokmah and Binah meeting eye to eye. They are the pillars at the entrance to the temple, and the entry is Kether, where the snakes meet mouth to mouth.

CHESED-GEVURAH-TIFERET

The triad of Chesed, Gevurah, and Tiferet holds the middle part of the Tree—Tiferet is in the center of the Tree, both horizontally and vertically, and Chesed and Gevurah are above it, the second horizontal pair. Whereas the top triad is concerned with vast concepts of time and space, the conversations that the divine has within itself, and the very formation of the Tree, this middle triad is involved with different energies. Chesed is all outward flow and force, Gevurah its strict opposite in containment, limitation, and form, and Tiferet holds the middle way of giving and receiving, the heartbeat at the center of the Tree. Thus between them they describe three different ways of interacting with the world—we could say to give, to receive, and to dance between. Or, the breath out, the breath in, and the still place between breaths.

This triad holds together a little more tightly than the top triad, perhaps because the form of triads is now established, perhaps because we are farther down the Tree and things are becoming more tangible, or closer toward the realms of tangibility. At this triad we can begin to understand or even measure ourselves within the dynamic. We might reflect, for instance, on whether we are more of an introverted person (Gevurah) or an extroverted one (Chesed), and we might study Tiferet for ways to find the balance between the two. Do we abide strictly by the rules or do we live more within the free flow of the moment—Gevurah or Chesed? As parents, lovers, coworkers, leaders, and artists, are we permissive or restrictive? What is the ideal middle point for any of these things?

Whereas the pairing of Gevurah and Chesed creates strong opposites—even if it is opposites who cannot do without the other—when Tiferet is added into the mix, everything changes. Tiferet reminds us that we can create balance not just by swinging from one extreme to the other, but by working these different energies together, in harmony with each other. A recipe, for example, calls for precise measurements of different ingredients, particular cooking styles and temperatures; one could say it is all about form, restrictions. A recipe is a clear example of Gevurah. Yet why is it that every person following a recipe will create something slightly different? Perhaps we are only using the recipe as a guideline, and much of what is happening is more Chesed-like. Perhaps we are more generous with the spices—or our spices come from a different location or we balanced them differently within the dish. Perhaps we added a secret ingredient, known only to us, or we followed our grandmother's way of whatever it was. An impossible number of factors mean that each person's Persian love cake or pumpkin soup will be different, and in this mixing we can see Tiferet.

A recipe is a micro examination of the combining of these sephirot and their influence on each other. For a macro example we might look at how a country is managed. Is this government laissez-faire, anything goes, or totalitarian, everything is controlled?

Probably neither are very attractive to us. We want some boundaries, guidelines, and rules of fairness and order. We want some generosity, freedom to make choices, a sense of plenty. We want both of what are essentially opposites, and we want them at the same time, thus the mediator, Tiferet, comes into play. Tiferet is continual flow, yet at the same time is always boundaried. The heart is a great metaphor for Tiferet—always moderating. It is endlessly giving of life, always in flow (or else we die), and at the same time strictly regulated: so many beats per minute, so much blood pumped here and there.

Examining this triad, it seems as if the three cannot do without each other, yet there are subtleties within their ordering. If we are progressing up the Tree, we come first to Tiferet, holding and releasing everything in each moment. Then comes the defining order of Gevurah, to regulate, to control. We can almost feel Tiferet being examined, distilled, and refined. Then comes Chesed to expand and allow flow and creativity again. It's a process of becoming increasingly rarefied, going up the Tree. In the opposite direction, coming down, we have the magnificent flowing tide of Chesed meeting the abrupt forms of Gevurah, followed by the moderation of Tiferet, rendering beauty between opposites.

Or another view—the yin of Gevurah and the yang of Chesed flowing equally into the circle of Tiferet. Perhaps the tightness of this triad is because Tiferet is part of it. Kether, the sephira on the middle pillar in the top triad, is concerned with the beginning of the world, the top of the Tree, and vast otherly things such as the connection with the Ain Soph and the lurking field of Da'ath. Malkuth and Yesod, down the bottom of the Tree in the middle pillar, are concerned with anchoring the Tree into life, onto Earth, and into reality. Tiferet, and to some extent the central triad, could be said to be solely involved with the internal connections of the Tree itself.

NETZACH-HOD-YESOD

Netzach, Hod, and Yesod form the bottom triad of the Tree, leaving Malkuth to stand alone outside this triple arrangement of triads. Malkuth is balancing or supporting or growing from all of them, like the roots of a great tree or the single known origin on a family tree or the sole inheritor. Because this is Kabbalah, it can be like all of those things; we don't have to choose between them. This lowest triad must take everything that has occurred before and funnel it into Malkuth. Or, heading up the Tree, it must transmit everything that has occurred in Malkuth, almost splitting it into its various components—unmixing it, as it were, and passing it upward. This is a relatively mundane task if we compare it to the other loftier triads, yet essential if the Tree is to function. For us, in the realm of Malkuth, it is our most obvious concern.

Of the three triads, this one is tightest and most intermingled. Instead of great schisms of space-time separating them or representing the polarity of energies, this triad has to work closely together to create the conditions for manifestation. We could say that Netzach has the ideas, Hod draws up the specifications, and Yesod handles the transmission. Or, in the other direction, Yesod receives all that has occurred in Malkuth—like a very complex, tangled, and unending dream—Hod decodes it into discreet units, and Netzach allows those pieces to flow together into coherent meaning. Hod and Netzach are in synchronicity with each other, rather than the opposition or complete otherness of higher-up pairs.

The concept of chaos and order is a way to more closely examine what is happening within this triad. Netzach is the glorious, fertile chaos from which all things arise, while Hod is the clarity and precision of order. There cannot be all order or all chaos—one leads to stagnation and the other to incoherence—and in the vessel of Yesod they mix together, molten, magical, and potent.

When we work with dreams and the realms of the unconscious, or subconscious, we need language. Perhaps it is the language of imagery, so we paint or sculpt these visions, or maybe it's the language of sound, so we create music or dance, or we write or speak aloud what we have glimpsed or sensed. Whether it is a nighttime dream or a dream-like vision of the future—a future relationship, community, way of life, or political system—to understand it ourselves and to communicate it to anyone else, we need two things. We need to be able to identify at least some but preferably many of its components, and we need to be able to convey the felt emotion or overall sense of it.

If we are describing a vision of a community, we cannot only talk about the shared ethical values and the sense of belonging, camaraderie, and creativity. We must also address the practical details of location, finances, and decision-making processes. One without the other is only halfway there, which is to say it's not there at all. It is Yesod, the facilitator of the dream, who can most gracefully bring these two things together. After all, in a dream impossible things happen all the time, and opposites can belong with each other. I think about the story of the creation of the periodic table of the elements, which appeared in a dream to the Russian chemist Dimitri Mendeleev, who, once awake, then drew it. It's still the way we understand the elements' relationships with each other. Such precision—Hod; such vision—Netzach; delivered within dream—Yesod.

This lowest triad almost has the job of explaining the upper triad. We live in the wild, interactive, endlessly complex realm of the natural world—we may be walking along the beach, climbing a mountain, walking through desert, farmland, forest, wetland, or gazing at the stars; this is Netzach. We understand at least a little of what we see, perhaps enough to know how much we don't know; Hod. We experience a glimpse of eternity through comprehending a small part of it; Yesod.

Theoretical Triads
HOKMAH-BINAH-DA'ATH

David Cooper suggests that the top triad, instead of the conventional Kether-Hokmah-Binah, might more aptly be Hokmah-Binah-Da'ath, although he calls them triplets and draws them in a straight line rather than a triangle (Cooper 1998, 89). In this possibility both Kether and Malkuth would be left outside of the triad structure, respectively holding, or bracketing, the top and bottom of a Tree containing three downward-pointing triads. Hokmah, Binah, and Da'ath are an interesting combination because they are each so clearly commentaries on Kether. Hokmah and Binah each realize different progressions of the divine, or the development of light, as it extends—and Da'ath holds the complete opposite, the mysterious black hole in the system. Black holes, it is supposed, might give birth to galaxies or possibly be entry points into other dimensions. Even if Da'ath is only the hovering non-entity of a sephira, it is opposite to Kether. Where Kether has become, Da'ath has not become. If Da'ath did come into being, perhaps it would swallow the entire universe.

NETZACH-HOD-MALKUTH

This is another theoretical triad, the idea that Netzach and Hod have more in common with Malkuth than with Yesod, or that they all three relate to each other through the medium of Yesod, which is held in the center of their triangle if we draw them as a triad. We can see how the realms of Netzach—all possibilities—and Hod—all particularities—resonate and interact so clearly within Malkuth. And Malkuth is the balancing place for those two forces, so that a certain poetry starts to occur. Yesod is nested within these three dynamic and powerful entities that are not in conflict with each other, but rather supporting and enhancing; it's a beautiful image. We can imagine the realm of dreams and the unconscious, including the collective unconscious, feeding and being fed by these three like a fetus curled within a womb.

However, to call this a triad unbalances the system of triads, which has been neat and clear down the Tree, a horizontal pair matched with the single sephira nearest to them in the middle pillar. The differently shaped triangle that this triad would create is not consistent with the geometry of the Tree, so, having considered its possibility and learned something from it (that image of Yesod in utero will stay with me), we return to the conventional triads in set formation down, or up, the Tree. Malkuth remains alone at the bottom, anchoring the triads like an inverted mountain peak or a spectacular feat of strength in a circus act of balancing many others on one pair of shoulders. Like a Kabbalist.

trance | The Cave

Caves evoke fear, curiosity, excitement. We recognize them as shelter; we remember the early human paintings and dwellings that have been preserved within cave systems, away from abrasive light and weather. Caves feel primal, shelters within the body of the earth that promise a return to the chthonic world, with an accompanying emphasis on body and the present moment. In a cave we are hidden away from the outside world. Meditation, retreat, and silence are promised by thoughts of being tucked away in a cave. Literally and metaphorically caves are places of initiation, birth, or rebirth, and also death. Caves have often been tombs.

TIME: An hour or longer; 30–40 minutes within the trance, then time to reflect and journal.

YOU WILL NEED: Your journal and pen. Any sacred objects you choose. A flashlight if you are going somewhere dark. Cushions, blankets, and darkness if you are doing this inside. If you have access to a natural cave, you can do this ritual there (you might want to take something to lie on and a blanket for warmth).

Decide where and when to do the ritual. Possible locations include by your altar in a nest of blankets and pillows, in a small/quiet/dark room, in your bed, in a cave. Possible times include at dusk, in the evening, at midnight, overnight, or just in a darkened room at any time. If you need a refresher on trance, there are notes in the appendix.

Begin by making your space as cavelike as possible. If you are actually in a cave, you will want to make it comfortable enough to lie down! Keep your journal and pen nearby, and arrange any sacred objects in a way that seems good to you. If you wish, you can set a timer or gentle alarm for thirty or forty minutes from when you begin the trance.

Prepare yourself for an inner journey that will last at least half an hour. Perhaps you will take off all your clothes and wrap yourself in blankets or do a few stretches followed by some slow breathing. Maybe you'll want to cast a circle; invoke the gods, your ancestors, or the Great Mother; cleanse yourself and the space; or something else.

When you are ready, begin by relaxing, breathing gently, and feeling into each body part, one by one. Often we start with the feet and toes and slowly move upward. Where you find tension or pain, take a few extra breaths as well as adjust your posture if necessary. Continue until you have reached the crown of your head.

Then bring your entire focus to your breathing. Feel how the breath moves through you on the inbreaths and the outbreaths.

With your eyes gently closed or in soft focus—slightly open but not really looking at anything—allow a sense of being in a cave to emerge. Perhaps you actually are in a cave and can breathe the quality of its air, feel the ground underneath you, or perhaps you will have to imagine these things. Some of us are very visual, while others work more with body sensation, emotion, sound and smell, or memories. Find out how you can create this feeling of being inside a cave.

Stay aware of your breathing, encouraging it to be soft and slow as you trance more deeply.

How does it feel to be held within the earth, to have it supporting you and all around you? What emotions, thoughts, and sensations arise? What is this experience of being in a cave like for you? You might feel safe, claustrophobic, drowsy, anticipatory, or anything else. Just notice what arises for you, and if it feels challenging, send some breaths into those feelings or thoughts.

We were all in our mother's womb for nine months. Perhaps you will trance back to that time, maybe rocking yourself gently. Perhaps you will reach out to your ancestors on either or both sides of your lineage. You might ask for their guidance and support or find that they have a task or question for you, or you might just receive a sense of their presence. Perhaps your trance will take you far back, to the birth of life on this planet, within the womb of the great ocean. Or your imagination may arc even further back, to the birthing of stars in the dark universe.

You can consciously guide your cave trance journey or let it take you where it will.

Sometimes a trance ends by itself; our breathing changes and we start to move parts of our body and stretch without a conscious wish on our part. Or maybe our alarm goes off and we are jolted back. Other times we have to bring ourselves back deliberately, returning stage by stage: completing what we were doing in the trance, reminding ourselves of our cave surroundings, becoming consciously aware of our breath again, and coming back into the body, then finally opening our eyes, stretching or wriggling, and sitting up. Some people also like to pat down the outside of their bodies, shake their whole body, or stamp their feet on the ground.

After you've returned, spend some time thinking through what you experienced. Write down the pieces you want to remember in your journal.

process | Unseen Parts of Self

We get so used to the stories in our minds—I heard the other day that our brains can process nine hundred words per minute, which is mostly our own thoughts—that it can be hard to break out of them. We tell ourselves *Oh I'm a delicate and shy person* and thus avoid understanding that we are actually extremely competent and others regard us as solid, reliable, and a strong communicator. Or we have a story along the lines of *I find it hard to connect with others* and let this thought sabotage our every interaction. Or we tell an outdated story, *I always choose the wrong relationships,* failing to notice how much we've grown in our self-knowledge and ability to make good choices. Sometimes we condemn others for characteristics we deny in ourselves.

So how do we grow past this? How do we learn to see in the dark, to throw light into our areas of shadow, and ideally to unpack, update, and integrate all these stories? We can actively engage with them to provide insight and a path to begin this work. There are many ways to do this, including but not limited to mindfulness, honest reflection from others, journaling, shadow work, working with tools such as Reclaiming and Feri's Iron Pentacle or emotional expression, and dream work. The method outlined below engages the dynamics of the top triad of sephirot within the Tree of Life.

TIME: 1 hour

YOU WILL NEED: Journal and pen

Settle yourself in whatever way seems best to you—at your altar, outside, or at your desk. You might want to ground and center, take a few moments to breathe quietly, or stretch your body.

Take up your journal and write the heading *Hidden Parts of My Self.*

Jot down the following as lists:

- ▶ Some characteristics in other people that have been really bothering you lately
- ▶ Some stories you repeatedly tell, either silently or aloud, about yourself
- ▶ Some beliefs you hold about your limitations or doubts about your capabilities

My list might look like this:

- ▶ A's unreliability, C's endless talking about themselves, F's lack of clarity
- ▶ I'm socially awkward, I can't get over my childhood, I never change my mind
- ▶ I'm not kind, I don't put myself out there enough, I'm too old

Pick one to begin with—usually the one that feels most crunchy or sticky or uncomfortable. Set your page up to have three columns. You might need to turn the page sideways or use a double page.

In the first column, write down the details of this item; for example, if I pick *A's unreliability* the details might be: *A cancels whenever they feel like it, A changes their mind a lot, A stays undecided until the last minute, A can't be relied on.*

If I pick *I'm socially awkward,* I might write: *I feel stressed at large social gatherings, I prefer to be quiet than to talk, I don't enjoy social chitchat.*

If I pick *I'm not kind enough,* my notes might be: *I have high expectations of people, I prefer people who are independent and self-sufficient, I can be brusque or cool to others.*

In the third column (leaving the middle one blank for now), reflect the opposite truths—these are things that are still true but appear to be opposite to what was written in the first column. For A's unreliability, I will focus on my own unreliability. If the characteristic is already my own (such as socially awkward), I will write down ways that I am socially competent. For example:

I'm unreliable in that I don't stay true to my feelings, I persist with an arrangement no matter what. I'm unreliable in that sometimes I stay polite rather than truthful. I'm unreliable in that I can agree with something to placate someone else.

I'm socially competent because I'm an attentive listener. I'm socially competent because I organize and manage events. I'm socially competent because I'm a great friend.

In the middle column write the synthesis. Breathe into the opposing statements and find the truth, the middle way, the composite. For example:

I'm reliable as far as keeping my word and commitments go, but I could become more truthful to how I'm feeling (like A) and that would be a different sort of reliability. I could learn to blend the two.

In social situations I experience some discomfort, especially if there's a lot of people and expectations. But I still carry myself well and relate deeply with people.

It is really up to you what you do at this point. You might want to dance or shake out your emotions; you might want to write more deeply into what arose for you; you might want to make some resolutions or action points. The fundamental idea is to hold both sets of realities and find a way to integrate them or come to a more holistic or truthful understanding within yourself.

You can follow this process with many different issues or just one at a time, whichever seems most useful.

Memoir: *The Source of Love*

I meet with a friend I don't see often. We have coffee and speak in a jagged way. I am filled with awkwardness, thinking we have outgrown this never-realized love affair, but then we walk together and he takes my hand on this gray autumn day so remembrance of our connection seeps back into me. I start to feel some pleasure in the tangibility of this skin-on-skin, hand-holding-hand and the conversation stills and reorients. We find a park and walk through it, crossing back and forward in several directions, talking. It's quite cold. We stop at a bench built in a circle, with its back around an oak tree losing its leaves. We sit close, he puts his arms around me. All the parts of our bodies chill, gradually, except where we are touching, my right side and his left. His arms are over and around me, we are holding hands as well, we rest our heads against each other, and I could probably stay forever, taking in the autumn of us, the still-quiet-warmth and some long unmet promise.

There's a man twenty years younger than me and quite beautiful, with long gold-and-silver hair and a soft and curious manner, who asks me out on a date. We have a drink at the quirky bar he chooses and he asks if I will visit the Caravan of Love with him. It's an old-style, tiny caravan parked in the back yard, with cushions and hangings, and I am so delighted, almost overwhelmed by even the idea of it, so we lie together on cushions in the Caravan of Love with our glasses of wine and talk and kiss. Kisses. Like the beginning of the world. Oh, kisses—I remember this. I flare into life, in total wonder—a kiss is such a precious thing. So transitory and incendiary. Everything is lit up.

I walk a labyrinth of ice: magical, like a fairy tale, with ice hearts and altars and twists and turns—I face a forest of maple trees stark in their winter bones, then low human buildings of warmth and shelter, and on a turn the ice lake, pristine and glittering. Around a bend there's an ice bench, like a throne with a carved back set into the wall of the labyrinth, facing the lake. There's someone already seated on it, and because of the layers we wear—coats and scarves and hats—I can't actually tell who it is, but they make room for me, sliding over, and I sit beside them. Now I see they are the beloved of a beloved and I smile and hold out a gloved hand and they take it in their gloved hand and we sit, holding hands like the regents of a magical realm. Slowly I let my head fall toward them and they move toward me in response so that we rest cheek to cheek, holding gloved hands in the land of snow and ice. The moment is as pure as a frozen flake of fresh white snow.

It's a kissing workshop that is playful and a bit serious; we practice kissing hands and cheeks, we kiss with eyelashes, with intention, we kiss foreheads and inner arms and finally the invitation is to kiss on the mouth. I meet a woman in the swirl of things and she asks if I want to kiss and I prevaricate. I ask *What sort of kiss?*—I am panicked and desirous and a little overwhelmed—and she says *Oh on the mouth and maybe a bit of tongue* and she's laughing with it and I laugh too and ask *Can we go slow?* and she says *Yes* and leans forward and starts the kiss. The shape of her lips against mine. The softness of them. The take-your-breath of it. The tiny, tiny moments of her mouth as she breathes trembles lives, like a butterfly's wings, the pivoting of all my attention into each second of this kiss, mouth to mouth, the first I have had in a year or more, while the world rewrites itself—always, in each moment, but here and in me—and still it is delicate, the breath of it, the barest touching of me and her. My mouth softens, smiles, as we kiss.

A local Tantra evening, a dozen people and some dancing, connection, sharing; I start to loosen all through. Oh, if my life held this every day, perhaps I could survive not having a lover. At the end we are supposed to find a partner for the final exercise, and I hesitate so I am left to pair with the facilitator. He invites everyone to find some way of holding and being held, if they wish, and I ask him to lie down with me, my back to his chest with his arm around me. He checks in several times, *Like this? Is this okay?* and then we just lie there and I am half-transported, falling into the holding. He says quietly, into my hair, *I've got your back,* and I'm startled into tears. There's so many people I support that to have someone hold me, have my back—I am astounded at the power of it. I'm crying in his arms and he says it again: *I've got your back*. A moment later he says *Fuck, this floor is hard*, and I laugh. Laughing and weeping, I rest against him and something small, like a valve or gateway or belief, shifts within me.

It starts to break through to me. What these moments, these tiny, perfect intimacies have in common, is me. I'm the common factor. They're my relationships, my connections. None of these moments would have happened without me—or the other person, of course, but there's so many of them. The park, the Caravan of Love, the frozen lake, the kiss, the hard floor—these are me. This is the way I relate. I am the source of this—I am the source. It's like receiving love notes from the universe: *You are not forgotten.* Here you can connect, and here, and here. With this one and this and that one and this one also. Into each moment offer your love, receive love. It's so delicate, so nearly intangible, and the gaps between these moments so vast—weeks or months—but they start to happen more as I bring myself closer to the awareness of them, into the invitation—I am the invitation. I start to fall in love with the universe again, not theoretically but sensually, within each moment.

Sparkling with this awareness, I go to a night devoted to sacred relating. There's forty people and as I walk in the door I see a man over near the fireplace, thin and intense, wearing age in his face, though probably he's younger than me. The fierceness of him scares me a little so I take a seat across the opposite side of the circle, though there was an empty cushion next to him. Through the first part of the evening I run into him in the mill of people and it's there, the connection. We exchange names and up close he isn't frightening, though I see that his face literally has two sides, one with pain etched deep in lines and the other side more open. Later for an exercise we find each other and reach out, take hold. You, yes. You.

We lie together, fully clothed and gazing into each other's eyes. His arms are around me and he strokes my hair. This is what I asked for and I cry a little in the receiving of it. I want to lie there for hours, and my five or ten minutes do seem like a long time but then there's a break, setting up for the next part of the evening. The men are invited to lie down, naked, around the edges of the room. The women move about softly, nearly silent. We gaze, meet the eyes of the men, don't touch. When I come across him, lying near the door, I look at his face and he has tears running out of his eyes. I see the rest of his body: it is perfect—in this realm they are all perfect. It's a blessing. His body looks like it belongs to him—slender and wiry, a little older than he probably is. I gaze at it and can imagine living with it, loving it, being joined with this body.

Then the women also do this—I do this, lie naked and revealed for the men to walk through the room. This man comes by me and holds my eyes, gazes briefly at the rest of my body, at the women's bodies; he seems overawed by the room, the ritual, himself. We are within a temple. Afterward, in the next break, I see him outside, changing his sarong for jeans and a T-shirt. He's leaving. I go out to him.

He says he's going home, he has a long drive. He comes and takes my face in his hands and thanks me, says that he came tonight to meet me. I don't want him to leave; I want to have tea and conversation. He thinks for a moment and then tells me that he's about to go into rehab, in a week, for six months. That he's an addict, he's been off it before for a long time, but he had a bad patch and now he's going to fix it. He says he will see me after, in six months. I know that in six months I'll be away, in Europe; suddenly it seems that this is all I will have of this man. I almost ask *Couldn't you visit me and make love before you disappear?* but it seems disrespectful of his process or what's actually offered in this moment. Instead I ask if he wants a kiss and he says yes, so we stand on the veranda under the night sky for one kiss before he leaves.

There's a young man I've met for coffee, we had a fierce intellectual conversation and I thought he definitely wasn't interested in me but at the end there was a slow hug and I felt him suddenly, he brought his whole self into it. He's a large man, Viking-like, intense and abrupt, but I like him and talking with him, and then in the hug I understood that men significantly younger than me, twenty years younger, take me seriously as a potential lover. It's something I've struggled to believe but this interaction somehow convinces me so that I stop apologizing for my age or making allowances for it. When I was their age, most of my friends and lovers were older than me. I feel young, younger than I did when I was actually young.

I go to see him one evening. He's still at work in a small-scale honey factory. The floor is sticky with honey—the air is filled with honey. His clothes, when he hugs me, smell of honey. There's a bee, dazed, against the side of the vat, overwhelmed—he lets it crawl onto his hand and then opens the flywire over the window so it can fly free. There's great drums of honey, a whole honey process winding down, which he can't leave until it's finished. I've walked into a honey world. We sit and have tea, with honey, and tip into a conversation about children and parenting and my mother's death, and he is very present and connected in it, revealed, raw, intently aware of what I'm saying. He touches me, on the arm, my knee—earlier he touched the small of my back—and at some point he kisses me. His kisses are defined, warm, still, and offering, not taking. Outside as I'm leaving he holds me again in the dark—everything about him still smells of honey—and kisses me again. It seems—not a promise, exactly, but a gift. From the night, the bees, from a young man who can stay present. From the universe.

In the new year I turn up to a four-day workshop on love and relating. It's adver-tised for couples and singles but almost all the work is couples-based. One of the singles leaves immediately, another leaves within the first day. Two of the remaining singles pair up to become a couple. Quite quickly there are only four single people left, and one of the two men I feel such a fierce boundary with that I hold him at arm's length every time we are paired together. On the second day one of the facilitators says to me that they've spoken to the other three and, if I agree, they will pair me with the other man for the rest of the time. He is young, ferocious, and clear. He speaks to me, says he knew this would happen, and he's okay with it.

For me he is a gift. He is probably the most difficult participant, constantly correcting the facilitators, arguing the point, rewriting the activities to suit himself, so that I'm glad I'm not teaching him, but to pair with he is wonderful. His communication is so clipped and astringent sometimes I laugh at the ferocity of it. One time I am explaining that the chocolate I've brought to share is vegan when he picks up the packet and waves it about. *Are you trying to pretend that this rainforest-destroying product, imported from the other side of the world, produced with child slavery, and wrapped in foil and cardboard is vegan?* he sort of shouts. I remedy myself, hastily, *Oh well, this product contains no animal or dairy products,* I rattle out and he says, astounded and still at high volume, *What are you doing? Don't edit yourself to please me! Say whatever you like!*

He is a small man, slender, with longish fair hair. He has a biblical name. He holds himself with perfect posture; although he is only my height, his presence is tall, calm, powerful. Massaging him, I follow the line of his name and think of those early proph-ets, of Christ—how difficult he probably was as a personality, what a pain to be around perhaps, but it was worth it for his vision and clarity and power. I see how his followers could be so devoted: here is a man unafraid of the truth. His words and actions, even his body, carry it. I feel myself expanding, flowering within it, sparking with light to be met so clearly. We form an alliance, we arc through the exercises with power and grace; unlike the couples all around us we have no agenda, no history to trip us up and not much investment in being cautious with the other—well, he has none.

We hold each other naked, suspended in the pool, and I feel him as the earth anchor-ing me while I float in water, sunlight and air on my skin. He rewrites the entire partner yoga practice to meet his own requirements. We do an exercise describing in minute detail the other's genitals. In the middle of mine he stops his very precise and certainly not flattering cataloging, looks into my eyes, and says *By the way, you are absolutely beautiful.* In the evenings we walk down to the carpark together, talking easily, and hug goodbye, soft and slowly. I esteem him. In the closing circle, each person speaks what they have learned or gained from the workshop. When it is his turn, he does not speak into the circle but instead turns and faces me, rearranging his whole body. He sits upright, graceful, and says he was honored to be my partner; he speaks of my qualities and does not address any of the questions of the checkout and I am softened all through, delighted; it touches my heart. No one else does that; he is like no one else.

In the days following I go and swim in the river feeling anguished. Which of them should I allow myself to love? The man from the temple night who I'll probably never see again but felt made for me? The Viking honey man who kissed and talked with me? The young yogic man from the retreat who I know has no interest in me? My heart feels as if it's breaking in the confusion of it, and then, in the river's flow, I know. Love all of them. Love each for what we shared, for who they are. Love them as fully as I can, with everything I've got, and that way I can't hold on to anything. Love is the river in flow, and I flow also. It doesn't hurt when I love them; it's trying to stop the love or limit it that hurts. Let it go. Delight in them, each of them—and I feel my heart full and touched and open. I love them. For seeing me, the shared moments, for exactly who they are. The depth I had with one, the openness with another, the intensity with another. Love costs nothing, and restricting love costs everything.

Fall in love with the world and each iteration of it that is granted me to see. My friend from the autumn park, the man in the Caravan of Love, the meeting in the ice labyrinth, the woman I kissed, the man who held me on the floor, the temple man, the honey man, my tantric partner—and all the others, too, that I've met in workshops or on dates, that I've passed in the street and our eyes have caught, those who I've listened to or watched—all of them.

Each a spark of the universe, as am I, each a part of the mending, of the great becoming, the formation of matter and life on its way from stars and on its way back to stars. I am the source of love. I breathe it in and out, each moment and each person a gift, a reflection, a piece of the whole. Love them all as well as I can—it's simple. I swim through the river like tides of stars. I can hold nothing. I am in the twist and flow of it, I am essence, a particle, and each breath—look—touch—word—is love, the birthing of love into the world, and I am the source of it.

activity | The River of Life

Inspired by a River of Life activity created by Jarrah Staggard.

The river of life contains the Milky Way, from start to finish, and everything else we can name or imagine, flowing on more or less endlessly. Our personal river of life is more finite and contained. It begins at our birth, carries all the events and experiences we are part of, and finishes with our death. We might regard our ancestors as tributaries to our river and our descendants as the great delta or ocean that our river feeds. Perhaps you are used to thinking of your life this way or perhaps it is a new concept for you.

We can imagine our own river as a map with the different events, influences, and relationships as geographical features along the way. Or we can look at our river as a living system, studying a moment in time—for example, this moment—and analyzing all its components: the philosophies that are feeding us, the relationships we're committed to, and the living things, such as gut bacteria, that are part of our river. This exercise emphasizes the *flow* aspect of a river—as if we were the banks of the river, containing and allowing the river's stream. Life flows through us. Our lifetime is a landscape through which an expression of life happens.

This is a creative exercise, although you also might want to meditate with it; create ritual around, through, or after it; or have it as a discussion with a group or with various people at different times. Choose a creative expression that feels right to you. Possibilities include poetry, painting, drawing, dance, music, collage... The instructions are written for an art piece on paper, but adapt them to your chosen expression.

TIME: 45–60 minutes (or more, depending on your art modality)

YOU WILL NEED: Art materials. Journal and pen optional.

Spend a few minutes grounding and centering yourself.

Lay your art materials out within easy reach. If you are working with another medium, put out what you need.

Now allow yourself to drop deep within, following the breath. Imagine there is a seed place within you—a speck of stardust, perhaps, or the memory of your connection to all things, the seed of your soul purpose, or your living link to the divine. Breathe with this idea for a while, however it is for you. It may be an image, a feeling, a sound, or something else entirely. Let your breath feed this place and notice its response.

Next imagine the source of a river, its very beginnings, and find the river source within your seed place. Perhaps you can feel it welling up or starting to flow. Watch, listen, or feel this river as it comes into being. Encourage its strengthening, widening, deepening. Perhaps you will feel your whole body carried by the flow of this river. Or perhaps you can imagine it sweeping through you, from the crown of your head down to your feet and out beyond you.

You can imagine the events of your life carried through you on this flow. Even things you have been very attached to in the past—such as personality attributes, relationships, and places—you may be able to observe how they washed into you, were part of you for a while, and then flowed onward and left you. You might do this generally or very specifically, even choosing to focus on situations that were painful, challenging, or limiting. You might recall things that were dearly loved but left your life, or patterns, relationships, or situations that you moved on from.

Where does this river come from? Where is it going? Does this matter to you or is it more about being present with the part of the river flowing through you right now?

What is flowing through you currently? You might experience this as colors, flavors, or feelings or as ideas, life circumstances, current explorations and relationships. Explore the connection of your personal river to the greater River of Life. Take a few moments to focus closely on the details of your river at this moment in time, before bringing your awareness to your art materials.

Find a way to represent your river as an art piece. Perhaps you will create a collage with different patterns, words, and images representing the river as it is flowing through you now. Perhaps you will draw or paint a picture depicting the source of the river. Perhaps you will make a poem, song, cartoon, or textile representation of the river.

When you are done, spend some time contemplating what you have created. What is your relationship to the source from which all things flow? How do you feel about accepting the River of Life into yourself and letting it flow on beyond you? Are there parts of your life you can feel getting ready to leave or parts that are just arriving? How does it seem to experience yourself and your life as part of the manifestation of the All? You might also like to journal about the River of Life.

activity | Creating the Third Disk

As you complete the work of this section, make sure to create a disk to represent the sephira you've been inhabiting. This will be your third disk. Perhaps you are traveling down the Tree from the top, so you spent the first section concentrated on Kether and are now up to Binah; in that case, it will be the black Binah disk you are working on. Perhaps you began somewhere else in the Tree, so the disk you are making now is for Malkuth, Tiferet, Chesed, or any other sephira.

TIME: 30–60 minutes

YOU WILL NEED: The appropriate colored disk (see page 69, "Creating the First Disk") and whatever art materials you wish to work with, such as colored pens and markers, paint, oil pastels, collage materials and glue, stickers

Begin by recalling the time you have spent in this sephira, including looking through your journal notes, recalling any Kabbalah exercises, processes, or rituals you did and especially how these related to this particular sephira, as well as the general mood and events in your life during this time. It will probably be distinct in feeling and awareness from the previous two sephirot.

Allow images and words, feelings and ideas to arise. You might hold these in your head, immediately begin work on your disk, or jot down notes or a sketch.

You can begin by marking the name of the sephira—I use both its name and the English translation—onto the disk. If your language is not English, use the appropriate word in your language. I use a gold, silver, or white marker for the Binah disk, which is already black, and a black marker for all the others.

Then decorate your disk. You can use poetry or the words of a song or chant. You might work with shape and color or

examples of completed disks can be seen at janemeredith .com/disks

draw or paint a scene such as your River of Life or symbols or patterns that make sense to you. You can cover the whole or part of the disk with collage, cutting or tearing out pictures from magazines, greeting cards, and wrapping paper. You can cut shapes out of colored foil and glue them on or stick other things onto your disks—sand, bark, feathers, petals.

Your disk might be complete within itself or it might reference other sephirot that are close by or in the same pillar. It might contain an image of the Tree itself or a reference to this sephira's position within the Tree. Often I have one theme, such as butterflies or shards of light, running through all my disks. I usually create a strong edge around the disk with paint or oil pastel.

You might complete your work in one session or come back later to add details or another layer; for example, an arc of glitter.

falling through darkness, all
guts and decay, brevity and
disintegration ... I turn myself
inside out for life and death and
there are no alternatives but to fall
impossibly far ... lifetimes—still
I remember but—beyond reach,
tumbling down, away, beyond,
through light refracting into
infinitely small pieces and all of
them falling, falling, falling ... the
dust of universes born and dying,
great nurseries of stars, graveyards
of stars—veils beyond veils
concealing, revealing

falling, spiraling through time
and darkness and stardust, in a
heartbeat of the possible a butterfly
flies and falls ...

. . .

THE ABYSS

*they say there was a dragon inside
an egg before the world began—it
was born, raging fire exploding
the singularity and echoed out
becoming even to the edges of the
universe holding darkness within
itself—Kether—Hokmah—
Binah—and now all falls away
falling the shattered shards of light
from the first moment of the Fall,
the All in pieces, petals, stars and
sparks falling falling through time
and infinity, darkness and into
matter light in extension extending
through the unknown through space
and time this is the great Abyss, the
unknown, even with Knowledge
nested at the heart of it—there's
an island between two rivers and
a garden planted there, the Tree
of Life and the Tree of Knowledge
or they are the same tree—and
there's flashes of all the worlds, the*

*structure of molecules dissolving,
giant gas clouds, the arc of light, the
wing of a white cockatoo the falling
of dark space we're swept up by
interstellar winds where galaxies
are formed and torn apart, eaten
like the stars themselves it's all fall,
all falling and there's no place to
arrive, it's the fall*

even stars fall

*this is the end this is the All
this is the nothing bound and
separated forever all dissolves,
releases, shattered*

*falling through vast space, endless,
an imagining becoming, a butterfly
potential whirled through space
and nothingness an abyss beyond
knowing, falling*

4

Pillars in
the Tree

Hokmah

THE ABYSS

Chesed

The fourth sephira emerges below the Abyss and directly underneath Hokmah. Immediately Chesed, named Mercy or sometimes Loving-kindness, creates two things: the existence of the lower Tree stretching below and beyond the Abyss, and the introduction of lines of descent from the top triad as it begins the right-hand pillar. It's almost the start of a whole new Tree.

The previous sephirot have existed both singly and in relation to each other—they have evolved from and with each other—but there has not been such a direct descent vertically. What will emerge out of these top sephirot, below the Abyss? Where triads blend energies, pillars separate and differentiate. The next several sephirot, the three directly below the top triad (forming a triad themselves), create bridges between the upper and lower Tree. They show ways that the celestial energies from the top triad can transform into something approaching our comprehension.

Pillars are a powerful construct within the Tree. What pillars will eventually do when they are fully arrived is give us direct ways to travel between heaven and earth, between divine and human realms.

Chesed: *Flow and Force*

If Kabbalah is about receiving, Chesed is an exemplar of that. Each sephira can be said to receive all that has already been from the sephirot above them, but Chesed is unique in receiving, via the lightning flash, the entirety of the supernal triad. Chesed shows us that we have literally received everything—the atoms that make up our bodies; a life; each breath, mouthful of water, and food; each kiss and caress; each moment. There is no place to stop on this lightning flash into existence until Malkuth is reached, so the receiving of everything necessitates the giving of everything. Chesed demonstrates that to receive is only half of the dynamic; the other half is to give. Jewish religious thought places a great deal of emphasis on giving to others and actively improving the lives of those around us, and Chesed epitomizes this by an outpouring equal to what it receives.

Chesed answers our questions about how much to give. We receive everything in order to give everything.

Chesed is the pivot between the top triad and the lower Tree whichever direction you are traveling in. It is the clearest example of what each sephira does as it pivots, like a hinge or directional channel both receiving and then passing on the energy, information, or light—whatever it is that is moving through the Tree. Hokmah is the all-important first functional pivot in the Tree of Life, between Kether and Binah, while Binah pivots between Hokmah and through the Abyss to Chesed, as well as from Kether into the left-hand pillar. Even Kether is a pivot, between the Ain Soph and eventually (or within a split nanosecond) the beginning of the Tree with Hokmah. When Chesed enters the Tree, this technology of pivoting is at its most evident; Chesed does it more, or is more entirely involved with it, than any other sephira.

Imagine carrying the weight of the world upon your shoulders; what about the weight of all future worlds to come? What is it like to receive the download, the blueprint, the instructions straight from the divine or from the beginning of time and be solely responsible for implementing them? What if you were barely imaginable by the higher powers, who could not really conceive of your existence, but you were also so distant from those you were responsible for that you could hardly project your thoughts that far? This is Chesed's position as the gateway between heaven and all of existence, the linchpin between all that is above and all that is below. Perhaps this is akin to our own position between our distant ancestors and our distant descendants.

Chesed is tied forever between the upper and lower parts of the Tree, endlessly responsible to both and yet somehow powerless to do anything but the task of reception and distribution. It could be said that reception and distribution is everything, and indeed, to some extent, all other sephirot also are part of that process, each receiving and passing on or passing back these energies, information, and states of existence. But Chesed's unique position magnifies this role. Directly beneath Hokmah, with a vertical download of all that emotion, love, and loss, Chesed catches, receives, and is the future transmitter of all that comes from the top triad, fed both by Hokmah and along the lightning flash by Binah, set on the business of generation.

What to do with all this information? Chesed is in the right-hand pillar, so this sephira does not turn to systems, qualifications, and categories to manage it. Operating instead on compassion, expansion, loving-kindness, or mercy, Chesed simply receives and distributes perfectly, without pause, hesitation, or reservation. Perhaps it's like being at the top of a waterfall. All of the river must be received: there's no place to turn some aside or sort out what should and shouldn't go over the edge—it's all going over. And what is received down the length of the waterfall and at the bottom is everything. The top of the waterfall doesn't keep anything back for itself; it is constantly resupplied but retains none of it. When I say *perfectly*, there's a sort of generosity in this right-hand pillar where things are total, complete, unending. Not like the left-hand pillar, which includes full stops, commas, and question marks—limitations, conditions. No, Hokmah, Chesed, and later Netzach are the endless flow of force. In this we could see them as representing the wave aspect of light.

Where Hokmah is a reflection of Kether and so seems always focused upward, into the Tree, Chesed is by necessity focused downward, toward the lower Tree. All seven sephirot of the lower Tree, including Chesed itself, fall into the domain of receiving the energy/information/force that channels through Chesed. *Force* is an interesting term. I think of life force and how relentless that is, continuing despite wars, ecological devastation, pollution, and suffering. Still the life force plunges on, around-through-over. There's a measure of compassion in that it's distributed so unconditionally. Even though we all are servants to it, each eventually meets a moment of release, when the unstoppable force flows over and past us onto—the next generation maybe. Even though we are served a full measure of life force while alive, regardless of our desire for it or not, we are also given just the right amount to live our life until our death.

Imagine being in charge of that—endlessly feeding the world. A further consideration is that what comes from the upper Tree and what is distributed to the lower Tree are very different. Within the top triad there is only the beginnings of the concept of creation. It is all action, reflection, reaction. Yet the lower Tree is tasked with actual creation—the bringing together of force and form into manifestation. So all the undiluted rawness of the upper Tree must be digested in order to be received by the lower Tree. To some extent each sephira does this, transforming whatever it receives into progressively less rarefied states as we head down the Tree. But Chesed alone has the task of digesting and transforming the entirety of the top triad's transmissions. Within the pillar system, the whole middle triad has a similar task—Gevurah digesting and transmitting from Binah, Tiferet from Kether (possibly via Da'ath), and Chesed from Hokmah. But in that format each is doing it only within a pillar, whereas within the lightning flash Chesed does it for the entire lower Tree.

Heading up the Tree the task is the opposite: to compose and refine everything one is and has received before passing it on. Once again each sephira does this, and within the pillars, Tiferet, Gevurah, and Chesed are all responsible for passing this information up through the Abyss. But in the lightning flash it is only Chesed responsible for this mammoth task of transmitting all of the lower Tree into the upper Tree. True to the nature of Chesed, everything flows through, to some extent raw and undifferentiated, although Gevurah previously no doubt has had a hand in formatting it, and the Abyss may yet shred it to pieces, turn it inside out, or simply eat it.

Chesed is depicted as blue—a generous, faultless sky blue that one could fall into forever. It reminds me not just of sky but water and the flow associated with water. Oceans, where life was born. The tides, pulled by lunar forces, washing and cleansing everything forever, reshaping the world in increments. The rock pools where life began. The outpouring force of Chesed ensures that there is endless experiment, variation—enough water, sunlight, chemicals—and if not in this particular rock pool, then the next one and the next, along nearly endless shorelines and throughout nearly endless time. Constraints of space and time do exist within Chesed, but they are vast, nearly immeasurable, and somewhat elastic. In local realms these constraints could be said barely to exist, or they exist in the same way that the mathematics of the wave exist, determining height, velocity, the point of crash or collapse, but nothing of the life within the wave.

I think of Chesed as a river—of stars, of force, of water—changing all the time but always in flow. Stepping into the river, let alone bathing or swimming, one becomes part of the flow, carried by it, surrendering—and this is the force of life that sweeps one along endlessly in its own direction. This is the mercy of Chesed, both the endlessness of it and also that one doesn't have to do it oneself. We are carried by a greater force, and it doesn't matter if we're doing well or badly, we are still carried. There's an aphorism about how each time we spoil a page of our lives, God grants us another page; this is the type of mercy Chesed has, endlessly forgiving and endlessly moving on, endlessly granting the next piece. Until there is no next page, one of those pages is the final page and that, also, can be seen as mercy. Our children and inheritors bathe in the same river of life although it is new for them; it is always renewing.

A river is a potent image. When creating magic I sometimes think of myself as standing beside an enormous river, the life/force/magic of the world. My spell or intention is a little boat I've made, perhaps from a bit of twisted bark, a twig, and a leaf. If I cast it into this great river, I'm expressing my wish and asking the river to carry it for me. If I try to send it upstream, against the current, it has no chance. Even if I want it to cross to the other side, it's not very likely. But if what I'm asking is for the river to support my little boat and carry it along the current, I may be successful. It will partly depend on my skill in shaping the craft and how, when, and where I place it into the river. This helps me shape my intention. If, for example, something has happened that I don't like, I could try casting a spell with the intention *Make this never have happened.* That would be going upstream, asking time to go backward, which we probably understand doesn't work. If my intention is *These circumstances will never reoccur*, that feels a bit like trying to send my boat straight across the river, which might occasionally be successful. But if my intention is *Let me find ways to make the necessary changes so this does not keep happening to me*, then it feels like I'm standing in the river, releasing my little boat onto an eddy that can keep it upright, sailing down the river of life and drawing on the magic of the river itself to assist my intention to shape the future.

Chesed's color, blue, has various divinities associated with it, including Mary, mother of Christ, who is often shown wearing a blue dress or blue cloak. As Hokmah is associated with Sophia, goddess of wisdom, placing Mary in Chesed, below her, is a nice touch. But more often I think of gods with blue skin, as well as the dancing Blue God of the Feri and Reclaiming Traditions. The Blue God in this creation story is the first of three to emerge once Miria is swept away into the vast distances of space. The story perfectly mirrors the arrangement of these sephirot: the Star Goddess, who is all things (Kether), looks into the curved mirror of dark space (Hokmah) and draws forth Miria the beloved (Binah), who then is swept away far beyond reach (the Abyss) and transforms into the Blue God. The Blue God is not just water and the oceans that birth life but those beginnings of life; life force freed into a world—the lower Tree—where it can become, dance, and transform.

The Hindu god Shiva is the divinity I most associate with Chesed. Often shown as white but sometimes as blue, Shiva carries the integrity of this sephira: maturity as well as compassion, mercy, love. Wolf-Deiter Storl writes of him in *Shiva: The Wild God of Ecstasy and Power* that "he is the lover of lovers and the devotee of his devotees" (Storl 2004, 1). There's a generosity in this, the opposite of a jealous or greedy god demanding worship and subjugation. Shiva dances the worlds into becoming and unbecoming. Shiva dances—the Blue God dances—the sea or a river dances. It's easy to see the connection with Chesed. Past the Abyss is the birthing of endless galaxies, the blossoming of stellar gas clouds, the self-fueling stars and the dancing spill outward, outward as the impacts continue, rippling the edges of the universe on through the nothingness into somethingness. Expansion is another word for this force, this mercy; an endless expanding of stars, of life, of possibility, as the light from the top triad keeps extending.

Like Chesed has with Gevurah, Shiva has a corresponding force in the goddess Kali—one without the other would be so unbalanced as to make the world impossible. There's a myth telling of Kali's righteous rage ferociously destroying everything, piece by piece. Shiva lies down in front of her to be destroyed, knowing that this is the only thing that will stop her. Sure enough, when she realizes what she has done, she stops and restores him to life. The balance is returned. This laying down of one's life, the offering of oneself unreservedly, is very much Chesed. For all its mightiness, its position as the top of the lower Tree, Chesed is totally of service in the flow of what we could call love, as is Gevurah, the fierce warrior divinity bent on destruction. It takes both of them. The blue expands; the red contracts. In their different, opposite, but complementary ways, both are in service.

When we describe the right- and left-hand pillars as *force* and *form,* this is true for the entire pillar. Yet the middle sephirot of those pillars, Chesed and Gevurah, have the purest or most entire expression of that. Yes, Hokmah is about force, but force is only just born. Similarly with Binah, where form becomes possible but hasn't quite arrived. But with Chesed and Gevurah, force and form are fully present. By the time we reach Netzach and Hod, force and form have evolved into multiplicity, complexity—so they are still there, guiding and shaping—but at Chesed and Gevurah they are realized. There's almost nothing else at this middle level of the Tree than the force of Chesed, the form/s of Gevurah, and the meeting and blending of those within Tiferet.

Chesed and Gevurah have the strongest polarity across the Tree. Binah and Hokmah are different from each other—at that stage of the Tree everything that happens is profoundly different from everything else because hardly anything exists. Netzach and Hod are also different from each other but so closely entwined one can hardly move without the other, like the legs of Adam Kadmon, the human figure superimposed onto the structure of the Tree; both legs are needed in order to move. But arms or hands—the positions within the body of Adam Kadmon where Gevurah and Chesed rest—are relatively independent from each other. They can cooperate, work together, or they can do entirely different things, even oppose each other. One can rest entirely, while the other is active. The hand itself contains the idea of opposition with our opposing thumbs, so crucial to our ability to make and use tools.

This almost opposition with Gevurah assists Chesed to be what it is. To go to the edges, so to speak, as if they balance against each other, both leaning outward, and the weight of the other allows each of them not to fall out of the Tree entirely, into wild nothingness, or be sucked into the unmaking vortex of Da'ath. So Chesed, though it sounds so mild—mercy, loving-kindness—is extreme. Extreme in perhaps a way we can't imagine. The saints come to mind, but this is not a human kindness. This is not tempered by reason, personality, or the constraints of the world. It is unending. Well, there may be an end to it, but like the universe or the waterfall, we can't tell where or when that is, and it's irrelevant to the actions of Chesed. This force, on its own, would be terrifying; it is more or less unstoppable except by its equal and opposite, Gevurah. Back to Shiva and Kali, water and fire, expansion and contraction, force and form.

In the grip of Chesed alone we would constantly be in an outward trajectory, always in torrent, overwhelmed with input, receiving everything—torn apart, really, by the outward forces of the universe. We would become a person who says *yes* to every offer and request indiscriminately; we would travel everywhere, accept every lover and business deal, taste everything, reply to all that spam in our inboxes—we would never stop. Our children or parents would be no more precious to us than a stranger in the street. I doubt we could stay fixed in houses, jobs, or locations, let alone relationships; we would be one with the endless wave form of particles or like electrons mysteriously present in each potential place equally and impossible to pin down.

This is a barely imaginable science fiction world and it's hard to put together with concepts of mercy and loving-kindness. So perhaps it is Gevurah's intervention, Gevurah's limitations, that allow these qualities of Chesed to be the mercy in the world. Because without Gevurah, Chesed would run amok in much the same way that Gevurah would without Chesed. These Chesed qualities are divine—to forgive everything, to be endlessly kind—and it's easy to see the place they hold in the Tree, the direct recipient of the inheritance of the top triad, the one responsible for distributing all that is generated there. Chesed is the summation of the divine from the supernal triad and its distributor to all of the lower Tree.

This distribution, an endless act, is a vital aspect of Chesed. So yes, it receives, momentarily contains, and is filled by everything, and then it releases. Like being present in each moment—we can be utterly filled with it, alive only now—and then pass on to the next moment. If I were to fully inhabit this moment—receive all of its input through all of my senses, imagination, memory, and experience—how long would it take to fully realize all of its subtleties and complexities? Instead I have the moment, only, to focus, discriminate, and select so that what filters through is a very edited, somewhat functional edition of the moment. But imagine not having those filters or discriminations or prioritizations in what we receive. That is Chesed.

Being at the top of the lower Tree is like being the eldest of a large family. Immense responsibilities are conferred with this position that more or less define Chesed. As the highest of the lower Tree—strictly speaking, Gevurah is at equal height, but in the lightning flash of the descent through the Tree Chesed absolutely comes first—Chesed could be understood as sorting through, channeling into seven channels all the undifferentiated material (or light) that it receives. The other six sephirot of the lower Tree depend on these abilities of Chesed. Because, we can imagine, they don't rely purely on an undiscriminating flow of energy from Chesed—although that also—but on a differentiated particularity in what they receive.

While all receive equally, they also receive differently, just the right thing for them. We can imagine these differences as rays or colors, all the white-gray-and-black of above turning into the blue, red, yellow, green, orange, purple, and brown, or see it as differing qualities or bandwidths. Perhaps it isn't Chesed that differentiates; perhaps it is the distance those rays travel and what they pass through along the way that turns them into different things. But in any case Chesed, by virtue of its hinge position through from the top triad, is responsible for them, the way the oldest sibling is somehow always responsible for their younger siblings—how they do at school, their general behavior and whereabouts, and, after they're grown, maintaining family ties and responsibilities.

Chesed does not have a personal choice in this and cannot play favorites or punish or limit those it may be less aligned with. It must be done perfectly, endlessly, with no hesitation. There's a certain ruthlessness in this, a pure, utter quality of impersonality and non-judgment that perhaps we can see as loving-kindness taken to its most extreme. It's the opposite of Gevurah's judgment, and this divine force ensures that everything continues regardless. Yes, you have to still wake up the day after your beloved died. Yes, the sun shines or the rain pours equally onto the most noble and the most degenerate humans. Yes, wisdom, insight, and magic are available to each one of us, regardless of age, circumstance, or the time and place we are born on the planet. Yes, atoms, electrons, light—the forces of the universe—continue unimpeded, even while we destroy the beautiful planet that gave birth to us and nurtures us. Always, until Gevurah steps in with finality, there's another chance, another breath, another moment. This is mercy at its highest level.

Seven days of Creation. Seven colors of the rainbow. Seven veils, seven gates, and in the old—and mythic/occult—system, seven planets in the solar system. All of the lower sephirot: Chesed itself, Gevurah, Tiferet, Netzach, Hod, Yesod, and Malkuth receive the same unending attention and energy poured from above into the below. Each receives exactly what it needs to become and express itself. All is apportioned perfectly, as it must be. Chesed is responsible for this with no choice or discretion. It is indiscriminate but perfect.

Reminiscent of Hokmah's yearning love and loss story, Chesed's outpouring of mercy and love just continues. The force, the wave of this right-hand pillar does not stop but needs form imposed on it to pause or change, and that does not occur until the left-hand pillar comes into play. It offers a certain sort of comfort. Chesed says that life continues, the sun will rise again, there will be a time past the current grief or trauma or pain, that we are all held in divine love. Chesed is Shiva dancing the world into being, endlessly, or Mother Mary gathering us under her cloak to offer ease from suffering or the river ever washing clean, the waves of the ocean continuing to crash upon and thus shape and reshape the shore. It offers both challenge and reassurance. Chesed's challenge is to give as much as we receive, while it reassures the world that mercy is unending.

Pillars in the Tree of Life

Pillars are a central construct in the Tree of Life. By comparison pairs and triads, although they can be worked with to help the mechanics and flow of the Tree, are very minor in the attention they receive or the importance ascribed to them. Pillars are where it's all at. Perhaps this is the way our eyes work, picking out strong vertical lines, or perhaps what we are all yearning for are some clear paths between the earthly realm and the divine. Pillars speak to the culmination of the Tree, where pairs and triads are the building blocks—what it took to get there, rather than the final outcome. So if pillars are so important to understanding the Tree, why have we waited until now to examine them?

Pillars don't really exist until the fourth sephira, Chesed, arrives. That is, what turns out to be the tops of the pillars have existed—Kether, Hokmah, and Binah—but they weren't pillar-like on their own, and those three weren't forming pillars together. Instead, the existence of each of them enables a pillar to be born; they are each the seed of a pillar: Kether of the middle pillar, Hokmah of the right-hand pillar, and Binah of the left-hand pillar. The Tree is always read right to left, as is written Hebrew. Thus the first pillar starts to form when Chesed arrives below the Abyss and directly beneath Hokmah.

The right- and left-hand pillars both contain a top sephira, a middle sephira, and a lowest sephira, which form pairs across the Tree. Within the pillars the bottom pair holds the lowest emanation of that pillar: the most realized, or closest to the material world. The middle pair, while holding a transition space between above and below, is also the purest or strongest expression of that pillar. The top pair holds direct transmissions from Kether. The middle pillar has its own geography, including special inclusions of Da'ath, and Malkuth at the very bottom. If we discount those two for a moment, we can see the middle pillar also has a top, middle, and lower sephira inside it that work in similar ways to those within the left- and right-hand pillars. We could say that the middle pillar also includes the possibility of nothing, or the unmanifest (Da'ath) and the everything, the manifest (Malkuth). The left- and right-hand pillars, with their simpler formation, brace the middle pillar, which has so much going on inside it.

Pairs have a straightforward power balance—especially the horizontal pairs of Hokmah-Binah, Chesed-Gevurah, and Netzach-Hod—and triads have a shifting shared-power dynamic, but pillars have an up-and-down arrangement that looks immediately hierarchical. We are used to thinking of operating systems, whether in governments, workplaces, or even families, with heads that hold and wield intrinsically more power, and those below (often, but not always, in a pyramid-style structure) who have less power and are at least somewhat obliged to follow the directions of those above them. Power in the pillars, where one sephira is placed below another, and then another below that—and for the middle pillar, another below that again—at first glance looks very straightforward.

However, this is Kabbalah, so everything that can be read in one direction can also be read in the opposite direction, and usually both ways are equally true or useful. While the heads of the pillars do have particular powers that are disseminated or offer direction to the sephirot below them, that's only the first piece of the dynamic. If a sephira is third or fourth on the pillar, they will receive these directives and information not just from the sephira directly above them, but from the one or two above that, as well. Thus being at the bottom of the pillar looks like a lot of work with not much power. Well, that's what it looks like, but it's not really so. Or—it is so in one direction, but then there's the other direction...

Energy and information flow equally from earthly realms to the divine as they do the other way. One could say that the whole point of Kether is Malkuth—that without Malkuth, Kether cannot be fully realized: the Crown has no Kingdom. And Malkuth is on the lowest possible rung, below all the other sephirot by two spaces, or rungs. We can examine this in various ways, for example: cosmologically, philosophically, energetically. In cosmological terms Kether exists practically outside time or perhaps before time, while Malkuth is solidly within time. That moment of original singularity—if it were constant, never changing—that would be pure Kether. If it winked out of existence again, perhaps that would just be Kether with its perfect opposite, possibly Da'ath, and maybe that will happen eventually. But in the meantime so much else has happened! From our perspective, on the earth, all that has happened allows us to exist.

Time—even if not time as we know it—began as events unfolded past that singularity. One of the many effects of all of that unfolding of the universe was the existence of a small planet, locally known as Earth, in a perhaps unremarkable solar system on the outward edge of one of the arms of the Milky Way galaxy (so called), and in this place life-as-we-know-it occurred. Evolved. It happened and is still happening. Does what is happening here—at my desk, for instance, or in my garden outside with the breeze blowing through the tree ferns and the pademelons hopping about—feed back, in any way, to the beginnings of time?

Departing from cosmology and moving into the entangled particles of quantum physics or religion and mythology, we can answer *yes*. Those particles are still resonating with each other. As for the gods, all the stories and teachings say that the divine ones, those not of earth, care deeply about what happens here and are affected by it. It is not just a one-way system. Inanna, in ancient Sumeria, might demand temples and scribes and courts and rules of land usage and sacred holidays—but equally, Inanna is fed by the service in her temples, by the words of the scribes, the rulings of the courts, the grain and animals bred and cared for, and by the ritual feasting, drinking, and love-making at her festivals. This is just one example. Humans, and life on earth, experience and accomplish things that gods never can, thus all those stories about gods, angels, and demons taking human form to learn what they cannot otherwise know. Sometimes, in the stories, the sensations and physical existence are so intoxicating that there are not just visitors but even defectors from the heavenly to the earthly realm.

The information or experience of our realm in various forms is believed to be fed back to the gods. Possibly in much the same way that entangled particles work, we are never entirely separated, however separate our experience might seem to us. That experience of separation is the effect of being down at the bottom of the Tree, but it's a local condition and not indicative of how the whole system works. A phenomenon known as multiple independent discovery—scientific breakthroughs that occur concurrently in different places in the world, between individuals or teams that have had very little or no contact with each other—is thought to be due to an evolutionary-style model of scientific thought, a zeitgeist or moment in history that provided readiness, or even the mathematics of probability. But perhaps another way of expressing it is the inter-connectedness of particles and the instantaneous flow of information throughout the entire system. If we took that as the benchmark, everything that happens in Malkuth and on earth is simultaneously happening in Kether—possibly because they have never really been separate. What happens here touches all the worlds.

The pillars have names—not just right, middle, left, but actual names. Being the Kabbalah, they have many names, so you can take your pick, really. The right-hand pillar is often known as the Pillar of Mercy; another name for it is the Pillar of Creation. The left-hand pillar is the Pillar of Severity, also known as the Pillar of Rigor. When two pillars are shown in occult works, such as on the Rider-Waite tarot card of the High Priestess, the right-hand white and left-hand black pillar reference these pillars in the Tree of Life. The middle pillar is commonly called the middle pillar but is sometimes known as the Pillar of Harmony. The left- and right-hand pillars, in particular, work in synchronicity with each other, both upward and downward. The middle pillar contains, distills, and disseminates all.

A helpful lens to use while focusing on the right- and left-hand pillars is that of force and form. The right-hand pillar brings forth emanations of the *force* of the universe and Kether and all things—the splintering of singularity with Hokmah, the endless managed flow of Chesed, and that continual production of possibilities in Netzach. The left-hand pillar is concerned with *form*—time and space with Binah, laws and limitations with Gevurah, and the minutiae of classification with Hod. Force and form create an interdependent dynamic between them; endless force is clearly useless without some sort of form, and form on its own is dead without force to animate it. The play between them—the exact degrees of force and form, in any one thing, or any interaction, as well as the level it's occurring at—creates a delightful mixing bowl of potentiality, not that we were at any risk of boredom in the Kabbalah. The middle pillar is the mixing point, or vessel—from the exploding star of Kether to the chalice of Tiferet, the womb of Yesod, and the cauldron of Malkuth; maybe even throw in a black hole at Da'ath—the places where force and form mix and combine, to create.

As ways of differentiating the energies of the right- and left-hand pillars, "force" and "form" are much more constructive—and understandable—designations for these pillars than the old-school "masculine" and "feminine" of many books and Kabbalistic debates. In that system, the masculine pillar is the right-hand pillar, with its expansion and outward force, and the feminine designated to the left-hand pillar, with its form and inward contraction. We will examine this concept more deeply in the next section's "Polarities in the Tree of Life," but I will just say briefly, and as a feminist, that I consider all gendered terms and terminology currently in flux within the wider social

▲ Left-Hand, Middle, and Right-Hand Pillars

and political debates of the early twenty-first century. Clearly they are more representative of the society they emerge from than absolute, and as terms of definition they are not particularly helpful in this or many other contexts.

Middle Pillar

The middle pillar is visually the most obvious of the pillars. It contains both the highest point of the Tree, Kether, as well as the two lowest points of the Tree, Yesod and Malkuth. It also contains the heart of the Tree with Tiferet, and even the ominous not-quite-there presence or non-presence of Da'ath. Whereas the other two pillars consist of three sephirot, the middle pillar holds four sephirot, with space for five. It has the beginning and the end, or we could say the alpha and the omega, of the Tree. It has the very barest, newest leaves forming at the tips of the highest-reaching branches, as well as the deepest roots, whether you see the Tree as upright (to our eyes) or upside down, with the roots in Kether and the branches growing toward us, in Malkuth. The middle pillar has it all going on.

It's quintessential as far as pillars go because it's the most obvious example of how pillars work. Pillars channel—more directly than crawling through the whole Tree or even than flashing lightning-like through the whole Tree—energy, essence, information from the top to the bottom and from the bottom to the top. Pillars are highways, through-routes, avenues for direct transmissions. So what is the middle pillar transmitting? There's even more directness about this pillar than the others because it runs from Kether to Malkuth. The All of Kether—the undiscriminated, the singularity, the totally entangled particles—runs all the way through to the everything of Malkuth—the completely discriminated, defined, with its separated-out (although theoretically still entangled) particles via a few interesting stations along the way. In the other direction, the middle pillar condenses and refines the utter endless complexity of Malkuth through various stages and eventually up into the refined simplicity—singularity—of Kether.

There are three other stations, one of them a sort of non-station, along the way. Da'ath is both the great nothingness, the potential unbecoming, of the Tree and everything else—and also, mysteriously, Knowledge. It's like a black hole, the place where light vanishes. Possibly it leads through to a different universe. Possibly it foreshadows the ending of this one. Perhaps if we understood dark matter and, in particular, dark energy, we'd know what Da'ath is. It's both there and not-there in a sort of reassuring way. That it's there, even in the usual dotted outline, is reassuring because it restores the symmetry and pattern of the Tree—without it, there would be a hole. Well, perhaps it is a hole, but anyway, a hole that's on the diagram instead of just a gap. It's also reassuring because usually we don't have to think too much about it—it's not really there, after all. So we can continue on in our little lives, gardeners in paradise who don't ask too much about that tree at the center that we were mysteriously warned against... Well. There's a story there.

What have Kether and Da'ath to do with each other and, most particularly, the formation of this middle pillar? We don't know. But then, we don't really know much about Kether, and even less about Da'ath. So we might have to say it's a mystery. But both Kether and Malkuth, in different ways, contain absolutely everything, whereas Da'ath, perhaps, contains absolutely nothing. And not only nothing—the Ain Soph, after all, was varying gradients of nothingness—Da'ath also seems to loom as the potential to bring about nothingness, to render something—maybe even everything—into nothing. To swallow the world. Serpent imagery is attracted to the Tree and perhaps nowhere more so than Da'ath. The Tree, the serpent, knowledge... the serpent that eats its own tail... the serpents who weave their way up the Tree around the middle pillar like a caduceus... these images find a home within the beckoning mystery of Da'ath.

The power of this—Da'ath's potential undoing—holds the opposition to the power of Kether. When the energy of Kether moves to either side, creating Hokmah and Binah and thereby the other two pillars, in its own pillar it seems that the direct force of Kether, applied downward, results in a black hole. Perhaps our universe was born out of a black hole. Perhaps it will die in one. At any rate, they seem a fitting statement for each other. The brilliance of unending light (remembering that we don't actually know what light is) balanced by or progressed through to utter darkness, the type whose raison d'être is to swallow light.

Moving on down past that impossibility, we come to Tiferet, the heart of the Tree. Tiferet is the heart in so many ways, but here, in the progression of Kether-(Da'ath)-Tiferet, we meet another way. What can bring resolution to these two absolutes, strung together through the possible worlds? How to move beyond that; how to integrate this pillar? Beauty. The heart. Like a balm, a space for all things, the remembering of beauty—even in impossible light, even through unknowable darkness, in moments, in particles, in mystery—Tiferet. Straddling the division between the top and the bottom halves of the Tree, Tiferet is the center of the center and offers mediation in all directions. It even provides a way for those impossibilities at the top of the middle pillar to translate into the very possible, entirely real lower parts of the bottom of the pillar, Yesod and Malkuth. If Kether and Da'ath are two aspects of beauty unimaginable, then Yesod and Malkuth are beauty imaginable.

In the context of the middle pillar, Yesod looks like it's doing all the work. If Tiferet has made the energy of this pillar conceivable, Yesod needs to make it possible. The realms of dreams, the unconscious, magic, the inner planes, the liminal places where invisible worlds meet the visible ones, sexuality, conception, birth—these are domains of Yesod. Above it, light ... dark ... beauty; Yesod lays the foundation for these to come into manifestation. If you can dream it, it can exist. As above, so below. In the words of what I was taught is a Native American prayer or chant: *I lay my vision out before me, walk the path of beauty that my ancestors laid out before me.* These words could describe the path from Tiferet through Yesod into Malkuth.

At Malkuth, at the furthest sephira from the beginning, everything stops. It's the conclusion, the great becoming. Life and death occur here. All of light, all of darkness translated into this rich, beautiful complexity we are inextricably a part of and yet question and examine so ferociously. Malkuth receives everything from the middle pillar (and from the entire Tree) so literally we are the reflection of the I Am. Working with the mystery of *As above, so below,* we should be able to understand the whole Tree from this perspective or at least receive the whole Tree. As tiny sparks of existence, we can transit up into the realms of dreams, imagination, and mythos; into the great heart of the world; up through the cold reaches of the Abyss holding the possibility of Da'ath, knowledge, into the All, the crown, the unknowable light and the spark that became all things. Like Eve in the garden, tangling with the serpent and tempted by the fruit of knowledge, we can choose—or not—to bite into the fullness of life and discover the nature of paradise and being human.

Right-Hand Pillar

The right-hand pillar begins with the second sephira, Hokmah. Hokmah's wisdom is about reflection. To gaze at or be conscious of reflection, we are already learning, comparing, seeking. So when Kether's gaze or will or extending of itself creates Hokmah, this seeking is already occurring. Hokmah carries both the burden and the gift of that. Whereas Kether's action or direction could be seen to be all about itself (even if itself broadly extended), Hokmah is about relationship back toward Kether, onward toward Binah, and down into Chesed, as the right-hand pillar starts to form. Hokmah still is a raw godly force, barely veiled, and so what pours into Chesed, even having passed through the Abyss, is immense, a Niagara of information, a transmission of the entirety of everything. It is still very pure, not particularly distilled—just-received from Kether.

Chesed receives this, as well as a more processed download from Binah on the diagonal (although this has also passed through the Abyss), which has made form possible. Chesed's job is then processing and distributing this into the lower Tree. Chesed is a powerhouse of forces. The vastness of it is almost inconceivable, yet somehow, unlike Hokmah or Kether, we can conceive what is going on there—or, at any rate, imagine that we do. The direction this force is initially heading is downward, into the Tree and manifestation, so Chesed takes the force of the unknowable and transmutes it, with mercy, into places where something can occur.

Netzach is directly below, holding the bottom of the right-hand pillar. This is a sephira of wonder, where force explores myriad possibilities as infinite as the constraints of time and matter allow. Netzach is the application of force into the design of the world. Tied so closely to its pair, Hod, the two operate together, but it is Netzach who is the visionary, the imaginer of worlds, the architect of desire. The power of this pillar floods through Netzach into particularities: the sunlight life force that beats through us, animating the pademelons and tree ferns, whose fires created the rocks, whose gases created this atmosphere we breathe, whose rich complexity make possible the soil from which we feed.

At Hokmah there's a flash of brilliance that goes on and on and on, out to the ever-expanding edges of the universe, an outpouring of endless energy from the Big Bang. The echoes of it can still be seen and heard, here, by us. Passing this energy down into Chesed, physical reality becomes possible and potentially unlimited, as the forces of raw matter—gases, stars, space: light transformed—come into play. This is passed through to Netzach, where every conceivable possibility exists, permutation upon permutation, and life itself blossoms. What is sent back up this pillar, from Netzach to Chesed to Hokmah? From life's grandeur at Netzach, the forces that create life can be discerned at Chesed, and in Hokmah we behold the emanation of the divine.

Left-Hand Pillar

Binah is the top sephira in the left-hand pillar and the place where the possibility of form arises. Perhaps what has already happened in the Tree has created space for this. At the level of Binah, the form we are talking about might be giant gas clouds, matter, dark matter, and dark energy: the forms that create the shape of the universe. Without these forms we would have no other forms. At Binah light and dark are separated, or differentiated, which is crucial to the construction of the universe.

It's only because matter is clumped unevenly throughout the universe that there are forms at all. If matter was spread out evenly, it would be too sparse and thin to create anything. So these vast and original forms are crucial, the birthing places of stars and, therefore, of everything else. From these operatic playing fields another sephira evolves, Gevurah. The form of things in Gevurah starts to be more cohesive; the concept of edges or boundaries, or this as distinct from not-that, comes fully into play. What with the pressure from Binah, above, to give birth to form, and raw power like a raging river surging across from Chesed, Gevurah's forms require boundaries so they are not either blasted apart or carried away on an unending flood. Things become distinct. Star systems, for example. Trajectories of comets or planets. The life cycles of stars. More complex, heavier atoms start to form and further forms occur, following what we term universal laws.

Those laws play out in increasingly smaller and refined directions, as well as sweeping out to the ends of the universe, so we arrive at Hod. Hod lies in the application of—and, from our point of view, in the observance of—these laws. Laws of energy, mass, and time. Laws of categorization, such as our periodic table and taxonomic classification, as well as the structures themselves; of DNA, chromosomes, molecular structure, the progression of the elements. Hod is so concerned with form that without its close comrade Netzach we'd be reduced to lifeless classification, like those numberless trays of dead insects pinned out in an early botanist's study. Hod's close association with Netzach creates the realm we live in; each of them feeds diagonally down into Yesod, and finally to Malkuth.

At Binah form and distinction are born and particularity becomes an essential condition, differentiating light from dark, matter from non-matter, and something from everything. In Gevurah these forms are forged, purged, tempered, and defined. Arriving into Hod, categories and systems evolve to define, classify, and condense all this information. In the other direction, the minutiae of details surrender into classic, economical patterns of purity and simplicity such as wave forms, symmetries, and fractals. Ascending still further, the pulsing on-off patterns of life-death, light-dark, becoming-dissolving are contained in Binah.

process | Left-Hand Pillar: Resolving a Problem

The original form of this exercise was co-created with Deb Gutteridge.

The left-hand pillar specializes in discernment, limitation, analysis. Form comes into being and clarifies itself progressively down the pillar. In the other direction, the minutiae of form dissolves into the structures that make forms as we know them possible. The left-hand pillar is a great place to bring complex problems or muddy thinking.

This is an exercise in guided journaling, accessing the severity of the left-hand pillar. These words—severity, limitation, boundaries—often have a negative connotation, but that is not how they transmit in the left-hand pillar. On the contrary, to bring severity into a problem is to have clear guidelines, support, and the expectation of a successful outcome. To place a limit on oneself—perhaps limiting our attention to this exact problem rather than catastrophizing or attempting to solve everything at once—actually assists our investigation. Boundaries help hold the edges, keep the problem contained, and work with rules that assist the process.

TIME: 30 minutes

YOU WILL NEED: Journal and pen

Settle yourself somewhere you will be undisturbed for half an hour.

Choose an area of your life to work with that you are currently undecided or unclear about. It could be a problem or just something you'd like to investigate more deeply. For example, it could be about deciding where to live, gaining clarity on a relationship, focusing on a difficulty at work, a question to do with your spiritual path, or a family issue.

Once you have chosen your issue, write it down as clearly and simply as possible. For example: *I don't know where I want to live* or *I'm unsure if this is the right job for me* or *My current spiritual practices aren't fulfilling* or *I wish I could relate to my parents better.*

Underneath this write the heading *Binah*. A third of the way down the page (or on a separate page) write the heading *Gevurah*. Two-thirds of the way down the page (or on a separate page) write the heading *Hod*.

Then, setting your pen and journal down, invoke or invite the presence or energy of the left-hand pillar. You might visualize this as an inner judge—one who truly has the clarity and understanding that will assist you—or your higher consciousness. You might call on the sephirot of the left-hand pillar, Binah, Gevurah, and Hod, or their qualities of understanding, justice (or power), and glory. You might invite this into the left-hand side of your body or into your left hand, you might retain a sense of it within yourself or visualize it. Perhaps you can just trust it will be present. Breathe with this for a few moments.

Binah

Let your mind and senses open to the field of Binah. This is where form begins. It might seem as wide as the night sky or as essential as a star. In the severity and simplicity of Binah, read aloud what you wrote down as your issue. For this moment, filter out any emotions or stories and allow yourself to see the situation for what it is as if you were not a part of it. Imagine what this problem would look like to someone who didn't know you and had no attachments to the outcome. Take up your pen and describe it as simply and completely as you can, without in any way attempting to resolve it, under the *Binah* heading on your page.

For example: *There are two places I feel very drawn to living. I'm emotionally attached to both. They are 800 kilometers apart. In one of them I have friends, family, and most of my belongings. In the other place is my house and cat and a sense of potential community. This is where I physically am right now.*

Gevurah

Take a breath or two. Now let yourself receive the powers of judgment, justice, and boundaries from Gevurah. Perhaps you will sense a red-hot flood of energy pour into you or you might imagine picking up a sword of clarity and direction. Read over what you have already written: the naming of the issue and the description of it. Dissect this problem. What can you see or feel as the bones of this issue? Are there underlying assumptions discernible? What is your desire or the specific problem? Take up your pen and list these insights under the *Gevurah* heading on your page, still without attempting to resolve them.

For example:

- I don't want to be confined to one place; I yearn to expand and feel expansive
- I feel inadequate and under-resourced in both places
- Everything is just disorganized, not operating as a plan, so neither place is functional

Hod

Breathe for a moment. Now allow Hod's abilities of taking action and making choices to arise within you. Perhaps you will imagine the order of a beehive, the fractals of a fern frond, or the patterns light and air make upon water. Read back over everything written on your page so far. What are the most obvious, immediate, and straightforward actions you could take in this situation that will assist toward clarifying or even resolving this issue? Some of these actions may be internal and others may involve interacting with others or taking an action. Write them down under the *Hod* heading.

For example:

- Maintain my current house and living situation
- Allow myself to begin imagining what it would be like to live between both places

- ▸ Organize my belongings so I have what I need where I am living
- ▸ Make some regular visits to friends and family to stay connected

Completion

Read back through your whole page. Feel free to underline, circle, or asterisk parts, add in more information, or put notes at the bottom. In the Hod section you might wish to place timelines on particular actions or order them in a way that feels logical or supportive to you.

Take some time to thank and acknowledge the left-hand pillar and the sephirot of Binah, Gevurah, and Hod as they exist within you, as well as entities or concepts in their own right. Then release your attention and, with a few breaths, shake out that energy, stand up, drink water, or do whatever seems best to complete this process.

ritual | Right-Hand Pillar: Altar of Compassion

The right-hand pillar creates and emanates compassion, expansion, and generosity. This pillar can be thought of as channeling force—that which gives energy to the whole of creation. From the top it spills down from the divine. From the bottom upward it contributes to the intricacies and richness of life. These attributes can assist us in expanding our thinking, relaxing our tensions, and being in the flow of life.

This ritual is contemplative and works in the mind's deep recesses. It reminds me of sand play, moving small objects about in a tray of earth or sand while telling a story, and the mysterious power that has to rearrange our thinking, as well as our relationship to what is happening, or has happened, in our life. It seeks to hold, recognize, and validate our experience.

TIME: 30 minutes

YOU WILL NEED: Your journal and pen. An altar: this can be an altar you already have, cleared for the occasion, or any area, inside or outside, that you dedicate as an altar for the length of this ritual. You might like to put down a beautiful cloth or in some other way mark the edges of your altar; for example, drawing the outline in sand if you're at the beach or edging it in colored leaves, flowers, or pine cones.

OBJECTS FOR YOUR ALTAR: If you are outside, you can take a short walk to gather natural items—usually fallen leaves and flowers rather than picking those still living—as well as interesting stones, shells, bits of bark, feathers. If you are inside, gather together some of your favorite ritual or sacred items, along with a handful of other things from your kitchen, desk, or bedroom. These could include spices or herbs, chocolate, perfume, jewelry, a small mirror, and any little objects of meaning to you.

Settle yourself in front of your altar, with all your potential altar items close at hand.

Choose an issue, person, or area of your life where you feel stuck, limited, closed, or in pain. This could be something from the past or something current. For example, it could be a past relationship, a lack of self-love, a challenge in your work, or a sense of blocked creativity.

Once you have chosen this, write it on a fresh page in your journal. For example: *My boss irritates me so much I can hardly listen to her* or *I'm frightened to tell my partner my true feelings* or *I don't like my body.* Then place your journal to one side.

Bringing your attention to your altar, find a way to divide it in half. You might divide it diagonally, horizontally, or vertically, or make an inner circle and an outer circle. Just do what feels right for you in the moment. Mark this division in some way (a line in the sand, a ribbon or thread or some other way) or just hold the division in your mind.

Choose one half of your altar to represent the right-hand pillar.

Take a few breaths and allow yourself to imagine the enormity of Hokmah, the first moment of separation from the All. Perhaps you can feel the vastness of Hokmah and the mystery of separation and love. Breathe into this feeling or awareness. Then allow yourself to pick one or more objects to represent Hokmah. Don't think about it too deeply; without too much direction from the mind, you might even allow your right hand to pick the items. I might pick, for example, a small mirror and a love note someone gave me. Arrange these items on your altar in the right-hand pillar section.

Now return your awareness to your breath. Breathing quietly in and out, allow yourself to gaze at the altar. Let your awareness open now to the second sephira in this pillar, Chesed. Take a moment or two to allow the blue of Chesed to wash through you, remembering its qualities of mercy and loving-kindness. From within this awareness, let yourself choose one or more items to represent Chesed and place them, also, within the section of the altar reserved for the right-hand pillar. They might mix among the Hok-mah items or they might be in their own place. For example, I might choose a seashell and a candle.

Once you have done this, breathe again, gazing at the altar as it is now. Drop down into Netzach, the lowest sephira in this pillar. Let Netzach's qualities of eternity, the vibrant multiplicity of the possibilities of life, arise within you. Breathing into this, choose one or several objects to represent Netzach and place them, also, into the half of the altar that represents the right-hand pillar. I might select a twig of flowering native bush and my necklace. Once again, these objects can be grouped together or spaced out among the other items already there.

When you are done, take some time to sit with your half altar, letting yourself bathe in or receive its qualities. You might want to write a few words in your journal or even sketch or photograph the altar as it is now.

Then move to the second half of the altar. First, look at its emptiness. Perhaps this emptiness represents the often brief moments we have where everything seems perfect, resolved, and simple. Or perhaps it represents the moment of each outbreath where we join up to the universe, releasing breath, tension, and the previous moment.

Choose an item to represent yourself, and place this into the empty half of the altar. I might choose a small goddess statuette.

Take some breaths. You may notice how simple this item is compared to the fullness of the other half of the altar.

Then contemplate your original problem or issue; you can go back and reread it if you like. Choose one or more objects to represent this situation, and place them on this second half of the altar, also. I might choose a photograph.

Look at your altar again. Breathe into this second half of it as it is forming. Then ask yourself: What underlies my part of this problem? Is it jealousy? Fear? A feeling of unworthiness or unlovableness? A fear of not being enough or being too much? A lack of self-love or a measuring of self against others? A deep unhappiness?

For each thing that you feel a strong *yes* for, choose an item and place it on the second half of the altar. For example, I might choose dried rosemary, one of my rings, and a little pink glittery heart. These items can mix in with the rest or remain together.

When you are done, take some moments to sit with this half of the altar. You might want to write something down in your journal or make a small sketch of how it looks.

Then let your gaze widen to include the whole altar. Remove the divider between the two halves, if you had one. Letting your gaze soften and your breath come and go easily, begin to rearrange the altar. Let your hands do the work.

Maybe I will let the necklace trail through the whole altar, like the curves of a snake. I might place the mirror near the center and the note underneath it, maybe adding my ring and the pink heart. I might put the photo in the center, beside the statuette, and the flower and candle in front. The rosemary and shell go to the sides.

When the altar feels right to you, spend some time with it. You might wish to journal, meditate, or tell yourself a story about what it means. Most importantly, breathe deeply into this mixing of the right-hand pillar into your own life and challenges. Feel if anything changes, shifts, or can move more easily within you.

You might leave your altar there for a while or clear it up when you've finished. Maybe you will take a photo of the final arrangement, sketch it in your journal, or just choose to hold it in your heart.

Over the coming days or weeks, when this situation arises in your mind, allow the memory of blending the two sides of your altar to return. You can also call directly on the powers of the right-hand pillar to be present with you.

Memoir: *The River and the Ring*

I'm standing in a French river, at night, under the full moon. The current, pushing against my legs, is far stronger than I thought it would be. I left my sandals on the bank with my sarong and the key to my room tied into it. I wanted to go in nude but there are people nearby so I'm wearing bathers because I thought I might get washed downstream and have to walk back. At this moment that seems quite likely. It's summer, though the water isn't warm. It's not the temperature that worries me but the ferocity of this current, although I'm just a few meters out from the bank and only knee deep. Really my idea was to swim in it and offer the river a gift that I have clutched in my hand, my right hand: a silver ring with an opal in it. French rivers, moonlight, silver, and opal. Chesed and the great rush of force, the release of love. That's my spell.

pillars in the tree

My journey with this ring started a few months ago in England. There's a precious piece of my history tied up in it, but I can't carry it any longer and I thought this river, this night, this combination of magics was the ideal repository for it. People have been throwing jewelry into water since time immemorial and I like the idea of keeping an ancient Pagan ritual alive even as I'm abandoning a precious object, freeing myself of my past. If someone finds it—if it gets washed to shore and discovered amongst the sand and grit, or it's hooked up on a fishing line or found by someone picking river stones off the bottom—it will be washed clean by then, reduced to silver and opal, pieces of precious earth. A gift for whoever discovers it and if not—then a tithe to this river and the rivers of the world, their gods, spirits, and blessings.

This particular river, at this point, is really two rivers. The confluence is just meters upstream from me, which perhaps explains the force of the current. There's a double bridge arching over them just before they meet, east of me with the moon above them, an elegant though unusual-looking arrangement. This is one of my favorite places on earth so I've spent some time considering it, down here by the water's edge, writing and thinking for hours on end. The confluence of the Vézère and the Dordogne Rivers, right at the bottom of the tiny hill-fort town I'm in love with, Limeuil. What I really don't understand is that when they meet, where I'm standing and from this point on, the river's only called the Dordogne. What happened to the Vézère?

The Vézère—a perfectly good river in its own right, vibrant and rich with waters—somehow just vanishes, at least in nomenclature, as soon as it meets the Dordogne. Perhaps that's what all this disturbance is about, that I'm standing in, thinking of swimming in, the waters protesting as they lose their name and get submerged into the larger river. I studied this section from the bridge today—from both bridges but particularly from the bridge over the Dordogne, which isn't the closest river to Limeuil, to the bank where I left my things, or where I sit, day after day, writing at a picnic bench on my computer under the trees. But that bridge had the clearer view of downriver, where I planned to be tonight with the ring. Apart from long stretches of green waterweed, reminding me of a nereid's hair rippling just below the surface, I thought it looked calm.

I'm downstream from the waterweed and it's not calm. Not at all. Swift. The rocks cut my feet on the way in. I couldn't see well and they're sharp, small black rocks, the sort it would be easy for a ring to sift its way down through, seeking rest. It's not a beautiful ring. It's a man's ring, roughly made, not like the delicate silver creations that usually cover my fingers. I'm not wearing them tonight; I thought this river—one ring, why not two or three?—might be greedy. Especially in its newly unsettled form, the Vézère eaten, unrecognized past this point.

Is this what happens to rivers? They give over to the greater force, swallowed by the one they've been journeying to meet up with ever since they were born? I can feel the Vézère writhing and protesting against my legs, and I'm not even far enough into the water yet to feel what happens when it really meets the Dordogne, when there's no chance of distinction between them any longer. These underwater ripples are just the beginning. It's flinging itself into this conflict, this love affair, this merging, as if there were no regrets, holding nothing back. Every drop of water it hoarded all along its journey is spent here, to swell the larger, calmer river, to add to its depths and breadth but right now—just here—that will be noticed. I've often wondered about what it might mean to a river to lose its identity, thinking it gave itself up with so little fight. Apparently not, under the surface.

The man who gave me this ring left me a long time ago now, sixteen years or more. It was the relationship that made and broke each of us. He was filled with regrets and recriminations, and I thought I would never get over it and was determined to get over it. Occasionally we met during those sixteen years, but more often I avoided meeting; easy to do since we were mostly on opposite sides of the world. I am probably doing things I would never have done if I was still with him.

He was older than me by sixteen years. I'm more or less the age he was then. But I feel younger than I was then, with a small child and a broken heart. Now I'm free to roam the world and make up my life exactly the way I want it. In England I met with him; we ate lunch in a place I would never choose: elegant, formal. We talked, sometimes awkwardly. When we were together, our age difference didn't seem so severe, but now he's seventy—it's a big age. I feel the difference yawning between us. We went in opposite directions after we parted. He's become softer and inwardly turned; he leads a quiet life. By my standards, a very quiet life. Whereas I ... have blossomed, gone up and outward, become active in the world.

After lunch we walked down to the river. The Thames. We sat together on a bench, not close. I turned to face him and decided to say something that I don't even know if it's true, any longer, but I wanted to see if speaking it would change anything. So I say *I never really got over you leaving me.* Just for one moment the air and the river and the tide between us carries that, and I can feel the truth in it but also how it's a statement of the past. It's a long time ago, so even though the ripple continues forever, it's far, far away from the source by now.

I don't think I was expecting him to answer—the point of speaking was to let it go— but he answers, only one heartbeat later. He says, calmly but with a hint of intensity, *I never left you.*

I laugh a little in the absurdity and surprise of it. The whole of our interaction for a decade and a half has been in the aftermath of him leaving me. Time and the world as I've known it shift around me, rearranging themselves into an alternate history. In his mind, or his version of events, he never left. Well, that explains why he never understood what I was going through. It even makes sense of his strange behaviors through the years. It is utterly clear to me, suddenly and as a gift, the exact weight and measure of spending sixteen years getting over something compared with sixteen years hanging onto it. Oh and I'm so grateful I was the one getting over it, even if so painfully and incompletely. There's a division between us, so deep now it can never be overcome. *He never left.* But I left, long ago, walking away from that pain and grief and disappointment. I left a hundred times in resolution, in forward movement, in deep healing and release. I've been gone forever, and he's still there.

We don't talk much more about my grand statement or his absurd reply. We watch the river, always moving on, tidal as well as heading to the sea, all that flow and relentless change, washing even history away. Then we walk back into the city. There's a small church nearby, built by Christopher Wren; he says he wants to see it. Neither of us has ever been here before; it's tucked away. We enter the courtyard but there's a man standing at the open side-door into the church. He tells us that we can't go in, there's a wedding happening.

A wedding. How perfect. We can't go in to the wedding. What a mythic occurrence. We never married. I would have been his third wife and was resistant even to the idea, one wife in a string of wives—and he was running away from, not toward me. So we can't go to the wedding. If we'd stayed together—or even parted on better terms, in kinder ways—we'd be in a slightly parallel universe and might be granted our own moment in this mystical church, but as it is we are merely reminded of the trajectory we took and gently turned away. I feel free, almost laughing.

I saw him again, a few weeks after that. He asked if he could give me a ring, just as a present. In all those years of passionate, deep, and ecstatic relationship, he never gave me a ring. But I thought maybe something might be healed by it. So I said yes.

When he shows me the ring, I recognize it. Oh, that ring. It's a man's ring, silver with an opal. He had it made when we lived together, for himself. He says he doesn't wear it, and he'd like me to have it. It feels like a relic. I had imagined a pretty ring chosen for me, something I might like or wear. It's too big for my hand, and all I would ever think of, if I looked at it, was him. I say I probably won't wear it and perhaps the disappointment shows on my face. He says I can do whatever I want with it, and on those grounds I accept because it feels, in the moment, that refusing would be cruel.

He speaks about how big my life is, and I know I've told him only a fraction of it, maybe a tenth. He says it helplessly, as if he has no way to relate to it. I don't even feel sad, more that the man I loved left long ago, and this man is someone who maybe remembers that man, was close to him once, but they've grown apart. All those years I needed someone with me, active and involved, not loving helplessly from afar. It feels like a failure, but it's a failure I can't do anything about.

I take the ring with me as I wander through France and then come to my favorite part, Limeuil. I first came here with him, and my son, twenty years ago. It was one of the tiny French villages we discovered traveling through southern France. I have a photo of me standing in front of one of the stone arches leading into the village—I'm laughing and look so happy, with the place, with him, with our travels. I think we only spent a few hours here but I remembered it as my favorite, seared its name into my memory, and when I began coming back to France regularly, I dragged that name out and found it on a map and came here again after a gap of fifteen years or so. Then I came again, and again. I come here to write. I come to feel a part of the landscape, to feel the French part of me rise up and just exist, live here for a few days or a week.

Limeuil. The ring. The river. There's a river flowing through me, of desire and loss and love. We were sitting by a river when we said those things: *I never got over you. I never left*. The ring from that time in our lives, unwanted by him, by me. Rivers eat rings. I've lost rings to rivers before, not willingly. Jewelry tossed into the waters—as offerings, for divination, as a spell. For the dead. There's a full moon while I'm staying here. The river. The moon. The ring. It's coming together. There's another piece of the spell too. I'm holding the sephira of Chesed this month. Dancing Shiva, blue waters, expansion and flow, the force of unending change.

So I came down to the river, under the full moon, at Limeuil. With the ring. I waded out, over sharp rocks and rushing water, and now I'm thigh deep and struggling to stay on my feet. I'm sort of wearing the ring, sort of holding it, so it doesn't slip off. I cleaned it with a silver cleaning cloth. I spoke to it. I said, this was a place where we'd been once, in love. I said that rivers wash everything clean. I said, it can be a treasure at the bottom of the water, it can remember we were happy, how in love we once were. That, for many reasons, here and now is the perfect time to let go of any thought that we will ever be together again, in any way. The ring can hold all that and the river can set it free.

But so far I'm just within the stream of the Vézère, and I really wanted to be in both of them, the ancient Dordogne as well, or where they're mixed, at the center. Also it will be deeper, maybe not as rough as right here, and the ring will have a better chance of resting undisturbed, on its own, for a decade or two, a century or so … maybe forever. After this bit of beach, which I'm wading out from, the river narrows slightly, collecting the waters of both rivers and mixing them together, but there isn't such a good getting-out place on this side for another hundred meters or so. I checked this afternoon. I can walk back barefoot, from downstream or from the other side over the bridges if I have to, but it's not ideal.

I think about just throwing the ring—I thought about dropping it from the bridge over the Dordogne earlier today—but that's not the point. I'm not trying to discard it, though to an observer it might look like that. I'm trying to release it, let it glide from my hand into the watery realms. I start walking upstream, against the current, so that when I get carried downstream I'll still be able to get out, and it's immediately easier.

As if now the river accepts me or I was just at a particularly tumultuous spot. Now the water's smoother, more coordinated.

I get to the river weeds and they look long and complicated. I don't really want to tangle with them, so I drop into the water and swim out strongly, cross-current and carried down. I'm actually doing it!—swimming under the full moon in the Vézère-Dordogne—I turn and hold my fist with the ring in it up toward the moon and then drop it down into the water and I speak the end words: *There's an offering, a spell—dissolving all the worlds—freedom-love-joy surrender ferocity*—I let go and am carried past it…oh, that's interesting. I didn't think of that, that it was silver and would sink while I'm carried along the top of the water, moving on, and then I strike out back for the shore and make it, more or less. I do a bit of undignified crawling over half-submerged rocks and then I'm walking ankle deep through the shallows, back to my belongings.

My feet are cut in so many places I don't put my sandals back on but walk barefoot instead, limping slowly, wounded, to the road and then up the silent cobblestoned hill, rough under my feet so I feel each footstep. I think of leaving blood on the stones. I think of the ring settled there, deep, and I feel satisfied all through me. I've done a thing that feels magical and right; I feel whole in it, bleeding but whole. This French river in the landscape of France and my ancestors. I'm released, freed forever, and yet still knowing my history, belonging to this place and swimming through time to be here again and again.

I write and tell him what I did with the ring. Then it's done, and it flows on forever, both of those things. The piece of the magic that's coming with me is the moonlight, the river, my bleeding feet, and only afterward do I think, as so often, oh perhaps that wasn't very safe. Night swimming in a strong river by myself in a foreign country. Essential, yes, but out at the edges of what is considered sane or wise. I rewrote a piece of the universe and myself and I felt carried at the time, by Chesed and my love of this place. The river runs through me. Jewels lie at the bottom of it. The rivers blend and merge and carry me on, through time and history and landscape.

trance | Middle Pillar: Journey of the Initiate

The middle pillar integrates opposites. Like breath it expands outward to the left- and right-hand pillars and also contracts inward, into itself. Just as creation—the singularity of Kether—has exploded into force and form at the beginning of time, there's an aspect of creation occurring at each other point where the force of the right-hand pillar and the form of the left-hand pillar meet: in Tiferet, Yesod, and Malkuth.

In occult pictures and writings where two pillars are referenced—often a white and black pillar—these are the right- and left-hand pillars. Between the pillars the mysteries are held. These left and right pillars beckon us forward while guarding what is within. If we think of the diagram of the Tree as three-dimensional and allow the left- and right-hand pillars to come forward while the middle pillar recesses slightly, we can see the middle pillar as held within this temple. We can also imagine it lying down, like steps that lead progressively inward and upward between two upright pillars. Or we can stay on the bottom step, gazing up at the pillars, and wait to see what emerges or descends toward us.

This is a trance, or contemplative meditation, which you can do moving among your disks or lying down. If we lay our bodies down on a diagram of the Tree, our spine would be resting along the middle pillar. Our connection to the heavens is here, as well as our rootedness in the ground. When the human body is imposed on the Tree, it is imagined as face downward, thus the right-hand pillar correlates to the right-hand side of the body and the left-hand pillar to the left-hand side of the body. As an entry into the mysteries, no particular answers are expected in this trance, although you are invited to form an intention for your exploration.

TIME: 45–60 minutes

YOU WILL NEED: Your journal and pen. Optional: your disks or a walking diagram of the Tree, coloring things.

Settle yourself quietly and comfortably. Have your journal and pen, and coloring things if you choose, at hand.

Allow an intention to form. Perhaps it is simply *To experience the middle pillar* or perhaps it is more focused, for example: *To learn more about the ascending stages of the middle pillar*, or more personal, for example: *To work with blockages around giving and receiving love.* Record your intention in your journal.

Begin by relaxing. Perhaps you will choose to briefly visit each part of your body with breath and awareness, inviting relaxation. After that spend a few moments feeling or visualizing your spine as it holds you upright and connects your head to the lower parts of your body. Then concentrate on the breath. Travel with it as it enters and leaves your body, following its ripples, tides, sensations, contractions, and expansions. Perhaps you can feel it as a channel within you, bringing life force with each breath.

As you drop more deeply into trance, become aware of your left-hand side and your right-hand side. Perhaps you will focus on them one at a time or feel both at once. Be aware of how they complement each other; breathe into your bipedal nature. Allow yourself to feel their differences: perhaps they have different strengths, appearances, and capabilities. Perhaps you associate certain attributes with the left- or right-hand side of your body, or even traumas, challenges, or difficulties. Continue breathing through these awarenesses as they arise.

Now imagine these two sides of your body—the right and the left—as two pillars, containing and supporting the middle part of you: your spine, your breath, your awareness. *Feel* yourself as a triple-pillared being, just like the Tree. Breathe into the middle pillar in your body. Imagine a cord dropping from the Ain Soph into your skull, down along your spine and then into the earth itself, so you are held between earth and heaven. Breathe with this for a few moments until you can hold this image, sensation, or awareness while also deepening your journey.

Continue breathing consciously and holding the imagery of yourself as the triple pillars of the Tree as you imagine yourself approaching a temple. The temple has a pillar on each side of the entry. If you are physically walking through a diagram of the Tree, approach Malkuth from below. When you feel or imagine you are close to the entry, stop.

Approach as a supplicant, one who would enter within and have the mysteries revealed. Notice the two pillars that guard this place. On the right is the Pillar of Mercy, and within it are contained the forces of Hokmah, Chesed, and Netzach. On the left is the Pillar of Rigor, containing the forms of Binah, Gevurah, and Hod. You might also feel how these pillars resonate within you in the right and left sides of your body. What would it mean to pass within these pillars?

Stopping between and in front of them is the first stage of this journey. We call this place Malkuth. Here we can contemplate the pillars within our own bodies. Breathe with this. If you are physically walking the Tree, move onto your Malkuth disk.

Do you wish to go further? Sometimes simply becoming aware of the mystery and contemplating it is enough for one journey. Let an answer arise from within you—*Yes, I wish to continue* or *No, it is not my wish to continue now.*

If your answer is to stop, slowly bring yourself out of trance and return to your awareness of your physical body and the room around you. Take some time to journal.

If your answer is to continue your journey, feel or imagine yourself moving up to just before the pillars, almost in the entryway. This is the position of Yesod. If you are walking, walk up to or stand on your Yesod disk.

Take some slow, deep breaths here. This position—at the threshold—might be where questions are asked or challenges are issued. How does it seem to you, awaiting such questioning? Take a moment to recall your intent for this journey.

Ask yourself, or the left- and right-hand pillars, *Is there a question for me here?* If so, what is it? Let yourself receive it. Upon becoming aware of the question or absence of question, you have a further choice—to proceed or turn back, finishing your journey for now. If you choose to proceed, hear and answer the question, if there is one. If you turn back, acknowledge the question (or absence of question) and answer it if you wish, then take your leave of this place for now. Return to the Malkuth position and then step out of the Tree, slowly bringing yourself out of trance, and return your full awareness to your body, the space you are in, and your journal and pen waiting for you.

Perhaps you will choose to enter the portal, passing between the left- and right-hand pillars, along the path of the middle pillar. Take some breaths as you do this, feeling how it is to pass through this gateway, into the temple. Perhaps you can feel it in your body as an emotion or sensation. Perhaps you will have visions, hear voices, or become aware of different things. You might perceive yourself as traveling upward, inward, into other dimensions or some combination of these. Your destination is the center of the temple.

Once you arrive at the center of Tiferet, spend a few moments breathing and receiving any thoughts, images, sensations, or understandings here. It may appear to you as an empty space, an altar, a pool of water, or some other way. Feel how it is to be in the center of this temple that is guarded by the right- and left-hand pillars; perhaps you can still feel their presence on either side of you. Tiferet is at the heart of the Tree, and it may be your destination in this trance. If you are carrying an intention with you, remember it now and release it. Watch, listen, or feel what happens to it.

Perhaps your trance is complete now, and you choose to return back, outside the temple portal to the Yesod and then the Malkuth position. Bring yourself out of trance, back into your body and the room, and then spend some time journaling your experiences.

If you continue the journey along the middle pillar, prepare to cross the dark threshold that exists between you and the final inner sanctum. This is the Abyss; crossing it, nothing is certain. As you move further up the middle pillar, you might feel yourself disintegrating, letting go of everything, becoming sparks, or being absorbed into darkness or speeding through like a light beam ... Continue breathing, trusting the pattern of the Tree.

Kether is the final place that can be visited on this journey. Perhaps for you it is an altar at the very back of the temple. Perhaps it is an inner room, reliquary, or crypt. Perhaps there are curtains you need to part to reveal it or you have to close your eyes in its presence. If you have made it this far, spend a few minutes breathing within the presence of Kether. Remember the journey you have taken to get here—your intention and the narrow path between the right- and left-hand pillars. You may experience revelations, questions, inner peace, or something else.

If you have an offering, a vow, or a request—remembering that such a request, made here, would have the power to change your life in ways perhaps unforeseen—you can make that in this place.

Be aware of how much time passes in the real world, even if you feel no need to return. You do actually need to return, so gather yourself with a few extra breaths and take your leave of this place. Return back through the Abyss and the middle temple with Tiferet, back out the doors to Yesod, and further back to Malkuth. Bring yourself back to your breath, your body, and the room you are in.

Spend some time recording your trance experience in your journal.

activity | Creating the Fourth Disk

As you complete the work of this section, create a disk to represent the sephira you've been journeying with. This will be your fourth disk. Perhaps you are traveling down the Tree and spent the first section concentrated on Kether, and you are now up to Chesed—in that case it will be the blue Chesed disk you are working with. Perhaps you began somewhere else in the Tree and so the disk you are making now is for Hokmah, Yesod, Kether, or any other sephira.

TIME: 30–60 minutes

YOU WILL NEED: The appropriate colored disk (see page 69, "Creating the First Disk") and whatever art materials you wish to work with, such as colored pens and markers, paint, oil pastels, collage materials and glue, stickers

Begin by remembering the time you have spent in this sephira, looking through your journal notes, recalling any Kabbalah exercises, processes, or rituals you did, and especially how these related to this particular sephira, as well as the general mood and events in your life, during this time. By this fourth sephira you will be increasingly aware of this sephira's relationship to the others you have inhabited.

Allow images, words, feelings, and ideas to arise. You might hold these in your head, immediately begin work on your disk, or jot down notes or a sketch.

You can begin by marking the name of the sephira onto the disk or doing this at the end.

Decorate your disk. You can use a piece of writing from your journal or other words. You might use paints, colored pencils, charcoal, marker pens, or pastels to draw pictures, symbols, or patterns. You can cover the whole or part of the disk with collage, cutting or tearing out pictures and sticking them on. I like shapes cut out of colored foil from chocolate wrappers.

Your disk might be complete within itself or it might reference other sephirot that are close by or in the same pillar. It might contain an image of the Tree itself or a reference to this sephira's position within the Tree. I sometimes choose a theme

examples of completed disks can be seen at janemeredith.com/disks for my disk, such as a garden for Netzach, and everything on the disk contributes to that.

You might complete your work in one session or come back later to add details or another layer; for example, words etched around the edge in a continuous circle.

stars or angels exploding endlessly the
perfection of the fall each piece counted or
falling beyond and through, seen, held even
in freefall each one beloved, each one known,
the clarity of pattern each portion of light
shining, utter, received and distributing
endlessly the river of atoms, particles of light
into the darkness the grace of it the utter
dance, precision endless flow

falling, the idea of the butterfly opens its
wings and gifts the universe a glimpse
of light pouring forth, refracted in blues
cadmium azure cerulean cyan ultramarine
lapis lazuli cobalt turquoise sapphire ocean
it ripples forever—and falls...

5
Polarities in
the Tree

The fifth sephira emerges within the left-hand pillar, and the pattern of the Tree solidifies. Gevurah is below the Abyss—everything from now on will be below the Abyss—and directly across from its pair, Chesed. Now there are two sephirot in each of the right- and left-hand pillars, like corners of a square. The fifth above them turns them into points of a pentagram, the splayed fingers of a hand, or da Vinci's Vitruvian Man, arms held out, legs spaced apart, head upright. This new sephira will receive the emanations of the top triad distilled through Chesed along the lightning flash. It will also be responsible for manifesting the special flavor and qualities of Binah, directly above it, into the lower Tree.

The origin of the top triad or the upper Tree is singular: Kether. The initiation of the lower Tree and its future direction is carried by both Chesed and Gevurah. These two cannot work except with each other, yet also, at the center of the Tree, they are the most polarized of pairings. Like magnets they are equal and opposite forces, holding each other at arm's length, otherwise the Tree would collapse in on itself. But also like magnets they are attracted and bound to each other. With only repulsion, the Tree would be torn apart into the vast interstellar spaces and distances of nothingness; this simultaneous attraction-repulsion creates space for existence.

The dynamics of the Tree are evolving with Gevurah's pushback to the previously prevailing forces of expansion and endless flow. Gevurah highlights polarities in the Tree. Conflict, power, justice, boundaries, inclusion, and exclusion are its territories.

Gevurah: *Boundaries and Justice*

Gevurah marks the halfway point through this Tree of ten sephirot. It sits directly below Binah in the left-hand pillar and across from Chesed; together they form a powerful pair, holding the line underneath the Abyss. Each of them are the central sephira within their pillar and in many ways each of them is the clearest representation of that pillar. Gevurah's name is variously translated into English as power, justice, judgment, rigor, strength, or severity. All of the sephirot are unendingly powerful, yet this is one is *named* for power.

Gevurah is both an inheritor of law, from Binah, and an imposer of law within its own realm and all that will come afterward. It is the ideal of law—both natural laws, those informing mass, time, space, the organization of shapes and events, from the greatest star clouds down to the tiniest particles, as well as less absolute laws. The laws of the wild, of attraction, of cause and effect. Human laws: political and historical laws, the laws of the land, bylaws and local law—and at some point this begins to merge into lore, that which is known, passed on, and forms the guidance or rules by which we understand the nature of things and choose our actions accordingly. The lore of a tradition, the lore of culture, of heritage, the lore of a community or place. Folklore. Spoken lore: the ballads, the druids' mysteries, the sagas. Written lore: sacred texts, local records about weather and harvests, births and deaths.

Natural law operates independently from humans—there is nothing we can decree or create that will change it—and also we are completely enmeshed within it. We are a part of nature. How have we imagined ourselves separate, to the extent where we are acting directly against it? Yet within nature there are parasites and predators; there are ecosystems that collapse and die or change irrevocably when something gets out of balance. From what we can tell, even an ice age or a mass extinction is recovered from; in time the balance is found and life goes on. We are a particularly destructive species, intent on wrecking not just our own habitats, but every habitat on the planet, including the vast northern tundras, the ice fields of Antarctica, the ocean, the deserts, the weather, the atmosphere, even littering the space around our planet with debris and junk ...

As we wonder if the planet will, at some point, simply shrug us off—warm half a degree too much for our delicate constitutions or release a plague or microorganism to spell our doom—we're feeling into the weight of Gevurah. How far out of kilter can this entire system be pushed before it collapses entirely or bites back? This concept of justice is one of divine justice—not a conscious righteousness, but the what-must-be of the holistic, the volcano responding to internal pressure, spewing forth living flame that demolishes all, leaving incipient fertility in its wake.

Gevurah is the warrior. Where Chesed is compassion, ever-giving, Gevurah brings fierce restriction, even destruction. Thinking back to the formation and evolution of stars, we can see Chesed in the creation of increasingly complex elements within those stars, with denser and denser elements being formed by pressure and heat—an endless force. This happens until the elements arrive at iron, when the star explodes and its components are scattered into the universe again. Gevurah. There's a limit. A star such as our own sun burns its energy—endlessly, we might think, from our vantage point; how Chesed-like, giving off all this light and heat—until suddenly that's it, the finite amount it had to spend is gone, and it collapses. The very act of giving, spreading its energy out so ceaselessly, has caused its demise.

Limits. Boundaries. Changes of state. Undoing. In the human world these are often cast as negatives. We even see them as harsh, unnecessary, punishing. They can indeed be punishing to those caught up in them—that star, for instance, or life on earth when our sun reaches its limit—but not maliciously. They are simply the laws in action. Although we might all prefer to be a person who often, mostly, regularly says *yes*—to life, to desire, to answering the needs and wishes of others—we also need to be able to say *no*. What about those emails that flood our inboxes, asking for our banking details or to sell us a thousand things that we don't want and perhaps don't even exist? No, thank you. Maybe just *no*. There's a limit. There are boundaries of good sense, time, resource management, appropriateness. *No* is just as useful a word, and attitude, as *yes*. In fact, one without the other wouldn't mean much at all.

The Wheel of Consent, developed by author and teacher Betty Martin and detailed on her website www.bettymartin.org, is a brilliant model for redefining our relationship to *no* and boundaries. Working within this system, we learn to receive someone else's *no* not as a message about our inherent worth, but as a statement concerning their valid choice. When we can both hear and respect this *no,* we come to realize that it protects us. Imagine asking someone for a kiss, to be their friend, or to live the rest of your lives with them, and them saying yes—not because they wished to, it was their truth or what they desired, but merely to avoid hurting or confronting you. We would then be kissing someone who didn't really want that kiss, or even living the rest of our lives with someone who didn't want to offend, disappoint, or confront us with their truth.

Bring on the *nos*—they save us, every time, from pursuing or enforcing an unequally desired situation. They free us up to follow our desires, which surely are more about being met, loved, and enjoying mutuality than some level of power or ownership over another somewhat unwilling party. In the Wheel of Consent, we learn to ask for what we want; how revolutionary! Many of us have been taught our whole lives not to ask for anything, certainly not to express any desires; more along the lines of, if you're lucky, if you wait long enough, if you do all you can for others, maybe you'll get some of what you wish. A haphazard and ineffective system, it turns out. So not only do we learn to ask for what we want, we also learn to hear and receive a *no* and actually be grateful for it. We've been taught all this time that getting what you want from *a particular person* is the important part: the person we married, our parents, our lover; it turns out that wanting that person (any particular person) to fulfill our needs causes massive problems.

When we feel obliged to give a person something because of our relationship to them—not primarily because we desire the interaction ourselves, right that minute—we are ignoring our internal *no*, pretending a *no* is a *yes* or forcing it to become one. Thus it starts to become hazy, both to us and the other person, about what a clear *yes* really is. Soon enough we may not have good access to our inner radar and become unsure ourselves: *Do I want that? What am I actually feeling?* We can begin to bypass this inner radar entirely, becoming someone who goes along with whatever is wished for or required; perhaps always wondering why we don't feel fulfilled, connected, or even that happy. We don't know what we want, and we're almost certainly not getting it. We don't know how to say *no* and therefore have lost the capacity to give a wholehearted *yes*.

Gevurah is the master of boundaries and therefore of the *no*. The *no* actually creates space for the *yes*; in boundary work we learn that unless we have a clear *no*, our *yes* has little value. One of the ways we can reset these within ourselves, which does require some discipline—how Gevurah—is to take every response that isn't an extremely clear *yes*, sometimes called an *enthusiastic yes,* as a *no*. Both listening to others' responses and also registering our internal responses to situations, we learn to act as if every *well, maybe*; *okay*; *if you like*; *all right*; and even a mild *yes* are, in effect, *no*s. Suddenly the world reshapes around us. Sometimes we even miss out on something we may have wanted because our connection to our *yes* has been so weakened.

Once we learn to enthusiastically say *Yes! Yes, please! Definitely yes!* we are left with this problem of what to do about the *no*s. Perhaps by this stage it's becoming clearer that a whole lot of those vague *well, if we must*; *okay*; or *fine then* should really be *no*. How to say it? Do we say it gently, kindly, fluffing about a bit, *Well, maybe a little later on … I'd really love to, but … I'm terribly sorry, but I can't right now …* Sometimes this is genuine, in which case we can make it clear: *Today I can't do that, but next week I'd love to. Let's make a time.* But when these vague not-reallys are masking an actual *no* this often leads to confusion, with the other person mistakenly believing our words and therefore coming back to us again or pressing harder with their request. It's as if we don't trust ourselves or the other person with the truth. The truth is *no*. We're also trying to control the situation: *I don't want to do that thing, but I want the other person to think that I do.* We don't get to do that and keep a strong *yes* and *no*, which it turns out is vital for living a really functional, let alone happy life.

Gevurah honors the *no* and will even teach us how to use it. In creating clear boundaries, defining the edges, space is created. Chesed, and the spilling-out-forever, can be formless, vague, even torrential. It might be immersive, but it's hard to get a sense of where it begins and ends, or how or where anything actually happens. Gevurah puts a stop to all that. Here are the edges. Of the boat, to ride the ocean in. Of my skin, so I know where I finish and the rest of the world begins. Of my boundaries, so that whatever happens between us has my full consent. Of this sentence, so that it has a beginning, structure, pauses, and an end. Even of this book, eventually, otherwise it might possibly go on forever.

Gevurah can make us weep. Oh, the end of that relationship. Death. The end of a job, maybe one that we loved; a child leaving home; a parent losing the capability to live independently. Even much smaller endings and limits—the closure of our favorite café, a friend moving away, the end of summer—can leave us with a strangely deep grief. We don't have a strong tolerance for endings, boundaries, limits. Why is that? For anything to function at all, both Chesed and Gevurah are needed in their full strengths. What is this prejudice we have? Why do we shun and avoid one while hailing the other? This is a general malaise in our culture. Part of it has a commercial basis; capitalism, the protection and increase of assets and capital, requires an endless growth-related incline.

Yet our lives are finite. Seasons change. When we hold autumn and winter to be just as precious as spring and summer, when we honor death, when we make space for grief, pain, difficulty, and fear—that's when we become free, within the cycles, to celebrate and honor each part, each moment, whatever it brings. While we cling only to the light, to expanse and increase, we can't ever experience them fully; we rely on them without knowing their opposite or recognizing that they are not eternal. Transience, change, endings; such profound domains that Gevurah holds. Perhaps Chesed unfolds the sacred landscape, but it is Gevurah who guards it, who contains and nurtures it. Paradise is a walled garden. Whose are these walls? Who builds the safety nets, the agreements, the contracts and commitments? Gevurah. Who is discerning, measuring, critiquing? Not Chesed—Chesed is consumed with pouring forth, with offering.

Gevurah is red—like fire, like blood—and associated with powerful, fierce gods and goddesses. I think of Kali, dancing her rage of destruction, and the Red God of the Feri creation story, representing all the red-blooded ones, including humans. The hunted and the hunters, the bleeding ones, the mammalian ones. Under this red umbrella comes also war and the warriors. War has been so emblematic of human experience: our wars over land, resources, ideology, religion, governance. Our civil wars and our wars of independence. Our military coups and our foreign interventions. Our border wars and wars of attrition. Our World Wars and unnamed wars of propaganda, colonization, and genocide. Our wars against whole classes—women, dark-skinned humans, the poor and dispossessed. Our wars against nature and the very land, air, and water that nurtures and sustains us.

There are wars we might feel more predisposed toward—wars on terrorism, against children living in poverty, domestic violence, drugs, drunk driving. There are ecowarriors, teaching sustainability and taking action, breaking human laws to uphold natural law as they attempt protection of the earth. There are the Red Rebels of the Extinction Rebellion movement, reminding us how precious life is. War is seriously out of kilter in our world, frighteningly so as we begin to burn up this precious planet. This is Gevurah out of balance. And why is it out of balance? Not because we honor the light, the right-hand pillar side of things, expansion and mercy and kindness—although one could argue there can't really be enough mercy and kindness. No, it is because we don't recognize and hold sacred the qualities of the left-hand pillar, this very one whose energies are in rampage.

The Reclaiming Tradition model of power breaks it into three types: *power-over*, *power-within*, and *power-with*. Viewing power this way allows us to claim and develop our powers. We don't have to disempower ourselves worrying that all expressions of power are bad, evil, or destructive. Power is akin to life force and essential to magic, so it's not about refusing to have any part of it. Instead, we can analyze the types of power at play in any situation and choose how to interact with them.

Power-over is currently running rampage in our world, with its anti-life agenda as it destroys habitat, drives uncounted species into extinction, changes the makeup of our atmosphere, and alters not just the surface of our planet but its very climate. But power-over doesn't have to be destructive. It can be functional: when, for limited periods of time and to achieve specific tasks, an individual or small group is designated to act on behalf of the whole group. This is how representative democracy is supposed to function. We elect leaders to act for a specific time on specific tasks. However, it's gone awry. Even within apparent democracies there are powerful forces acting on the same stage as governments—corporations, religions, private interests—who are not elected and can't easily be un-elected, or removed. Those elected only rarely act on behalf of the whole group, more likely acting on behalf of those like themselves, completely unrepresentative of the whole, as well as being unduly influenced, even controlled, by the other powerful, non-elected interests.

Within this challenging scenario we individuals, who make up the masses, have certain powers remaining to us. There's power-within. Generally explained as the power that no one can take away from you or the power that each person has, equally, within themselves, this power-within is the place from which power-with springs. Power-with is where individuals join their powers together to have a greater effect. I have the power (indeed, in Australia, the obligation) to vote in elections. I have powers to join with others in protest, even highly organized protest, and to lobby. I have the power to spend my money and resources almost however I choose. I have the powers of free speech; the power to stand for election myself or support others who represent my view to do so; to join or even start a political party or pressure group. I have the power to create alternative bubbles of reality—festivals, WitchCamps, communities, creative projects—with others, and the power to spend my time and energy devoted to what I believe in, even if that is a radically different world than the one we live in.

Operating within, underneath, and beside our operational and governmental systems of power-over, power-with can achieve a lot, especially within a democracy. In other systems of government—military, dictatorship, punitive, monarchical—our power-with may be drastically curtailed. For example, when we are not allowed to gather in groups, when free speech is either banned or severely punished, if fair trials don't exist or it's treason to speak out against the government or leaders, power-with is forced to operate underground. It still does operate—all of the subversive movements of history prove that, from the Underground Railway before and during the American Civil War to the Resistance in France during World War II to the Viet Cong and countless others, some presumably still unknown.

Cries for justice and the redistribution of power resound across our globe. Some notable justice movements in the last decade have been sparked by single emblematic incidents. These caught the world's eye, causing a tipping point into powerful movements of social unrest. I think of the naming of Jyoti Singh, a young Indian woman gang-raped on a bus in 2012, who later died from her injuries. Under Indian law rape victims cannot be named, but Jyoti's mother publicly named her, declaring there was no shame for Jyoti or her family, only for the perpetrators. This case received worldwide attention and outrage, with mass protests in Delhi and throughout India for better security and laws to protect women.

The Black Lives Matter political and social protest movement exists in the United States as a response and desperate call for awareness and change in the face of continual killings of black people—mainly men and often young—by police, usually in entirely unprovoked circumstances. In 2020, when George Floyd was killed in the street by police and the 8-minute, 46-second-long murder was filmed by a teenage girl on her phone, the movement flared into days and weeks-long protests all across North America, as well as internationally, with the dead man's repeated phrase *I can't breathe* expressing a generations-long violent oppression. In Australia this movement lent power to ongoing First Nations protests about deaths in custody, a struggle that challenges the apparent tolerance for the appalling statistics of Indigenous incarceration and deaths while incarcerated. Police brutality and indifference to the suffering of those in custody, the unequal punishments meted out to Indigenous people by police and in the court systems, and the neglect of Indigenous health, education, housing, and employment fuel this unjust system.

Also in Australia the callous, monetized, and short-term thinking of giant mining corporations destroying historical, sacred, and cultural Aboriginal sites has come into focus again, with the willful destruction by Rio Tinto in 2020 of two ancient rock shelters in Western Australia, causing not just local but global outrage. In the United Kingdom the protest movement Extinction Rebellion, a collaboration begun between environmental activists and academics in social and environmental sciences, took to the world stage in 2018 and 2019, demanding that governments tell the truth about the climate crisis and take decisive action immediately to avert catastrophe. They achieved a worldwide following, with mass protests and some political victories, including the British parliament declaring a climate emergency. Greta Thunberg is a Swedish school-girl who inspired the worldwide Schools Strike for Climate. She leads a demand for change and justice for those who will have to live with the consequences of older generations' inaction on the climate emergency, and at age seventeen she is a formidable world figure.

We have to turn our eyes to justice; not just the tame sort that suits us, a system of courts and laws within certain so-called civilized countries, but actual justice. Clean water for all, for example, including for the rivers themselves and all the animals, birds, fish, and plants that depend on them. Education, health, basic living conditions; why are these spread so unequally across the globe? Justice for the elderly, the young, the sick. Justice for people of all skin colors, all ethnicities, all genders, ages, religious and political beliefs. Justice for living things other than ourselves—for the Great Barrier Reef in Australia, the Amazon rainforest, the polar bears, the thousands of species on the critically endangered species list. Climate justice. Justice for generations yet to come—and not just generations of humans, but generations of fragile rainforest trees, native frogs, bees. Justice for the deserts and the ice caps, the tundras and jungles.

Justice and mercy seem turned in the wrong directions in our world. We offer compassion for those who are suffering and helpless yet act to empower governments that continue that same suffering. Perhaps we should try turning it around, using the powers of justice to right the balance and offering mercy and sympathy to those who have failed us so badly. Our whole justice system, including the jailing of individual criminals, seems guaranteed not to create any broad justice. Corporate crime, government misdirection and criminal action, and the exploitation of peoples, resources, and land for the short-term benefit of the very few are endemic and largely go unaddressed by a justice system that those same governments, businesses, and private interests created. We have given our version of mercy—attempts at fair hearings, reviews and remand for good behavior of those sentenced, livable jail conditions—to those who actually need justice. We are unbalanced. Every part of our world screams this.

Our oceans rise along with our temperatures, while increasing numbers of unprecedented weather events and natural disasters occur. Australia and California burn up while Pacific Islands drown; fires and floods, droughts and storms increase in intensity, duration, geographical spread, and frequency. Exponentially, one event feeds the next—fire ravaging so much forest that the rainfall drops, for example. Perhaps it will be plagues next—the Black Plague in the fourteenth century killed around half the humans in Europe, and that was when the fastest mode of transport was ship or horse and most people didn't travel at all. (I wrote that sentence before COVID-19. But imagine a disease that infected 90 percent and killed 97 percent of those infected. It's possible.) According to the World Health Organization, mosquito-borne diseases account for more than one million human deaths per year, and as we continue to make our environments wetter and warmer, we surely can't imagine that number is going to decrease. There's a very real threat that increasing pressures of climate disaster will result in political instability, the further erosion of democracy, and potentially in resource wars and civil wars.

The law and forms of Gevurah actually hold space, when in right relationship, for creativity, choice, liberty, and flow. Gevurah can be the red warrior who comes to defend or protect us at a time of need. It can be the unalterable guidelines of what creates a livable environment for humans. It can be the discovery of natural laws. It can be boundaries we create and practice with each other and with the world. It is the recognition of form and containment, of discernment and separation, of conclusions and ending. Gevurah is justice—it is the sword that severs, the elegance of form, the ideal of law. It is clarifying, it is precise and unapologetic and rigorous. In itself, Gevurah has no mercy, no discernment, no softening, but it is always bound to its partner in the Tree, Chesed, and so the two dance together—power and mercy, form and force, particle and wave, stillness and movement, law and liberty.

Polarities in the Tree of Life

To come into the Kabbalah blithely claiming that the main binary operating through the right- and left-hand pillars is gender based, male and female, or often termed *masculine* and *feminine*, is deeply problematic. It's so inherently problematic that I think it's better just abandoned, politely perhaps, as a historic misdirection, which then allows for those oppositions or polarities to be examined much more broadly. Even if we take into account that the middle pillar—the central one, the one with the most sephirot— is non-gendered within that system, assigned to neither masculine or feminine, it is still reductionist and inherently flawed to automatically or casually associate the so-called masculine with one pillar and the so-called feminine with the other.

Opposites are a persistent dynamic for humans and we operate within many powerful binaries. Binaries in our world are not treated as equals. Rich and poor, for example. Black or colored skin/white skin. Able-bodied/people with a disability. Housed/homeless. Employed/unemployed. These polarities are based in power and privilege, and the side we find ourselves on is often impossible to change. Sometimes the privileges or power accorded to one side of the polarity do change; for example, cultural change has occurred over time in our attitudes toward gender. Sometimes legislation or active support and justice work intervene and create change; for example, around how different classes of people are treated in education, housing, or the justice and social welfare systems.

Feminism has spent two hundred years arguing for equality that treats all adults the same way, with the same opportunities, risks, and rewards regardless of what gender we are. A more radical analysis calls for not just equal opportunities, but equality of outcomes. In intersectional theory these demands intersect with analysis around race and class, with each of these three determinants—race, gender, class—in effect being viewed as a class, or within the class system. This enables us to learn more about the particularities of each person's circumstance, as well as to analyze oppression itself. We understand, for example, that a black woman is less privileged than a white woman, although both have less privilege than a white man. Assigning part of the Tree to an oppressed or disadvantaged sex, race, or class mires us in dynamics of prejudice and injustice almost as if that was part of the blueprint of the universe instead of an unfortunate human predisposition or willful, exploitative, and systemic perpetration.

I find the current movement of LGBTIQA (lesbian, gay, bisexual, trans*, intersex, queer, and agender) peoples exciting personally, sociologically, and politically. This is surely part of what feminism has always fought for—the ability to define ourselves free of imposed conditions due to gender. Or for that matter, marital status, sexuality, and fertility. There still remain serious, fundamental issues of race and class, as well as other concerns; for example, the relatively deadly nature of being female-bodied or female-identified or being raised a girl in a society that covertly condones rape, incest, and sexualization of children. Even so, this current, early twenty-first century flowering of the possibilities and complexities of gender identity is, to me, a delightful explosion of the binary system that existed as the imposed norm for so long.

Queering the Kabbalah—a term I am gratefully using that I first heard spoken and expounded upon by Charlie Wellington, a student of mine at the time—is a dynamic topic that throws into the air all gender- and sexuality-related assumptions about the Kabbalah, the sephirot, and their relationships to one another. We can look into one of Charlie's questions a little more closely: Does the Kabbalah even require any action from us on the queering front? Firstly, what is our definition of queer? It has historically meant odd, unusual, strange. It can mean to deliberately alter something; for example, queering an election or sporting result. That which is queer is outside what was expected, or it has been tipped off kilter and come through differently. According to Charlie, the Kabbalah, and in particular the sephirot, are already significantly queer.

There's the middle pillar, for a start. If, according to some, the right-hand pillar is masculine and the left feminine, where does that leave the middle pillar? Does it include both masculine and feminine, and thus is quite queer? Is it genderless, agendered, or belonging to some mysterious third gender? All of these options also fall into the category of queerly gendered. The middle pillar contains both Kether and Malkuth, which are often thought to be the most obviously gendered of all the sephirot—Kether as masculine, the endlessly emanating light, and Malkuth as feminine, the endlessly receiving fertile earth. So how does it work for them to be in the only non-gendered pillar? Not very well—a little queer, we might say, using several definitions of the word at once.

The most interesting part of this now-outdated system of assigning genders to pillars is that the qualities of the right-hand pillar, the so-called masculine pillar, are only partially those qualities we currently associate with the concept of masculine. So yes, in societal terms we can agree that the masculine concept is outwardly inclined and associated with light—but love and compassion? And while we might agree that the so-called feminine in our culture carries the qualities of inwardness and darkness, in the Kabbalah the left-hand pillar is the ferocious one, with rigor and power as essential characteristics. So this whole concept is provocative even within gender-stereotyping scenarios. There are mystical, impartial, and even godlike qualities associated with these polarities, and bringing them to bear on our assumptions, our daily lives, and our interactions and discussions around gender can be fruitful. But placing masculine and feminine as fundamental binaries—possibly anywhere, but certainly within the Tree of Life—now seems irredeemably passé.

Queer theory—exploring and questioning the dominant paradigm, especially as it relates to sexuality and gender—seems to go perfectly well with the Kabbalah. We already have this strange experience of needing to understand the so-called feminine pillar as the one with ferocity, severity, and limitations, and the so-called masculine one as the source of mercy, kindness, and expansion. But when we look more closely at individual sephira for traces of these concepts of masculine and feminine within it, it gets even more complex. Both Judith Laura, in *Goddess Spirituality for the 21st Century,* and Rachel Pollack, quoting from and building on Laura's thesis in *The Kabbalah Tree,* do this. They point to the clue of the Hebrew names of the sephirot because Hebrew words ending with -ah are feminine. This includes the word Kabbalah as well as Hokmah, Gevurah, and Binah—two of them on the left-hand pillar, but one on the right.

Having brains composed of two hemispheres may predispose us to recognize and create binaries, to work in terms of either/or, and to divide things into two—usually opposing—categories. Thus we can make long lists of what we consider meaningful polarities: left and right, up and down, inward and outward, night and day, introvert and extrovert, dark and light, positive and negative, mind and body, masculine and feminine. Endless trouble has been caused by these polarities, especially when one whole list—for example: light, mind, positive, masculine—has been held in opposition to another whole list: dark, body, negative, feminine.

Gender polarity has been assumed as fundamental. This simple fact—whether one is born with a female body or a male body—can determine much of what happens to us in life, in different degrees of severity depending on where and when in history one is born. As a polarity, gender is both crucial and problematic in a number of ways, even before it gets put into the Kabbalah. The division of human bodies into male and female, and the subsequent categories piled onto that division—such as intellectual/ emotional, powerful/weak, decisive/indecisive, serious/frivolous, career-oriented/ relationship-oriented—have caused deep damage to almost all individuals suffering under them. It has also been a cornerstone for an integrated system of oppression which, coupled with capitalism, has informed and controlled our culture, our institutions, and our personal, work, and social lives.

Associating less privileged or favored characteristics first with each other, and then in contrast to more favored characteristics, clearly entrenches the polarity. It is also a direct cause of, and feeder into, sexism, racism, desecration of the earth, disdain for the body, and ignorance of the dark, both the hidden and the mysterious. Thus it has helped create and sustain our current systems of entrenched racism and sexism, class discrimination, and inherited privilege—interpersonally, between nations, and in how we treat our planet—endangering our very survival.

We are born, mostly, into male or female bodies. Some of us are born into more ambiguous bodies, and that remains part of this debate. If the whole world operates one way if you have a female body and another if you have a male body, what happens to those who do not clearly fall into these definitions? Statistics range widely, with possibly one in a thousand births corresponding to unclear sex identity at birth, although one source says up to one in sixty and others, one in every fifteen hundred or two thousand. But if it happens at all, it throws out the precept that all humans fall into one or other of these categories, so it's problematic.

Our world also includes the trans, nonbinary, and agender communities and individuals, who may or may not have bodies that can be categorized strictly as male or female and may or may not intersect with the category of those born intersex, or not clearly gendered. Currently there is a political movement, a generational change, and a defining moment in debates around gender. Some spiritualities and psychologies have always claimed and worked with the understanding that we have both male and female within us (they often use the terms masculine and feminine), and to a certain extent this may be helpful, particularly for those stuck in very rigid, narrow, or problematic versions of gender-assigned roles. But then do we also say that each of us has a nonbinary part? Clearly we should, yet I think it shows up the assumptions within that thinking, which more deeply confirms gender roles rather than challenges them. Perhaps it's more functional to leave the whole question open—we can hardly abandon it, since it's so fundamental to our upbringing, work and personal lives, outlook, opportunities, and privilege—and simply ask each individual *How are you with gender at this stage in your life?* This would be revolutionary in itself.

Even what we "traditionally" know as masculine and feminine—and using that term, I'm very aware of its limitations, for clearly there are differences in what we now assume belong to those categories than what Jewish lore of a few hundred to a few thousand years ago might have assigned to them—the sephirot look all mixed up. Kether is all and everything—it surely then must contain all traits, all potential, all possibilities. While we can see Kether as some kind of God—the Jewish YHWH or the version in Islam or Christianity—and thus assume masculinity, we can also see Kether as the Star Goddess, She who began and birthed all things from Herself. Or take away gender completely and see it as the singularity from which our universe unfolded/exploded. Hokmah is the mirror reflection of Kether and so might be called feminine, the Sophia—but it's the top of what has been regarded as the masculine pillar, although with that feminine -ah ending. Gevurah is the warrior within the system—and yes, there are powerful female and feminine warriors, but within current dominant cultures it is an archetype usually assigned to the masculine. Tiferet—the golden heart of beauty—sounds incredibly feminine in our current terminology, yet it is the sephira associated with Jesus, and not just him but all hanging, dying gods: Odin, Tammuz, and Dionysus, and it's within the middle pillar.

It's a puzzle. But not so much a puzzle if we simply ask how it makes any sense to try to impose a binary, or human genders, on a system that is tenfold, inherently triplicate, and unendingly complex and nuanced? How can we possibly limit any one of these sephira to our notions of *he* and *she* or even the broader terms of masculine and feminine? The sephirot are vast, ages-old, and refer far more closely to the unfolding of the star maps of the universe than gendered life-forms here on earth; their inclusiveness and grandeur surely needs to be graced with terms far wider and more essential than those. Gender in the Tree, in other words, may be useful to us individually as we seek to navigate our own experiences and may be useful for deconstructing current social assumptions around gender and may, in fact, support or add further analysis to queer theory, but it's of strictly limited use to help further our understanding of the Tree.

Instead, as we address polarity, let us look at some other terms. *Expansion and contraction* is a description I find useful when applied to the right- and left-hand pillars. Hokmah expands; until now, everything has been held by the one, the All, Kether, and Hokmah doubles that. Binah contracts, as a third defined sephira that will begin to channel this unformed All into the particulars of creation. Chesed expands, receiving from the top triad and channeling that out through the rest of the Tree. Gevurah contracts, selecting, shaping, and cutting away what isn't needed. Tiferet holds the balance between, and then Netzach expands again, into the garden of possibilities. Hod contracts, sorting it all out, classifying and defining. Stars expand and contract, systems expand and contract, life expands and contracts.

We are creatures of expansion and contraction; with each breath our lungs expand as we breathe in and contract as we breathe out. This expanding/contracting is part of our communion with the world, with the air that sustains us but also with the green life on this planet with which we literally exchange breaths. A powerful meditation is imagining a tree, or the earth itself, breathing in simultaneously with each of our outbreaths, and their breath out being the breath that we take in. Our heartbeat can be experienced as contractions and expansions, the working of this muscular organ so intrinsic to each moment of our lives, as it pumps blood through our bodies. The process of birth is a series of contractions and expansions, as the baby is propelled outward from the mother's body. Life itself, we could say, is an expansion, and dying, a contraction.

There are also parts of that cycle of contraction and expansion where we can recognize pauses, or stillness; sometimes we even deliberately build that in. Breathing is like this—we breathe in and then can pause, holding the fullness of the breath; we breathe out and can pause again before the next breath. If we think of the pillars of the Tree, these pauses can represent the middle pillar holding space between the polarities while the two outer pillars are the extremes of fullness and emptiness, the far ends of the pendulum.

Chaos and order are a well-known polarity that fits the Kabbalah. The chaos of Hokmah, Chesed, and Netzach with everything unfolding, still in formation, exploding outward in all directions, and then the order imposed by Binah, Gevurah, and Hod as they distill, limit, and clarify. In the middle pillar we can feel the yin-yang of it, how all of Kether, Tiferet, Yesod, and Malkuth have chaos and order side by side or turning one into the other, momentarily balanced. Order and chaos seem like the dance of the gods, both much more precisely descriptive and also far grander than the muddy terms of masculine and feminine. These wider, more universal, less weighted and vexed polarity languages apply much better to the Tree and its sephirot.

Mercy and justice can be posited as a polarity—in the Tree they are, with the right and left-hand pillars sometimes assigned those characteristics. It's an interesting polarity because one is so clearly in deficit without the other. Both are deeply valued qualities in the Westernized world—values to aspire to, held up, even idealized. One can be seen as soft and giving, the other as harsh and limiting. Yet which of us would desire to live in a world that had only one of them? Who would appreciate a justice system that had no mercy or a social care system that did not have justice as a core value? How could we raise our children with only one of these values? The balance of mercy and justice is a fine art; no fixed formula can adequately meet it, and many situations require all our sensibilities to get it right or at least approximately right. We want both, at their full extent, perhaps not realizing how completely interdependent they are.

Force and *form* have become my favorite terms for the polarity in the Tree, as represented in the right- and left-hand pillars. Force in the outward wave of expansion and energy with Hokmah, Chesed, and Netzach in increasingly refined doses, and form as the manifestation of matter, time, and space, as well as actual forms, through Binah, Gevurah, and Hod as force is boundaried, shaped, and refined. As everything ripples

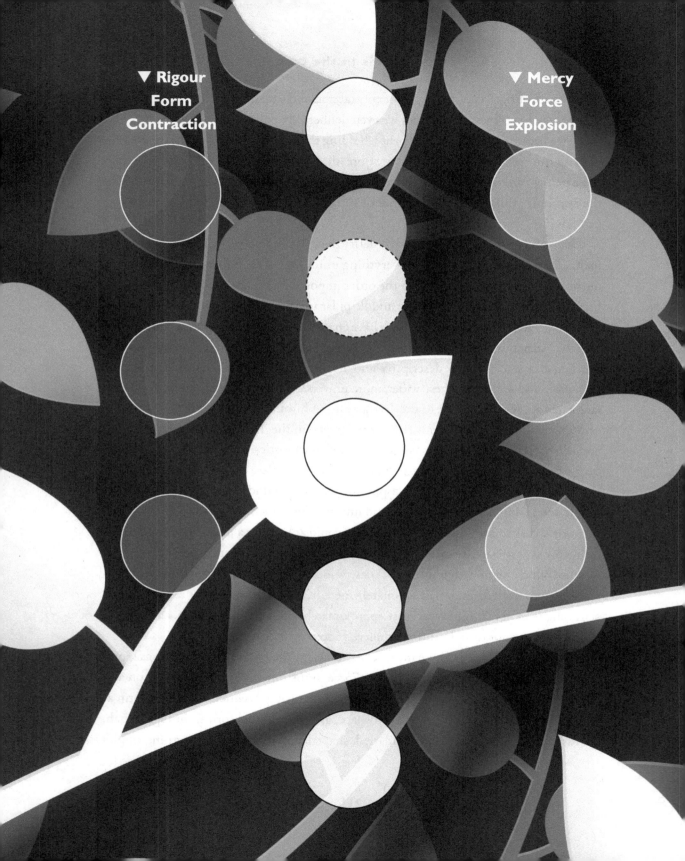

▼ Rigour
Form
Contraction

▼ Mercy
Force
Explosion

down from Kether—which is both prior to and also containing all of force and form—Hokmah gives us the force of absolute expansion, the unending moment past the singularity of time, space, and matter. Binah sorts that, discerning stars, gases, atoms, matter and dark matter. Chesed explodes into being as the initiator of the lower Tree, bringing everything, unformed and ungraded, past the Abyss before Gevurah wades in wielding a sword and discerns, selects, qualifies, and quantifies. A moment of balance with Tiferet and then, at Netzach, all possibilities shimmer toward life, multifold and unending, until Hod brings in descriptors, relationships, progressions, and systems. This distills into Yesod and arrives, finally, at Malkuth, the perfect alchemical mix of force and form in synchrony.

Force and *form* also looks quite like *waves* and *particles*, with force representing the waves described by quantum mechanics and form representing the particles. Waves are patterns that tend to be infinite and continuing, whereas particles are defined points. Wave-particle duality is a fundamental way of examining the microscopic world of quantum physics tripped up, as discussed earlier, by light itself, which behaves both as a wave and a particle depending on how it is observed, and is thus essentially inexplicable: the middle pillar in evidence.

So we can see waves to the right, particles to the left, and in the middle—light. The light that beams straight from Kether all the way down to Malkuth. Or it can travel via the lightning flash, dodging back and forth from one state to another, but with this central constant that everything else is measured by. Light. How the universe came into existence in the first place, how light birthed itself, emerged from darkness or how any god or goddess cohered to allow this force-and-form to be birthed through them. The polarities that stretch everything apart, making room for existence, add the play, the complexity. They might seem almost to cancel each other out—if one looks for particles in light, one can only find particles; if one is searching for waves, there are only waves to be found. Yet when taken together, separated (and joined) by the great middle pillar, all of creation can exist in a series of perfectly imperfect balancing acts.

practice | Boundaries and Consent

Boundaries are not bad things. If used with discernment, they create containers that support us. Having strong, responsive boundaries can ensure that we ask for what we want, accept invitations that delight us, and dare to grow our edges when it feels right to do so. We can gather strength and insight and cease relating within abusive situations or relationships.

When I've done boundary work earlier in my life it often involved drawing diagrams with circles on them, placing the names of people in my life in the circles to show how close those people were to me. This may have been an interesting exercise, but it didn't help me to establish strong boundaries or even know what my boundaries were or to have any sort of flow in the present moment, where boundaries might be changing. It also didn't help me to talk about my boundaries with other people or even realize that was something I should be doing.

Usually we practice boundary and consent work with others. But a lot of the time I don't have others around, so I'm keen to create ways we can practice on our own. If you have other people to work with, great! Please adapt the following exercises to work with a partner or in a group. But perhaps also make the time to practice on your own. After all, the person who needs to understand and be able to implement our boundaries is ourselves, so practicing by ourselves makes sense.

Finding Our No and Our Yes

It's impossible to do any sort of effective boundary work without recognizing what a *no* and a *yes* feel like to us emotionally, energetically, and in our bodies. This requires awareness and trust. Self-awareness and self-trust. If we are out of touch with them, it can take a while to establish, reestablish, or build these within ourselves. This exercise does exactly that.

The awareness we build is by tuning in to our responses to a situation, suggestion, or action. Doing this, we take the emphasis off any consequences and focus solely on our response. We can do this by setting boundaries beforehand; for example, by saying that none of these suggestions or invitations will be acted upon: this is purely an exercise.

Trust comes in when we have to pay attention to our response, not ignore it, damp it down, or shove it to one side, as we have probably been doing for most of our lives. Children are only rarely left to follow their own responses, instead constantly being schooled to meet others' expectations or requirements and follow others' responses rather than their own. We have all been children, for many years, and our adult lives, where nominally we have more say over our environments, relationships, and choices, came after these childhood years, usually without a thorough debriefing in between.

TIME: 30 minutes

YOU WILL NEED: A pen and paper or your journal. Some sort of line or divider on the floor such as a ribbon, a drawn line, or a stick.

Consider what you might possibly do in the next twenty-four hours and write a list of suggestions. Include quite ordinary suggestions such as *Have lunch* or *Go to bed early*, as well as more ambitious suggestions: *Finally tackle that piece of work I've been postponing all week* or *Make that difficult phone call* or *Go out for a really lovely evening by myself.* Include a few extreme or ridiculous suggestions, such as *Take a balloon ride* or *Start learning a new language,* as well as some things you would really love to do, such as *Have a bath* or *Ask my friend to schedule a catch-up.* Write at least twenty suggestions down.

These suggestions form the basis of the exercise in finding our *no* and our *yes*, and they will not be acted on at this stage, regardless of what we answer.

Now place the dividing line on the floor, making sure there is room to stand on each side of it. The right-hand side will signal *yes* and the left-hand side will signal *no*.

Stand at the bottom of the line so that with one step you can step equally easily to the right or left side.

Speak aloud for this exercise—we are all used to voices in our minds and often are much more free with what we say there than what we speak aloud. However, this exercise is to accustom us to speaking our *yes* and *no* aloud and hearing our own voice speaking those words.

For the first round of the exercise, you will answer *no* to every suggestion.

Read aloud your first suggestion, take a breath to consider it, and then answer *no*, stepping into the left-hand *no* side of the divider. Notice how that feels. Perhaps you are saying *no* to something you didn't want or plan to do anyway, or perhaps you are saying *no* to something you actually intend to do or would love to do. What does it feel like to say *no* to this?

Return to your start position. Continue down the list, reading aloud each suggestion, pausing for a breath, then answering aloud *no*. Continue stepping each time on the left-hand side of the divider. Notice your internal responses as you continue to answer *no*.

When you get to the end of the list, pause a moment. Reflect on how it feels to be answering *no* to every suggestion. Perhaps it is very familiar. Perhaps it is deeply strange. Perhaps you have mixed feelings. Breathe with this for a moment, then return to your starting position. You might like to stamp your feet, shake your body, or have a drink of water before continuing.

For the second round of the exercise, you will answer *yes* to every suggestion, although with the understanding that you will not carry through these suggestions as a result of this exercise.

Read the first suggestion aloud, take a breath into it, and then answer aloud *yes*, stepping onto the right-hand side of the divider. It may feel quite different from when you answered *no* to this same suggestion, or you may feel disconnected from the exercise or yourself. Notice what you are experiencing.

Return to your start position. Then read out the rest of the suggestions aloud, one by one, pausing for a breath and then answering aloud *yes* to each one, stepping onto the right-hand side of the divider.

Notice your internal responses. How does it feel to be answering *yes* to these suggestions, some of which you may not at all wish to follow through on? Perhaps this feels very familiar or quite alien, disconcerting, even upsetting or numbing. Read and answer through to the end of the list.

When you get to the end of the list, pause again. Reflect on what it is like to answer *yes* to every question. Breathe with this for a moment. Again, you can shake yourself, breathe, stamp, drink some water.

Spend three or four minutes writing down your impressions about how it felt to be answering *no* and *yes,* regardless of how you might have wanted to respond.

For the third round of the exercise, you get to listen to your internal response and answer truthfully. You still will not carry through with an action; just feel your honest answer and respond accordingly, learning what it feels like to do that. Remember that in consent work we interpret all half-hearted, conditional, or unclear responses, such as *maybe, all right, I guess, okay, sure* as a *no*—only an *enthusiastic yes* qualifies as an actual *yes*.

Stand at the starting place. Read aloud the first suggestion on your list and take a breath before answering it. What do you feel? What do you want to reply—maybe because it's automatic or you feel obliged or you want to get this exercise over with? What is your true answer, the truth within you? When you know this, answer aloud and step to the left if the answer is *no*, to the right if it's *yes*. If you do not have a clear answer, practice assuming that it is a *no*, and answer *no* and step to the left.

How does that feel? Notice your responses, and perhaps the process you went through to speak it aloud, get an answer, and take the step.

Now return to the starting place and read the next suggestion aloud. Again, take a breath and spend a moment feeling into your truthful response to this suggestion. Perhaps your stomach clenches or your throat feels constricted or your feet are restless. Perhaps your mind glazes over a little or tries to skip ahead to the next thing. Perhaps you feel anxious, bored, or irritated.

What is your response to this suggestion? Is it something you want to say *yes* to or something to which, truthfully, your answer is *no*? Regardless of the reality or consequences of this suggestion, try answering with your truth, remembering that an unclear answer or a conditional sort of agreement such as *oh I suppose so, if I must*, and *okay then* actually counts as *no*. If these responses are occurring to you, try speaking *no* aloud instead, and see how that feels and how it feels to step to the left of the divider, even though in real life your answer might well have been taken as a *yes*.

After you've answered, and felt how that is, return to the starting position and read the next suggestion aloud. Continue in this way, suggesting, pausing and feeling into your response, and answering aloud and with a step to either side of the divider, reflecting how that feels, for the entire list.

At the end, write what you have learned in your journal. These may be such things as *I'm not comfortable with saying no, even when it's my truth; I find it hard to give a clear yes; It's easy for me to know what I want but it's sometimes impossible to speak it aloud; I prefer to give excuses and reasons rather than a clear no; I don't really like having to give an opinion at all.* These are starting points for learning about how to work with boundaries.

Over the coming days, practice this in real-life situations, both solely by yourself and with others. Try not to respond to any pressure you might feel to reply instantly; instead really hearing the suggestion, request, offer, or wish and locating your truthful response. Then answer from that place.

If it's another person asking, you may choose to add a reason to your *no*, although depending on circumstances, this can lead to your reason being debated or disputed—that is, your *no* isn't heard. Many of us also do this internally. When you feel one of those *oh well maybe, sure, why not* sort of responses, you might want to say something along the lines of *I'm not feeling a clear yes just yet, but can we talk about it more?* or *I'd love you to explain how this would work before I answer yes or no* or to unpack it into parts if you have a mixed *yes* and *no*, maybe agreeing to part of it and not another part; for example, *I would love to have lunch with you, but not today. I could do that tomorrow.*

This practice with boundaries, as well as strengthening our *no* and *yes,* will bring a lot of clarity into many interpersonal situations—insights and empowerment and a strengthening of our ability to hold clear boundaries that respond to our internal truth. It revolutionized my life, and maybe it will do the same for yours.

process | Life Priorities

Gevurah can support us to reorganize our lives, update our priorities, and decide where and how to spend our time and energy. It's easy to get waylaid by demands that don't actually support us, meet our passions, or lead us in the directions we most want to go. It sometimes seems as if most of our life force is given to unrewarding activities. Some of these we have little choice about, such as turning up for work, running a household, and meeting family obligations. But it can be interesting—even empowering—to examine what our choices look like, both as we live them currently and how we might organize them in the future.

TIME: 30–60 minutes

YOU WILL NEED: Pen and paper or journal

The Process

1   Write out a list of the activities you currently spend time doing. Some of these might be grouped together, for example *household stuff*, rather than listing separate items. Some of them you might want to separate out, such as *teaching work, writing work, work admin, work meetings*. The main criteria for grouping or separating things is how much you love them, so as I pretty much equally love (or not) all aspects of household stuff, I've grouped it together, and as I'm passionate about some aspects of my work but much less so about others, I've separated them out. For the initial list, use your gut feeling. You can always adjust the items later.

2   Go through each item on the list, feeling into your relationship to it and rating it honestly. Use a star rating system—this was my definition of the star rating, below. Yours might be slightly different. I drew the stars under my items; you might prefer just to use a number, a color, or some other method.

      5 stars = I passionately love this ★ ★ ★ ★ ★
      4 stars = I mostly love this ★ ★ ★ ★
      3 stars = I can take it or leave it, it's okay ★ ★ ★
      2 stars = It's bearable ★ ★
      1 star = I'd be happy to never do this again ★

3   Rewrite all the items in groups of star ratings, so you now have a group of 5-star items, a group of 4-star items, and so on. Check if you need to make any adjustments to where various items appear; for example, I had initially given only 4 stars to something that, on reflection, was really one of my highest priorities. When I changed it to 5 stars, it felt daring and confronting but true.

4   Look at the group of 5-star items. Consider what your life would be like if you organized everything else around them.

5   Look at your 4-star and 5-star items together. What would your life look like if these were your priorities? What changes would you need to make?

6   Look at your 1-star and 2-star items. Can you get rid of any of them? What steps would you need to take to do that? Do you want to take those steps?

7   Look at your 3-star items. Can you minimize any of them or adjust them so that they become 4-star or 5-star items? What would you have to do to make this happen?

8   Now you can undertake visioning, spell work, or planning. Perhaps you will do a spell around this, or dream or vision how it would be if your 5-star items were your central priorities. Perhaps you have a practical approach and want to draw up lists or make a plan.

9   Write your 5-star items on a new page or piece of paper—maybe you want to decorate it in some way—and come back to it often.

Memoir: *The Red Thread*

I walk slowly around the circular temple space holding a small twig of needle-like leaves in my hand. There are mattresses to either side of me with people seated on them. We chose randomly from a plate of flowers-stones-leaves to find partners; we were told the choice is always perfect. At the doorway I turned right, so I walk around the entire room before I see my partner on the immediate left of the door, waiting by a mattress covered with a sarong, his branchlet of little leaves that matches mine on a cushion beside him. An Israeli man I have mixed feelings about. He's a meditator, a yogi, he's been cool to me throughout the week, barely answering when I've spoken to him. His hair is silver, making him look far older than he is; mid-thirties looking fifty. He wears it scraped back in a knot on his head. I hesitate as our eyes meet and he leans forward into my gaze. *I am totally here for you*, he says fiercely, leaving no space for equivocation. *I will not leave you. I will be with you whatever happens.*

· · · ·

We're in the Italian countryside outside Rome for a weeklong sacred sexuality intensive. It's summer. It's just so fallen out that the sephira I'm holding this month is Gevurah and I'm a little grudging about it. Chesed I imagine would be gorgeous—or Tiferet or Netzach ... but no. I'm with the warrior and the red blood. I revere the red—the red thread of my mother's mother's mother's ancestors that has birthed me, bleeding into the French landscape. Further back, part of that family came from Italy, where I am now. So I'm here to dance with the red, with my edges and heartbeat.

I haven't bled for a year yet I feel vibrant, more open than I've ever been and searching for how to be with this ferocity and passion. When I was young, in my twenties, I felt ancient, crone-like, whereas now I've got no interest in being a crone. I'm doing it backward. I was old before, and now in my fifties I'm young and possibly getting younger; mid-fifties feeling thirty. I turn up to this workshop and learn about boundaries and how to go to the depths with whoever is seated opposite me, about grace and trust and surrender.

We do a session on mothers but I cannot even get to my mother yet; there's something more pressing. My friend who died two years ago now but I'm still in mourning, she tidied up everything: her paintings, her computer, her belongings. For a year she'd been sending me files and photos, which I know she deleted off her computer once I had them. I imagined her doing it with twenty people, with fifty. She knew a lot of people. She didn't have a partner and had only one child, a daughter, whom I know, a little, from being friends with her mother for twenty years. But after my friend died I learned that this daughter did not have a clear, healed, strong relationship with her mother, that instead my friend echoed my own mother in her neglect and mismanagement of that relationship, and all that tidiness as she prepared for death was not really what needed tidying, at all.

You left a mess, I weep and shout at an empty cushion, while all around me others scream and pound and wail and shake, *you left a mess*. Perhaps it's also my own mother I'm accusing of this—*What a mess you left in dying*; perhaps we all do. A part of life, the messiness, and dying—all that's different is that it has to be picked up by someone else or stay a mess. I weep and pound the cushion, my rings piled carefully to the side. *Oh how could you? How could you die and leave your daughters in such a mess!* Gradually the shock and outrage leaves me until I am just sad all through, weeping for mothers and their daughters. I pick up the threads of the living, my own and those of other daughters, other mothers. The red threads. I lie on the mattress and feel held in this container.

221

Another day we're in triads. For once I was proactive, finding a woman I haven't worked with yet but I like her quiet composure and an American man I've been allies with; we've offered each other support of the type I'd usually only receive from a close friend. We are re-creating a family dynamic. I would call this a piece of reparenting, although they don't call it that. We take turns to be the child, mother, father, and—maybe to get it over with—I volunteer to go first as the child. The gentle German woman becomes my mother and my friend takes the role of father. We tumble into the process wide open and all of us cry at some point. At one stage I am nestled into her body while she strokes my hair and whispers to me.

When the instructors say the people in the child role have to stand up and walk into the center of the room away from those parents, I stand up but can't walk forward. I am clinging to the hand of this woman as if I could never let go, and she's clinging back. She walks with me to the edge of the mattress. I'm supposed to go on without her, but I can't. Finally I take a very small step or two but I'm still holding her hand, our hands are behind me, on the left-hand side, my left hand is holding her right hand as if it would be death to let go. Tighter and tighter I hold her, and she's holding too; I have tears pouring down my face. My mother died three years ago. I see again that vision I saw then, hovering in the doorway, me on this side and handing her across, but she was a baby in my arms and I handed her through to death, oh I remember. And now I have this red thread by the hand and then—

Our arms are stretched, mine back and hers forward, still clinging, and I don't know how I'm imagining it will progress from here but there's a movement behind me and my hand is broken free and I'm apart, separate. I almost stumble; I didn't choose it, wasn't ready. I couldn't have let go, maybe ever, and I turn and look back and she also is crying and one of the other women in the circle comes forward and wraps me in her arms. Oh, the loss. Later she says she would never have let go, she felt my mother's death there, but one of the facilitators came up and very quickly forced her hand open. We are in wonder at it.

• • • •

The next day, or maybe the day after, we gather around a mattress on the floor in the center of the room. We are watching a ritual with two of the facilitators, a man massaging a woman. She lies down naked and he begins the massage. There are forty-five people watching as he brings his whole focus and attention into his hands onto her skin. It is late afternoon, a hot summer's day. We've been keeping long hours, doing deep emotional work for days, and now we surrender to this process, its slow intensity, the gravity of them at the center of the room. We are on the floor and she's lying down, he's bending over her. We can't see very much but we can see his devotion, his absolute attention, and when she turns onto her back and he arranges her legs on either side of him, he is kneeling before her, she is the altar and he the devotee, we are transported with them into some wild field, ancient temple, present moment of sacred offering.

Sometimes he tells us something or checks in with her, but mainly it is silent, just our breathing in the space. He's quite young, Italian, and I feel that he's bringing through grace for all the ways men have treated women through the years, for the neglect and violence and fear and horrors; he's undoing it piece by piece, moment by moment, touch by touch. I have tears running down my face for the stilled, held grandeur of this devotion. It's almost as if it's me lying there—I am receiving it, held by it, and I lie back so I can see even less but still feel as if my eyes are so wide open they can never close, having seen this. The red thread that weaves through everything, that gave birth to us, that survives and heals and I see her there, his hands on her, in her, as she journeys deep and he is present for it completely. The only other Australian, a woman, happens to be next to me and she sees the tears falling out of my eyes and reaches her hand out so we lie there, holding hands, in the presence of a deep healing washing through the room's hot summer air. The container of this time and all its attendants—us—holding space; the pillars of the temple; receiving, receiving.

• • • •

I meet his eyes as he leans forward promising his devotion. That intensity. Okay then—here we are. I sit down on the mattress with him, cross-legged; we gaze at each other, piercing. I say I want this massage as a magical spell. He nods. I say that I'm okay with touching everywhere, but not with the latex gloves. I only want skin or else don't touch me at all. Staring, blue-gray eyes fierce into mine, he spits out *There will be no gloves. I hate gloves.* I have brought tiny altar items and I set them up by the mattress: a rosebud for Eve, a shell for Aphrodite, a candle for Freyja, my mother's blue silk scarf, a tiny wooden goddess from Glastonbury. I pile my rings there. He asks if he can call his spiritual ally, and I say *of course*; then he says it is Shiva. Of all the gods in all the realms. Shiva. He calls to Shiva. He of the blue, of Chesed, and here I am, going into the red and Gevurah. Of course, of course. This container.

• • • •

There was an earlier ritual where we were naked in the temple. The men had gone first, standing like statues in the room as we walked through, marveling. We met their eyes, some of us wept, some of us asked to touch. I placed my hand against a naked man's beating heart, gazing into his eyes. I crouched down and placed both my hands over the feet of another man. I ran my fingertips over the shoulder blades of another, he was one I had danced with in the mornings. Dancing, we grabbed hold of each other, pushed and backed away; provoked, we growled. He pulled me into his body so I felt all of him against me and we moved, eyes boring into eyes, twisting, turning, hands caught together and then again—all of him/all of me—and flung away. I stripped off the selves that have kept me hidden, cautious, unsure. Eye to eye in the dance, this moment's beloved. Now I behold him naked and his shoulder blades are like the beginning of wings.

When it was our turn, the women facilitators and assistants began, before the men came in, lying there naked for us, the five or six of them. Legs open, revealed to their essence. There's so much here—so much I'm learning. How to teach—this way. From the utter core, nothing held back, nothing hidden. Literally. This is the red, carving its way through me like veins, like blood. I cried seeing them and had no question that I'd do it. We lie on mattresses and cushions around the edges of this beautiful room. First we looked at each other. A woman gazing at my vulva, weeping, says to me *This is the most beautiful thing I have ever seen.* Then in deep reverence the men enter the room. They can approach one of these temples-that-are-women to sit before her. She might have her legs open or she might open them. Or not. He might just sit with her. She might show him her innermost secrets.

The man with the shoulder blades comes to me first, straightaway. Kneels before me and looks at all of me, my eyes and face, my breasts and arms and belly, hips and legs and sex, slowly, in his spacious way. In this presence I open my legs and he bends forward, kneeling, forearms on the floor, head lowered toward my vulva, and looks at me. Gazes.

After quite a long while he asks if he can hold the lips of my vulva apart, and I nod. He touches me. The first man in years to touch my genitals. He's so gentle, reverent, and then—he just looks. It's as if I am a painting in an art gallery or a sculpture of the goddess and he has brought himself to learn, to be imprinted. I feel transported through time and place, dropping through all the worlds. This is the gaze of the devotee, of the beloved. I have tears pouring down my face. Time deepens around us, carries us, carries me. Back to a place where my body is revered. He bathes me in that gaze and I am returned, somehow, in this temple, ritual, reverence; into the place where sex is sacred.

• • • •

This ritual, the massage. With the fierce Israeli man, the Shiva worshipper. I want something strong enough to shift this pattern I've been stuck in for years now with no lovers, and before that a long time since I had sex I could bring my whole self into. I'll rewrite anything for that; everything. I'll put myself into the alchemical crucible and be wrought anew, and this ritual seems like it might have the power to do that. We've cast a circle, called to our gods, spoken our agreements, and now it starts.

As soon as he touches me, I realize that I spent all my time talking magic and none at all about the mechanics of the massage. I completely failed to mention that I like gentle, sensual massage. As he begins a painful deep tissue massage with lots of staccato tapping, my body jerks and flinches, shudders, and I weep and weep just to have someone's hands on my skin, to have his full attention devoted to this. I surrender. When I turn onto my back I start calling the Tree into my body, especially the path from Gevurah to Tiferet to Netzach. Remembering he is Israeli, I ask him to name the parts of my body in Hebrew. He starts reciting them as I chant aloud sacred names and I'm falling, falling through the Tree. My arms and legs are tingling as if I were over-breathing, but I'm not, I'm very carefully not, and I start sounding louder and louder and eventually he sits between my legs, still naming my body, looking at me, meeting my eyes again and again, checking and asking—

He's still naming me and I feel like we're at the beginning of the universe and at my request he's called to Shiva, asking him to bring lovers into my life, he did it in Hebrew, and by now I am singing, sounding, the *I Am That I Am,* and he says, startled, *We have that too* and I say *Of course, it's Kabbalah, it's Jewish* and I am shaking, my body vibrating with impact, it's like an earthquake, a volcano, a comet, he moves one hand to my stomach, my womb, my heart while his other hand touches me and both of us are chanting in a mix of languages, there's a spell weaving about us, our eye gaze is unrelenting—

I see two sparks born in the breaking of the worlds right back at the beginning of time and they've been spinning, falling through space always and just now in this moment have met again—

I see years unspooling in my life—those years of not being touched, not having lovers, there's been a purification and stripping away of everything and now—

this is how empty I had to be to receive it—

this is how open I had to be to let it in and rewrite me—

I'm holding the distillation of power, the power of the whole-unto-herself, the red thread: I accept it—breathe deep—I live and release it—

the whole of our lives, to bring us here—I see through aeons of time every second, each one is actually like this, all the universe was born to serve just this moment (each moment)—

we're sparks—spinning, falling through time, through the everything and collided now, particles entangled again and recognizing each other but they never forgot—

I'm suspended vibrating with energy coursing through me I'm the river I'm fire burning up—his eyes still holding mine the arrangement of our bodies old as time and still we are chanting, Hebrew, English—the names of gods, of goddesses, of the Tree of Life—it's searing, not even remotely erotic other than that it is happening in and through my body, with his gaze, his words, his hands, all his focus-life-energy and I invite it into every cell and I spin it out to the distant corners of time, singing—

My body is the body of the goddess
I am that I am
We are stars we are stars we are stars

We are sparks, entangled, joined. We fall through time, remembering and held within a moment—bound together with the red thread and searing, falling—

Eventually it ends. I push his touch out and away from me in increments, in breaths, rewritten to some deep pattern of my self. He lays a sarong over me, even my face, and sits next to me, waiting. I drift, I float. Among the specks of dust, of light, a mote, an arrangement of atoms, of vibrations, a particle, a wave. I am red. I let life surround and hold me, the light pierce and claim me; I am remade. Within the crucible, the ritual, the hands of the beloved. The red threads woven through me.

ritual | Divided Self

Gevurah and Chesed are considered the sephirot with the strongest polarity within the Tree. Each of them is a clear distillation of the pillar they belong to: Chesed the right-hand Pillar of Mercy and Gevurah the left-hand Pillar of Rigor. Between them they hold force and form, expansion and contraction, water and fire, life and death.

Divisions and polarities are rarely so clear in real life. Everything gets muddied up, even in large impersonal organizations such as the justice system, let alone individual lives. This exercise offers a way of working with polarity to learn about balance and imbalance. This can inform our understanding of a situation and offer a way to create change.

TIME: 30 minutes

YOU WILL NEED: Journal and pen

Choose a situation in your life that feels unresolved or one where you have questions about your role in it. This could be a relationship with family, a lover or partner, a friend or work colleague; it could be a project or ambition you have, a spiritual matter, or a community issue you are involved with.

Sit comfortably and begin by bringing awareness to your breath. Invite yourself to relax.

Focus briefly on each area of your body, imagining your breath moving through that part, clearing it of stuck energies and patterns. You might visualize the muscles, veins, bones, and tissue as you go, or perhaps it is more of a felt experience. If you work with sound, you can think of a bell or gong sounding through that body part.

Imagine yourself lying facedown on the Tree: your head resting within the top triad, your shoulders over Chesed and Gevurah, Tiferet in the middle of your chest, Netzach and Hod under your hips, Yesod around your genitals, and your legs descending through Malkuth. Perhaps you can feel the sephirot correlating with your body parts. If you like, you can physically lie down, face downward.

Imagine or feel your right hand dipping into Chesed. Allow your left hand to bathe in Gevurah.

Imagine a line down the center of your body, top to bottom. You might feel this as a narrow band of the middle pillar, or perhaps you recall the notion of a thread that connects each one of us to heaven and earth, running through our crown, down the spine, and all the way into the center of the earth. Allow this division to become quite solid, a barrier. Imagine, for the moment, that it holds the right and left sides of your body separate from each other, self-contained.

Still holding that central division, concentrate on your right hand. Let it begin to actively receive Chesed's blue energy, and allow that blue to flow up your hand, into your arm, and all the way up to your shoulder. Perhaps you can see this in your mind's eye, feel it in your arm, or you may have another way of experiencing it.

Let this blue energy continue flowing into the right-hand side of your body until that side is completely filled, completely blue, still respecting the central division.

Now concentrate on the left hand—reach out with it and open to receive Gevurah's red energy into your left hand. Allow it to flow up your hand and arm to your shoulder. Be aware of any sensations or visual impressions you receive. Allow the red to continue flowing until it has completely filled your left-hand side.

By now your body is colored red on the left, blue on the right. Spend some time strengthening these feelings, dipping your awareness first into one side, then the other, and allowing your impressions and sensations to build. Continue to hold the dividing line up the center of your body, separating the blue from the red. You might imagine or feel the words or the energies of *severity, rigor, limitation* on the Gevurah side, and *mercy, generosity, expansion* on the Chesed side.

Observe—look and feel more closely—how does each side seem? Are they a similar strength and vibrancy? Is there any movement within the sides? What type of movement? If you imagine dipping into one, tasting it—how does it seem to you? The other side?

Now return to the whole concept—your body, the dividing line, the Gevurah energy and the Chesed energy, and allow yourself to recall or introduce the situation you brought into this process.

Let the situation float over the surface of your body, as it is divided between Gevurah and Chesed. How does that seem? Does one side or the other react, enlarge, or grow stronger? In what way? Is one side more vibrant and one less so? Which one?

How does this situation feel within your body? Does one side respond more or respond differently? Do the sides feel balanced? What is that balance or lack of balance telling you?

Try asking a question about the situation and feeling or watching your responses to it as this Gevurah/Chesed being.

Does this experience explain something to you about yourself or the situation, especially in regards to the balances of justice and mercy or contraction and expansion? Does it offer guidance as to how you might act? If so, spend a moment clarifying this guidance. You can check with your body, asking *If I were to do this or that, how would that be?* and observing what happens in each side of your body in response. You might be aiming for a balance between the two sides or to reinvigorate or heal one side.

Is there another question you wish to ask?

If it feels right, you can spend some time rebalancing your red and blue sides, feeding each of them in turn with breath and intention.

When you feel complete, thank these energies of Chesed and Gevurah and spend a few moments releasing them. Allow their energies and the colors to drain out through your hands and back into the sephirot held within the Tree.

Return to the awareness of your breath, allowing the central dividing line to fade away and your body to become distinct from the Tree. Perhaps parts of it will begin to twitch or stretch; we often encourage this as a way of returning from a trance state.

You might want to shake yourself out, stand up and walk about a little, drink some water.

Then spend some time journaling about your experiences and any insights or understanding you reached.

activity | Creating the Fifth Disk

As you complete the work of this section, create your fifth disk to represent the sephira you've been journeying with. Perhaps you are traveling from the top of the Tree and spent the first section concentrated on Kether, so by now you are up to Gevurah—in that case, it will be the red Gevurah disk you are working with. Perhaps you began somewhere else in the Tree, so the disk you are making is for Chesed, Binah, Malkuth, or any other sephira.

TIME: 30–60 minutes

YOU WILL NEED: The appropriate colored disk (see page 69, "Creating the First Disk") and art materials such as colored pens and markers, paint, oil pastels, collage materials, stickers

Begin by remembering the time you have spent in this sephira, including reading through your journal notes, recalling any Kabbalah exercises, processes, or rituals you did and especially how these related to this particular sephira, as well as the general mood and events in your life during this time. By this fifth sephira you will probably have a feel for its position within the pillars, triads, and pairs of the Tree.

Allow images, words, feelings, and ideas to arise. You can hold these in your head, jot down notes or a sketch, or immediately begin work on your disk.

You can mark the name of the sephira onto the disk. You might write it in Hebrew or another language or several languages.

Decorate your disk. Use words in any way that seems good to you. You might draw or paint images, symbols, or a whole scene onto your disk. You can cover the whole or part of the disk with collage or natural items.

Your disk might reference other sephirot that are close by or in the same pillar or be complete within itself. It might contain a sense of the paths that connect it with other sephirot, an image of the Tree itself, or a reference to this sephira's position within the Tree. My disks are often very simple within the top triad and become increasingly complex as they descend through the Tree.

You might complete your work in one session or come back later to add to it.

examples of completed disks can be seen at janemeredith.com/disks

received caught held in a moment
the ladders glimpsed for the
rising, for the falling, in spirals,
helix, double spirals patterns
perfect and revealed the shapes
through darkness, backlit like
fire in the night stars burning all
consumed, all offered the sparks
tearing themselves apart within
the furnace of creation the crucible
flamed ignited breaking—

the wings of the butterfly close as
it plummets, falls through lava,
through passion crimson carmine
wine scarlet ruby garnet rose
geranium maroon madder jarrah
vermilion it blushes, falling as its
wings catch fire with color, falling
falling

6
Paths in the Tree

233

Tiferet

O nce the polarity dynamic has been addressed, a new balance arrives within the Tree. This takes the form of the sixth sephira, the most balanced of them all. Tiferet, named Beauty, is in the exact center of the Tree. It belongs to the central triad. It is in the middle pillar below Kether and the Abyss, seen as emanating the direct rays of Kether into the lower Tree. If we fold a diagram of the Tree in half horizontally, the fold will go through the center of this sephira. This also happens when we fold it in half vertically, so that we see a cross formed in the center of Tiferet—the center of the center, the crossroads at the heart of the Tree.

As this sixth sephira emerges, the paths connecting the sephirot to each other multiply. Of all the sephirot, Tiferet has the most paths: a total of eight. Until now paths have been practical ways of traveling from one sephira to another or directing flows of energy back and forth, up and down. At Tiferet paths begin to look like spokes of a wheel, threads in a spiderweb, or the rays of a sun. Before there was a clear and gradual progression, with each sephira neatly slotting into a relationship with the one before it, locking into triads and starting the pillars. When Tiferet-of-the-many-paths arrives, suddenly it looks as if everything is connected to everything else—that every thing is part of every other thing.

The whole map of the Tree does not get any more complex than this. It continues downward, unfolding itself in more or less logical progression, but now toward resolution rather than further complexity, completing the triads, pillars, and pairs. Tiferet holds the center of the web in the Tree, radiating paths in all directions and inviting multiplicity.

Tiferet: *Heart of the Tree*

Everything about Tiferet arises from its position at the center of the Tree. This sixth sephira redesigns the Tree—until now everything has been coming from Kether and flowing downward in various ways. Tiferet offers an alternative to that top-down model. Now we can see rays emanating out from a center like the hub and spokes of a wheel. Nearly half the wheel is yet to come, but even so, Tiferet with the top five of its paths drawn in looks like a rising sun. Although the Tree began with the middle pillar, by now both the other pillars have two sephirot, while only that problematic Da'ath space haunts the middle pillar, where we might have expected its second sephira to be. Then Tiferet arrives.

Ever since there was more than Kether, the Tree has looked to be in a state of becoming—something—and now with six sephirot, Tiferet at the bottom balancing the impossibility of Kether up top, it looks as if this has been achieved. Tiferet carries a sense of completion—even though, as it turns out, the Tree is far from complete. That's another resonance Tiferet has with Kether: that really the Tree could stop at this point (either of those points) and seem complete. Kether began the Tree, and Tiferet—directly below it and in the heart of the lower Tree—will begin a whole new stage, the parts of the Tree that we inhabit. Within Kabbalist literature and teaching, it's generally thought that we humans can only know or understand realms of the Tree up as far as Tiferet, at the highest, although this book of embodied Kabbalah takes a different slant.

Often called the Heart of the Tree, Tiferet is in the center of the diagram; it glows golden and is named Beauty. It's also connected to most other parts of the Tree, just as a human heart is connected and vital to the other parts of the body. There are less flattering views of this middle sephira—Grand Central Station was a name someone in one of my Kabbalah groups gave it. At Tiferet everything is arriving and everything is leaving via all these connecting paths. There's a sort of barely constrained busyness, rush, and even self-importance that comes with being so central, so crucial, to the operation of everything. Each of those surrounding sephirot—Kether, Binah, Gevurah, Hod, Yesod, Netzach, Chesed, and Hokmah—in fact, every sephira except for Malkuth—both feeds into and draws from this great pulsing heart of Tiferet.

If Tiferet is the heart of the Tree, it's a heart that's shattering open in all directions. If we drew the paths of Tiferet right into its center instead of stopping at the edges of the sephira, it would be splintered into eight segments. I think of kintsugi, the Japanese technique of repairing broken porcelain with seams of gold. This technique makes a mended item even more precious than the original unbroken version of itself; both metaphorically, with the rescuing of a precious object, and literally, with the addition of gold. The image of molten gold rivers mending the broken heart is evocative. In Kabbalah, where dualities coexist and even support each other, it's perfect that the center of the Tree would not just be connecting everything together but also shattering it apart. This shattering carries a reminder of Kether and the Big Bang, the beginnings of everything.

Tiferet's yellow color fits perfectly with the image of a sun, or the radiant center of the Tree, with the other sephirot as planets in orbit around it. Although we now know that our sun is not the center of the entire universe, still in effect it holds that role for us on Earth. Without the sun we would not exist. Our planet circles it, paying court and keeping its distance both at the same time. All of life pays homage to the warmth and light that feeds and bathes us unendingly, as far as we are concerned. If we raise our eyes beyond our local sun, we find myriad other suns, stars, unimaginably distant from us in the night sky. Seeing them we can perhaps conceive of a giant star explosion that birthed them all, scattering these shards about in the darkness, whose shining paths stretch outward in all directions. So in recognizing Tiferet as the beauty and grace that touches our human lives, we can cast our eyes further up the Tree, glimpsing other sephirot and guessing, theorizing, the existence of Kether.

Tiferet is sometimes depicted as the mystical rose, with the many petals, deep scent, and invitation that belong to a rose. It's also the rosy cross, the rose at the center of the Tree, that we get when we fold the image both horizontally and vertically. That intense potential of a tight bud waiting to unfurl… and then the first petals open. It comes into full blossom entirely itself, offering its heart and perfume to the world, exposed and luscious. Then the falling away of pollen, of petals, as it drops to earth and is even then still beautiful. That's Tiferet. Its beauty, the rose's petals representing the many paths, the invitation that lies at the heart of the Tree. Look upon beauty, breathe in beauty. Allowing each soul enough light in its life to unfurl, to blossom, to reveal the fullness of itself.

Tiferet completes the second (middle) triad with Chesed and Gevurah, a radiant resolution to the extreme polarity of those two sephirot. All that opposition and balance and extremes—and also this, the center point, where everything comes to rest and is completed. Whatever uncertainty may have been left hanging from the balancing act between Gevurah and Chesed is resolved here, at the downward triangle point of Tiferet. It holds the same position as Kether in the top triad, although completing instead of initiating the triad. The middle pillar's job is to balance everything. The Tree at this point is very neat: six sephirot, two in each pillar, forming two triads and all evenly arranged around a central mysterious space of Da'ath, the missing sephira. The nothing of Da'ath, or the specter of Knowledge, the reference point that is no reference point, is held within the six of Beauty, Mercy, Wisdom, Crown, Understanding, and Power.

The Star of David can be drawn through these six sephirot. This six-pointed star was recognized as a Jewish symbol long before being used by Nazi Germany as the token required on the clothing of Jews, making them instantly recognizable and visible targets within the deadly anti-Semitic regime. Like Tiferet, the color of this cloth badge was yellow. Like the shattering of Tiferet by its many paths, this particular use of the Star of David adds another layer of complexity to the star, a composite image that holds both the proud history of the Jews as a self-identified and identifiable people as well as the memory and warning of genocide, grief, and suffering experienced by Jewish people within Hitler's Germany and its conquered territories and countries. Like all symbols it has multiple interpretations that build and layer over time.

On the Tree of Life, the Star of David is composed of a downward-pointing triangle of Hokmah, Binah, and Tiferet bisecting an upward-pointing triangle of Chesed, Gevurah, and Kether. In this version of things, Chesed, Gevurah, and Kether are flowing up, heavenward, and piercing through veils—Chesed and Gevurah piercing through the Abyss with the help of Kether's upward pull, and Kether itself penetrating into the Ain Soph. Hokmah, Binah, and Tiferet are concerned with downward motion toward Malkuth, manifestation, and the evolution of the Tree. The Star of David combines opposites of above and below, heaven and earth. Once again Da'ath hovers at the center, and once again the complexity of this image overlays the already quite complex arrangement of the Tree. At Tiferet we have a cross, a rose, a sun, a star, a multitude of paths, and a second triad. We cannot hold on to a single image for Tiferet; it insists on multiplicity.

Tiferet holds the lowest point in the Tree so far, and thus another image that visually arises is that of a cup or bowl within which the essence of the higher sephirot arrive and are held. All of the sephirot are sometimes depicted as chalices, following Isaac Luria's story of the great shattering of vessels. Luria, from the 1500s, is one of Kabbalah's most famous figures; many of his teachings and stories changed forever the way Kabbalah was understood. He taught that the light which spilled from Kether into the lower vessels (sephirot) was too much for those below the supernal triad, and each of them shattered, scattering shards of light. There is much more to the story than this, including a continuing debate on whether this was or wasn't what brought evil into the world. Malkuth, as the final vessel, is said to be the only one of the lower seven not to shatter with this force of light.

When we attend to this concept of the shattering of the sephirot, there is a moment where each is whole and unbroken before breaking apart. So each has the experience of firstly containing the light, and then of being shattered by light. As the heart of the Tree, Tiferet especially demonstrates this great contradiction. Yes, it is whole and complete unto itself; yes, it receives the rain of bright sparks from above and contains them; and yes, it shatters into infinite pieces. Tiferet is both containment and receptivity, shattering and heartbreak.

We can allow this as a reflection of how our hearts are broken. Simply by accepting and welcoming the beauty that comes our way, we also must be torn apart by it—by the demands it makes on us and the grief and pain that come with its loss. Hopefully after loss, following repeated invitations of beauty in the world, we can open and give our hearts again, understanding that brokenness and loss are essential pieces of living. Relearning love after having one's heart broken is a hard, hard lesson. Perhaps the instinct becomes to close the heart, to protect oneself from ever going through that again. However, this also closes us off to allowing the life force to run freely through us, so eventually most of us open our hearts again, accepting that death, loss, and change come in to all lives.

The cracks, the breaks, are what allow fuller expression, as with the seams of gold mending broken porcelain. They would not be there if the item was still whole. The light—the gold, the yellow of Tiferet—is part of it now, the part that holds the shattered pieces together. We usually consider this as a personal thing—my heart, my love and pain, my breaks and mendings—but the Kabbalah is about more than our own lives, even the heights and depths of them. Tiferet is the heart of the world, the heart of the All that has been, is, and will be. Shattered by light and held together by light. Looking at the state of this world we are intrinsically a part of, how could our hearts not be breaking?

Suffering leads to compassion. Not just sympathy, being sad for another in their plight or for ourselves, but a heart-based feeling—perhaps it is love—that embraces suffering and the sufferer, holds space for and with it, not seeking to deny what is happening. Chesed is sometimes named loving-kindness, and this aspect of Tiferet is fed by that, as well as informed by Gevurah's discipline; a heartfelt acceptance as well as the ability to keep loving even while suffering. These things are not learned lightly. The broken heart can be closed, afraid, cautious—or it can be open, loving, free. When we are broken open by love, everything can flow through us.

This is beauty as a fragile, resilient, flowering heart that resides within the center of the Tree of Life. It has paths like seams of gold that hold each segment distinct and yet joined to the others. It's the moment of the full chalice breaking and spilling. It's a rose at the transient moment of perfection, it's the heart that weeps, breaks, and still loves. Tiferet is the place of gods who break and are broken, who die before their time or sacrifice themselves—Christ, Odin, Tammuz. It's a place of surrender and offering, where everything is released and yet, through that release, everything is held. It's a transition point from the bottom half of the Tree through to the top half—or the other way, the blessing of the top of the Tree as we descend to the realms we live within, earthbound.

Yesterday I walked a labyrinth. All these winding, nested paths, the turning back and forth, covering every inch of ground, and then—the center. The simplicity of being in the center after all that complexity. It reminded me of Tiferet. This labyrinth, on the land of the Gadigal people of the Eora Nation in Sydney's Centennial Park, is modeled after the Chartres Labyrinth in France, but with an unusual centerpiece. At the very center there's a circle, just as Tiferet is both a center in its own right, of the whole Tree, as well as referencing that original center of Kether. Around that is a ring, divided into four, with the divisions pointing into the four directions. Tiferet has paths in all directions and connects up to all four corners of the Tree. Around that are the classic six petals of the inner part of a Chartres-style labyrinth; Tiferet is the sixth sephira. Around all of that wrap the eleven circuits of paths, reminiscent of Tiferet's so-many paths. Eleven is also the number of the sephirot when we add Da'ath into the equation.

Where are we when we stand at the center of a labyrinth? What does it represent, and why is it considered healing to walk all the way along that layered path to arrive at this simplicity? Back at Kether, time and space barely existed. But beyond the Abyss, and by the advent of Tiferet, they certainly do. All of those paths—all those possibilities—of the labyrinth and Tiferet exist within a multiplicity. Yet I'm reminded of the refrain in "Zero," one of my favorite of Wendy Rule's songs: *All space is here, all time is now*. This is surely the center of the labyrinth, reminding us that the Big Bang happened—right here—and the only moment of time we truly have is this one, now. We are at the center of existence. This is always true (for everyone/everything and at every time), but a circle, and a labyrinth, reminds us. All space is here. All time is now.

There's a simplifying aspect to Tiferet in that everything arrives here; there's also the complexifying aspect that as rays of light, the paths, the inclinations toward becoming, all radiate out, everything gets increasingly further apart and increasingly differentiated and diverse. This was happening between Kether and Hokmah, or we could say between any of the sephirot, but it is Tiferet that invites the multiplicity. When we focus on Tiferet, we see all these things happening at once, not in a particular order. Yes, the lightning flash passes through Tiferet, as does the middle pillar; yes, there are paths heading in eight different directions; yes, the Tree folds in half through Tiferet to divide the top from the lower halves of the Tree—but that's all simultaneous, concurrent, and possibly of equal importance. Unlike when we begin at the top—or the bottom—of the Tree when an order is implied by our downward or upward motion, from the middle and radiating out there's no logical progression other than, like a heartbeat, it's pulsing, and everything's affected by it.

Our hearts, while we are alive, are relentless in their expansion-contraction; that's a condition of life. Kabbalistically this pulls in themes of the two outer pillars, which Tiferet rests between. The contraction, pulling everything in toward the middle pillar, holds the Tree together (so its disparate parts don't fly off to the distant ends of the universe), while the expansion keeps them far enough apart that the outer pillars don't just merge into the middle pillar. We yearn for union and court it endlessly, while throughout our lives we seek individual expression and experience. In different ages, cultures, and individuals, the balance between these two is set differently; and the ways each of us achieve this balance is different. In some cultures union is experienced with family, ancestors, and tradition, while within contemporary Western culture we primarily seek it through romance and consumerism. Individuality is highly prized in one place and time, and not at all in another. Still these opposite drives run through us; still our hearts beat, pulling us close to others with love and union and pushing us apart from each other as we follow the individual journeys of our lives.

If Tiferet is the heartbeat of the Tree, that makes the farthest reaches as crucially a part of its system as its closer-in parts. This is a whole-system simultaneous approach, as in those moments when we realize—not just intellectually but entirely—that the unique being of us, just a fleck in time and space, is met and matched by countless other equally unique beings and we all exist simultaneously, separately, and yet are inextricably part of the same thing. The parallel lives of generations through time or of humans alive in this moment or of ecosystems as they evolve and change or stars as they birth and die within explosions of light: each moment a Tiferet, the beating heart and the beauty of it—this force that we call love.

Hearts and the ♥ symbol are tied to romance and love in our popular culture. Yet, more deeply than that, hearts tie us to life. But we can't experience love without being alive. Kether, on its own, has to *be* love, as it is everything; but can it *experience* love? Surely it takes separation, and the existence of Hokmah, for love to be experienced. Thus before we were born or after we are dead, we may very well be part of love, belong to Love, be indivisible from it, but to actually experience love we have to be alive within individual lives. This is reminiscent of what we learned in Binah, with sleep or death rendering us indivisible from the All, where life and awakeness leave us separated. Tiferet continues the great work of the Tree, reminding us that at the heart of everything is our experience, not just of separation but also of union. Life as we are separated out from the All, and Love as we yearn for union again.

There's a lot happening in this Gordian knot at the center of Tiferet, fed from all directions and held so firmly and entirely within the Tree's paths and workings. Three words arise over and over again, three concepts woven together in many ways and places but most especially here, at the center of the Tree. Light. Love. Life. All begin with the letter L. The website hebrewtoday.com has this to say about L in Hebrew: "The Letter Lamed (ל). This letter is the tallest letter of the Hebrew alphabet. Since it stands taller than all the other letters, it represents royalty. In fact, it represents the King of all kings, the Almighty." It looks like a lightning flash. One might say there's a trace of Kether running through it.

The shape of the lowercase L in English—l—is also tall and straight enough to be the middle pillar itself—representing the journey from Kether all the way down, through Tiferet, into Malkuth. In Hebrew it doesn't quite do that, although according to walkingkabbalah.com, "The shape of the lammed is an undulating movement, and the lammed represents constant organic movement, constant change. Lammed is the lightning strike of energy descending down the two sides of the Tree of Life." Taking the overlap of English and Hebrew together—and why not? this is Kabbalah—we get the middle pillar overlaid with the lightning strike, beginning to look serpent- and staff-like, or even serpent- and tree-like. If we double the lammed, in mirror form we get something very like the caduceus double-snaking its way up the trunk of the Tree. In our world that's currently used as a symbol of healing and medicine. Mythically this interplay of images shows us the serpent within the Tree of Life, in the Garden of Eden, and the apple—in this case, the heart or the rose, Beauty—at the center of it. We could continue with this: roses and apples belong to the same family and symbolically can reference each other … Once we start layering symbols and meanings, the mysteries rise up, living, around us.

Love, life, and light. Of these, light is the only quantifiable force. Love is subjective, a felt emotion or interpretation. Although when we analyze it, it begins to look very like the impulse of the life force itself, that great inclination toward becoming. Life—we might think we have a clear idea of what it is and what it isn't, but we don't, really. If my body dies but millions of microorganisms continue living with and on this body, consuming parts of it and lending to their life, where's the dividing line exactly? How did life begin—wasn't it from non-life? How does that even make sense? Our concept of life has a localized meaning from a human perspective, but once we take it wider we begin to lose the edges of the definition. We talk about the life of a star or a solar system. And so many things—molecules, energy, chemicals—are moving back and forth between supposed living and supposed non-living things that it's very confusing on a micro level.

So it turns out I can't be definitive about light, although I know it is the inexplicable constant in our universe. I can't exactly or objectively define love, although we all experience it; and we also don't have a definition of life that holds up on close inspection, although we most definitely consider ourselves to be alive. To add to the confusion, *love*, *light*, and *life* are frequently conflated, or one is used to explain another, or they are used interchangeably. Within the Tree we place *light* in Kether. The aspect of light that we are calling *love* is found most utterly within Tiferet, having leapt across the impossible Abyss. That light/love is filtered down into the crucible of Yesod, and then to Malkuth, where we are well and truly full of this *life* thing, living as expressions of love, or light, grappling with philosophical, psychological, and emotional concepts of love as well as quantum physics and astro-scientific examinations of light.

Clearly we know next to nothing, but we do have this diagram of the Tree of Life, and to me it's suggesting—let's work with this. Let's begin imagining these three great forces—light, love, life—are dimensions of the one thing, and that they are more or less pure emanations of the All, of becoming, of the great leaning into existence. Were we to need or wish to distill them back to essence, we would be talking about that original light. Simply that. The light in the darkness, the Great Expansion, and the mystery of why darkness or even nothingness is not all there is, forever. How is there light at all? How love? How life? What are these things that we exist completely within?

Tiferet cannot be separate from the Tree; it is not discrete, entire-unto-itself. It is utterly of and within the Tree: it's made from it and makes it—as all the sephirot do, perhaps—but this one intrinsically, like a model for the others, to be so connected, so in the midst of emanating and receiving, to be the pulse, the throb of it, in motion, in moment; that's Tiferet. Its name, *Beauty*, is reassuring. Perhaps, for at least some of the time, we can stop asking how and what and why, and simply rest within this place, at the heart, the place of beauty. Golden and defying the dark, sending out messages in all directions regardless. Loving, offering, receiving; born into light and life and finding, choosing, being met with love, the life-long love affair of life itself, the opening, the breaking of it, the multiplicity.

Paths in the Tree of Life

One way to see the paths of the Tree is as rays of light. Certainly Kether is all light, light is the constant in the universe, and all the sephirot can be understood as emanations of different frequencies of light. Thus it would make sense that the paths linking them to each other are also made of light, and perhaps even the radiance coming off one sephira is what leads, path-like, to the next sephira. Rays of light, however, spread out once they've left their source; they diffuse through space. But the paths on the Tree don't spread out; that would make the whole map just a blur of light.

Or perhaps this does happen: there are particles of light everywhere, strengthened between the sephirot by the double direction of the paths, so making a path-like bridge of flecks of light to travel along. It would be like looking at the pathway between two stars—does that contain more light than the rest of the background? One can imagine that it does, and probably that pathway is the most direct and obvious way to travel between two stars... An amazing image on the web called "Kabbalah Memebrane Animation," created by P. L. Kopecky, shows what this might look like; see https://www.deviantart.com/plkopecky/art/Kabbalah-memebrane-animation-379410816.

Essentially, however, as we use the term, paths are contained at the edges. The idea of a path that blurs out forever and indistinctly merges with the general landscape isn't really a path. A path is a way that lies between places, and on the Tree paths are the way to get from one sephira to another. They are not shown as going into or through the centers of the sephirot—they stop as soon as they meet the edge—but that is their trajectory: from the center of one to the center of another.

There are various implications of using the word *path* rather than road, highway, canal, bridge, ladder, avenue, shipping lane, or all sorts of other ways that can be used to travel from one place to another. A path conveys the idea that we're traveling by foot, although it could also be a bike path or a bridle path. But it seems unlikely that we're on a large form of transport, such as a car, train, boat, bus, or plane. We are possibly alone, then, or at most with a few companions. Although concrete, brick, and wooden paths certainly exist, the word *path* hints at an earthen way, perhaps one that wanders across fields, over a hill through some trees, down by a river, possibly over a footbridge and continues, rarely in a ruler-straight line. A path has personality, gathered from the places it passes through, the terrain, the type of soil—clay, sandy, hard-packed, rocky—that it's made of: the *terroir* in French, the taste of the particular earth.

Paths are poetic in a way that roads rarely are. Paths are laid down over time and not necessarily permanent; if they're not in use, most of them would fade back into the forest, meadow, or landscape. Paths summon up a communion with nature: with hedges and with animals that use them, live nearby, or even created the paths. Paths are often quite narrow—even if there's only two of us we might still go in single file. Paths imply a journey—an adventure—and organic paths are never one way. We can travel along them in either direction or in both—first one way and then the return.

Sometimes one meets other travelers on these paths. Perhaps they are moving slower or faster than we are, and overtaking occurs. Or we've stopped for a rest or a picnic and they catch up to us. Commonly we meet travelers coming from the opposite direction, at which point we might exchange news. *What's the path like up ahead? How long did it take you? Does it get muddier than this?* Or maybe we just pass them by, but in Australia we'd meet their eyes and say hello or nod at the very least, acknowledging this camaraderie, this sharing and choosing the same journey. We might even pass the same people several times as we overtake each other in turns, meet at rest points, or pass each other in both directions, so that they will come to seem like companions on the path.

Paths have often been associated with magic. In Greek mythology there's a path, or paths, that lead into the Underworld, as well as the path through the labyrinth on Crete, where the minotaur lives. There's magic's left-hand path—and presumably the right-hand path as well—and they correspond interestingly to the Kabbalah's right- and left-hand pillars, with the left-hand path being the sinister—certainly in the original and possibly also the later meaning of the word—secretive, inner one, and the right-hand path being the bright, bold, daytime magic. There's Tao's middle way—called a way rather than a path, but it sounds very path-like to me—straight up the middle pillar, no doubt, feeling and balancing the energies of right and left, mercy and judgment all the way, but falling to neither side. Think of all those paths in magical literature—Frodo's path to Mordor in *The Lord of the Rings*, the path through the whispering woods that leads Enid Blyton's characters to the Magic Faraway Tree, and the paths in fairy tales: little Vasalisa treading through the forest to Baba Yaga's hut, Hansel and

Gretel's doomed path of breadcrumbs, Gerda's path through the four seasons in *The Snow Queen,* and the path of moonlight over the ocean that various characters miraculously tread.

All of these paths have to be walked on foot. Paths are like pilgrimages. When we apply this to the Tree of Life, maybe we learn that paths are a journey in themselves, not an instant transit system. That is, labor is required to pass along them from one end to the other. Energy must be expended. We don't just press a button or hop on a convenient mode of psychic transport and arrive at the other end. What, then, is this labor that's required to travel the Kabbalistic paths? And is it the same in one direction as the other? Looking at worldly or even mythic paths, we can say definitely not. A path might be uphill, meaning that to travel back is downhill, for instance. Think of Vasalisa, sent trembling into the dark forest to steal fire from Baba Yaga or returning triumphant with a burning skull! The classic hero's journey always entails growth, maturity, and some type of initiation before the return journey.

So does this resonate with our paths on the Tree? Absolutely. One could even say that the level of mindfulness and the integrity one brings to the path will result in what type of destination we reach—or our ability to understand it and participate in its magics. Because one can arrive at a destination prepared for what might be there or not. There is an argument to be made that we can never fully prepare for the unknown; however, when we have done the preparatory work, we are much more able to understand what's going on, take in what is offered, and benefit from our experiences. Paths in the Tree are the networks, almost the veins, that join the sephirot to each other, so they are shaped by the sephirot at either end. Just as the way a path between a pine forest and a beach will be sandy at one end and have a lot of pine needles at the other end and in between will go through a series of transitions, our paths between two of the sephirot will be distinctly flavored at each end while experiencing some melding, mixing, and cross-pollination in the middle.

The most common form of examining Kabbalistic paths is following the Golden Dawn's assignment of thirty-two paths, which is what I have done here. They name each of the sephirot as a path—numbers one through ten—and then the actual paths that link the sephirot are numbered eleven through thirty-two. Each of those twenty-two

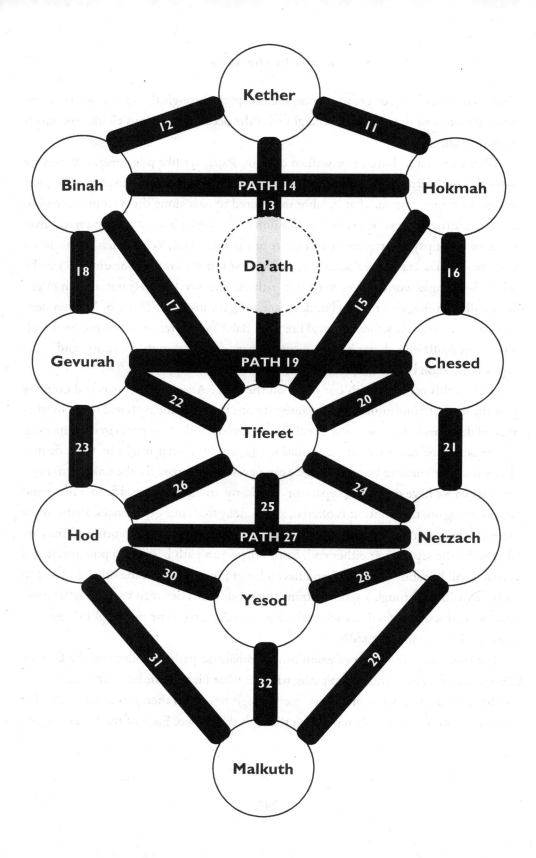

paths is guided or informed by a letter of the Hebrew alphabet, and in the Golden Dawn system also assigned one of the tarot cards from the Major Arcana. We will look at the tarot associations in the next section. For understanding the letters of the Hebrew alphabet and their resonance with each path, I recommend Rachel Pollack's *The Kabbalah Tree* (Pollack 2005, 136–156). An irreverent, hilarious, but incisive commentary of the Hebrew letters for the paths can be found in *The Chicken Qabalah* by Lon Milo Duquette (Duquette 2001, 44–65).

Path 11: Kether to Hokmah

This path holds the experience of leaving Kether and the first segment of the lightning flash. Presumably this path came into existence on the instance with Hokmah, resulting in a space or time that lies between the two sephirot, which this path facilitates. If we travel from Kether to Hokmah, we are leaving the origins of everything to discover whatever occurs past that. In the other direction, Hokmah to Kether, we are releasing the last pieces of individuality to move into the great Oneness, the All. This path feels narrow and precise.

Path 12: Kether to Binah

This is the second path, so by now we know that paths are a thing the Tree does or that we do while in the Tree. This path could be seen as a back way because mostly we concentrate on Kether's connection to Hokmah or to Tiferet. Kether to Binah seems immediately less romantic and tragic, more focused on productivity than Kether to Hokmah. What will happen after the Big Bang? Where are we going now? The other direction, Binah to Kether, also seems like a shortcut: the Great Mother folds us all into the hands of death, the dark cave that leads to unending light.

Path 13: Kether to Tiferet

This path leads straight across the Abyss, laying claim to the division within the Tree: from the strongest of emanations in the upper Tree to the strongest of emanations in the lower. The path seems to defy space and time as it travels over or possibly through a black hole, an empty space, dark energy—and it's the longest path in the whole Tree, long enough for two normal paths. Kether to Tiferet is the descent of heaven into—if not earth itself, at least the realm of earth, like the journey between the Big Bang and the existence of our own sun. The reverse path, Tiferet to Kether, feels like the path of utter surrender—perhaps to death, initiation, or the divine—as it passes through or over Da'ath.

Path 14: Hokmah to Binah

This path, a segment of the lightning flash, links these two powerful sephirot together. One could even say they are the most powerful, as even though Kether is All and everything, it actually does nothing except exist, and it's not a state where one can do anything. The Hokmah to Binah path channels force into form for the very first time—a concept becomes a reality, or, more accurately, this far up the Tree, the possibility of concept becomes the possibility of reality. In the other direction, Binah to Hokmah, what has been form or the idea of form dissolves into its essence so that it might reunite with the All, toward the direction of Kether.

Path 15: Hokmah to Tiferet

Cutting down on an angle through the Abyss from the right into the middle pillar, this path brings Hokmah's wisdom—that original separation, loss, desire, and passion—directly into the heart of the Tree without going through the tempering that following the lightning flash brings. It's an arrow to the heart, piercing, an invitation to discard the veils of illusion and reside in truth. In the other direction, Tiferet to Hokmah, there's a passing of the beauty and fullness of the lower Tree up into the top triad, where it can blaze forth unrestrained.

Path 16: Hokmah to Chesed

Directly down the first segment of the right-hand pillar, this path is powerful and straightforward. It crosses the Abyss and thus includes a transmutation from the ethereal, untouchable top triad into aspects of the world we know. All that is Hokmah is distilled and passed into the place where it can emanate out into the world, through Chesed and its endless pouring forth. In the opposite direction, Chesed to Hokmah, there's a stripping away of all that has been and surrender into the infinite.

Path 17: Binah to Tiferet

Another angled path, again crossing the Abyss and bringing a strong nurturing energy from Binah into Tiferet—a balance to the mystical surrender that Hokmah offered. This path could be seen as crossing very directly from the dark to the light—Binah's dark cave to Tiferet's bright sun—and as such this path moderates and informs that blazing sun, underwriting it with subtleties and sensitivity. In the other direction, Tiferet to Binah, the path is a ray of light, penetrating into the deep mysteries of Binah, the generative force.

Path 18: Binah to Gevurah

This path is the top section of the left-hand pillar, descending from the top triad, across the Abyss, and into form. The swirling mass of Binah—stars forming, atoms enriching, cells growing into being—is rendered comprehensible in Gevurah, which immediately begins limiting, governing, and winnowing so that forms can arise. In the other direction, Gevurah to Binah, precision and complexity are rendered or dissolved back into the essences of form, the parts and pieces randomized again, perhaps by passing through the Abyss, into a great soup of potential.

Path 19: Chesed to Gevurah

A solid building block of the Tree, this path is the center one of the three horizontal bars in the lightning flash. The path braces these two powerful sephirot, both drawing them together and holding them apart. The feeling is one of deep trust, as from Chesed to Gevurah everything that has been realized from the top triad is passed across as a flow in order to be chopped apart. In the other direction, Gevurah to Chesed, all these beautiful and precise forms that have existed travel into a realm where they dissolve into pure force.

Path 20: Chesed to Tiferet

This close and intimate path—from mercy to beauty—feels like a delight to travel along. In one direction, Chesed's pure force gets distilled into the more gentle radiance of Tiferet's love and beauty. There's a worthiness in Chesed that's missing in Tiferet, which seems so the-center-of-things, though both are involved in the functioning of the

Tree that all sephirot are in deep service to. In the other direction, Tiferet to Chesed, we can see the relinquishment of balance, a willing surrender back toward the All.

Path 21: Chesed to Netzach

The second, and final, section of the right-hand pillar is this path from Chesed to Netzach. There's a further distillation and clarification occurring but also a release as the perfection of Chesed pours down into the immense complexity and experimentation of Netzach. Force explodes into endless possibilities. In the other direction, Netzach to Chesed, there's a discipline imposed, a refinement, as the multitude of possibilities find their way back to their common roots and diffusion resolves itself into clarity.

Path 22: Gevurah to Tiferet

Another short angled path, this one feeding the warrior spirit into the heart of the Tree as part of the lightning flash. The ferocity of Gevurah travels into the beauty of Tiferet and bolsters it, offers an inner strength to withstand and remain pure. This path reminds me of romantic stories of the Knights Templar: *Here will be the defenders of the kingdom of righteousness.* Tiferet to Gevurah, in the opposite direction, brings a heart and warmth into the precision and what might be, but for tempering influences, the ruthlessness of Gevurah.

Path 23: Gevurah to Hod

This path forms the second and final segment of the left-hand pillar and so locks the evolution of form firmly into place. Form came into potential in the swirling of Binah; passed through a stage of testing, precision, and boundaries in Gevurah; and reaches its full expression in Hod. Gevurah to Hod is as if an architect handed the blueprints of a building to the builder: all the practical necessities will now be evaluated and calculated. In the other direction, Hod to Gevurah, the minutiae fall away as we arrive at the grand vision of what is to be.

Path 24: Tiferet to Netzach

One of the rays of Tiferet and part of the lightning flash, this path linking the middle pillar with the bottom of the right-hand pillar is a bursting excitement of beauty—in Tiferet we are still modest, somewhat contained and rational, but in Netzach it's nothing barred. Like the bud to the flower, all unfurls. In the other direction, Netzach to Tiferet, there's a refinement of purpose and focus; the path narrows but not excessively. What has been a wild abandoned beauty steadies itself, perhaps to resound more deeply.

Path 25: Tiferet to Yesod

The path from Tiferet to Yesod drops down toward the lowest part of the Tree. It's on the middle pillar, still bringing the essence of Kether strongly through, even though it's been distilled by Tiferet and altered by its journey across the Abyss. Radiance pours down to light up the murkier, hidden realms of Yesod; thus we recall moments of insight and clarity that we receive in dreams, visions, and our spiritual and creative practices. In the other direction, from Yesod to Tiferet, there's a surrender typical of this upward movement through the Tree: specifically, a surrender from complexity into purer, simpler concepts.

Path 26: Tiferet to Hod

Another ray from Tiferet, this time out to the bottom of the left-hand pillar. The Tiferet to Hod path brings beauty and grace into what could be rigid systems. I'm thinking of the beauty of clockwork, the grace of the elemental table, or the way languages take on their own characters, and how each of the petals on a flower will be just slightly different. In the other direction, Hod to Tiferet, beauty is informed by precision—yes, each petal is different, but only within certain parameters, saving the whole thing to remain true to its form.

Path 27: Netzach to Hod

The final of the three horizontal paths in the Tree that all are part of the lightning flash, this path braces the lower part of the Tree, allowing the pendulum of Yesod and Malkuth to swing below it. Netzach and Hod are a close pair, perhaps the closest; thus the path between them is both tight and one of extremes. The grandeur, impossibility, and variance of Netzach narrows quickly to the precision, perfection, and exactitude of Hod. In the other direction, the tightness of Hod relaxes into the generosity of Netzach. This intimate and constant exchange between force and form moves quickly, like the shuttle on a weaver's loom.

Path 28: Netzach to Yesod

This path brings the wildness and chaos of Netzach into the unconscious, our dreams and visions, and the potential of this world. These might be divinely inspired moments: events or visions that lift us completely beyond our usual dreams and imaginings, as when we pierce through the veil of illusion to recognize the immense impossibility and complexity we are contained within. In the other direction, Yesod to Netzach, we have an opportunity to seed our most powerful imaginings or creations into the collective unconscious as future potentialities for the unfolding of time and fate.

Path 29: Netzach to Malkuth

A long outside path, not always included in lists or diagrams of paths, the path from Netzach to Malkuth drops a direct line into our world from the right-hand pillar. Forces we can barely understand or not directly perceive shape us and our world, and sometimes we catch a glimpse of them. In the other direction, Malkuth to Netzach, the reality of what must be lived in some way tempers or informs the excesses of Netzach, perhaps reminding it of purpose and outcome.

Path 30: Hod to Yesod

The left-hand pillar, via Hod, feeds into Yesod along this path as part of the lightning flash, imposing form and thus meaning into its dreamlike realms. Taken literally, perhaps this path means that however wild our nighttime dreams may be, usually they occur in a language we understand, with objects or places that are familiar, or at least comprehensible to us. In the other direction, Yesod to Hod, the edges are pushed and rigid boundaries questioned and perhaps sometimes expanded, rewritten, or more deeply understood, thus adding to Hod's complexity.

Path 31: Hod to Malkuth

The second equally long outside path, also not always included in diagrams of the Tree, this path from Hod to Malkuth brings the influence and powers of the left-hand pillar directly down to the bottom of the Tree. Form is imposed, not arbitrarily but according to divine systems that create and order matter, mass, light, and time. In the other direction, Malkuth to Hod, the living world informs the systems that seek to define and understand it.

Path 32: Yesod to Malkuth

For humans, the path from Yesod to Malkuth is probably the most important and certainly the most immediate path. This is the final segment of the lightning flash. On some versions of the Tree, this is the only path that connects Malkuth to the rest of the Tree, and following the lightning flash this is the path that channels the distillation of all that has been down into the world we inhabit. From Malkuth to Yesod all that exists in the manifest world—its information, energy patterns, and experience—is fed into the Tree via this path. All of our inner journeyings, our reaching out to the divine, our access to the collective unconscious, and our participation in the mythos occur as we travel from Malkuth to Yesod, which operates as our bridge into the entire Tree.

Path of the Lightning Flash

The lightning flash can be seen as a series of linked paths, one of which—across the Abyss—is a path that exists only within the lightning flash (see illustration on page 12). The lightning flash can be seen as one long continuous path that passes through every sephira. In the downward direction it travels from Kether to Hokmah to Binah, then across the Abyss and through Da'ath on the diagonal to Chesed, across to Gevurah, on a long descending diagonal to Tiferet and Netzach, then across to Hod, down to Yesod, and finally straight down to Malkuth. In this direction it brings the essence of the Great Above all the way into the Great Below.

But the lightning flash also travels upward, originating in Malkuth. In this direction it looks like the soul ascending back into the realms of the infinite—material substance dissolving back into the atoms that created it. If you watch a slowed-down video of a lightning flash, it has a gradual branching-downward motion, but once it connects to earth there's a strong, direct return back up to the cloud when it flashes, which is what our eyes pick up, although it's so fast we can't track the upward movement.

The zigzag motion of the lightning flash in the Tree of Life, as well as the way it elegantly links all the sephirot into one line or movement, adds a certain zap and flash to paths in the Tree, distinct from staid pillars or sturdy crossbars. The lightning flash promises speed and excitement: it's the shortcut through the Tree rather than the scenic route plodding along through pillars, pairs, and triads. Once we have done the solid work of learning individual sephirot and paths, the lightning flash is attractive;

otherwise, it's like being on a very fast train, with the countryside flashing past too quickly to be properly seen. But if we know the terrain we're passing through, if glimpses of it remind us of rich experiences and journeys we've previously taken, and even offer hints of future delights or experiences we might have at some other time, then it's a thrill and a fast way to get where we're going.

The lightning flash is not a formal Kabbalistic path; it's the not-so-secret shortcut, away from the signed paths, cutting corners and slipping through fences. Its emphasis is on the entire length of it, not the individual segments. Nonetheless, when we use the term *paths* as meaning a way to get from one place to another, the lightning flash qualifies. It's certainly a way to get from one place to another within the Tree. I'm reminded of Enid Blyton's Magic Faraway Tree (in the book of the same name) and the character Moonface's slippery-slip, a hidden slippery-dip or path actually inside the trunk of the tree that spiraled from the very top all the way to the bottom.

Of course the slippery-slip was mainly a downward path—or at any rate, that was the usual direction. Once when the tree was besieged with angry elves, Moonface let a rope down through the slippery-slip and the children climbed all the way up it in the dark. Perhaps Blyton's onto something here—heading down the Tree of Life can be so rapid we barely know what's happening, though it's a thrilling ride. Heading upward, however, is laborious work, hand-over-hand in the dark, and we're not quite sure what will meet us at the top.

The Narrow Path

There's a concept I know as *the narrow path*; perhaps you know it by another term. Maybe it's also the path of righteousness or the holy way or the Tao's middle path, but I learned it as the narrow path.

Each time we are faced with a decision or set of choices, if we apply our values and all that we know, and if we ask to stay true, to be of service, and behave in alignment with our deepest understandings, we take a metaphoric step forward. When we begin bringing our awareness to this process, the choices and possible paths can seem overwhelming, as if we could branch off in many different directions. But the more we do the work and make our choices accordingly, the narrower our band of choices becomes—or the further we have traveled from the extraneous and default settings that throw us off course. Something happens, anyway. The path starts narrowing. We are faced with a dilemma or a choice and there appear to be only a few options, and possibly even most of them we know we won't accept. Soon enough there's really only one choice—sometimes a hard one—but we feel the pull of it, it's right in front of us, and...well, by now we're on the narrow path.

There's not much straying to either side. We take the next step. Things continue to simplify, to provide their own answers—our answers, cleared from the detritus of whatever-it-was we cluttered our lives up with beforehand—and the path gets simpler and simpler to traverse. Not easier, necessarily, except in the decision-making arena. But clearer, cleaner. Faster. Narrower.

No one else is on this exact same narrow path—it's our own path. Maybe that's what makes it easier: it's so deeply recognizable. The narrow path is like having your soul singing to you and you're singing back, taking each step.

Strictly speaking, the narrow path isn't a path on the Kabbalistic Tree of Life. On the other hand, in a very Kabbalistic way, it's exactly what it's all about.

process | Creating Path Sentences

There are books with whole pages devoted to each path of the Tree of Life. In the previous section you can find a paragraph for each of the paths, but it's a beautiful exercise to create your own path descriptions—one brief sentence for each path in each direction. I prefer these to lengthier descriptions as they distill in a poetic style something of the essence between these two sephirot and what it means to travel between them. These path sentences don't rely on our knowledge or the tarot or other references or any expectations we may have of what we think a path should mean; they rely purely on our experience of what is alive for us in that moment on that path.

The idea is to do this exercise twice—once in each direction through the Tree— upward and downward. If you're working with others, you can split it up so each of you do some of the sentences. This creates a beautiful group resonance, especially when you split up the different directions; so, for example, I might be writing the downward-path sentences and my friend be writing the upward-path sentences. They can sound call-and-response-like when read aloud.

You can do this exercise without getting up from your desk, but for its fullest expression I recommend laying out your disks on the floor and walking the paths, pen and journal in hand. You can do the exercise now, while studying paths in the Tree, but also after you have completed your work with all ten sephirot; it will be even richer then. It's different each time we walk the paths.

TIME: Allow 30 minutes for each direction

YOU WILL NEED: Your disks or a map of the Tree; your journal and pen

Lay out your disks on the floor or otherwise draw a map of the Tree, adding in lines for the paths.

Choose a direction to begin with either starting at Kether heading downward or starting at Malkuth and heading up.

Physically stand at the sephira or put your pen on that part of the page. Take a few moments to ground yourself, then allow your relationship to that sephira to arise within you.

Take a step onto, or next to, the sephira and look at the first path and the sephira it leads to—all the paths are listed in order below, though you don't need to walk them in this exact order.

Letting out a breath, walk the path slowly or move your pen along the page between the two sephirot. Let some words arise; speak them aloud. Allow them to be in the first person and present tense. If the sentence seems too long or not precise enough, refine it a little. As you arrive at the sephira you were heading toward, review the sentence. Does it summon some of your emotional response to this path? Does it make sense to you, resonate with your ideas and knowings of these two sephirot? It may be surprising or unexpected but still should hold that resonance of your empathy with the path between these two sephirot.

Write it down. Then draw a breath and turn to the next path.

SAMPLE SENTENCES

Tiferet to Netzach: *Rays of sunlight reach through the worlds to you.*

Gevurah to Chesed: *I bring walls to contain your boundlessness.*

Malkuth to Yesod: *Every detail is released toward the numinous.*

Kether to Tiferet: *This is the arrow of light to the heart.*

Tiferet to Kether: *I send love and beauty into the ever-burning spirit.*

Tiferet to Gevurah: *I receive your strength as a gift.*

Tiferet to Yesod: *I transform myself in service to the dream.*

PATHS IN ORDER

Kether to Hokmah/Hokmah to Kether

Kether to Binah/Binah to Kether

Kether to Tiferet/Tiferet to Kether

Hokmah to Binah/Binah to Hokmah

Hokmah to Tiferet/Tiferet to Hokmah

Hokmah to Chesed/Chesed to Hokmah

Binah to Tiferet/Tiferet to Binah

Binah to Gevurah/Gevurah to Binah

Chesed to Gevurah/Gevurah to Chesed

Chesed to Tiferet/Tiferet to Chesed

Chesed to Netzach/Netzach to Chesed

Gevurah to Tiferet/Tiferet to Gevurah

Gevurah to Hod/Hod to Gevurah

Tiferet to Netzach/Netzach to Tiferet

Tiferet to Yesod/Yesod to Tiferet

Tiferet to Hod/Hod to Tiferet

Netzach to Hod/Hod to Netzach

Netzach to Yesod/Yesod to Netzach

Netzach to Malkuth/Malkuth to Netzach

Hod to Yesod/Yesod to Hod

Hod to Malkuth/Malkuth to Hod

Yesod to Malkuth/Malkuth to Yesod

After your path sentences are written, read back over them and make any edits you feel are needed.

When you've created path sentences for both directions in the Tree, there are a couple things you can do:

- On a large map of the Tree, you can write the sentences along the paths so the words actually form the paths in each direction.
- You might include some of the sentences on your disks.
- You can also read the sentences aloud and even record them to play back later, during a meditation on the Tree. So your reading would be like this: *Kether to Hokmah—light extends forever. Hokmah to Kether—this is the journey home. Kether to Binah—I unfurl into worlds. Binah to Kether—infinite variety returns to the infinite*, and so on.

trance | Path Journey

In the Tree of Life the sephirot are usually considered the main game. The paths exist essentially to connect the sephirot together, sometimes in various shapes or patterns, such as triads or pillars, and sometimes because we want to get from one place to another. If we're traveling from Kether to Malkuth, for instance, we don't take a helicopter out of Kether, skipping over everything else until we reach our destination; we take paths to travel there—perhaps down the middle pillar or along the lightning flash or some other, more obscure, back roads.

But each path is a landscape rich and nuanced in itself. If these paths were in the real world—maybe country roads, possibly winding up mountains or lingering around a lake—those journeys would be full of experiences. If they were pathways—boardwalks over mangrove swamps, cliff-top paths, a canal tow path, a narrow track across a high plateau, a path set by stars across a desert at night or compass-led over an ocean—they'd be so bursting with sounds, sights, smells, and complex, shifting territories that they'd be at least as interesting as the place we left from or the place we arrived at.

There are a lot of paths in the Tree of Life. This could take some time, if we were to do it thoroughly. Perhaps, instead, we'll be like a visitor turning up to a National Park and studying the map ... Oh, there's a day hike departing from here, but I'm not really equipped for that. A gentle twenty-minute stroll by the creek ... probably I can be more adventurous than that. One of the paths closed by rockfalls—avoid that. Oh look! Here's a challenging-in-parts, medium-grade, two- to three-hour walk with amazing views, with a lake and a forest along the way. That looks perfect. To translate that into the Tree: What intrigues and potentially delights you? It might beckon with delight (Tiferet to Netzach), shimmer with a deep mystery (Yesod to Malkuth), or intrigue with an as-yet-unknown dynamic (Kether to Binah).

When you've tried this path exploration once, you can continue it with other paths, including some intrepid exploring and also gentle strolls through fields of delights or questing for the more closely guarded mysteries that lie among these networks. It's most effective when exploring the connection between two sephirot that you already have some understanding of.

There are several ways of exploring. You can trance, physically walking or sitting within the Tree of your disks. You can trance or do automatic writing with just your journal. And, my favorite way, you can explore your chosen path out in the world, where you take an ordinary walk—for example, between your house and the local park, the office to the lunch shop, or as you walk the dog.

The exercise given here is as if the journey were done solely within the mind, but feel free to adapt it to the other methods. Keep in mind that when one is outside, walking either in bush or along roadways, only a very light trance state can be safely entered.

TIME: 30 minutes

YOU WILL NEED: Journal and pen, coloring things optional, disks optional

Settle yourself to begin trance work.

Choose a path to explore. Perhaps you will be guided by your intuition or you could use divination or perhaps you are setting out to resolve a question you've had for a while.

Breathe for a moment or two and let yourself find or create your intention. Perhaps this will simply be *to explore* or it may be more specific, such as *to discover how the expansion of Netzach becomes the order of Hod*, or it may be personal, for example: *to travel the path from Tiferet to Gevurah to learn about practicing self-care*.

Begin at the sephira you are setting out from. Orient yourself there, perhaps spending a few moments feeling into the color, images, words, and associations you have for this sephira.

Then locate the beginning of the path. You might visualize this, feel it inside yourself, or speak aloud or silently. Perhaps you will feel the energy of the sephira on the far side of this path or name that destination or just know that if you head out in this direction, that is where you will end up.

When you begin traveling along the path, let yourself move slowly. Open to or inquire about what sights, feelings, and experiences lie along this path. You might like to think of this in terms of geographical features or questions provoked; you might notice physical sensations in your body or have memories or thoughts arise. I allow for moments of whatever arises, as well as asking myself questions: *What can I see? What emotions am I experiencing? If this were a landscape, what landscape would it be?*

As you travel along the path, notice how it is changing. How does the mix of sephiric influences blend and change as you move further away from your starting point? Your inner landscape might be changing from early morning through to afternoon; perhaps you have left a temple for the wilderness that surrounds it; maybe you have shifted from feeling comfortable to feeling challenged. Perhaps the path has become rocky, steep, broad, or sheltered. Let your attention be drawn to different aspects of this experience as you continue traveling.

One could spend an infinite time exploring each path; however, this exercise is set at around twenty minutes. As that time approaches, bring yourself right up to your destination sephira. Notice how the entry point seems to you, between the path and sephira itself. Are you facing a door? Just a seamless transition from path to sephira? What are the characteristics of this juncture?

Once you've arrived, breathe for a moment or two with this sephira before gently bringing your attention back to your physical body and surroundings.

Make sure to journal your discoveries, questions, and path. What did you learn? You might want to draw your experience of the path like a map, with the different features and your questions recorded on it. This can give you a starting point for further exploration of this path, possibly in the opposite direction, and also offer a deeper glimpse into the two sephirot you've journeyed between, as well as how this particular path functions.

Memoir: *The Open Heart*

I am in Paris. Paris where I once was with my beloved, the one whose ring I've dropped into the Vézère and Dordogne Rivers. He sang me songs of love on a bridge over the Seine; that was still two years before he left me. Paris, in France, land of my mother's ancestors. Paris, where I was when my mother died, when I heard the news of her death. I went to Notre Dame, the cathedral built on an island in the middle of the river and lit a candle for her, a burning gold flame among hundreds of others. Paris, a city to take your heart and break your heart, city of jewels, of the night, of love, of lights. The city of light. I am in Paris and deep in the Kabbalah, immersed, drowning in Tiferet with my longings that aren't met in the world and I'm full, bursting, flowering but unseen, still invisible. If there's anywhere I can break through, surely it's here.

I'm in a little apartment—originally a stable. There's an entry level with room to sit, a tiny kitchenette and a toilet. In the middle of that petite space are stairs, with a shower off the landing, a few more stairs and then another level, with a clear Perspex floor so you can see down. There's a desk and another half dozen steps to a loft bed over the shower. It all works like a small miracle—only just, but I adore it. *J'adore.* It's in a row of stables, repurposed, off a passageway closed off from the street. The residents have filled the passage, both sides, with potted plants and trees and herbs, making a narrow garden, one could say a walled garden, with doors and windows placed along it so everyone looks out and down into this hidden greenery.

I've spent a month with Tiferet and I'm due to move on further into the Tree, to Netzach, but I want to do magic first. I want something to change. Not just within me but in the way the world meets me. To create a shift and surely Paris and the heart of the Tree is the perfect setting. The heart of the Tree in the city of light. I've always been shy, cautious, careful; even though I burn within, I rarely show it on the outside. It comes out in ritual, in writing, in love, but I don't wear it like an aura in the world. Surely now it's time, but I don't know how to bring it through and yet the gold in the seams of Tiferet, the broken heart, the open heart, whispers to me.

There was a man in Rome, the one with the shoulder blades. I'd seen him before, at a festival, and written him off as a surfing type; all tanned skin, blond, fit and careless, laughing at the world. Wearing his youth like a right. He turned out to be my group leader at the intensive—how could it be any other way? So I got to watch him close up. He's bright and fierce, like a lion with his coloring gold and burnished. From the very beginning I was confronted by the way he threw himself into processes, whole-hearted and clear, transparent as you could ask. I watched the amount of labor he did—not glamorous, noticeable, or profound, just hours of lugging mattresses and fiddling with sound systems and at everyone's beck and call; he's of service. Strong and putting his strength to use. Untiring and unstinting. Even though I saw him doing more than most people, I never saw him rushed, it never feels like he's rushing. The moments I talk with him I have all his attention—one hundred percent, maybe one hundred and ten percent.

Through the days he was incredibly present for each person in our small group, exactly in the moment they needed it most. One of his default looks is slight bore-dom—as if the world doesn't quite hold his interest—but I watched it flip, again and again, when someone was in a deep moment of vulnerability, revelation, or need. He flings himself in there as if this were the person he loved most in the world. It seems in that moment that they are. Each person. I saw him again and again with people who irritate me, who I avoided for their clinginess or awkwardness, and he just fronts up, radiating presence and joy, and relates to them softly—he's so much softer than me. He's a lesson to me. He's utterly beautiful by every standard one could think of and seems to have no judgment at all, no reservations about those who are older, less beautiful, brittle, hurting, afraid. He didn't bring himself into interactions as a teacher but just as a human presence, simply.

I always noticed him, first in and then curiosity, then awe: this man who gazed on me like I was a painting, whose shoulder blades reminded me of angels. Now I'm seeking Tiferet magic, the heart of the Tree, to shine golden like that, through and through, not to be afraid of the breaks that show but trust those seams of gold that mend me. Take him as an inspiration of how to live in the heart, how to let the radiance through. Let it infuse me and blossom, flower within and pour out, find the turnaround to the open heart. Tiferet magic in Paris, in this tiny apartment I love so much.

I have my disks with me, and late at night I lay them out on the only floor that has room for them, the mid-level see-through floor, so they hover there, already between worlds. They take up the whole floor, there's nowhere to be but within the Tree, there's not room for me at the top or bottom or sides. I have to be within it. I'm traveling with just a small case and search through my belongings. I find three tealights, exactly; one red, one blue, one yellow. I put them on the disks, red on Gevurah, blue on Chesed, and yellow on Tiferet. Perfect; I am doing triad magic. This is the path I have just come down: a month in Chesed, a month in Gevurah, and now my month in Tiferet, ending tonight with this spell that I haven't quite created yet, a spell to open the path to Netzach.

I lay out little tokens for Freyja, Eve, Aphrodite on the Tiferet disk and then I start singing and humming, rocking back and forth, and I ask the Tree to take me in. I cast a circle, circles within circles: Paris, the see-through middle floor room with the walled garden, the Tree, Tiferet. I light the candles: blue, red, yellow, and they burn. The night shimmers about me and I feel on the edge of something, great things even, and I take a pen and write and write across a page in my journal, all my wishes. Then I write over the writing again, sideways, the yearning, the tearing-apart seams of me, and then diagonally over those words another layer, pouring out in passion all my longing the depth the intensity of it *oh take me in open with me show me let me be revealed to it, change I want change whatever it takes*—the words now dense and matted on the page, unreadable except in spell language, and I take up the candle and drip wax over them, sealing them in yellow drops and it gets everywhere, on the see-through floor, on the Tiferet disk, on my hands and pen and I don't care I'm burning now in this intensity and I sit and study the map of disks; I hover over it I loom and I see but don't see—what's happening—why can't I change it? I'm an hour or more into this ritual and still it feels like work, not that it's come alive. Tiferet is the heart and I'm in the heart and then I see.

I'm calling and calling for lovers, to be within that field of the heart and sensuality, to find these people, draw them to me, discover them. Within the Tree each of us is utterly the beloved, I know that, I even feel it, and the universe is sweeping in, closer and closer around me, I'm dancing with it, in blue rivers, in red rituals, I'm so there but something's missing and you know what? It's me. If I'm in Tiferet, or the part of me that is Tiferet, or the lesson that is Tiferet or the piece of perfection that is this golden heart of the Tree, then it's up to me. Not just to be ready, open, longing, to offer everything, but to live it. Now. Each moment. Each of these possibilities, each of these people and moments, they are my beloved ones. To walk through the world—or dance, or fall—in love with each moment and being; to offer unreservedly my heart, this heart, that's to shine like the Tree, to radiate, to live love.

This is the turnaround. Not that it will come to me or I will move to it but *I am that*—That—already, forever. To offer my heart as fully as I can to each of them. Not just each dear one or potential lover, but each girl at the supermarket checkout, each beggar in the street, each office worker on the bus, each radiant being walking past me. Oh, I was on the right track when I said that my friends could be lovers, if they would. Each one a burning spark, falling—it doesn't matter if they return it or not, though presumably some of them will along the way—but this is me doing the ritual, me calling for Tiferet, me becoming lover and beloved and living open-heartedly, all the crossroads open, all the paths running at once, the multiplicity, the streaming outward, the rays of Tiferet. I see it and now I'm feeling it as well. A lover to each of them—oh yes—but not privately, secretly, just those ones who touched me deep: all of them. In that moment beloved, in that moment reflect and soothe and delight and be my fullest self which is love as if I was already in love with each one and simply, oh so simply, bring myself to that, act from that place, the heart. Each act, ideally.

If I do that, then I'm reflecting what it is to be the beloved of the universe. What it is to live as love, radiantly, falling. And there's so many—it's so impossible—it kind of doesn't matter what happens. Just keep radiating. Just improve that person's day one bit. Just offer all that I am in that moment and there's no room for fear and I'm suddenly coming out of myself in so many directions at once, I can feel it within me, the ritual's turned around and I'm under the skin of it now, it's burning through me in gold rivers, oh this is the gold. This being a living piece of the universe, it's not passive. I learned long ago that giving is receiving, that it's when I offer love I feel love and so— just do that. Be fed by these blue rivers of Chesed—*offer everything*, remember—and red flames of Gevurah—*I am that I am*. I am the beloved not because I receive love, but because I offer it; I am love in motion. This heartbeat into the universe.

Tiferet is the heart, but it's the open heart, and not just open, it's broken. The sephirot break, of course, except Malkuth—that's how the next one gets filled—and so Tiferet isn't the heart, entire, Tiferet is shattered, scattered, broken into pieces and all the paths carving into and out of it they break it, endlessly. It's not about being complete, whole, it's in multiplicity. It's not holding back until the right one appears or the right moment or the right anything it's throwing myself, whole-broken-heartedly into each and every interaction, love, person, event. The moment is shattering through me—I'm in the essence of it and I want to remember it forever, code it onto my being so I can't forget it, can't ignore it.

There's a ring on my finger—many rings, but this one I've worn for twenty years. It's a woman, a goddess, the Star Goddess even, twisted with the silver of the ring, her body the circle of it, arms above her head, and she's holding a moonstone, the moon and her legs spin into stars at the end which meet the moon where they join; she's the circle of life, life and death, becoming and unbecoming, she's holding and birthing all that is and I've always worn her on the first finger of my left hand and for twenty years I've kept the secrets of her body—her breasts, her vulva—tucked between my first and second finger, hidden, and let the stars and moon display on the outside. I take her off now, still in the ritual, and turn her around and put her on my finger showing herself, giving herself to the world. It's a vow, it's a promise, a declaration. It's the spell.

Oh I've opened now, maybe forever—I've turned around my patterns of hiding, sheltering, waiting, and I'm going out there. In each interaction, to the depths of my potential. I'm feeling this love/light/life of the universe and offering it, like a conduit, straight through me. This little Star Goddess on my finger, she's reminding me every moment I'm out there that this is what I'm doing. She's showing the arc of her body, she's revealed she's becoming, she's entering into life with every fiber and scrap of the universe and all that is. It's all the same, pulsing, living, and it doesn't matter who receives it, if anyone does, it's the force of it into every form, the burst of it, the heart of it all and I'm in it, it's in me and I feel unstoppable now. I am the lover of the universe and I bring that into every moment.

It's always about becoming, the Kabbalah, not receiving, although becoming is receiving. As the light tumbles, force and form woven together down the Tree, serpent-like I receive, open, become, offer all of it. The note of me harmonizes with the universe. I am becoming a woman who is beloved of the world, I am becoming a lover to the world; the world and each tiny piece of it is my beloved. I cannot stay small, I cannot hide anymore—all the brokenness is only cracks to allow this flow, this beating heart to receive, to be the impulse outward, the contraction-expansion that is all of life and this moment here in the heart—in Paris, on a floor that looks through to Above and

Below both at once, with the trees outside, the walled garden, and me eating of this fruit, blue and red candles burning witnessing the yellow and the heart of me cracked open, mended with gold. I'm shining, and I know if I live this, incidentally but inevitably there will be lovers, human lovers, and also it doesn't matter at all.

Take this blue fountain of life force, this river that pours through the world, feeding the Tree, light a candle for it in Paris and between the worlds. Take this red chalice, this perfect form that holds a ritual, moment, connection, the shapes of the Tree itself—and light a candle for it, in Paris, between the worlds. Break open this yellow-gold heart of the world, the one that's beating there, in your chest, in mine, pulsing through sunlight and the sap rising in the trees, the bees, the salmon in the rivers and the bears that eat them, the berries ripening, the birds in nests and cracking out of eggs, the frogs in the night, the waterfalls, the kisses and sex of it all, the whole bloody mess of it, the delights the heartbreak moments and the soaring, too, the innocence and desperation, the crying in the night oh the great rendering of human souls and the endless beat of nature becoming, becoming, becoming. Light a candle for it, yellow flame in yellow wax, in the Tree, the center of it between the worlds and in Paris and offer oneself, now, always, into the open paths of being beloved of the universe, the lover of all and every, blue and red holding and shaping the gold, all feeding in, pathways, and pouring out, out and down through life through the Tree into the world.

My ritual's come alive, fed with life, and it's inescapable, the beat of it, my own heartbeat. Perhaps I'm living stretched on the Tree with all the rivers, all the paths and flames of it running through the center of me, as intimately as a lover would—this is the lover, the beloved, *I Am That*. There's a separation, still, I'm not entirely one, not yet though death brings that at the end of time and I feel the magnetism of it, why atoms hold together, the force of them and love that falls like light through empty space of each second past the singularity of All and it's written through every cell of me and the ring on my finger, her body arched outward to the world like she's giving birth, making love, dying, the Star Goddess, and she reminds me, each moment, how to be. To bring all of myself, to offer all that I am—beloved, broken—to each piece and delight in the freedom, the dare and necessity of it and hold nothing back, as everything was already let go of, long ago at the beginning, so the stars could even be.

ritual | The Inner Column of Fire

The Inner Column of Fire is a powerful healing ritual meant for extreme distress, especially when pain or trauma seems lodged in the body, as with sexual abuse, rape, and other violations. I encourage even those feeling impossibly wounded to try this healing ritual.

It's a high energy ritual calling on the powers of the middle pillar and our intrinsic resonance with that pattern, most especially in the human spine and the shaft of starlight or divine light that is often imagined to enter from the Great Above through the tops of our heads, fall straight down through our spinal columns, and then continue downward, perhaps as far as the very center of the earth.

I imagine this light as about the width of a sewing thread, metallic silver, and unbreakable. It's a thread of life force, both within us and beyond us. I believe nothing—not even death—can sever us from belonging to both the earth and the stars or, in Kabbalistic terms, Malkuth and Kether.

TIME: 1 hour, plus nurturing time afterward. This ritual can be broken into two pieces several days apart.

YOU WILL NEED: An undisturbed space, journal, pen. Coloring things optional. Whatever helps you to feel safe, comforted, and cared for—including but not limited to cushions, a soft blanket, drinking water, a lit candle, a cup of tea.

Begin by getting comfortable. This might include showering or bathing, stretching, dancing, yoga, meditation, grounding, casting a circle, calling upon your spirit guides and allies or ancestors, cuddling up in cushions and a blanket, or listening to some gentle music.

The effectiveness of this fundamentally very simple ritual is in the level of focus and conviction we bring to it.

Part 1—The Thread of Light

Allow yourself to conjure up an image, feeling, or concept of the thread that holds you into life. Imagine its origins in the stars, perhaps in the very first moment of the universe, and how it now runs like a string through your body, anchoring itself deep in the earth. You might imagine it as silver, gold, blue, white, or some other color, or for you it may be more of a vibration, musical note, gut feeling, or something else entirely.

Spend some time—even ten or fifteen minutes—breathing into and with this thread, feeling or imagining the whole length of it, but most especially the part that runs through your body. You might experience it as waking up, sparking, vibrating, buzzing, humming, brightening, or responding to your attention in some other way. If it seems stronger in some parts of your body than others or it fades in and out, let your breaths travel the whole length of it, repeatedly, until you can even out the flow within it. You could do this in either direction or both—whichever feels natural to you.

Allow yourself to recognize this thread or ray as pure, divine, and undiluted by your history and experiences, let alone by anyone else. We might experience it as a compass, a guiding light, an inner knowledge, or recognition of how we are all born from stars and are inseparable, ultimately, from everything that exists. It cannot be tainted. It is divine, our birthright and lifelong companion. This thread is within us but also much greater than us.

Gradually allow the thread to vibrate as your heart beats. Then begin to feed it with your breath, allowing it to expand within your body. It might become as thick as a cord or the spinal column itself as you breathe, focus, and send energy into it. Allow sensations to accompany this expansion; they might include shaking, a sensation of heat, of pins and needles, or something else as you feed it with your breath and focus. Every cell, piece, and memory of you that this thread meets as it expands will be transmuted. You cannot hold onto even the most embedded experiences while focusing on this and doing this work.

You might choose to have a break here and spend several days integrating this awareness of the strength and unassailability of this inner cord of light. If you do this, when you begin again, progress through all the early stages of the exercise before moving on. If you choose to continue within the same session, know that you can repeat the whole process another time to help strengthen the imagery and rewrite what is held in your body.

Part 2—Becoming a Column of Light

You might feel the wish or desire of this cord, this middle pillar of yourself, to keep expanding—to essentially fill or consume your whole body so that you will be encased in a burning, vibrating, sparking, ecstatic white-light column made of star-and-earth force. Or you might need to gently encourage it to continue to expand. As it expands it will burn through anything the body is holding that doesn't align with its purity, that fierce divine thread of life force.

You might express strong emotion—tears, sobbing, shouting, panting; singing, sounding, shaking—as you invite this force to burn outward from the initial thread and expand to encompass your whole body. Feel yourself filled with it, your own thread of divine life force. This healing-from-within has the power to push out, to displace, or to burn anything lodged in you that is not of your essence and not in alignment with the divine, including wounds of the body, soul, and psyche. It can touch what a healing-from-without cannot reach. Let it expand beyond the confines of your body so even your skin is bathed in it, and you are held entirely within its aura.

As you continue to breathe, to vibrate with this thread of starlight-to-earth that you are, you might experience flashbacks, images, spoken or remembered words, or other phenomena. Continue breathing and allow the healing to happen, reaching out to the stars and earth through your thread so you are always held between them. There will come a peak and then the intensity will begin to lessen. You might let the sensation and idea of being encased in this column of fire, starlight, or life force dissipate or contract back to its original eternal thread that links you to Above and Below; a shimmer of it may remain throughout your whole body in the coming hours or days.

When you feel complete for now, take a break. You might drink some water, move your body, or change position. Record your experience in your journal.

• • • •

You may feel this process is complete in itself or you may wish to repeat it once or more through the coming days and weeks. If you did not reach a stage where your whole body was encased in and consumed by the middle pillar force the first time, it is worth repeating the process at a later time.

activity | Creating the Sixth Disk

When you complete the work of this section, create a disk to represent the sephira you've been working with. This will be your sixth disk. Perhaps you spent the first section inhabiting Kether and you are now up to Tiferet—in that case, it will be the yellow disk you are working with. Perhaps you began somewhere else in the Tree and so the disk you are making now is for Gevurah, Netzach, Binah, or any other sephira.

TIME: 30–60 minutes

YOU WILL NEED: The appropriate colored disk (see "Creating the First Disk," page 69) and whatever art materials you wish to work with, such as colored pens and markers, paint, oil pastels, collage materials and glue, stickers

Start by recalling the time you have spent in this sephira, including rereading through your journal notes, recalling any Kabbalah exercises, processes, or rituals you did, and especially how these related to this particular sephira, as well as the general mood and events in your life during this time. By this stage you will probably have a strong feel for the unique qualities of this sephira.

Allow images, words, feelings, and ideas to arise. You can hold these in your head, immediately begin work on your disk, or jot down notes or a sketch.

Mark the name of the sephira onto the disk, as with the previous disks.

Time to decorate! By now you may have a theme running through your disks; they are all paintings, they all use collage, or they each have a mix of found objects, words, and symbols—or each one may be different from the others, representing what you found particular or unique about this sephira. Your disk might contain a sense of the paths that connect it with other sephirot, an image of the Tree itself, or a reference to this sephira's position within the Tree. My disks tend to be very simple within the top triad and become increasingly complex as they descend through the Tree.

You can complete your work in one session or come back later to add more details.

examples of completed disks can be seen at janemeredith .com/disks

impossibly long ago this light was born
on rays in all directions speeding piercing
penetrating the forever, burning the finite
and in a dream a heartbeat, a wingbeat past
it was lovers with the source, inseparable,
born in the same moment yet flung far apart
by longing, falling like hearts broken open
the passion and reignited burning each
particle in bliss of becoming—

as it falls the butterfly tears one fragile wing,
falling, into the heart citrine cadmium
amber lemon daffodil saffron sunshine gold
and fragments fall, fall, falling—

7

Embodied in the Tree

275

The seventh sephira arrives as the lightning flash continues its diagonal descent from Gevurah through Tiferet and now to Netzach, called Eternity. As with each new sephira, Netzach reveals increasing complexity and the next stage toward embodiment. The Tree has been gaining substance, refining and defining itself, moving toward ever more solid states of being throughout its long—or instantaneous—journey from Kether. That was All, being the first and only, shimmering in the barely conceivable. Next Hokmah, still in the mists but differentiated from the first, adding gravitas toward this evolution; then Binah, whose triangulation acted to solidify the tremulous and unquantifiable nature of what was happening.

The descent through the Abyss—another inexplicability—occurred, and on the other side, Chesed with the pouring through of the all that is and Gevurah shaping and containing. Then to Tiferet and the beating heart, a direct expression of what began at Kether. Now even further, tipping down the Tree like a waterfall into Netzach. This seventh sephira initiates a further level of complexity and development as it begins the third and final triad and horizontal pair.

Netzach is at the bottom of the right-hand pillar, underneath Hokmah and Chesed. One of the pillars has reached the ground—or as far toward the ground as it can go. Fed by the downward thrust of the lightning flash through Gevurah and Tiferet, Wisdom, Mercy, Power, and Beauty all directly contribute to the composition of Eternity.

Netzach: *The Garden*

Netzach leaves the perfection of Tiferet's center-of-the-center in order to complete the right-hand pillar, its third and final sephira. With Netzach we are entering into the lowest triad, the one from which Malkuth will be born. These three—Netzach, Hod, and Yesod—between them make a space from which creation can occur. That downward-pointing triangle is a symbol used to denote the vulva, the powers of generative fertility and sexuality. Netzach's green color, a mixture of Chesed's blue, from directly above, combined with yellow from the previous sephira on the lightning flash, Tiferet, makes this sephira look instantly alchemical, as well as brimming with life. This is the green world we are so intrinsically a part of.

The lower four sephirot—Netzach, Hod, Yesod, and Malkuth—are understood as the landscape of our human lives and as far as our minds can reach, although Tiferet is spiritually accessible, or at least can be glimpsed in some moments. But the entry into our field of existence on the downward path is Netzach, and this involves embodiment. For us there's really nothing else—everything we do and say, imagine and experience takes place within the body. Embodiment in the Kabbalah is sacred, it is spiritual; there is no division. The Tree is embodied in our own bodies and we could say in each being and thing and even each atom; collectively we are the body of the Tree. But it's one thing to know that and another to live that way. Embodied Kabbalah goes beyond acknowledging that all we've really got is the body and that everything we learn and experience comes via that medium, into joyously placing our body within the Tree, inviting its magic to flow through our veins, rewriting our thoughts and behaviors, and opening paths we have always longed for, as well as ones we never would have expected or thought to seek.

By now the sephirot are close to our world, and the multiplicity of Tiferet finds expression in Netzach with myriad experiments. Netzach invites us into this flow—not just of the stars or great forces we might glimpse at the edge of our understanding, but into the moment-to-moment flow within a life. The transmutation of sunlight onto water; life occurs. We find ourselves in the garden of this green sephira, before anything has been named or cataloged, and know ourselves part of living creation. The Tree has moved from abstracts such as light and love into the imaginable green realm; embodied life in a great tumbling of becoming, held between Tiferet's beauty and the precision yet to come of Hod. Netzach is the ever-moving moment of life blossoming.

The Tree itself has been gaining body and complexity ever since we were marveling at its arising out of the Ain Soph, the Great Nothingness. This whole miracle of existence is resonant with the mystery of our individual lives. How easy it would be not to exist! For our parents never to have met—or our grandparents or great-grandparents—for one of those oh-so-important beings to have died before they reproduced, for war/

starvation/genocide/plague to have taken out the whole family/village/tribe at any point, for circumstances to change just slightly, for that month's egg not to be the one fertilized or not with that particular individual spermatozoa. And in any other time and place—which is to say, almost entirely all times and places—we don't exist. Yet here we are, embodied.

The Adam Kadmon is a vast, ephemeral, and conceptual symbolic body that lies over or through the Tree of Life, but us miniature parts of the Tree (people) can also map the Adam Kadmon onto our bodies. This is a whole mystical study in itself; so many lines of Kabbalistic inquiry lead into different worlds and realms. If we draw out a map of the Tree or lay our disks out on the floor and then lie on top of that, facedown, we can begin to feel the magic of this Kabbalistic embodiment. There's an intimacy in lying facedown: we are embracing the Tree, arms open to it, becoming and unbecoming with and within it. Our feet are in the mud and our heads crowned with stars. We are making love with the Tree, the universe, the All and the I Am; each one of our tiny lives a love song to its vast impossibility. And then—magic. This is life magic, sex magic, this is dynamic union, this is the dance: the stars becoming each one of us in the form of a tree, a human, a life. This is how we work, embodied, facedown, joined into the Tree of Life, and the green sephira of Netzach takes us there.

According to author David Abram, the whole of nature is in constant, continual conversation with all its parts; only we, the humans, have cut ourselves out from that conversation, being somehow interested exclusively in our own species. Exceptions to this might include children, natural scientists, our relationships with our pets and gardens, and us Pagans in constant dialogue with the seasons, elements, and the land around us. But the way Abram describes it in *The Spell of the Sensuous* is not an abstract concept or a singular conversation or set of conversations that we might have or miss out on, but as an each-second awareness and response to the living world we are immersed in. If I were to try this now...

That breeze—its direction, strength, humidity, seasonality, scents, variance— and at the same time, that birdsong—which birds? How many? Number of species heard within a few heartbeats? What directions? Saying what—excited about food, the morning, a predator in the area, general life exuberance? Are

they in the sky, in a tree, on the ground? Different bird from a different direc-
tion—what bird, where, doing what? Cow in the background, lowing, some dis-
tance away—getting closer? Just one of them? Is it missing or looking for its calf
or just making sound? The sunlight dims, there's shadows of trees on the lawn, a
cloud—what type, will it rain? Sun strengthens and breeze picks up, bird group
in possibly the southwest, slightly quieter, other single bird silent, cow making
more sounds, same distance away—fern fronds waving up and down in breeze,
lomandra leaves still, they are closer to the ground than the fern fronds—third
different bird, loud sharp sound, close by—first group of birds very loud again
and now a swirling around sound—

That's about one minute. I edited out the human sounds of music from a nearby
house and a distant car, and I could only capture a fraction of what I observed and felt
through the open door. By now there's a black cockatoo somewhere close and low, circling, which would explain the way the sound is behaving. I can only see to the north
and a little west outside this door, and that breeze has left. The cluster of birds (they're
out of sight) who were noisy has faded, but there's still occasional chirping from them.
A different chirping bird flits its way across the small screen of my attention, heading
west. That's the next thirty seconds or so, but already considerations from the human
perspective are starting to irk me.

I've come up against my limitations in participating in this conversation of the world.
I'm inside, so even though I've got the door open, the visual and kinesthetic information is coming only from one direction, about 90 of the 360 degrees available. The
aural—I'm receiving it from all around, but it's hard to locate precisely because turning
my head doesn't help clarify the direction. I can't match up the aural to the visual unless
it happens to occur within my 90 degrees of vision. Actually, that 90 degrees is cut off at
the top by an overhanging roof eave and at the bottom by a veranda that hangs out over
where otherwise I could look downward. So I really—literally—only have a window
onto this world. My immersive world is this room, with its desk, computer, printer, piles
of paper, boxes of books, et cetera.

Even if I was outside—let's imagine for a moment that I take my laptop and transition to that slope I can see from my window. That way I'll have 360-degree vision and

sound and can match the two together much better. I'll also feel the ground underneath me—is it soft, hard, damp?—and have a close-up of the grass. Those baby bangalow palms will be on my right with the lomandra row in front of me, at the bottom of the slope. I'll be able to feel the air—or wind if/when there is one—not just if it comes from one direction but from any direction. I'll be on intimate terms with any leeches or mosquitoes searching for blood, and the tiny black grasshoppers, and those clouds of white moths that seem to rise from the grass these last few days will be next to me, on me, around me. Plus the sun, or lack of, won't just be a visual light and shadow on the plants and lawn but an actual effect on my body. If it were to start raining— which wouldn't be good for the computer—I'd feel it, not just those actual raindrops when they arrive but that sigh of cool air before it, the slight misting of the breeze, that tremor through the air around me.

But here's another problem: I'll only experience any of those sensations on small parts of me: my face, my hands and forearms, my throat and neck, and my bare feet. The rest of my body will be blunted to sensation because I've got clothes on. Why do I have clothes on since I'm on my own and it's not cold?

When I have been outside nude, I enter a whole different world. There's 360-degree information, and that doesn't even cover it because it's not just from all around but from above and below as well. Skin is incredibly sensitive. When I haven't got clothes on, I have discovered that I can tell—not even by thinking of it, but immediately, instantly— which exact direction a breeze is coming from and every slight shift in direction and intensity. The intervals of sunlight and cloud aren't just patterns I watch on the ground or moments when I have to shield my eyes or squint; they are caresses over my body like a warm hand or a cool cloth. All over, all at once. I am in a sensual bath, and not only that but a bath everything around me is participating in: the trees, bushes, birds, and any other humans I'm with.

But now the real problem: these conversations I'm involved in are with myself. This is what David Abram posits: that there's a great, continual, rich, ever-changing conver- sation that life is having every moment, and we're disconnected from it. The most we can hope to do, usually, is observe some of it, and almost always we're not even doing that. But this conversation of life with itself—even sitting outside, in amongst it, I'm listening, registering, feeling, opening my senses—but am I responding? Am I actually participating? Almost certainly not if I'm writing on my laptop at the same time. I might look up from the screen, turn my head occasionally or my eyes in certain directions, flick a leech away if I see it coming too close, or adjust my position to get into or out of the sun. But what is that like in this multidimensional world of living?

It looks like a severe autism. A sort of locked-in syndrome, one where I have the capacity to respond, engage, partake, but I don't. I don't have the understanding, the habit, the tools. I don't know how to do it well, so I don't do it at all. The conversation of birds flicks so fast I struggle to even follow small parts of it. Insects a hundred times faster. Trees—I can just about keep pace with trees. Rocks and the mineral world generally are slow to communicate, wearing away through weather, rising up through volcanic action, shifting in plate tectonics, but they're completely there for the conversation. I'm part of the so-called animal kingdom, but as an animal this inert, this unlettered in basic dialogue, we're like shadows. Ghosts. How does it feel when I lean into it? Lonely. Cut off. Alien even; how would I, could I understand or respond to any of this activity?

That's extreme. Gardeners, of which I am one, are in dynamic conversation with their gardens. Farmers, sailors, bushwalkers, bird watchers, people who work with animals, microbes, and weather are all in conversations with their worlds. I am someone who talks to plants and birds and animals aloud—I'd love to think there's a lot more of us, and I assume that the Pagans, Druids, witches, and others likely to be reading this book are among them. But so often our conversations arise from an authoritative place of knowledge and (relative) power or from simple, even naïve wonder. How have we allowed this to happen? One can imagine a child, maybe four or five, turned loose in a garden, forest, or field engaging in an in-depth conversation, listening, talking, questioning—and in times of ritual or ecstatic experience I've been able to return to that. I do have some deep relationships, such as with the river I swim in during summer. Over years I've built up a conversation with that river, but I don't live every minute in that world. I've chosen houses, clothes, and computers instead. I've chosen to be illiterate, non-vocal, and mostly deaf to the life I'm intrinsically a part of.

Reading *The Hidden Life of Trees* by Peter Wohlleben made me see the world differently. It taught me things I can't unknow about trees from the perspective of trees—

or a closer perspective than the usual human one. That book taught me that copper beeches, which I've always loved, are a genetic mutation that humans cultivate for their beauty, but the dark leaves make photosynthesis much harder. They're trees living with a disability that we imposed. In natural selection they might not be selected. Trees are meant to be in forests, I knew that. But Wohlleben explains what it means to a tree not to be in a forest and instead to be in a park, street, or even a garden. The cost of that, to a tree. To be without the physical protection of other trees close around it. To be isolated, stranded, without others of its species or even any other trees at all, and so unable to exchange nutrients, information, and not, in effect, go through the natural cycle of trees, which have completely different lives in their own setting. Did I realize we were torturing trees? Turning the world into a sort of zoo for trees, with our captives displayed along city and suburban streets and in green spaces we imagine are somehow natural? No. But now every time I see them I wince at our arrogance and ignorance, and mutter apologies under my breath.

Other writers have also ventured into this landscape—one that's right before our eyes, but we have removed ourselves from it so completely that we don't even recognize what we're seeing most of the time. In *Being a Beast*, the record of an outrageous and often hilarious experiment, Charles Foster spends years trying to literally become four different animals, in turn a badger, a stag, an otter, and a swift. We can read the greater commentary that we've forgotten how to belong. That perhaps the only way to begin to reclaim our own animal nature is by identification, mimicking, inquiring so closely into aspects of nature that we can imagine merging with them, like the stories of shamans in the great natural religions. Speculative fiction has often crossed these borders—there's Ursula Le Guin's *The Word for World Is Forest* where a whole planet and all that live on it are essentially one being, a theme that also occurs in James Cameron's *Avatar* movie. Amy Thomson's novel *The Color of Distance* places a stranded human traveler on an alien planet that reshapes her to allow her survival, with the unspoken reference point being our essential alienation from earth. And Joan Slonczewski's *Brain Plague* brilliantly goes in the other direction, seeding intelligent microbes into human brains so that a world can be discerned by the reader as one living, interdependent being.

The Garden of Eden is a key component of Kabbalah. This story of our origins, of the biblical paradise humans were expelled from, operates on many different levels. It is mythic: a story to explain the beginnings of humankind. It is mystical: containing occult lessons for the initiated. It is moral: with cultural and religious lessons about obedience, temptation, and shame. And it is metaphoric: elucidating our estrangement from both nature and the divine. The great temptation at the center of the garden, the tree and the fruit of knowledge, and the invitation to dare, to ingest, and to *be as gods* hovers around any discussion of Eden. Notions of body, sex, union, separation, and punishment all feed into this pivotal story of the original garden and its original inhabitants. Current readings of this story could include those of dispossession and colonization.

There are two significant trees described in the first chapter of the Old Testament of the Bible: the Tree of the Knowledge of Good and Evil and the Tree of Life. Possibly they are the same tree. Neither of them allows a simple interpretation; the serpent promises Eve that, if she and Adam eat of the Tree of Knowledge, *thou shalt be as gods.* There's an immediate reaction from the One God (oh—such a significant contradiction, and so early on!) directing that humans must leave the garden immediately, for having eaten of one tree, what's to stop them going even further and eating from the second tree, thus conferring eternal life upon themselves? *As gods,* indeed—and when we begin to unpack all this somewhat contradictory information, to view it as hints, as partially concealed/revealed knowledge (maybe even Knowledge), we can drop deeper within this mythos.

This green sephira of Netzach is deeply concerned with the unfolding patterns of life, or potential life; of gardens, or mythic gardens. Its name is commonly translated into English as "eternity." Netzach is the place where the endlessly flowing generosity of Chesed pours straight down, like a waterfall; it is the inheritor of Tiferet's golden rays of light—and we all know what happens when sunlight interacts with the waters of our planet. Life. Life is so mixed up with death—how can life constitute eternity, in any way? I think—maybe contradictorily or Kabbalistically—that participating in life (and therefore death) is glimpsing eternity. That without participation in life, knowledge of life, eternity is flat. Maybe it doesn't even exist. If everything stayed at the Kether level or the Ain Soph level, yes, maybe it would literally be for eternity. But no one and nothing would experience that eternity. Instead, we are made aware of eternity by our non-eternal lives, just as we are aware of (and long for) union only from our state of separation. We (collectively) participate in the eternity of each moment, and our individual moments and lives are part of the great eternity.

There's an interesting piece of linguistics here—in English we can correctly use the phrase *an eternity*. Something lasted, or will last, for *an eternity*. We don't say *the eternity*—meaning there are more than one eternities. My eternity—all I can ever be and know and do—is confined to my lifetime. It's an eternity, my own eternity. I'm conscious of greater fields of eternity all around me that I coexist with and within, that I'm a participant in. The eternity of the garden I create, which can easily continue after my death. The eternity of my child and potentially a line of descendants through him. The eternity of the words I write, even these exact ones here, which have a different type of, and length of, eternity than my own. The eternity of these atoms, molecules, chemicals that make up me, that have been and will continue to be in so many other things, places, and in times I can't even imagine, backward or forward. Myself as a piece—a scrap, but never mind—of divinity, and as some sort of mirror to that divinity; that's eternal. That's me participating in eternity, surely.

Netzach is wild—it's chaos—however sheltered the paradise is, this garden isn't tame; it's raw creation, the works of gods and all possibilities unfolding, pouring endlessly out of the great nothingness and the starbursts through time and space into the endless potential arrangements of those atoms, those elements, those particles. Stephen Jay Gould's great work *Life's Grandeur* is a thorough debunking of the human-centric view of evolution. He demonstrates how we have created a view that puts us front and center stage, whereas a more objective view shows us seriously off to the side, up a small, obscure branch, with the real business of life in amongst the slime molds and bacteria. In fact, the biological tree of life diagram has the entire category of *Animals* as just one of many offshoots of one of the three main categories: *Bacteria*, *Archaea*, and *Eukarya* (we're a twig of a twig off that branch).

That we are an arrangement that can comment on these conditions, on other facets of the garden, and indeed on ourselves, and even speculate on the philosophies of the whole situation—well, that's a random factor and nothing to congratulate ourselves for. Instead we find ourselves, as it were, out on the edges of existence and somewhat cut off from the rest of it by this very attribute. We position ourselves as outsiders on the planet we live on and are dependent upon. Outsiders have the best critical view, but with their detachment from and lack of identification with what they're observing, how useful can they be? As artists, philosophers, magicians, yes. Will that be enough to change the course of our history as we currently appear intent on destroying our own ability to exist on this planet?

I'm writing this in the first months of the coronavirus pandemic, an interesting and pertinent time to be considering the powers of nature, the concept of eternity, and what humans might discover by reconnecting with the great conversation of the world. It's unresolved whether viruses are categorized as living or nonliving, but within Netzach it's all living; a rock, a volcano, an ocean is living; the stars live, all existence is alive. This virus is a stark reminder of the powers that are beyond human control within this garden we inhabit. Within three months it has become the most powerful thing in our world, shutting down economies, altering the course of governments, and changing the daily lives of most humans. It's part of the endless variety produced in the garden of life's grandeur.

I'm listening to the black cockatoos calling, high and circling, as they do, coming in on the gusts of wind signifying a weather change—I can sense it in the damp, scented air, brushing my shoulders through the open door. I've mostly given up on clothes, seventeen days into my near-total isolation. I live on my own and I've left the property twice in that time for supplies. Maybe soon I won't be here in front of the screen, but living in the garden again, talking with those bangalow palms that I planted when they were a handspan high and which now stretch far over my head, watching their fronds in the breeze and so learning more about this wind, and the black cockatoos won't just be telling me about the coming rain but we'll be conversing about what trees are in fruit and seed and where they are. I'll be feeling the wind, sun, and rain on all parts of my skin and in a dialogue with them about the unfolding day. It will seem to me, as I go deeper and further into this exploration, this garden, as if I had forever in this paradise, and even if I die out there my body will still be a part of it, a part of the conversation, for all eternity.

Embodiment in the Tree of Life

When we speak of embodiment, we are talking about living as fully as we can, in the body we have, in this time and place, with these limitations and these gifts. We are part of the business of being conceived by other bodies—and then being born and living, growing, changing, eating and defecating and bleeding and weeping. Singing and dancing and working and playing. To be alive in this world of wonders, of oceans and birds, of the gentle rain and the storms, of night skies, deserts, forests and mountains. To take part, farming or gardening or caretaking, meeting the beings of this world, making love, learning and teaching and nurturing, sometimes in fear and sometimes in hope. To create. To grow—to change—to be subjected to circumstances: war, poverty, wealth, plague, revolution, love, and also to choose every moment how to be, how to respond or initiate, how to inhabit this body. To die in it, of it, gifting all that we have been and even our bodies back to the cycle of life.

To live in the garden means to be present to this life, and thus present to all life that surrounds us, and thus present to Life. Knowing that Life is an expression of the All, of the I Am, and that we participate in it wholly. Mind and body are considered as at least partially separate in almost every philosophy I know of. What if they're not? What if this mind, the one writing or reading these words, is intrinsically a part of the body whose eyes are reading it, whose brain is processing it, whose fingers, in this case, are pressing small black plastic buttons to make letters appear on the screen or, in your case, is holding a book or e-reader, turning pages, or perhaps whose ears are receiving a stream of these exact words? I'm going to suggest that, effectively, the mind and body are one thing. Much as we could view the right and left hands as different things—they are—but widen the lens just a little and we see they are parts of one system; they both belong to the same body. More is gained by understanding them as expressions of the one thing rather than as separate.

We belong to the earth—literally. The atoms, chemicals, and all the particles that make up our body-mind were part of the earth before we existed and will continue as part of the earth after we've died. We are also part of the stars, stardust; all these atoms, chemicals, and particles came out of the hearts of exploding stars long before our earth existed and will return to the starscape when the earth dies. We are not separate

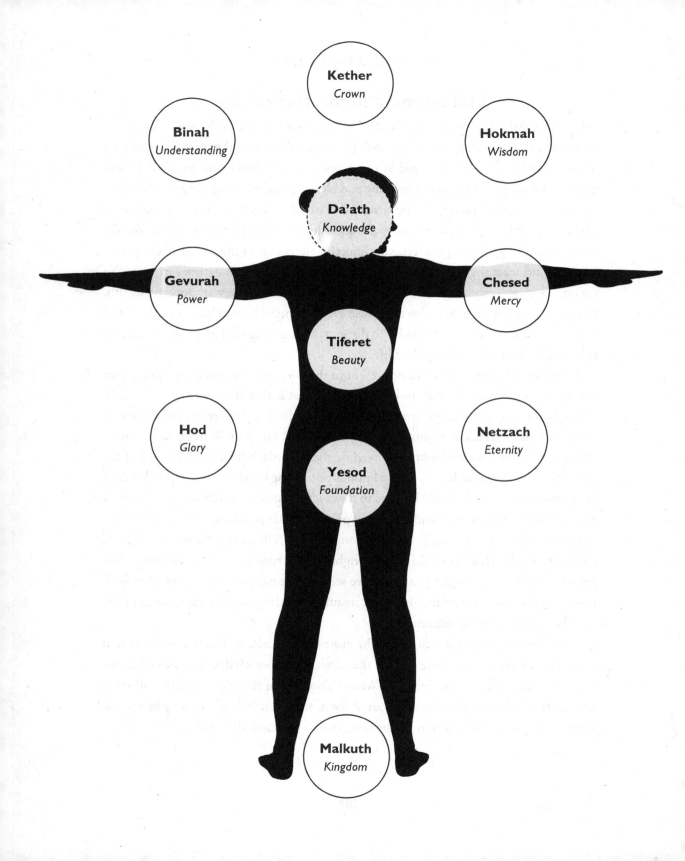

from this garden in the stars, this garden of earth. Our bodies belong to its body, living and dying. David Abram in his beautiful *Becoming Animal* argues that since the atmosphere is an intrinsic part of our planet—the earth as we know it is completely dependent upon its atmosphere—we could, instead of saying that we live *on* the earth, more accurately say that we live *in* the earth (Abram 2011, 100). He suggests this might change our whole relationship to our planet; instead of being something the soles of our feet are in contact with (sometimes), it would be immediately obvious that we are surrounded by it and completely dependent on and immersed within it. With this switch of a single word, the welfare of the earth becomes inseparable from what humans are apparently most focused on: our own immediate well-being.

Embodiment is something many of us struggle with. It involves so many challenges to anyone brought up to believe that the body is inferior to the mind, that women's/black/Indigenous/differently abled/older/larger/smaller bodies are less than perfect, that paying attention to the body or physical realm is self-indulgent/narcissistic/unimportant, to anyone who's experienced trauma, neglect, chronic pain, scarcity, rape, addiction, violence, self-harm, or homelessness, or to anyone who has followed religions or doctrines of disembodiment, ascension, or disdain or contempt of the body, from Catholicism to the New Age as well many others. Oh, I think that's nearly all of us by now, probably all of us. Is it possible to grow up in the West or Westernized world and not have to go through many learnings of how to live deeply in our bodies? Let's assume not. Let's assume that this is, in itself, a major piece of work, one with many healings, deep journeys, much practice, weeping laughing dancing and making love with ourselves and others along the way.

Embodiment—belonging to the Tree, the universe, the All, and therefore our own bodies—is a crucial piece of Kabbalah magic. Of course, we can't do anything at all without our bodies, but how much more powerful our experience—how much more resonant within all the worlds—is our magic when we know through felt senses and in every cell that our body aligns with the Tree itself, that we are an expression of it and it an expression of us? Within that experience we embody magic: magic for healing, for change, for pure celebration of life.

The sephirot are ten lenses, ten expressions of the divine, ten sometimes dramatically different doorways through which to experience ... anything. Let's dive more deeply into what each sephira brings to this discussion of embodiment. For once we're going to head up the Tree instead of down, starting with the ultimate embodiment, Malkuth.

Malkuth Embodied

The body is sacred. When our body is a temple and belongs to the temple (the All, the I Am), then each part of it is sacred. We make offerings to these body altars—of food, rest, exercise, pleasure, and reverence—and all of those are sacred. We make our offerings with prayers and blessings. With attention, with respect, perhaps with awe. Sometimes in need, in fear and longing, pain or distress, but also in hope, in love, in trust and joy. Imagine each meal—each mouthful of water—being given the mindfulness of an offering in a temple. Imagine how it will be when we make a commitment to our bodies as sacred and only allow touch or intimacy with those who respect that and treat their own bodies that way. Imagine raising children within this understanding. It's hard to change or even challenge the education, health, social, and economic systems we live within, to rewrite how they treat and understand bodies. But we can do it for our own body, we can insist on it within our intimate relationships, and we can raise our children to know this. We can embark on the work to take us through the wounded, disconnected, and frightened places we meet within ourselves when we commit to this. We can receive each drop of rain, each breath of air, each sun- or moonrise, each touch of the world as a blessing.

In the Adam Kadmon, this sephira is associated with our feet.

Yesod Embodied

To be embodied in any realm but Malkuth is problematic because these realms are not really about embodiment. But we can seek their gifts and learn to bring them into our embodied state. Dreams are often dismissed as unreal, but if we followed that logic, because they're only happening in our minds, we'd have to say most, even all things we experience are unreal because they also come through the filters of our minds. The inner realms, the inner planes, alternate states of consciousness, the collective unconscious, the mythos—these are states we can enter, interact with, and learn from. They are as connected to our waking state as we want to make them. Many of us—artists, magicians, poets, priestesses, mystics, and others—access these states often or even experience ourselves as partially living within them. We live alive to dreams and all the realms Yesod describes, weave their magics into our lives, open to their wisdoms, and call upon them for qualities and insights we need. When we access these powers not just within deep ritual or the creative process, but moment to moment—as we walk over land and feel its layers of mythos, as we relate to someone and recognize the archetypal resonances as well as the personal, as we create a song, garden, child, workshop, or relationship with the wisdom of our ancestors—we embody our magic and our dreams.

Yesod is associated with our genitals in the Adam Kadmon model.

Hod Embodied

The gift of Hod to embodiment is order, organization, and classification. What are our priorities? If we analyze our behavior, we may realize that we pour resources—time, money, attention—into things that are not the most important parts of our lives. Often this is necessity: the unrewarding job that pays the rent, boring household tasks that have to be done, being polite to relatives we'd never choose. When we examine our behavior, we may discover that large sections of our discretionary time and energy go into consuming media, whereas we value far more highly time spent with family and friends. Or we continually neglect our personal spiritual practice, our study or creative time, to fulfill social obligations we don't receive much joy from. Hod offers a strength of insight to reorder our priorities. Hod brings discipline. If we avoid our art or our magic because we're afraid, Hod will carve out the time for us to confront those fears. If we are stuck in negative or even destructive patterns of relating, Hod can get us to a support group, a therapist, open the journal for us to start writing our truth, insist on setting a time for that hard conversation. Hod can break a problem down into components and let us focus on just one step at a time. It's simple, pedantic, and glorious.

The left leg and foot are governed by Hod within the figure of Adam Kadmon.

Netzach Embodied

What do you do for joy? For play, for pleasure? Every time someone asks me this, I'm jolted into remembrance. I'm much more of a Hod-style person. But Netzach is my secret love. Oh yes, remind me to go swimming in the river, an activity I adore over almost any other. Oh, persuade me to dance—and feel delight, a physical tide of it. When I'm in the garden—a very Hod-like, disciplined pursuit—I receive joy from the soft air, that flock of silent pigeons sweeping low over the hill, their wingbeats their only sound, from the growing things I planted and the ones who surprise me, springing up on their own. Netzach asks us not just to have joy at the fringes, the little extra things we might get to if we finish everything on our list, but to make joy an essential, inspirational part of each day and maybe even each moment. To live in delight. To choose and prepare food that will nourish and also delight us. To choose company that brings us joy. To know that physical, sensual, and emotional pleasures are sacred.

In Adam Kadmon, the right foot and leg are held by the realm of Netzach.

Tiferet Embodied

What is your soul purpose, the heart of you? Usually searching for and learning about this unfolds throughout our lives so that the very journey toward it is the slow revelation of our deepest gifts. But we always have clues: activities that spark us to life, challenges that are deeply profound, and skills or talents so uniquely ours that if we don't enact them, no one ever will, not exactly like that. Tiferet speaks both to what is unique about each of us and also what is universal. To embody this—being of service that is utter joy because we are completely fulfilled by it—is something we mostly experience in glimpses, or moments, as rare events. But how would it be to work with this as a focus—to ask how each day and even each moment we could be fulfilling this passion, this service, this heart of the world, and to be basing our choices and actions on that information? I think that would be an embodiment of Tiferet.

Tiferet is in the center of our bodies; it is the region of our solar plexus and heart in the body of Adam Kadmon.

Gevurah Embodied

Boundaries are essential to survival. Our skin is a boundary; it holds the living mass of us separate enough from the rest of the world so that we can exist, and each of our cells has its own boundary of a cell wall. External boundaries—fences, laws, social conventions—are easier for us to understand and integrate than our personal boundaries.

Outright denial is where we say or even believe that we don't have boundaries. *I'm good with anything. I don't have any needs. I always have more to give.* Clearly this can't be true. We often don't know what our boundaries are or how to cope with someone else's. Learning this enables us to understand the field of boundaries: what they are and how they might work. Further, we often ignore our own boundaries even when we are conscious of them—that inner feeling which lets us know we don't really want to do something, but we do it anyway. When we learn to work with boundaries as allies, giving us valuable information and guiding us; when we pay attention to our own boundaries and respect those of others, then this embodiment of Gevurah, ironically, sets us free.

In the Adam Kadmon, Gevurah represents the left arm and hand.

Chesed Embodied

What else would we do with this freedom granted by understanding, respecting, and implementing boundaries than flow forth, out into the world? Where do you stop yourself, limit yourself, hold yourself back—not because of respecting your boundaries but because of some perception of what is suitable or acceptable? *Nice girls don't... I'm not good enough... As a child I was always told...* and all other versions of that. Where, how, and when are we not giving all that we are? Maybe we ended up in the wrong career or held back on self-exploration or artistic expression, but we can find a way to remedy that: to meet those passions and share those gifts with the world. When we embody Chesed, we are all flow and offering; it's not about the end product, it's about the expression of all that we can be and do in the world. We remain intimately concerned with others and the world, but from the standpoint of our fullest selves, which are constantly evolving.

Chesed is in the right arm and hand in the Adam Kadmon model.

Binah Embodied

What is it to give oneself the rest, the spaciousness, and grace that we need? The amount of sleep we require. The self-care: exercise, the right food, the hours we need alone, and the hours we need with others. What is it to nurture this body and the other bodies in our care, whether that is children, a partner, lover or lovers, elderly parents? It can feel very slow, embodying Binah. It is grounded. It allows space for many things—

even for depression, anxiety, and retreat from the world. There's a cave-like aspect to it, a womb-like sheltering and timelessness. When we work with Binah in this way, we are intimately aware of the needs of our body, and we respond to them. My lower back is hurting; I need to move or stretch. I didn't get quite enough sleep last night; let me make room for a nap during the day. This food that I love eating doesn't suit me; I don't digest it well. I need more exercise; let me find a way that works—the gym, dancing, a team sport, yoga. In nourishing, sheltering, and nurturing ourselves, we embody Binah.

Binah hovers near the brain and head in the Adam Kadmon.

Hokmah Embodied

How to embody the unembodied? I think Hokmah is about devotion. What are we devoted to and how do we embody that? I am devoted to my children; I feed and care for them. I am devoted to the earth; I plant a garden, I study earth sciences, I support my workplace to move toward sustainable practices. I am devoted to the gods; I have a personal practice, I create altars and ceremonies, I sing and dance for them. I am devoted to my art; I make time and space for it, I put in the hours, I center it in my life. I am devoted to my community; I step forward to fulfill vital roles, I support others in leadership, I do the hard work that needs to be done. I am devoted to a vision of how we could live; I do my best to educate others, to practice living by those values myself, to offer challenge and support to others striving for change. I am a devotee…

Along with Binah, Hokmah is associated with Adam Kadmon's brain and head.

Kether Embodied

Kether is both not embodied and containing all our bodies. In this Kabbalistic conundrum we can make space for mystery. We may seek to understand but also know that not everything can be known. We can bring awe, delight, and reverence into complex situations. We do not turn away from the powers of birth, sex, and death but instead allow those experiences to deepen our ability to hold space for the mysteries. We let our edges dissolve. We see our current life as a play we are involved in and our personality as a role we may step free of at any time, through death or because we hold to it only lightly, as long as it's useful. We see and interact with others who are in their own plays and roles. We see through worlds and realms; we feel their edges. We know the ordinary is not ordinary. We breathe the breath of the I Am, sing its song, and feel it singing us. We are alive as the vibrating pattern of the universe, becoming and unbecoming all within a breath.

Kether represents the crown position within the Adam Kadmon model, hovering above the head.

ritual | This Body Is Sacred

Although we are always embodied, much of the time our conscious awareness is not attuned to that. It's inescapable, yet we escape it in a thousand ways. Every time we forget to breathe deep, to adjust our posture to the situation, to provide for our basic needs, to remain deeply in the present moment—each time we turn to a screen, an idea, a thought of the past or present—we sacrifice some of our awareness of embodiment. We could say that the trade-off is worth it, but these things aren't in equilibrium, in so many ways, and it isn't entirely paying off, at least for the planet.

We are out of balance—out of balance within ourselves, and mostly not even aware of that; out of balance between poor and rich segments of the population; out of balance with the living system that sustains us, indeed, that *is* us, as we are particles of it. We are currently rogue particles, not in cooperation or even awareness of the whole system, even while being completely dependent upon it. But this ritual is not purely to correct an imbalance and an injustice; it is a celebration, entering into the garden of delights that our senses offer to us.

Like other Kabbalistic exercises and practices, it's not meant as a one-off, even though that's how it's presented here. I remember listening to a rabbi speaking about offering prayers of gratitude on a single breath as a daily practice, and the interviewer asked how many of these prayers beginners should aim for each day. The reply was one hundred a day. This was not the answer the interviewer was expecting, and in his momentary speechlessness the rabbi continued, saying that the end aim was that this prayer would be occurring with every single breath. He was making the point that gratitude and presence is a way to live, as essential as breathing. It is alignment with the All and essentially an alignment with ourselves. Similarly, the practice of mindfulness, a Westernized and nonreligious form of Buddhist practice, is not solely about practicing a technique that can bring peace in times of distress, stress, or unrest, but about changing the awareness we bring to each moment. This ritual is sympathetic to both these ideas, and ideally it's deeply pleasurable.

TIME: Allow an hour

YOU WILL NEED: A place where you can be naked, preferably outside. Something to cover yourself—a sarong, blanket, cloak. Drinking water. An apple or other piece of fruit. Your journal and pen.

HINT: Don't take this book with you. Read through the instructions and then just make it up, as seems appropriate, once you are in the ritual.

Find a place where you will be undisturbed by other humans for an hour. Ideally this will be outside. Perhaps your back garden, a nature reserve, forest, deserted beach, river bank, or another place.

Please do take into account your physical safety and well-being, as well as other practical issues. You might need to remain partially clothed throughout, or perhaps you choose to do this ritual in the company of others for safety or other reasons. I have sometimes gone to natural places (forests, beaches) that during the day are filled with people but are deserted at night. At times I have taken the risk to be naked there, and other times I've chosen not to.

If being outside is not an option for you, translate the ritual to an indoors setting. You might want to bring flowers, leaves, and other pieces of nature inside or collect all your rocks, crystals, shells, and feathers to place around you.

• • • •

Begin your ritual clothed, honoring the earth and the Indigenous peoples who lived and still live in the place where you are. Ground yourself into your body, this place, and this present moment.

You might cast a circle, if that feels right or necessary.

Spend a few moments with your eyes closed or in soft focus, becoming aware of your breath and how it moves through your body. You might wish to consider the constant exchange of breath between yourself and the world.

With your eyes still wholly or partially closed, turn your awareness to your other senses, one by one. What can you feel, physically, underneath you and all around you? Is the earth soft or hard? How does the air feel, or sun, shadow, breeze, rain? What can you smell? How are these smells related to the feeling sensations? If you open your mouth, can you taste this present quality of air or imagine a taste? What are the tastes? What do you hear? Try turning your head to find out what changes. How many sounds can you discern?

Now open your eyes and spend some time looking about you. Look close, far, and at middle range. What are you seeing? How are your other senses informing your sight?

Take your clothes off and repeat the process above, beginning with eyes closed or in soft focus and moving through physical sensations: smell, taste, sound, touch, and finally sight. What is different? How is it different?

Perhaps you will want to move around now, continuing to tune into each of your senses. Possibly you will want to dance, lie down on the earth, stand pressed against the trunk of a tree, immerse yourself in water if you are by the water, do some stretches, or even begin to talk, whisper, or sing to the world around you.

Explore your senses. Is hearing stronger when your eyes are closed? With your clothes off, does the rest of your body gain a similar level of sensitivity and information gathering that your hands and face would usually have? How is walking on the earth with bare feet?

Come to a resting place. Return to a gentle breath and pick up your water. Try smelling it with your eyes closed. Then tip it toward your mouth, very slowly, finding if you can sense its approach. Allow the water to touch, then enter your mouth. Drink some water, having as full a sensory experience as you can.

Pick up your piece of fruit. Feel it with your fingers, hand, and perhaps even lips. Smell it. Taste the outside of it without biting into it. Gaze at it.

Consider the fruit. If to eat of it is to ingest Knowledge, would you do it? What does this mean for you? Perhaps you will choose to taste it. What knowledge are you receiving as you bite into, chew, and then swallow this fruit of a tree, of the Tree?

Continue to let yourself explore this world of belonging to nature through your senses. If you can, spend at least thirty minutes naked and outside. Let the question of what it means to be embodied ripple through this time.

• • • •

When you feel complete or your time is up, record your experience in your journal—you might choose words or drawings. You might wish to cover up or partially cover up for this, or you might need to return inside. What has your experience been? What challenges, insights, or gifts did this experience offer you?

If you cast a circle, make sure to complete your ritual by releasing it.

trance | Healing Ancestral Lines

Ancestors can refer to our own immediate biological or more distant ancestors. It can also refer to the ancestors of a tradition, our spiritual or magical ancestors, or even the ancestors of humanity. There are entire bodies of work dedicated to communicating with ancestors. If this is your interest or field of experience, consider this an open invitation to try blending that knowledge or those practices you already have into Kabbalah work. If ancestor work is a curiosity for you, here is one small process that might open some doorways. Even if you have no immediate interest in ancestors, approach this exercise as a part of an exploration of the embodiment of Kabbalah.

Our bodies don't just arrive into their forms independently. Every aspect of our physical being is guided by what has been before. The lands our ancestors lived on, the foods they ate, the stories they told, the trees and animals they lived with, and the very water they drank helped create them and thus helped create us. Ancestor work involves our families, particularly the biological families that we were born into. Many of us hold a history of trauma in our bodies from experiences we had growing up with or growing up away from our biological families.

Ancestor work can be done much more broadly or with a different focus such as our far-distant ancestors from hundreds or even thousands of years ago. It can be done with those we consider our spiritual ancestors—people who began or continued the tradition/s we now belong to, whether that is Kabbalah, Goddess devotion, Wicca, Buddhism, Western occult magic, or any other. This is an opportunity for healing, although if we had traumatic experiences with our family of origin, we do not have to begin with the trauma straightaway. We can skip back to our grandparents or great-grandparents. Working with these generations can inform and support us so that if we do choose to work with our most immediate ancestors, our parents, we have the tools, resources, and support we need.

This exercise is written to explore the motherline—the line that stretches back through our mothers, from our biological mother to her biological mother, to hers, to hers, to hers, and so on, perhaps back just a century or so or perhaps much further. There are many different lines we could explore—our father's motherline, our father-lines, a line we happen to know of or one we know nothing of, regardless of the genders it travels through, not to mention all the other ancestors that are invoked with each generation we reach back into—all of the siblings, the aunts and uncles, cousins, children who grew up but never had children of their own, children who died young—the whole network of human beings, once alive, whose DNA we share in some way. If you want to explore ancestral work with a non-biological ancestor—perhaps a step-parent, a beloved parental figure, or someone from your spiritual or religious heritage, please do so.

This trance is titled "Healing Ancestral Lines," but that is a grandiose title for very humble work. We do not come out of this with any ancestral line healed, as such. We go in and offer presence and witnessing and then we return to our own lives, the current incarnation of the ancestors, as it were, and hope to continue that presence and witnessing, particularly in relation to how our ancestral work has informed us about ourselves. We are active in both worlds—the ancestral world we've accessed by trance and connection, and our own living-right-now world—but we don't expect this work to be simple, quick, or completed. It's sacred journeying with the intention of bringing healing, while understanding that healing is an ongoing process with many layers and subtleties.

TIME: Allow an hour

YOU WILL NEED: An altar for the ancestors. This could be very simple: a candle and flower, for example, or much more elaborate, with photos, icons, and mementos. Your journal and pen. Coloring things optional.

You can do this work in a deep trance and journal afterward or you can enter a lighter trance, taking notes as you go. Over time you can try both ways.

Set up your altar.

Begin your work in the way that seems best to you. You might begin with a land or Indigenous acknowledgment, then ground yourself. You might want to cast a circle, turn to the directions, or welcome the elements.

Address your ancestors. You can acknowledge how they live within you, even specific instances of this: for example, your hair color or body type, the language you speak, your occupation, talents, or passions, or simply that you are one of their descendants. You might know some names you wish to call on, particularly if you are following one specific ancestral line, or the names might be lost or unknown to you.

If you have a clear intention, state it now, to yourself and your ancestors. Examples of an intention are: *to follow the motherline, to travel back two hundred years, to follow my ancestral lines back to Spain,* or *to visit one of the sources of my family's trauma.*

Choose a method to enter into trance. Some possibilities include breathwork, drumming, dance, or visualization. Choose whether to go deeply into trance or more lightly.

Create an anchor into the present time and place so that you can easily return whenever you wish. An example of an anchor is a favorite stone that you can hold in your hand before you begin the trance and when you wish to return. The anchor does not have to be a physical object; it can also be a phrase, an image, or an action. The important thing is to connect with it before you start the trance and know that it will bring you out of the trance.

Begin the trance. Spend a few minutes deepening and relaxing into your trance state.

Within the trance, open a portal or doorway to your ancestors. Some possibilities include:

- Visualizing or imagining yourself climbing up a diagram of your family tree
- Entering into a strand of DNA within your own body and following the spirals backward
- Imagining opening a book or photo album and traveling through the pages
- Picturing or feeling yourself standing next to an immense tree and finding a doorway into the tree

Allow yourself to be guided by your intuition, your gut feelings, and your imagination. If you're on a spiral staircase and something tells you *every spiral is fifty years*, believe it, and act as if it were so. If you see a doorway to exit and something within you says *not that door,* keep moving.

Find the right place for this visit. You might perceive this as a stillness and depth, as an interactive scene full of action and conversation, yourself as an observer of a scene playing out in front of or around you, as hearing or having a conversation, a bodily knowing, a resonant image, or some other way entirely.

Here are some steps you can follow within the trance:

▶ Introduce yourself by your name, your ancestry, and the time that you come from. Offer your willingness to listen and understand, the desire to heal, and curiosity about your ancestry.

▶ Spend some time there. Perhaps you will be involved in or create a ceremony, perhaps you will have a conversation, perhaps you will observe and feel. If you are asking for healing or bringing healing (or both), make sure to symbolize or enact that in some way.

▶ There may be one particular person you are drawn to. You can ask who they are, what is happening for them, and what messages they have for their descendants.

▶ When it's time for you to leave, offer your blessings and thanks to the time, the people, and the land. If it's a place or time you intend to return to, you can state this.

▶ Return the same way as you traveled there: via your family tree, the DNA spirals, or through the tree, book, or photo album.

Connect with your anchor as you complete the trance. Then take a moment to return fully—patting yourself down, having a drink of water, standing up or otherwise changing your posture, speaking your name (and maybe the date!) aloud, looking carefully at the objects that are physically present.

Spend some time journaling about your experiences.

Perhaps you have been inspired to do a particular piece of healing work, which could be creating a more permanent altar, working on a creative piece, doing a healing ritual on your own or with others, or seeking support from or starting a conversation with friends, family, or a therapist. Record this intention and then honor it in the coming days. Bringing this work out beyond trance and into the rest of our lives is a way to strengthen the bonds, trust, and power, both of magic and working with the ancestors.

Memoir: *Art and Life*

I visit Musée de l'Orangerie in Paris, those big pools of oval rooms dedicated to Monet's waterlilies. The vast canvases curve in concave away from the viewer, so it's like falling into the pond to be in the room with them. Four in each of two rooms; two pools, eight aspects of waterlilies at dawn, night, daylight, the floating images the effervescence the almost religious quality of it all. I came here with Damon when he was six, my second visit; he drew nothing but waterlilies for days, weeks. So coming here again is also falling back into that time because, though twenty years have passed, here it is the same, the exact same waterlilies waiting to be viewed, admired, offering that same second of transcendence they've always had. The carpet's the same, the bench seats in the center of the room the same. I've been in this room at three or four stages of my life and I'm always different but it's always the same and it always offers me something new.

This time I learn that Monet designed the ponds and the gardens for the waterlilies, for the paintings. So I go to Giverny to see the original. The day I choose is a day many hundreds—thousands, probably—of others have also chosen: late spring. A good time for flowers and the countryside around Paris. I walk from the train within a stream of people. I queue for a ticket. I process through the formal gardens around the house and press impatiently on to the waterlilies. They have lasted, as have the paintings, long past the life of their creator. There's a strange brand of immortal mortality flowering here as if they're the exact same ones in the paintings, regardless of the deaths of those other ones. Although in this version there are a lot of rules: no food, no stopping for too long, stay strictly on the paths, and there are guards walking around to make sure we obey.

I cross a bridge that's famous for its painted version. It's real under my feet, I put my hands on the railings, I gaze into a painting that's alive. I'm within it. It's very strange, almost unsettling, but also quite magical. I'm in a river of people and it's hard to stop anywhere, to leave the current, but I find a bench with a space and sit down to gaze and ponder more deeply. There's a mother and a small girl, about seven years old, already on the bench; they speak to each other in French. The girl is drawing waterlilies on a pad of paper. She lays the colored pencils in a row on the seat between me and her and picks them up one by one. I am entranced by the echoes of Damon drawing waterlilies and now this girl and how many others, through the years?—when a patrolling guard stops by our bench and reminds us in French not to sit too long, I think that's what he says, but then he also says, to the little girl, that she shouldn't really be doing that because her colored pencils might mark the bench.

I can hardly believe that's what he's said, but sure enough, the mother starts gathering the pencils up and the little girl argues with her a bit—like me, she can't understand the sense of this directive in this place of color and life—in this place that was built to showcase color and life—in this place that was built to showcase color and life so that an artist might not just see it, glory in it, but create in this place that has no frames, like the artwork eventually has to, even if they're vast, immense, take up whole rooms, are pools in themselves—in this place with the 360-degree living art, vibrant and shimmering, sharing its precious moments with us, who merely pass through, in so many ways, here in this place only for a few hours, on this earth only a few decades—here in this place a little girl is supposed to not-draw-with-colored-pencils, not try to re-create this brilliance on the page, not try to interpret what she sees and how she feels about it—because one of her pencils might mark the outdoor green-painted bench?

What if she's another Monet? What if her heart and eyes are filled with color and life and she has a passion to put a glimpse of it on a page? What if this is the way she relates to this scene, through drawing? What if she learns not to draw when other people are around, what if she learns that the world disapproves of creativity, of self-expression, of art generally, of the color escaping onto the benches… what if she learns to keep it all inside?

I have such a strong reaction to this—stronger, probably, than the little girl, her mother or the guard—and my French isn't up to expressing it: What is this place for? Why is it even here and why are we here? Isn't this little girl drawing waterlilies while gazing at waterlilies the exact reason? What are we here for, to spend our lives doing? Coloring so carefully we don't mark the bench or preferably not coloring at all? But the world is rich, spilling over in color and sometimes we know that and other times it's art that takes us there. Art hanging in an expensive, purpose-built gallery or art created in landscape or art on the page using colored pencils. Don't get color on the bench! How much color, exactly, could a slip of a pencil—a pencil! we're not talking oil paints here, but a colored pencil!—get on a painted wooden bench? Perhaps he was just in a bad mood? Doesn't like children? Wasn't allowed, himself, as a child, to do such a free thing as sit on a bench and draw pictures?

I move on and I am asking myself now, gazing at individual waterlilies, gazing at the ponds, the surrounding garden, which I find more beautiful, more meaningful—these gardens or those paintings? The paintings capture layers of ideas, concepts about beauty and nature, as well as the actual sight, interpreted by Monet, one man, a painter, long dead. *Les Nymphéas: Reflets verts, Les Nymphéas: Les Deux Saules, Les Nymphéas: Le Matin aux saules.* The garden is its own thing. All those moods—painted—are within it. The actual *les nymphéas* are here. All those uncaptured not-paintings—*Waterlilies at Midnight, Waterlilies at the Winter Solstice, Waterlilies Through Tears, Waterlilies while Making Love, Waterlilies Seen by a Seven-Year-Old*—they are here, as well. There's a clipped and manicured aspect—the performance of the whole thing—which probably wasn't here in Monet's time. And all these people—he didn't have several thousand visitors a day tromping through his views and threatening to leave colored pencil marks on his benches.

The paintings take my heart because they show me the possibility of this. But this—the garden, living—is itself. The paintings seek to capture a moment—though they're composites of many moments, they're not photographs—and this is the moment, living. A moment. A moment that I happen to inhabit and even though I'm sharing it with hundreds of others, I'm not, really. It's my moment. That little girl had her own moment. I turn to philosophical musings and she turns to colored pencils, but we are both inspired by this raw living garden, as Monet's paintings were. Although the paintings—or the idea of the paintings—inspired the gardens, brought the garden into existence. They feed each other, but one—however nuanced, however masterful, transcendent, ever revealing of new depths—is essentially finished. One is unfolding, and that's my preference.

The garden with its death and endless change, the garden with its paths and rules, guards and little girls, the garden I inhabit in this moment, gazing at shades of pink as they blush up a single petal—the garden. I choose that. Watching this insect ripple the water, hearing waves of conversation pass me by on the path—French, English, Japanese, Spanish—rising and falling in words and waves, this tide of people seeking—something. Beauty, art, love. The garden. Art and nature meeting in both places, the art informing the garden, both in its original composition and now, through the eyes of the gardeners, visitors, the French tourist board no doubt, and the garden informing the art—Monet's magnificence and who knows how many thousands of others, including one little French girl on the day that I happened to visit. Art and nature making love on the page, on the canvas and out here, intersecting with the wild; the passionate embrace.

• • • •

Still in Paris I go to l'Atelier des Lumières for their immersive art experience: an hour wandering through a huge repurposed industrial foundry with a projected 360-degree artscape comprised of Gustav Klimt's work. The paintings move across the walls, enlarge, drift apart and reform, dissolving one into another, parts of them spanning across the floor while on different walls other parts of them move, hold still a moment, arrive brushstroke by brushstroke or shred apart and rain earthward, five, six, fifteen different things to look at and all of them in change. I dissolve in it, it's like lovemaking, it's ecstatic, fierce and wondrous and revelatory, the light is everywhere, my skin receives Klimt's patterns, colors, I am only and exactly that, a living canvas for projected light; how I carry it, display it—that is up to me. I lie on the floor, I walk through forests of art and shadow. I am swallowed up in darkness when the light leaves—I watch the scribbles of an artist's brush string across a man's white shirt. The paintings form and unform, we are in and of the gallery, the edges are all dissolved.

I am the meadow of flowers I sit amongst. I am the diamond-patterned floor, the light reflects off me, I am the forest. The trunks of silver-white trees slide over human bodies. I am seated on an arc of blue so heartbreaking—changing to yellow-green-purple—my paper is purple with light splattered, it is red, dappled, it is streaking gray, light. I am in an ocean there are tides of small boats sailing in the sea, it ripples under, over, through me it dances over walls and through the space I have purple I have gold and black and cross-hatched light, always the light, the light the dappling, curling unfurling purple and golds of light—there is a blotch of red across my page. Now a ripple of yellow, touch of blue—it is in serpents/writing across—I am in a striped world, I am a stripe, I am bands of stripe. I am a blue forest with green. I am an ant in it, swallowed by color; the green comes for me, the red paints over—

I am devoured, consumed, tasted—bitten into by color, again and again. I am saturated, full of color, so full I drip and spill it out again, it tips over my skin and clothes I am running with color, with light, it is all light and I have been eaten by it. I watch a city build from nothing onto the black, we are in the grid of it, the wash, the underpinnings—there's a sudden warmth of orange and yellow—I am in it—now I have words flowing over my skin. We are dappled—one hand is red/rose the other yellow with a stripe of blue—the faces are gardens of color we are revealed, purple striations carpets that sweep across the floor, swallowing all they find.

Klimt's golden *Tree of Life* beginning, I am watching the beginning. Spirals uncurling from spirals, slow and ecstatic, relentless never-ending each piece appearing in place and the unfurling of life becoming, art becoming life and the birds and the colors and the pieces, each one and it's happening on every wall, in every direction, it's inescapable I'm swallowed by it, I've become it, I'm a curl, a spiral, a speck of gold—I am in the garden, *Arcadia* I think the word and see it all around, the floor is dark until leaves of light scatter off the walls and drift over me/the floor and now it's falling—the gold is dissolving into specks, to sparks, to atoms and it falls, drifting downward and across, through the floor, we are falling—we are torn apart by the endless unfurling, by spirals turning back into gold, back to dust, the sparks of the universe, becoming and unbecoming, to the depths of the world, to distance and separation and all is loss and beauty, inseparable and the spirals of the tree gold and spiraling is breathtaking, sere and majestic, it is majesty—grace—breath.

• • • •

I had a lover; I thought of him as a gift from Paris. So much of Paris in this Netzach story, the city of light. I nearly didn't meet him because I was about to leave; I didn't think anything could come of it. But he was insistent and messaged me for days in quirky, invitational, open-hearted ways and I succumbed to curiosity. I met him in a small garden patch next to the station, it's the end of the line and a hot day. He loped up looking so French: dark hair, slightly long; dark eyes and a sallow complexion; all focus, calm, and welcome. We walked off the edge of Paris into the forest and spent the afternoon walking and kissing and talking. His English is good though sometimes he grapples for more complex words and we debate, between us, the nuances of an English or French word.

It's getting cooler and he invites me back to his place, says he can cook something, we can have a glass of wine. And the other invitation is there, running underneath like a gold and green thread, but I feel that if all I wanted was wine, dinner, and a few more kisses, he will be fine with that. We go to a Carrefour, a minimart, and he lets me choose the chocolate. I choose my very favorite Lindt Citron Vert and he gets another because you can never have too much chocolate. I feel the kindness of the world, embraced by this so simple thing of shopping with a sweetheart. It makes me want to weep, but really I'm shining.

At his apartment we talk more seriously over delicious wine. He says he doesn't believe in cheap wine. We talk about desire and sex and relationships, and everything he says I like. We go to bed, his messy, unmade bed, and we make love for hours and hours in a free-falling sort of way that ebbs and flows and never really ends. I adore it. I lose myself in it, I find myself, I am totally myself. Free and laughing and weeping and kissing and unfolding on this bed in Paris and his eyes always searching mine, his mouth finding mine, finding my skin, my delight, expansion dare edge embrace, his arms around me his hands on me, in me all over my skin and there are waves of intensity and lulls of deep rest but still in the flood of it and one time, late it's very late by now, long after midnight, he gets up to turn off the lights and music and he's gone long enough that I'm nine-tenths asleep by the time he returns and he enters the bed with such focus and intent, opening my body toward him again and I half-say *Oh I thought we were sleeping, are we still making love* and he laughs and says *Yes, we're still making love*, and I'm so deep in that I've lost any measure of reserve I might have had—

We finally sleep a few hours. I sleep in his arms in his bed in his apartment in his city and I've no edges, I've gone over the edges of the page and I'm leaving color everywhere and when it's sort of morning we're making love again really this is him, his focused intent, and I've cried a dozen times from the beauty of it, the freedom delight the finding myself here the overwhelming gift of it, and it takes up so much room I can't even fit in grief or regret at the fact that I'm leaving. It's all joy. Oh, the reminder that this type of sex, of love, exists—the type that doesn't stay within the lines. That it's possible—that others apart from myself worship sex in this way, court it to open the gates and fall through and through and through, spinning about each other in vast space—sex as the most embodied, the most free, universal, unlayered, and becoming—

Ecstasy of stars and birth and death layered there between us. Sex as the story that rewrites the stars, alchemical, the space that creates space, the art that creates art, the worship of the divine through another human. The garden we build, creating a space for life to flourish. The art of love that spills off the edges of the bed, over the edges of the page, the immersion of it, the breath and body of it, the unbounding quality, the generosity of it, the thousand kisses of it, all the possibilities that dance here the sheer unending dare of the physicality of it; take me places I've never been and let me become all things and your hands on my skin and your kisses unrelenting, bliss, we are an artwork off the page, we are the reason the page exists, we are the city of love, we are colors, flowers, forest, every atom vibrating, becoming.

ritual | Playing in the Garden of Eden

The mythic imprint of the Garden of Eden story, told in the first pages of the Old Testament, is the focus and fascination of much Kabbalah theory and debate. In this ritual we take pieces of the story and play around with them, in true Kabbalistic style, to see what happens.

One piece of the (untold) story that I am passionately fond of is a claim by Timothy Freke and Peter Gandy in *Jesus and the Goddess*. According to them, there's a mistranslation in the story of Eve's creation. They note that a more accurate translation for what we have written as *rib*, Adam's rib, is actually *side*; that God took one of Adam's *sides* to create Eve (Freke and Gandy 2001, 90). That is, half of him. They were two halves of one being. As in the left- and right-hand pillars … They were, in combined form, a replica, a representation of God. Beyond gender, pre-gender. There's still space for God, for the middle pillar, down the center, the spine, the line of divine light, the pole that runs through each of us from Above to Below. The spine of our central nervous system, the trunk of us. Divided right and left by our brains, our bipedal natures, by the splitting of one into two and joined again by their union. How Kabbalistic.

There are many ways to engage with this story. I am going down the ritual path, described below, but you might prefer to write a song, create artwork, plant a garden, or all sorts of other things. It's beautiful to play out myths with other people if you have some friends, coven mates, or Kabbalists who are available for it; otherwise you can do it on your own. Make sure to play multiple different parts and have everyone swap roles because that is when the human aspects lift and merge into the mythic, when we're experiencing not just one angle or interpretation but many overlaying each other.

TIME: Allow an hour

YOU WILL NEED: A tree, preferably living, but it could be the image or
impression of a tree or a constructed tree, using a branch or a pole decorated
with leaves and fruit, or even a person playing the role of Tree. Fruit—apples
or something else. An attribute to represent the serpent energy—it could be
a serpent mask, a serpent-like piece of fabric, or a snake's shed skin. Book of
Genesis chapters 1–3 (I prefer the King James Version, which is available online
in multiple places). Your journal and pen. Coloring things optional.

Begin by grounding yourself and making any land and Indigenous acknowledgments you feel called to. If you wish to cast a circle and recognize the elements, do that. You might wish to call to the beings of the story: the Tree, Eve and Adam, the serpent.

Read aloud the story of Genesis chapters 1–3. If you have other people with you, pass the story around as you go so that different voices read different parts of it.

If you are alone, spend at least a few moments reflecting in your journal about the most noticeable parts of the story, particularly Genesis 3:1–6. If you are with others, you may choose to discuss this rather than writing.

Now set your mythic scene up around the tree, tree image, or icon. Place the fruit (at least enough for one piece per person) and the serpent symbol or mask near the base of the tree or even in the tree, within reach.

Optionally (but I would) take your clothes off.

Now deepen into a trance state using breath, visualization, drumming, rocking, or whatever method you prefer. Go deeply enough that you can be aware of layers of reality so you can walk in both worlds, but not so deeply that you can't move around and speak easily.

If you are on your own, step into the scene and take on the serpent's role; otherwise, any person does this. Pick up the snakeskin, snake mask, or other symbol and try moving with it, seeking out snakelike movements. Let your body and mind begin to resonate with the serpent of this story. You might want to make sounds, singing, hissing, or toning; you might twist and writhe on the floor; you might dance. Try out your senses, remembering that snakes smell with their tongues, and feel the vibrations of movement very acutely. You might want to pick up a piece of fruit, imagining its symbolism and power, understanding it as the temptation it becomes in this story. Try speaking—or singing or whispering—the line *Thou shalt be as gods*. I like it repeated many times, in multiple voices, letting them overlap and rise and fall.

If you have others there, one of them can then step into the scene as Eve. If you are on your own, put down the serpent's role and anything you've been holding, step outside the immediate scene and shake or brush yourself down or stamp on the ground a few times before re-entering the scene as Eve. Eve is offered the apple, or piece of fruit. As Eve, allow yourself to wonder at the Tree, the serpent, and the offered fruit. Engage all of your senses. Recall the promise: *Thou shalt be as gods*. Will you accept the apple? Accept or not, as you feel. Bite into it or not, as seems right to you in the moment.

If you have others there, and the person playing Eve has accepted and eaten of the fruit, one of them then steps in to play Adam, who in turn is offered a piece of fruit by Eve. If you are on your own, again step out of the scene to release the Eve role before stepping in again as Adam. Allow the same time and process as with Eve.

If you have others with you, play the scene through as many times as you wish, maybe as many times as it takes for each person to hold each role. If you are on your own, you may wish to return to one or more of the roles. Before you finish, spend some time with the tree itself, letting impressions arise within you in whatever form they take.

Complete the session with thanking Eve, Adam, the serpent, and the Tree. If you called to the elements or cast a circle, thank, honor, and release these.

Put your clothes back on if you wish and record in your journal what you experienced. You might want to draw as well as or instead of writing. If you are with others, allow time for private journaling and contemplation, then complete the ritual with debriefing and discussion.

activity | Creating the Seventh Disk

When you complete the work of this section, create a disk to represent the sephira you've been working with. This will be your seventh disk. Perhaps you started at Kether and you are now up to Netzach—in that case, it will be the green Netzach disk you are working with. Perhaps you began somewhere else in the Tree and so the disk you are making now is for Hokmah, Malkuth, Hod, or any other sephira.

TIME: 30–60 minutes

YOU WILL NEED: The appropriate colored disk (see "Creating the First Disk," page 69) and whatever art materials you wish to work with, such as colored pens and markers, paint, oil pastels, collage materials, stickers

Start by contemplating the time you have spent in this sephira, including looking through your journal notes and recalling any Kabbalah exercises, processes, or rituals you did, especially how these related to this particular sephira, as well as the general mood and events in your life during this time. By this stage you will probably have strong ideas about the place and purpose of this particular sephira.

Allow images, words, feelings, and ideas to arise. You can hold these in your head, immediately begin work on your disk, or jot down notes or a sketch.

Mark the name of the sephira onto the disk.

Decorate your disk, aiming to create something that will recall your time spent with this sephira. Perhaps this disk continues a style or theme began in the previous one or the others in this pillar or perhaps its decoration reflects its unique essence. Use any art or craft materials that are available or call to you. Your disk may be very simple, with just a few words or a single image, or complex and layered. Allow yourself to experiment with styles you are unfamiliar with. You might complete your work in one session or come back later to add more details.

examples of completed disks can be seen at janemeredith .com/disks

*into the garden of all things, all
possibilities multiple transcendent
named and unnamed an ecosystem
of paradise and falling falling past
falling through on endless flow we
are the forest ocean starscape we
are iridescent with possibility with
becoming*

*flying, breaking, through paradise
through the green the forest field
garden orchard viridian moss
emerald the idea of the butterfly,
its image refracting in dew drops
on green leaves the saturated colors
of it, the feathers of it, falling and
breaking—fall*

8
Magical Systems
in the Tree

The eighth sephira returns balance to the Tree. With the diagonal downward run from Gevurah's restraint and boundaries to Tiferet's center to Netzach's unending spill of creation, it has been a one-way cascading arc of gravity with no hesitations, no checks and balances. Something needs to pull this up before every atom in the universe just pours outward and all form dissolves. The pattern of the Tree is to move from the right to left, so now it moves to the left-hand pillar. This new sephira will be informed by the need to grow out of, as well as balance, Netzach's wildness, drawing on the strictness of Gevurah directly above it.

Hod is the eighth sephira, known as Glory, and the number eight brings stability. There are eight main compass directions, eight paths from Tiferet, and eight is the number of both the sides and the corners of a cube—not a flat square but a solid object with vertex corners. Even though it's solid, this sephira is not simple. Hod is all about the increasing complexity we inherit as we move down the Tree, further and further away from the I Am. Hod and Netzach form the third and final horizontal pair, bracing the Tree yet again. Because they are at the bottom of their pillars, they look as if they are set on the ground, leaving anything further to drop within the earth, like the roots of a tree.

Hod is where complexities are understood, refined, and categorized. In Netzach might be unfolding brilliance and unending change, but in Hod everything will be analyzed, labeled, and cross-referenced. It's as if one can't take a breath during Netzach: it's so unending, so dizzyingly complex and entrancing, yet immediately past that one is impelled to pick up the microscope, the pen and paper, the charts, and start crafting ways to understand. This eighth sephira combines the ferocity and clarity of Gevurah with the radiance and reach of Tiferet. Here will be precision, definition, and pattern.

Hod: *Complex Systems*

Hod is the eighth sephira in the Tree of Life and it restores order. It balances out the pairs by coupling with Netzach, it completes the left-hand pillar and thus puts the Tree back on an even keel, and it restores the sephirot to an even number. All of the lower triad will have secondary colors drawing from the colors of those above them; Hod's orange is a combination of the red of Gevurah, directly above, and the yellow of Tiferet, above and to the right. If we combine the attributes of Gevurah and Tiferet, we are looking at the Severity of Beauty or the Beauty of Severity. For a sephira that is deeply concerned with order, information, and patterns, these are fitting titles. Hod's own name is Glory.

I imagine Hod as a library—not just an ordinary library, although they hint at the glories of what a library can be—but a great, possibly mythic library. The library of Alexandria or the Akashic Records. Libraries as they appear in fantasy novels such as Garth Nix's *Lirael,* where some of the books are alive; Lev Grossman's The Magicians series, where there's a book of each person's life; or the Old Town Library in George R. R. Martin's *Game of Thrones.* The closest I've been to one of these libraries is the library of the Klementinum in Prague, which looks as if it literally spans time and creates magic all by itself. Libraries like this speak entirely to the imagination because, even with the one in Prague, we can't go into them; we just stand at the edges of the *No Visitors Beyond This Sign* gilt rope or linger on the page, catch glimpses, and wonder. Their magic appears even more powerful by their restricted access; it reminds us that books themselves are magical items. A library is a wonderful image for Hod because of its order, but not only that: the ideas contained in books convey the depth of their powers—everything from education to revolution to revelation.

However powerful, wild, or magical the contents of a book or library may be, the whole system only works because of its inherent order. This order lies in many layers. The books are all in one room or a series of rooms. The books are on shelves. They are all roughly the same shape. The information on the spine relates to the contents and categorization, so they can take up minimal space while still being easily located. They are shelved according to an order, and the shelves are usually labeled. There's a catalog, and sometimes a librarian as well, to assist us in locating a book. Within the books themselves lies more order: contents pages, chapter headings, margins, sentences and words and paragraphs. An agreed-upon written version of a language. Sometimes an index, references, a bibliography.

Books and other systems of recording and categorizing information are very Hod-like. They take that ray of Tiferet's golden light, apply Gevurah's discernment, judgment, and limitations, and produce a system. A code. A pathway to understanding. Consider the mystery of a library to a non-reader. If we stood inside a library, looking only at the spines of the shelved books, how could we explain what they contain? That each one is utterly different, though from the outside they all look pretty similar. Language itself is a Hod-like device—all these little marks on the page that we've agreed on the meaning for, and then somehow you are reading—wherever and whenever and whoever you are—a thought that I am composing in my mind, translating into words, and typing onto my (image of) a page. Even as readers standing in that library we can have an idea of the span of knowledge contained here, but to access it we have to lift the books down from the shelves, open them up, and immerse ourselves word by word in their contents.

To locate the book that we want, we use another code, the alphabetical-by-author-surname code for fiction and the Dewy Decimal System for nonfiction. Perhaps we discover its location within the library—or even check if the library holds the book we are looking for—by accessing yet another code, the filing system of the library catalog, most probably stored on a computer hard drive and accessed through the portal of a website. All these interlocking systems, each with a precise order that we can discern and navigate, all in order to discover something as yet completely unknown: the content of this book we're searching for. Once we've found it, taken it off the shelf, and opened the cover, then we're back in the wilderness again. No amount of chapter headings, glossaries, and back cover blurbs can convey this to us—the actual content, the world of the book.

Although at first glance a library and a garden may look completely different, there's a lot of each of them in the other. The library appears ordered and the garden appears chaotic, but there is deep order within nature and deep wildness to be found inside a library. If the contents of a library were as ordered and predictable as its structure, it would be a dull place. And if a garden was completely chaotic, it could hardly survive; it is ordered either by human design and direction or, if we are talking about a wild, natural place, its orders are climate, geography, and the eco- and micro-ecosystems it exists within, as well as fundamental natural laws. Both the wildness of the contents of books and the orders inherent within natural systems display the intimate intertwining of Netzach and Hod.

Order within the natural world is a field of endless study and fascination, and countless books have been written about this. In Prague my son saw a woodbook; its topic was a single species of tree. This book was actually a box made from the wood of that tree, with the cover made from its bark. Within it were also samples of the roots, leaves, and fruit, along with its botanical description. There were sixty-eight of these books, each for a separate tree. The book is the tree but the tree is the book. In one of her astounding fantasy novels, Catherynne M. Valente has a wonderful image of a tree whose flowers are books, and in his extraordinary epic *Vellum,* Hal Duncan has his character traipsing across a map of endless pages, literally trapped inside a book. Books and the natural world, gardens and libraries, weave into each other on many levels.

Kether, although the All and everything, was much simpler than the complexity we meet as we descend through the Tree. By the time of Hod there are layers within layers; it's a place of the mind. Kether is both all mind and no mind, but Hod is actual mind, the type of mind we recognize, although vast and more aligned to a supercomputer of all possible combined systems than a human mind. But we have bridges into this set of concepts even if we discover, once across the bridge, that it's like Russian dolls: there's always another one inside. Or, just as we are about to understand something, we realize that is a further door into the actual mystery. This Tree of Life glyph, with all its multiple associations, symbols, and overlapping depths, could have been made in Hod, with Hod, by Hod.

Looking at complex symbols such as the Tree of Life, we recognize that this is not something we are literally taking to be true; there are not ten or possibly eleven large circles or spheres strung out in space with pathways between them and different states of being within each. We understand that it's a model, a map, and not even a strictly accurate model or map. It's not like a map of a city, where we would expect what's depicted to represent reality extremely closely. This is a mind map, a set of metaphors layered on top of each other—invitations to magical thinking. Not just a random letting-people-loose-in-the-woods type of magical thinking but structured, purposeful, and specific—while still exploratory—magical thinking. Having such sets of symbols allows our minds to begin to approach the concept so that when we talk or think about the symbols and their relationships to each other, meaning starts to be created or revealed.

To begin thinking about Hod, we layer together the English name of the sephira, Glory, with its color of orange—a secondary color composed of the red of Gevurah and the yellow of Tiferet—along with its position as the base of the left-hand Pillar of Severity, its pairing with Netzach (green, Eternity, the base of the right-hand Pillar of Mercy), and its position in a triad with both Netzach and Yesod. We already have a concept of Hod just by looking at all that. We haven't even had any direct experience of it yet or thought too much about the word *glory* and what that might mean or had time to delve deeply into any of those associations with the other sephirot. But we are getting a feel for it. Then, as we apply analytical thought—so Hodian—we see that the famous limitations and powers of Gevurah must be broken down to finer application here, and that what is in Hod must address that wild abundance of Netzach.

I think of biological taxonomic classification, which is an application of boundaries on a precise level to the natural world. We also classify cloud types, examine geological strata, and use such tools as microscopes, telescopes, mathematical formulas, and the laws of physics. We investigate gravity, motion, the structure of atoms and the formation of stars and elements within those stars. All those things are happening regardless of humans, but in Hod we seek to observe, test, theorize, and create the means to communicate these complexities to each other. Language. Music. Even critical theories of art, literature, history, psychology—all come together in Hod with this basic premise of trying to understand the world we are part of, as the influence of Binah flows down this pillar, to define pieces of it and create representative structures whereby doors are opened to think and communicate more deeply and more precisely.

This exploration could go into so many disciplines—history, biology, astronomy, geology, chemistry, physics, psychology, theology, sociology, mathematics, art theory, anthropology, archaeology... Within each of those disciplines there are ways to deal with information—mathematical formulas, principles, data analysis, experimental procedure, peer reviews, discourse, observation... There are charts, diagrams, maps, blueprints, graphs, tables, and systems. The periodic table of elements is an example of complexity rendered systematically into a visual scheme that gives us information more vividly about each component, and its relation to every other component, than a lengthy description would. We can also imagine an orchestral work, the engineering of a building, or the programming of a robotic instrument as elegant expressions of the complexities they seek to explain. The beehive of European honeybees is a wonderful natural representation of Hod, the precision of form within which all aspects of life can be efficiently and perfectly conducted.

This eighth sephira is the place of tricky questions, where examining these questions does not necessarily lead to answers but more questions. For example, where in the library should an autobiography about wartime experience and the art of the period be shelved? One library categorizes the book under war, another under biography, and another under art history. Another question: Can we ever truly know what human experience was like one hundred, two or five hundred, two thousand years ago, or even in another culture or body today? We can look at evidence anecdotal and scientific, through artifacts and records and architecture—many disciplines—but we will never know exactly… and in every era or place the question is examined, a different set of answers occur. The nature of Hod is to delight in complexity.

To undertake scientific thinking and analysis that appears to go against the dominant religion of the day has always been difficult and sometimes dangerous. People who have pursued this, including alchemists, astronomers, and naturalists, have often paid a terrible cost. In 1663 Galileo was imprisoned for life for promoting the theory that the earth moves around the sun. Earlier, in 1543, Copernicus died before he could be charged with heresy for his book, which also postulated that the earth rotated on its axis as it moved about the sun, as the stationary center of the solar system. Charles Darwin, in the 1800s, agonized for twenty years before publishing his findings on his theory that all species of life have evolved from common ancestors, due to the huge social and religious condemnation that he feared awaited him.

People have been burnt alive, drowned, imprisoned, and tortured for questioning, thinking, and pursuing knowledge. The 99 percent of scientists who claim that we are in a global climate crisis have frequently been ignored, belittled, and discredited personally, along with their work. This is the contemporary version of heresy: to propose that our current assumptions and use of wealth and resources is unsustainable, perhaps even immoral. Journalists have frequently been required to present a so-called balanced report, with climate deniers granted the same platform and equal say as global climate scientists. No doubt future generations will despair over this, just as we do over the struggle of those earlier groundbreaking scientists and thinkers.

This whole topic raises the specter of disinformation—ideas and views that are presented as fact but have no factual basis. Misinformation is simply inaccurate, but *disinformation* actively seeks to redirect thinking, to rewrite the narrative around what's happening. Disinformation, sometimes scathingly termed *alternative facts*, appears to be on the rise, fueled by social media, conditions of fear and deprivation exacerbated by the coronavirus pandemic, and deliberate campaigns aimed at spreading dissent, uncertainty, and even outright violence. It can be very difficult to know how to meet this propaganda, both when we see someone we know influenced by it and in the wider world.

Part of the confusion stems from the way we have allowed feelings to be not just as important as facts but somehow the determinant of what we consider to be the facts. This is typical of our world that values the right-hand pillar over the left. An example of how this works is when someone, especially someone in authority, claims that they *feel* that crime is on the rise. This comment is not fact based—maybe crime is not on the rise—but is an emotional appeal. We may already be worried that crime is getting worse, or the comment may play into our uncertainty or fear around quite different things. The comment invites anxiety, not analysis. It sets the ground for a powerful figure to come in and save us or for a mounting campaign of fear and instability or the frightening combination of both.

The skills that Hod fosters should be adequate to meet these situations, but these skills of rationality, critical thinking, research, and fact-checking are not those highly esteemed within our world or on social media. An emotive photo, a call to arms, a conveyed sense of outrage or emotionalism are far more appealing for a post that may have only seconds to make an impact. Hod represents scientific thinking—careful, critical, tested. Such a measured and pedantic approach is often met simply with disbelief by those not trained in fields that rely on such thinking. When someone tells me that the 5G network is implicated in the spread of coronavirus, no amount of facts will challenge this opinion because the opinion is not based on fact. Facts are not the point.

The laboratory of Hod—where precision, verification, consistency, and truthfulness rule—is considered a side alley of the world we live in, relevant mainly to academics and scientists who, as we all know, live far away from everyday reality. Watching the apparent disintegration of America throughout the final year of Donald Trump's presidency I was wishing, desperately, for an education system that valued and taught—rigorously taught!—critical thinking, analysis, and logic. Of course such an education does not mix well with faith-based religion, maintaining a consumerist culture, or enforcing inherent systems of inequality. The laboratory of Hod, learning ways of thinking and behaving based on fact and analysis, can upturn our lives. This type of thinking reveals some of the delicate balance crucial within the Tree of Life, as rigor brings us back to choice.

If Hod is a library and a laboratory, it's also to be found within nature. That intimate relationship of Netzach and Hod allows form to interleaf with force on the smallest—and largest—of scales. The nurseries of the universe—places where stars are born and nurtured, vast clouds of gas and dust known collectively as nebulae—don't operate randomly. There are precise sets of circumstances, a particular process that occurs for a star to emerge. When a star is in existence, burning the fuel load of its own body, the creation of progressively denser or heavier atoms follows a set pattern. There are rules stars follow—rules depending on various circumstances—but they're not arbitrary and they're not elective. This is the precision, the limitation and—from our end—the classification of Hod on a grand scale.

On a more local scale, our planet creates or allows for the formation of life, that is, carbon-based life as we currently know it, without excluding the possibility that other forms of life may exist elsewhere. But we'd have to hazard a guess that if it does, it will follow strict, irrefutable laws of its own. Meanwhile our types of life, and even those parts of the world we generally consider not-life, such as viruses, volcanoes, storms, all follow beautifully complex and precise laws. It is our delight to study and learn about them, knowing that we are intrinsically a part of these systems we attempt to observe. Doing this we discover an apparent contradiction, through a Hod-like lens, about the existence of life on earth: statistically, it appears to be incredibly unlikely.

James Lovelock's famous Gaia theory, published in various forms through the 1970s, explained piece by piece why it was so unlikely—the exacting requirements of earth-based life and of vulnerable humans in particular. Life on earth is completely reliant on the atmosphere, with an exact mix of gases in our air. Humans are very sensitive to temperature and can only exist within a very tiny range of temperatures. Our planet had to be around the right type of star, at the right distance, with the right chemical constituents to allow this type of life to evolve. It's easy to note, retrospectively, that it has these factors or we wouldn't be here observing it. The life that has evolved suits its circumstances. But Lovelock went further, suggesting that there were so many unlikelihoods involved, so many different delicate factors in interplay with each other, it looked as if they were working together to create these conditions, even when there's a higher probability of other outcomes occurring. He suggests that Gaia, the earth, is in the process of creating life—and life-supporting circumstances—systematically, if not consciously.

Again, this looks like a very close balancing act between Netzach and Hod—the magnitude of possibilities honed down through almost infinite complexities to a system that functions. The laws of Hod operate in the service of Netzach, and Netzach provides the raw material for those Hodian laws to interact with. Patterns are a part of nature, and in Hod we study patterns: the patterns of how stars form, how the tides move, ecosystems and weather systems and systems within communities. Perhaps the most basic pattern is chemical. This chemical coding underlies everything. The stars. Air. Our bodies. Every single thing we look at, use, ingest, and even the process of how we think. Chemistry. The protons, the neutrons, the electrons—and of course the whirling distance within and between all those things. But essentially, starting with hydrogen, which has one proton and one electron. The ones. This is the building block of the universe and of all other elements. Hydrogen atoms combine, in our sun or another star, to make helium. All other elements arise from this type of process, combining with others, sometimes gaining or losing electrons, to create increasingly heavy, dense, and more complex elements.

These codes run through everything. Often we seek to codify, or to perceive codes and patterns, not just in chemical or physical phenomena but in history, psychology, and philosophy. Sometimes we get inspired by natural codes—our understandings of how a successful ecosystem works might be something we attempt to apply to human communities, for example. Permaculture aims to create systems of agriculture, the cultivation of certain crops and animals essentially for human use, in a way that is sustainable within itself, thus becoming its own ecosystem. Bees and other insect colonies have long fascinated humans for their complex and efficient system of managing their own environment, with every individual participating in the system for the good of all. *Hive mind* describes a pattern not of an individual mind but the effect of a group mind that serves all and controls all, with little or no room for individual preferences, questioning, or deviation.

While we might imagine that human decision-making is much more complex and variable, sociologists, psychologists, and political and economic analysts devote themselves to studying the patterns and codes—innate or learned—that we appear to follow. The state of Hod is very familiar to us. Netzach also is deeply familiar to us—that wild state of belonging to nature and the immersion offered there. Both these sephirot are low enough down the Tree that they are accessible and known to us. Our bodies and minds respond to their symbols—the Library and the Garden—and the doors to these mythic realms open for us, both for mundane purposes such as study and relaxation, and as pathways to ecstasy and union with the divine.

The code-and-chemicals pathway to the divine is less recognized at this moment in time than states of ecstasy. But as we follow Netzach's wild ecstasy, seeking to embrace and be embraced by the divine, Hod is required, in full, to provide the form for Netzach's force. Imagine an artist who never picked up a paintbrush; a poet, musician, or composer who declined to write—maybe because the limitations of the forms available to them could never capture their imaginings, their visions, the songs inside their heads. Without form, force is ephemeral; it cannot change or touch the worlds. Force yearns for form, chaos needs order, Netzach courts Hod—study the markings on the wings of this butterfly, count the petals of this flower, register the notes of this birdsong, taste the waters of this stream—and learn. Partake in this great wonder. Bring the garden to the library, the library to the garden, and in these overlapping circles, tides of dance, imbibe the nectar of the gods.

Other Magical Systems and the Tree of Life

The Tree of Life is a complicated system with many dynamics: pillars and triads, pairs and colors, paths and polarities, fast tracks and slow progressions. It has a clear order—from Kether all the way down to Malkuth—but the order can equally be read backward, from Malkuth all the way up to Kether. And perhaps Kether's at the bottom, not *up* at all. Or possibly the sephirot are in intersecting rings, like the wood of trees or the orbits of planets, but no one's quite sure whether it's Kether at the center of the whole thing or Malkuth. Maybe it depends where you're looking from. Or they could be like dimensions, from the simple dot on the page ● and then all the way out into the depths of string theory. But they are ordered; no one's disputing that.

As well as being a system with an order, the Tree of Life is definitely, and perhaps most obviously, a pattern. It's almost impossible to write about or verbally describe without a diagram, whether we are waving our hands around in the air, sketching it on the back of a chocolate wrapper, laying our disks out on the floor, or drawing versions of it in our journals. The pattern of it remains steady: the circles, the pillars, the lines of the paths, the lightning flash. The sephirot are always drawn the same size as each other and the distances between them are consistent. Da'ath, in spite of being not really there, is always not-there in the same place, the same size and shape as the ten sephirot.

The Tree of Life is symmetrical: if you fold it vertically down the middle, it matches up perfectly. If you fold it the other way, horizontally, Kether and Malkuth match up, Da'ath is over Yesod, Chesed folds over Netzach, and Gevurah over Hod, while Binah and Hokmah fall into empty space on either side of the path between Yesod and Malkuth. Tiferet is left with a cross in its center from all this folding. All of these things give us information about the individual sephirot, their relationships with each other, and about the Tree. But these are internal patterns. The Tree is also envisaged as a blueprint of the universe, the pattern not just of itself but of many other things. Certainly the fundamental pattern of the unfolding of the universe and how existence came to be, but also such concepts as individuation on the way down the Tree and union with the divine on the way up.

Within Kabbalistic theory and thinking there are many other patterns. The Jacob's ladder version of the Tree is one, which is essentially the Tree four times, descending, with a total of forty sephirot (some of them overlapping from one Tree into another). There's the Dark Tree or reversed Tree that Israel Regardie calls the Qlipothic Tree, hovering as a mirror image below the one we're familiar with. Adam Kadmon—the map of a human body—fits more or less over the diagram of the Tree, with some artistic liberties. Correspondences for the sephirot include Hebrew Names of God and angels.

There are also the sephirot-within-sephirot that are called on in the yearly Counting of the Omer. That's a forty-nine-day process working with the lower Tree for redemption, both individual and for all humankind. In the Counting we imagine a smaller version of the lower Tree within each of the lower seven sephirot; thus the count begins with Chesed of Chesed, moving the next day to Gevurah of Chesed, then Tiferet of Chesed, and so on. The second week begins with Chesed of Gevurah, then Gevurah of Gevurah, and so on, for seven weeks. Each day each questioner asks themselves how they can reflect and improve on their thoughts and actions with this focus.

There are many other non-Kabbalistic systems that can be (and often are) laid over the top of this diagram of the Tree, both to enrich our understanding of Kabbalah and also to read another depth or layer into the other systems. These are magical systems that arose independently to the Kabbalah and are not intrinsically connected. One could argue glyphs that are central to one religion or spiritual tradition are often to be found in another and that this is not coincidence. They may arise from the deep collective, our historic shared past, or the mythos itself. Possibly they reflect patterns in our brains and how we process and understand the world. There is also much crossover—and at different times vigorous debate and cross-pollination—by students and seekers and scholars within and between religious traditions.

The tarot is the most well-known overlay used with the Tree of Life. The deck of seventy-eight cards falls into place on this Tree; unsurprisingly, since the current forms of both are due to the work of Western occult magic groups during the early twentieth century, essentially the Hermetic Order of the Golden Dawn and its descendants. The Golden Dawn was an influential secret society whose members included Arthur Edward Waite, Pamela Colman Smith, Aleister Crowley, William Butler Yeats, Maud Gonne, Annie Horniman, and E. (Edith) Nesbit. Both Dion Fortune and Israel Regardie were members of an offshoot of the Golden Dawn.

The circle and the cross is a very simple symbol that fits neatly and perfectly over the Tree. The Star of David can be drawn with the top six sephirot, leaving a simple cross below it. I have also known astrologers, people who worked with a traditionally Native American medicine wheel, and many others to find alignments and patterns that fit into the Tree of Life. I like to experiment with the magical tools of the Pearl and Iron Pentacles (as worked in the contemporary magical traditions of Feri and Reclaiming) in the Tree of Life, matching their ten points of Love, Law, Knowledge, Liberty, Wisdom, Sex, Pride, Self, Power, and Passion to the sephirot. If the Tree of Life is—or to the extent that it is—a blueprint of the universe, even if still in progress, no wonder we can find so many cross-references and alignments within it and between the Tree and other systems designed to seek enlightenment and map the world.

Adam Kadmon

The Adam Kadmon is a powerful magical concept and well-used magical tool within Kabbalah (see illustration on page 288). Malkuth is at the feet and Yesod at the genitals and womb. Netzach and Hod are the right and left hips-legs-feet, respectively. Tiferet is at the heart and solar plexus, while Chesed and Gevurah respectively hold the shoulders-arms-hands. Da'ath is at the throat. Some commentators divide Hokmah and Binah up as different parts of the brain or head, while others position Kether, Hokmah, and Binah all together in the brain and head, or sometimes it's said that Kether hovers just above the head.

The Adam Kadmon describes both the Tree as it fits within a human body—our own small versions of it—and also the vast, impossible figure of Adam Kadmon that is as large as the Tree, perhaps literally or else in mythic terms. Certainly one would not attempt or imagine to fit the whole of even a single sephira into our bodies—it would be like inviting several stars, perhaps a cluster, to inhabit my right shoulder or wherever—but I can imagine opening the etheric body of my right shoulder to receive some of the energy or flavor of Chesed. In that measure, it can be informative and supportive. But Adam Kadmon, like a figure sketched in the stars, has ten sephirot within the body. Or rather, perhaps the sephirot create Adam Kadmon as one of their (joint) emanations, an expression of the Tree.

We can work magic with this figure, either within our own bodies—an injury to my left ankle could be seen as a reminder to rebalance myself between Netzach and Hod, to rely less on the intellect and more on feelings—or within the body of the Adam itself; how is Chesed resonant of the right hand? If I wish to be more like Chesed, what practices can I do with my right hand and arm that will enhance that? As the figure of Adam ourselves, we can lie facedown either on our disks or the ground and feel for a moment or two what it means to be held within the Tree, paired with the Tree, perhaps making love with the Tree. At any time—walking around, lying in our beds, doing the dishes—we can contemplate what it means or how it feels to hold an echo of this Tree within ourselves.

The Circle and the Cross

The circle and the cross is probably the simplest system to lay over the Kabbalistic Tree of Life.

On a map of the Tree, draw a circle through the centers of Kether, Hokmah, Chesed, Tiferet, Gevurah, Binah, and back to Kether. Da'ath will be enclosed by this circle. Now draw a vertical line from the center of Tiferet down through Yesod and into the center of Malkuth. Finally, draw a horizontal line from the center of Netzach across to the center of Hod. This is the circle and the cross. Every one of the sephirot is involved, all in interesting ways. The top six have formed an inward-gazing circle, protective, sheltering, and equalizing. The bottom five have formed a cross or a crossroads, with possibilities leading outward in all directions. Tiferet is part of both circle and cross, the hinge and doorway from one to the other.

This glyph is the symbol for the planet Venus, modeled on the hand mirror of Venus and used to denote the female gender. Thus we could link it with beauty, the English name most commonly used for Tiferet, noting that this is not an external or visual beauty but a beauty of the soul, of the individual's reflection of the divine. We might recall the linguistic observation that in Hebrew the *-ah* ending of a word denotes it as feminine and note this applies to *Kabbalah*, as well as *Binah, Hokmah,* and *Gevurah.* Following this thought we can imagine that the generative aspect of Kabbalah, the Tree, and the whole of existence might be perceived as female rather than male.

What's most interesting to me is that when we fold our diagram horizontally in half, the cross of the lower Tree falls within the circle of the upper Tree. This circle and cross combined in one is known as a Celtic cross, referencing the sun (the circle) and the earth (the cross), as well as the four elements and the four quarters of the world. If you've literally folded the paper in half, you can't actually see this, so really you need to imagine the folding and then draw the cross into the circle. The center point of that cross—that before was floating in the air between Hod and Netzach—now rests in the center of Da'ath. So Da'ath is not just a circle held within a circle, but it also contains the cross, forming a miniature Celtic cross itself. Here is a mystery revealed, a subject for deep meditation, trance, or inspiration. Here we fix our gaze on Knowledge, that esoteric, secret knowledge kept at the heart of the Tree.

Tarot

Entire books have been written about the correspondences between tarot and Kabbalah, so this is merely the briefest glance at the subject. Essentially, the tarot deck commonly in use, regardless of its style, tradition, artists, or anything else, is a seventy-eight-card deck. It has twenty-two major cards and fifty-six cards in the minor arcana—four cards more than the usual playing deck because, as well as each of the four suits having the numbers one (or ace) to ten, it also has four court cards. These are variously named king-queen-knight-page, king-queen-prince-princess, queen-knight-prince-princess, father-mother-son-daughter, or variations on those. The twenty-two cards of the major arcana follow a set, numbered sequence, occasionally with minor variations in order or name but essentially consistent. They are numbered zero to twenty-one.

This is how to place the entire tarot deck into the Tree of Life.

The aces of all four suits go into Kether, the twos into Hokmah, the threes in Binah, fours in Chesed, fives in Gevurah, sixes in Tiferet, sevens in Netzach, eights in Hod, nines in Yesod, and tens in Malkuth. In this progression we can see the increasing complexity and division of numbers and sephirot as we move down the Tree. The aces are beginnings that hold the seed of what's to come, as does Kether. The tarot twos carry a balancing and duality, like Hokmah. The threes in tarot are dynamic, reminiscent of

Binah's gestation of matter. The tarot fours echo the stabilizing force of Chesed, steadying the flow of the upper into the lower Tree. Fives in the tarot suggest the limits of Gevurah; sixes, the rebalancing Tiferet brings to the Tree. Tarot sevens reflect the complexity of Netzach; eights, Hod's order. The nines offer a depth of the suit they belong to, just as Yesod does, and tarot tens carry almost too much weight, like Malkuth.

The court cards of a tarot deck are usually assigned in groups to particular sephirot (queens here, princesses there), but to me it makes more sense to place them in the four quarters of Malkuth, all bound to this earthly realm and adding to the complexity of this sephira. Also, Malkuth is often shown in four quarters, with four colors: olive, citrine, russet, and black. Almost always the court cards are human figures and so surely belong in the realm of Malkuth.

The major arcana unrolls itself along the paths of the Tree. Here are the paths, each with their attendant card and thus an indication of what lies on the journey between any one sephira and the next. To create a total of twenty-two paths, there are paths between Malkuth and both Hod and Netzach, which often don't appear on other diagrams of the Tree.

Paths one to ten are considered to be the sephirot themselves; therefore, the numbering of actual paths begins at eleven.

Kether to Hokmah—Path 11—The Fool

Kether to Binah—Path 12—The Magician

Kether to Tiferet—Path 13—The High Priestess

Hokmah to Binah—Path 14—The Empress

Hokmah to Tiferet—Path 15—The Emperor

Hokmah to Chesed—Path 16—The Hierophant

Binah to Tiferet—Path 17—The Lovers

Binah to Gevurah—Path 18—The Chariot

Chesed to Gevurah—Path 19—Strength

Chesed to Tiferet—Path 20—The Hermit

Chesed to Netzach—Path 21—The Wheel of Fortune

Gevurah to Tiferet—Path 22—Justice

Gevurah to Hod—Path 23—The Hanged Man

Tiferet to Netzach—Path 24—Death

Tiferet to Yesod—Path 25—Temperance

Tiferet to Hod—Path 26—The Devil

Netzach to Hod—Path 27—The Tower

Netzach to Yesod—Path 28—The Star

Netzach to Malkuth—Path 29—The Moon

Hod to Yesod—Path 30—The Sun

Hod to Malkuth—Path 31—Judgement

Yesod to Malkuth—Path 32—The World or The Universe

I invite you to get out the tarot deck, set up your disks on the floor, and take some journeys. Trance, create art, journal. It's rich, complex, layered, and quite possibly never-ending.

exercise | Tarot Reading

We can work with the tarot to meditate and explore within the Tree by laying the deck down on top of our disks or a map of the Tree or in the shape of the Tree, as detailed in the previous section. The whole thing might be a bit much; maybe we just choose one sephira and its connecting paths, lay out the relevant cards, and immerse ourselves in that landscape. From that point we can trance into a journey: as a landscape or inviting any figures on the tarot cards to speak or interact with us. We can create art in response to this, either visual or written or any other form; we can meditate, dance, or practice voice dialogue techniques. We can also use tarot cards for their most familiar purpose: a tarot reading.

This will be a tarot reading within the Tree, so every card will have not just its own meaning and not just our emotional or gut reaction to the card, but also Kabbalistic references. For example, if we turn up the Wheel of Fortune, we might reference its path between Chesed and Netzach. Further, if that card falls into the position of Tiferet, we ask: What can the path between Chesed and Netzach tell me about my relationship to

Tiferet? Tarot readings are almost always done in relation to a prompt or question, so if we have asked *How shall I deepen my spiritual practice?* we then have an opportunity to consider how our heart, and the beauty within us, might benefit by traveling more deeply the path between Chesed and Netzach, perhaps in order to understand or assimilate the variances of fortune, find internal balance, or cultivate detachment, depending on our take on the Wheel of Fortune.

TIME: 30–40 minutes

YOU WILL NEED: A deck of tarot cards, your journal and pen, a cloth or clean surface to work on. A blank map or diagram of the Tree.

Tarot readings usually focus around inquiry. Open-ended questions suit the complexity of the tarot, so we might ask *What things should I be considering at this time regarding my career?* or *What would be the consequences of returning to study?* and get a useful answer. If we ask a simple yes/no question such as *Should I take this job offer?* the cards are unlikely to respond with similar simplicity. Instead, we would get reflections on the pros and cons, the alternatives and the underlying issues, so we might as well ask the best question we can and expect to deal in complexities. The framing of a question is an important part of tarot readings.

For this reading, you might have a pressing issue in your life that you wish to investigate or you might ask a more general question reflecting on your learning of Kabbalah magic, such as *Show me my unfolding relationship to the Tree of Life* or *How can I engage more deeply with this work?*

Prepare the place you will conduct your reading. This is often on a cloth to keep the cards clean, but you might also choose to be by your altar, have one or more of your disks with you, or actually do it within the Tree, with your disks laid out on the floor and you sitting amongst them.

Shuffle the cards. I just mix them up on the cloth with my hands, stirring them around for a while, before gathering them back into a pack. Consider your question or, alternatively, let your mind become blank and receptive.

Some people like to cut a deck of cards once it's been shuffled, facedown and either into two piles or three, and then put the deck back together with the cut portion on top. Deal from the top.

This is a ten-card spread, following the layout of the Tree of Life. Following the diagram of the Tree or your blank map, lay the cards out facedown in this way: the first card will be in the Kether position, at the top; the second will be in the Hokmah position, down and to the right; and so on down the lightning flash to Malkuth. Leave the Da'ath position empty for now.

One by one, turn your cards up. Reflect or meditate on each one before moving to the next. Interpret each card in relation to its position in the Tree, as well as in relation to your question. For example:

KETHER—the question or situation at its most entire, somewhat beyond what we will ever access

HOKMAH—the reflection of the question or situation and the first glimpse of how to learn from it

BINAH—the depths and potential of the question or situation

CHESED—the amount and type of energy that is needed to address the question or situation

GEVURAH—the type of boundaries and power that are needed or that must be met

TIFERET—the gift this situation offers

NETZACH—what creative possibilities or challenges exist within this situation

HOD—the opportunity or necessity for learning in the situation

YESOD—the mythic, emotional, or psychic moods of the situation

MALKUTH—the practical and immediate needs of the situation

Alternatively, even though you lay them out from the top of the Tree downward, you might choose to read from Malkuth upward.

At the end of this process, you might choose to turn the next card off the top of the pack up and place it into the Da'ath position, sideways or on a tilt, if you like. This card can show a hidden potential within the situation, especially if it is a Major Arcana card.

Record your reading in your journal or on your blank map of the Tree, along with your question and card interpretations. Return to it in a week or two and add a further interpretation; this will always be deeper than could be seen the first time.

process | Drawing Other Systems onto the Tree

Perhaps you are interested in investigating more deeply how Buddhism's eightfold path might map onto the Tree of Life, or the Iron and Pearl Pentacles, or the shamanic concept of three worlds, or astrological correspondences, angels and archangels, herbs, or something else. You might choose a system you're very familiar with or one that you're not familiar with but are curious about. You can do this many times with different systems or keep layering one system over another, building up composite, extremely complex maps.

I recommend beginning this work in your journal, with a drawn map, and then later moving it to the floor, amongst your disks. You might want to add written signs, which you can place on or near the disks, particularly if you've chosen a system you're not familiar with. Once we are physically within the Tree in this way, a layer of body information, somatic experience, adds to our perceptions and understanding. Both this and the more abstract drawing of a map give us valuable insights and ways of relating to these overlapping magics.

TIME: 1 hour

YOU WILL NEED: Journal and pen; colored pencils optional (but useful); your sephirot disks; spare paper for labels/signs; ribbon, tape, chalk, or some other way of marking paths between the disks; information on the system you're seeking to correlate with the Tree

Begin with a map of the Tree of Life, just the sephirot and their names, with no paths drawn in. I usually draw Da'ath with a dotted outline. Take a whole page for this in order to leave room for notes and clarity.

Then draw your second diagram, or information, over the top of this map—possibly using a different colored pen or pencil.

I'm going to take as an example the eightfold Buddhist path, about which I know almost nothing, so I'm working from a diagram I found online. I'm intrigued by its eightfold nature, how that might sit over the paths radiating out from Tiferet and where each of its aspects will end up in relation to the sephirot. The eightfold paths and my alignments with the sephirot are: *Right Livelihood* (I aligned this with Yesod), *Right View* (Kether), *Right Intention* (Hokmah), *Right Mindfulness* (Binah) *Right Speech* (Chesed), *Right Concentration* (Gevurah), *Right Action* (Netzach), and *Right Effort* (Hod). Malkuth is left at the bottom, anchoring the whole system.

Spend some time with your system and map, writing, thinking, or dreaming into its layers. Where do the sephirot match up to these correspondences? Do they open new depths of understanding or contemplation in either or both systems? What can you learn from the overlay of the Tree onto your selected system? Do you also learn new things about the sephirot?

Now take this physically into the Tree. Lay out your disks on the floor, set up signs for the new system, including paths or lines if you wish—in this example, I would put in the spokes of the wheel, correlating with the eight paths that lead from Tiferet. Then walk into your system, move around and through it, contemplate it from different angles, spend time with places that seem less clear to you, and take notes as you wish.

You can ask a focused question or contemplation from within it.

Why stop at one overlay? It is possible to continue with another overlay or more than one—for example, the Wheel of the Year could overlay what I have already done, leading to yet more complex and labyrinthine explorations and considerations.

Memoir: *Multiplicity*

There's a multiplicity unfolding in my life, a complexity of layers and people and events I can barely keep track of, it's so many and overlapping and intricate. I still don't have any lovers but I've become the lover of the world, and face after face of the world shows itself to me.

• • • •

There's a temple night with over a hundred people and my energy is high, I'm delighted by it. We're in large double circles, doing exercises with person after person, consent exercises, yes and no, eye gazing long moments, move around to the next person, the next, the next. One of my partners is a narrow young man, dark hair, pale skin. I ask his name in the seconds before the exercise begins and it's a French name, he has an accent and I ask *French?* and he says *Yes*. The exercise is to play with energy without touching; we bring our hands close and feel the warmth, move them apart until we lose it, bring them back together again. I'm intent, focused. We move a long way back and I can still feel it, waves of warmth. I laugh with delight and when we come close this time it compresses, intensifying so we're in a bath of it but our hands are still the main focus, we try dancing with them, and at the very end we bring them together, palm to palm, both hands, and it feels sealed.

The evening sweeps on, more pairs, then the pairs join into fours and then eights and sixteens. I'm still enjoying it. Half of us are given blindfolds and told to find a partner. I see him nearby and I ask with my eyes and shaping the words through the noise, not trying to be heard, *Do you want to pair?* I'm hesitant in it, I leave space for him probably wanting someone his own age, someone else basically, but he smiles and nods. He speaks his boundaries, puts the blindfold on, and lies down on the wooden floor. I have ten minutes, or maybe even longer, to touch him.

His frame is delicate so my touch matches that. I trace fingertips up his arms in slow circling increments, I touch his hair, just barely moving fingers through the strands of it. I cup the palm of my hand against the side of his face, at first not touching, just the heat of it, and then the lightest touch I can manage. My fingertips trail down the open neck of his shirt and then I place my hand over his heart. Not the center of his chest, his actual heart, and this is where to be. He is trembling and I press my hand down a little so he will know I'm not leaving, I feel the warmth pouring through me and I put more weight into my hand as if I could press through his chest and actually be touching his heart. All my concentration is there.

Afterward he nearly weeps, telling me how strong it was for him—after he has touched me, light and delicate, running his hands over my limbs and body, not stopping anywhere but sweeping across me, again and again. After we have lain together on the hard floor and kept touching, holding, sinking into a shared delight toward the end of the evening while people walk around us. That French intensity, the grace of him. We take each minute given; holding, holding. I feel I could never be held enough. And we talk in brief pieces about France, about his travels and mine, and we don't want to let go. About half the people leave, so it's quieter, and then it's eleven, or whatever time it is, and they ask everyone to leave. I lean over him and kiss him, a whisper of a kiss, then we help each other up, hold each other one last time, then I find my things and go out into the night and drive home.

. . . .

A friend and I find ourselves in the same country—a country where neither of us lives—and agree to meet up. I arranged the accommodation and everywhere seemed to have just a double bed. I wrote and asked if this was okay and although my friend wrote back saying yes to the cute-van-in-a-field, the bed issue was not addressed. When I get off the train to be met on the platform, we are so pleased to see each other. We trek for miles, cross-country through fields and woods. We create dinner together at the tiny sink/bench/burner and we are coordinated, smooth, in agreement. We eat the same type of food; we prepare a meal the same sort of way.

We spend three nights sleeping beside each other—sleeping close, it's a small bed— and the days roaming the countryside, talking and not talking. Eating and sleeping and walking together—it takes my breath away, the kindness of it. Each morning my friend turns to me in bed and asks, first thing, *What did you dream?* It is such deep, stirred delight and anguish in me to have this asked, to be this close with another human. I feel almost stilled by this level of attention, of presence, something in me can finally breathe more deeply and I'm unendingly grateful.

. . . .

I meet this man for a date in a Sydney suburb. I'm a little incredulous he was so keen, partly as he's twenty years younger than me. He says *Oh, I knew I wanted to meet you* and he's soft and kind and good-looking in a bearded, golden sort of way. We talk about children's books and his work as a nurse. We end up sitting on a picnic bench in a park and I ask if he wants to cuddle, although I can scarcely believe that he might, but he does. He sits so that I'm between his legs with his arms around me, my back against his chest, and his arms are bare, I stroke them with my fingers and I feel so found, so reassured by the world. We stay like that a long time, maybe an hour, sometimes talking sometimes not. It sweeps deep reassurance through my skin and flesh and right at the end we kiss, little exploratory kisses of delight.

· I have dinner with him the next week and walking through the harborside streets of Sydney holding hands in the evening is perfection. To kiss by the water, to wander up Observatory Hill in the soft dark air, to eat a meal and feel his hand on my knee or holding mine on the table, to enjoy the mildly scandalized looks we attract—I cannot stop smiling. I take him back to my hotel room just to be somewhere warm but once there I find that we are not really a match—he is possibly used to women who throw their clothes off and have sex immediately—and I would have to teach him every single thing and I'm tired, too tired for this, so we say goodnight. A few days later I leave Australia for Europe.

· · · ·

I meet this man in Byron Bay, he's traveling for work and says he just wants someone to talk to. We get on really well, and the way he talks—about his mother who's ill, about his teenage children who are struggling in different ways, about himself—I really like him. This face of the universe. We have a drink, we have dinner, we walk on the beach. I'm always amazed at how people abandon the beach at night—it's nearly empty, though by day it's packed—now we have the majesty of it, the dark waves and salt air expanse to ourselves. We walk along the edge of the water, in and out of wavelets, and keep talking. At some point we take each other's hand.

We stand on the sand, with him closer to the waves so our heights are more even, and breathe until we are just nearly touching. Our breaths move us closer. I feel the heat of him in the night air. Parts of our skin—hands, arms—begin to touch, and I slow down. Slow down into the molecules of it. I let it unfurl like a flower, one petal at a time, until eventually we are standing, body brushing body, and so slowly, slowly I bring one of my arms up from my side and let it curve around him.

Back in his apartment he clears the couch, which he's been using as a wardrobe, and we sit and negotiate touch. I teach him to ask for what he wants—how sexy that is—and how to receive a no and be grateful for it. At each of these things he is amazed—at the erotic power of consent, that he's not offended or hurt by a no, at the layered texture and sensuality of simple, delicate touch. I rest against him and he strokes the skin of my arms lightly. It's late and this is a sort of bliss to be held in this space of touch and attention, one corner light on, in a tourist apartment in Byron Bay.

He asks me to stay and I won't, not trusting him yet. He asks to see me again and we make a few half-organized plans. He walks me out to my car and we stand in the street and kiss. He doesn't respond to the message I send the next day or the one I send a week after that, and then he deletes me off the app. I know the names and ages of his children. I know the messy details of his breakup, where he grew up and where he works, his relationship to his parents ... I wanted to see him again. I could have been his lover.

. . . .

In Paris I'm eating a meal in a small Italian restaurant, less formal than French, homemade pasta and a breezy feel. The waiter flirts with me, he's probably twenty-five, cute and very conversational. He asks why I haven't ordered wine with my meal, and I say I have to teach later tonight and he throws up his hands in French horror and brings me a glass of red wine. He smiles and says *You can be my teacher* and I laugh. He laughs too and lifts his eyebrows in invitation and I have to shoo him away. As I eat he looks at me every so often—it's early to be eating in France, and the waiters are mainly standing around with each other near the bar. He brings me a liqueur at the end of the meal and when he delivers the bill there's an extra piece of paper with his name and phone number scrawled across it. *I get off at eleven,* he says. *I'll meet you outside.* I laugh again, maybe blush, with this sweetness and attention, and I say that I can't, I really do have to teach, and he's incredulous—how could I give this up? and I am, too—how could I?

. . . .

London. A young man, a museum curator, very keen. Worried that I'll leave the country, he texts me saying if he doesn't act fast, he'll be left behind with a kiss dying on his lips. I laugh out loud. We meet for a picnic in a London park and he's sweet, with a heartbreak story about a mother's death and family dislocation. He's attentive, and I really like the way he touches; at first my hand and arm, and later, strolling through the early evening summer park, he stops and holds me a few times. We kiss, and he is a delicate and insistent kisser and I like it more than I thought I would. He wins me over.

He sends a lot of fun, flirtatious texts and I respond, so we meet again for dinner. It's raining and we can't quite find the grace of our first meeting: our choice of food, the matter of who's paying, how long to walk afterward and how far to go erotically are all awkward. We kiss and cuddle and that's the best bit but I don't feel any depth between us so that's it, really. I send him a few texts afterward but he doesn't answer.

• • • •

Still London, another young man, this one I almost didn't meet—he's going overseas himself in two days or perhaps tomorrow but he insists. We meet in one of the more depressing shopping areas of greater London, and when he's there, when he shows up, I suddenly get it. What's between us, why he wanted to meet, and he's both inordinately shy and very intense, as well as somewhat awkward, but he sees the world in such a peculiar, interesting way I could talk with him for hours. He's quite good looking—much more than his photos—and I like how certain he is about his attraction to me. We talk a lot, fast and deep, about travel and sex and relationships and life choices, and lately I haven't been able to imagine, at all, the type of person I could have a proper actual relationship with, but talking with him, I suddenly can. This type of person—deeply quirky, independent and somewhat of a loner, passionate, and revealed—I actually could have a relationship with someone like this.

We talk about touching and then we touch. He puts an arm around me on the bench we're sitting on, off the edge of the shopping precinct in front of a closed theatre. We talk about kissing and then we kiss and it's good, promising. I could keep kissing him for hours. Days, possibly. He's the standard twenty years younger than me but with him it doesn't show so much because he's intellectual, traveled, self-aware, socially critical. I want to keep him. But he's going away and right now has stolen time from getting ready, has to finish packing up his flat, has to go and see a friend he'd had a falling out with, and we talk about how alive it seems between us, how full of possibility, and in the end I tell him to go, get on with what he has to do, and it's a bit of heartbreak but we part.

• • • •

He's in Paris, he's Arabic, he's an academic, young and intense. We spend five months in intimate, demanding texted conversations. He offers, at a distance, adoration, challenge, stripped naked raw intimacy. He tells me explicitly what he wants us to do, and I burst into tears, again and again, at the relief of it, the remembrance, that this possibility exists in the world, of lovers, of bodily sexual lovers. He says we can kiss for hours. He has a hard edge and again and again drives me into a corner where I have to have a break from it; I can't agree or don't want those power dynamics and then a few days later, a week later, he sends a softer message. We're involved in a dance, maybe tango, it's so passionate and raw and strong—pushing our strength up against each other, the feint and play of it, the animal of it. I feel completely, overwhelmingly desired by him and within that my confidence is born again, my lightness to wear it into the world, and things change for me, he changes things. I never meet him.

• • • •

A young man sends me a text, saying *I'm applying for the position of your London lover.* I meet him on his lunch break by the Cupid statue in Piccadilly. He is tallish, rangy, with dyed blue hair. When he sees me, the first thing he says is *Oh, you're so beautiful.* We walk in the park and sit under a tree—he wants to touch me and I want to be touched. We also talk about history—his university major—and lovers and cats. He can't believe I haven't had sex for years, he wants to change that, he offers to change it and really, I'm accepting. He says he's going to make love to me with his mouth, that he loves to do that, he adores women. This whole world that he's opening, with his hand in my hair, with his mouth on mine, I want to fall into it, oh yes I want to be adored and I'm smiling and nearly singing with it. This face of the universe. It doesn't ever actually happen—but maybe that's enough?

• • • •

There's a man in Sydney who kisses the inside of my wrist so delicately, with so much attention, I think I might faint with it. There's a young man at a festival in Byron who pairs with me for an intimate massage; American and very sweet, I nearly didn't ask him because he was so good looking, but he also looked lost and relieved when I rescued him. There's a man I meet at a polyamory dating event who's magnetic and I like him a lot, African, I kiss him in the street before discovering his wife doesn't really want him dating other women. There's a man at a spa night, another American but my age, it's his last night in Australia and we lie holding each other for thirty minutes, melting into softness together; I wish he had time to come and visit me. There's a beautiful young

341

English man I kiss at a workshop and afterward he says that was his first kiss in over a year.

• • • •

Each one of them I'd take as a lover, every one of them. I almost feel as if I had. The universe keeps offering me glimpse after glimpse, taste after taste of what I want and every time it's not quite, not right now, not this one. Still I am alive in it, not dying any longer but in the realm of living and delight, deep in the pattern of it. I honor each one, every one, as my beloved.

trance | Journeying Through Layers

Traditionally the correspondences of the sephirot include angels, Names of God and attributes, the pillars, pairs, and triads, Days of Creation, and parts of Adam Kadmon's body. More recently they include the translation of the Hebrew names into English, colors, tarot cards, and astrological correspondences. Further we could add concepts of lower, middle, and upper realms, and doubtless many other systems or overlays.

That is the big picture, where we are looking at whole systems—the whole of the Tree overlaid with the whole of another system, or set of correspondences. It's as if we're standing back, widening our vision, trying to get as broad an overview as possible. But there's also the alternative: focusing our vision in on one location, one branch of the Tree, one sephira; deepening into our experience of what it means to have these overlays, these different flavors, references, correspondences. This is more or less never-ending—there are ten sephirot, so it could take perhaps many months if we were to address this systematically. Not to mention how many possible overlays there might be if we went seriously looking for them. Endless.

To confine the experience a little, we will begin with one sephira and between three to five overlays. This exercise starts with a trance journey and then moves into the creative realm.

> TIME: 1 hour for the trance and journaling plus 1 hour or longer for the creative section (these can be broken into two different sessions)

YOU WILL NEED: For the trance: a quiet place to journey, your journal and pen; optional—your disk of the sephira you choose to journey with. For the creative section: art/craft materials of your choice—options include paints, pastels, or watercolors for a painting; journal and pen for poetry; fabric and sewing things for a fabric creation; magazines, scissors and glue for a collage; musical instrument/s for a song.

Part 1: The Trance

Select the sephira you will be working with. Often we go with our instinct, our gut, what we're drawn to even without knowing why, but sometimes we might choose a sephira we find obscure, to get to know it better, or a sephira we love and feel comfortable with, knowing that the relationship we already have with it will support our experience.

Select the overlays you will be working with, choosing between three to five. Options include the name in English (or your most familiar language), the Hebrew name, the color, the number (i.e., Kether is one, Hokmah is two, Tiferet is six), the tarot cards, astrological correspondences, an Iron or Pearl Pentacle point, a body part of Adam Kadmon, the assigned angel, the Name of God, a Buddhist path, the Day of Creation, the pillar, the triad...

Order the overlays in the sequence you will explore them, perhaps from the most familiar or accessible (to you) to the least familiar. Write this in your journal in case you need a prompt partway through the trance. If my sephira is Hod, I might choose overlays of orange, the left-hand pillar, Glory.

Settle yourself in a quiet place. You might want to ground and center yourself before beginning to pay attention to your breath. Spend some time just noticing the breath—the ins and the outs—and be aware if anything changes. Sometimes we choose to travel inward with the breath or allow it to ripple outward from us, becoming aware of a stillness within. Find a way to let your awareness of the external world fade and the internal worlds be the focus of your attention.

Within these internal realms, remind yourself of the sephira you've chosen to journey with. Perhaps you will firstly be aware of the Tree, then locate the sephira on the

Tree, or perhaps you will immediately be in the presence of the sephira or even find yourself within it in some way.

For the first few minutes, simply introduce yourself to the sephira or let it introduce itself to you. This might include letting memories of your time or previous experiences with this sephira arise, letting questions you have about the sephira come to the surface of your mind, or simply breathing in and out with its name or whispering it to yourself. You might want to remember its location on the Tree and the geography of what's around it before focusing again more intently on the sephira itself.

When you feel deeply present to the sephira and yourself, open to the first layer. In my example with Hod, the first layer is the color orange. I allow this to wash over the sephira, or if it was already there I might be aware of a rippling, a deepening into orange. Perhaps I let it wash over and through myself as well. How does this feel? What am I aware of in the state of orange? How does orangeness influence and inform me? When I feel into my imagining of Hod, what effect does orange have on Hod, and how is Hod related to orange?

Spend some time within this exploration, wherever it leads you. You may feel very peaceful and serene or you may set off on an adventure or engage in an internal dialogue. Perhaps I will even ask Hod to show me what the color orange means to it.

Take at least five minutes with the first layer. Then, if you feel complete for now, open yourself to the second layer. My second layer for Hod was the pillar, focusing on the idea of form. So I open to this concept of form and feel and observe what happens both within my perceptions of Hod and within myself. I might immediately be flooded with images of honeycomb, for example, or I might begin to feel my edges quite strongly or I might imagine the word *form* dancing and expanding through the space of the sephira.

Spend some time exploring this second layer, as you did with the first.

After at least five minutes, if you feel complete for now, introduce the third layer. Mine was the name *Glory*. You may notice the layers interacting with each other or they may remain quite separate for you.

Continue the process with up to five layers or complete it with the third layer.

When you are finished, allow yourself to transit back through the layers, then out of the sephira, out of the Tree, and return completely to your own body and surroundings.

Record your experience in your journal.

Part 2: Creative Response

Begin by rereading the notes in your journal, even if you just wrote them. Then, in your chosen medium—which may have changed since you began this exercise—find a way to explore the layers of this sephira that you journeyed with.

Choosing a creative form we're not very familiar with can produce rich and exploratory pieces, so we might choose poetry if we usually work visually or a drawing with pastels or colored pencils if we more usually prefer words or some other form entirely, such as dance, clay modeling, or collage.

• • • •

This process can be repeated with all the sephira, or with one sephira many times, choosing different layers. It's as endless as the Kabbalah itself...

activity | Creating the Eighth Disk

As you complete the work of this section, create a disk to represent the sephira you've been spending time with. This will be your eighth disk. Perhaps you spent the first section inhabiting Kether and you are now up to Hod—in that case, it will be the orange Hod disk you are working with. Perhaps you began somewhere else in the Tree and so the disk you are making now is for Netzach, Kether, Gevurah, or any other sephira.

TIME: 30–60 minutes

YOU WILL NEED: The appropriate colored disk (see page 69, "Creating the First Disk") and whatever art materials you wish to work with, such as colored pens and markers, paint, oil pastels, collage materials and glue, stickers

Start by recalling the time you have spent in this sephira, including looking through your journal notes, recalling any Kabbalah exercises, processes, or rituals you did and especially how these related to this particular sephira, as well as the general mood and events in your life during this time. By this eighth sephira you will have clear ideas about the function of this particular sephira within the Tree.

examples of completed disks can be seen at janemeredith .com/disks

Allow images, words, feelings, and ideas to arise. You can hold these in your head, immediately begin work on your disk, or jot down notes or a sketch.

Mark the name of the sephira onto the disk.

Decorate your disk, creating an image, set of images, or words that recall your time spent with this sephira. Perhaps this disk continues a style or theme began in the previous one or the others in this pillar, or perhaps the decoration reflects its essence. Use any art or craft materials you choose. Sometimes I create a single image, such as a wave or honeycomb, and blend all of my colors, words, and images into that shape and theme.

You might complete your work in one session or come back later to add more.

into form and beyond form into synthesis
the worlds' imaginings multifold and
magnificent, magnified distilled dreamed
down into layers of existence all the realms
hovered luminescent waiting to be birthed
to be generated it's in lines and grids and
spheres, fractals geometry and motion the
perfection of it captured and set free

and the minutiae of butterfly, measured
and weighed in a library of each cell its
colors, the fragments, in tiger's eye in
gamboge burnt orange persimmon tangerine
it is here but broken, breaking, fluttering

falling

9
Magic in the Tree

349

The ninth sephira returns us to the middle pillar, momentarily creating a mirrored and balanced Tree, perfect but for the shadowy Da'ath. The middle pillar always carries a dynamic of integration, and by now there's a lot to integrate. The ninth sephira is a busy place, but unlike Tiferet, where the paths seem to be equally coming and going, Yesod is where things descend to and ultimately through. Yesod, called Foundation, extends the Tree below Netzach and Hod, appearing to gravitationally draw all of the Tree toward it. The three of them create a triad that mirrors the top triad of Kether-Hokmah-Binah and creates a funnel-like shape of arms lifted in prayer or revelation.

Yesod has nine sephirot to balance and process. Numbers are magical; their very concept and use is twined deep into magic and each has special qualities, but the number nine is often assigned the powers of magic. Nine is the last of the single-digit numbers so it's a tipping point, a fullness and completion in itself. In the supernal triad, where creation begins, the colors are shades only—light, dark, and a blend of the two. In the central triad, where the energies of the universe coalesce, hovering between what has already been and what's yet to come, are the primary colors, bold and clear and, to some degree, simple. This lowest triad, which Yesod completes, carries the secondary colors; the blending of previous colors, the subtleties that occur when differences are mixed together.

All of this feels alchemical, and it's easy to see Yesod as a crucible, a cup or V-shaped container with these influences pouring into it while it cooks up the potion, the secret formula, the spell … This ninth sephira is a place of shifting tides and sudden changes; clarity and confusion trade places seamlessly within it. It's a place of mythos, dreams, the inner realms, the collective unconscious. Its symbols and languages can be interpreted, like dreams, in many ways. Yesod is a well from which one draws water up from the deeps and journeys through the worlds.

Yesod: *Imaginal Realms*

Yesod is called Foundation, so for all its mystical qualities we are considering this sephira as fundamental to the Tree. Here is the foundation for all that we have and know, for the Kingdom of Malkuth that is yet to come. And what is this foundation? It is the place of dreams, of mystery, of walking between the worlds. This is the realm of consciousness that we can open our awareness to. This is where gods whisper to us, where our edges dissolve: a conduit for creation. Here we can seek the divine or the truth of our selves and discover these are the same thing. Here the spontaneous and lived nature magic of Netzach and the learned and disciplined temple magic of Hod weave together.

This ninth sephira completes a triad—the third triad—and so it is the third in a three that is third in a three. Binah, the third sephira, is said to bring the possibility of manifestation, the origin of form into the universe, and each triad brings this closer to reality. So Yesod, three-three-three, is its penultimate expression, completing the second of the downward-pointing triads and bringing even more gravitas, weight, and inevitability toward the final expression of the Tree, Malkuth. Like all in this lowest triad, Yesod has a secondary color: in this case, purple. Purple mixes Gevurah and Chesed's colors of red and blue, thus linking this sephira into the center of the left and right pillars and further accentuating its Y-shaped reach. Hod and Netzach were both directly next to the sephirot they drew their colors from, so this reach of Yesod tells us a lot.

Yesod returns the balance of the Tree to the middle pillar; if we stopped at this point, the Tree would be almost perfectly symmetrical. We can see at a glance how much of a mixing place Yesod is—the descent point of Kether and the middle pillar, the completion of a triad and indeed of all three triads, grouped with Hod and Netzach but drawing directly upon Chesed and Gevurah—Yesod has it all going on. We know that the Tree does not stop at this point but keeps going to Malkuth, directly below, and this gives Yesod its key function within the Tree: as a bridge, or birth canal, through to Malkuth.

Each sephira acts both as receptor for what has happened above it in the Tree and a distributor as it passes onto the next sephira all that has been; the only exceptions to this are Kether, who only pours forth, and Malkuth, who only receives. In this regard, Yesod is no different from seven other sephirot. What is different is its placement in the Tree—how deeply it completes the symmetry and logical structure, and that it is the most direct connector to the only outlier in the Tree, Malkuth. Yesod is so close to completion it almost is completion, like any nine. This is as full as something can be before tipping to the next level. Yesod is as full as can be, and all of that fullness has only one place to go.

In the opposite direction all that happens in Malkuth, which could be said to be the whole purpose of the Tree, can only transition upward on its long journey to Kether. Whether it goes via the lightning flash, sephira to sephira all the way up, or via the middle pillar (a seemingly more direct but possibly more dangerous route), everything must pass through Yesod. Yesod is a funnel with a wide mouth and a narrow stem, and we can sympathize with the difficulties of funnels. They are really structured as a one-way system; trying to get things up the stem into the mouth is not at all easy. If too much pours in at the top, it can overflow, so whatever we are pouring in doesn't end up at its destination. While the top V-shaped part of the funnel can be just fine with impurities and even large objects swirling about, the narrow stem will be blocked or disabled if something too large goes down it or if impurities build up the way cholesterol might in an artery, causing narrowing and constriction and, in the end, a loss of the flow of lifeblood. These are the dramas of Yesod.

So much of Yesod is in commentary with other sephirot. Even those far-distant sephirot such as Kether, Binah, and Hokmah have aspects of themselves alive here. Yesod's in the middle pillar, in receipt of a nearly direct transmission from Kether. It certainly has a strong dynamic with otherness, as Hokmah does, though in Yesod's case that other is Malkuth yet to appear. Whereas Hokmah brings such immediacy into that relationship with the beloved, Yesod is waiting, pregnant. Yesod is carrying the forms born in Binah, as closely as can be done, toward our world. It balances between Hod and Netzach, and also between Gevurah and Chesed. It is directly below Tiferet, reflecting its light and influence as the moon does that of the sun.

Yesod is about becoming, except there's no way to become but to dissolve. Yesod is dissolving, distilling; it's alchemical. It's not just a funnel but also a crucible, receiving everything from above, brewing; passing it through stages of transformation or transmutation until it becomes the spell that will be received by Malkuth. In the other direction, Yesod receives all of the muddied, endlessly complex, and possibly confusing information and experience generated in Malkuth—which it has to distill—before passing it up the Tree into increasing refinement. Yesod is the place for those who walk between the worlds, for seekers, dreamers, poets, visionaries, and artists. Yesod's world of dreams, of mythos, of the unconscious gives access to the entire rest of the Tree.

It's a liminal space. Things hover at the edge of becoming like the seed in the ground, the unborn child in the womb. That thought we can't quite—yet—catch, an understanding that is just beginning to unfold for us. We might deliberately work within these liminal realms to try to transport ourselves in either direction—into the numinous or further into the embodied realm. Daily practice is something many of us undertake to deliberately forge connection with the divine each day, courting the liminal with consistent attention. Engaging our creativity—whether that be with paint, words, fabric, or something else—is another way we might tread the liminal, inviting glimpses of the divine to inhabit more concrete forms. In Pagan ritual we experience the divine as embodied, drawing down deity into human bodies and seeing the whole of nature as immanent and sacred. We witness each other and the whole world as expressions of the numinous. In these and other ways we seek not to separate the divine from the mundane or worldly but to bring them together, with ourselves as the conduit. Yesod is what makes this possible.

Yesod is the land of dreams. Not just the place we visit inside our own heads when we are asleep but the immense repository of dreams, shared visions, the collective unconscious, the mythos, the land of fairy tales and imagining. These doorways are our access to the divine from our lives in Malkuth, and they are also the pathways of the divine into our world. There are two other access points, represented by the paths that stretch from Netzach and Hod down to Malkuth: the gateways of the natural world and that of study and application. However, the most immediate, obvious, and direct path is through Yesod. Imagination. Our minds constantly stray to the imagined worlds of the future or the past ... every single night we enter an inner dreamscape ... we read novels and tell stories and watch movies and listen to music, and all of these activities engage the imaginal. In these places we become aware of lives and experiences not our own. We can stretch outside the limits imposed on us by our earthly reality—fly in our dreams, envision the future we wish for, rewrite the past, speak with our ancestors, visit the Underworld, identify with other human stories, or trance to places we've never been. It's a place for magic.

All of us visit this realm constantly—indeed, partially inhabit it—and we can practice, strengthen, and hone our skills within that realm to become effective, directed, and even powerful. We could say this is the place of the magician, the witch, the shaman, the spellcrafter, the world-weaver. When we use the phrase *walking between two worlds,* Yesod is the second world we are speaking of. Mostly when we dream it isn't lucid—that is, we're not aware that we're dreaming and can't consciously direct what's happening. But lucid dreaming is an instance of walking between two worlds; we are in the dream but also aware of the dream and perhaps able to direct or influence it. At the very least we can observe it: the dreamer observing the dream. During trance, magic, and other practices, we also engage this two-worlds model, although the skill is in balancing the two: entering deeply enough into the Yesod realm while still remaining awake, fully aware of our bodies and the earthly world around us.

These states of conscious dreaming, or submersion in the other realms while fully awake, are effectively the same thing taken from different sides. They both allow our—let's call it subconscious—to interact with our conscious mind. Our individual soul or divine spark—which, although differentiated, is entangled with all other souls/sparks, or more precisely is part of the fabric of soul that exists through all time and space, the I Am—is in dialogue, co-creation, with the All. Within these states we have access to our intuition, our inner knowing: the potential we carry about with us daily but perhaps barely interact with. When we are in these liminal spaces, our minds are open, like lifting off the tops of our heads so the sparks from all of the Tree, all of existence, can rain down into us.

Yesod is a place of becoming, on the downward trajectory of the lightning flash, and of dissolving, on the upward. When working with Yesod, we might lose our sense of which way is up, where we are, or what is happening. It's easy to get so submerged in the universe and our interconnectedness as to have no perspective—no *I* from which to observe or hold a commentary. This is literally because the I—the individual one, wearing our own name and form—is still in the process of gathering itself together, of becoming or dissolving and possibly both at the same time. To retain a sense of self in this realm—including motivation, direction, and distinction between self and the collective—requires both inclination and skill, perhaps skills developed over many years. One way to inhabit this between-the-worlds space is consciously, by dialogue with the divine within, whether through prayer, ritual, psychological processing, trance, or another method.

The other way to inhabit the realm of Yesod is asleep and dreaming. We all dream, whether or not we remember our dreams. Some of us are, as it were, asleep to those dreams. Others may remember dreams or fragments of them but pay them no attention. Jeremy Taylor's wonderful and groundbreaking work *The Wisdom of Your Dreams* offers a system of understanding not just our individual dreams, but the way those dreams speak of and to the collective. Working with dreams following Taylor's method, we can experience others' dreams as if they were our own, drawing insight and understanding not based on any preset list of correspondences but from our emotional and bodily responses as we tell or listen to a dream. Our own dreams are part of the collective, and in them we can see not just personal messages but understand how they touch others, as well as comment on the social, political, and environmental realms we inhabit. Taylor posits that dreamwork is not just for personal healing and insight but is a revolutionary process that breaks down barriers between individuals and disparate social groups, and his insights offer a profound way to inhabit this in-between realm.

The way most of us live most of the time is that the wall between Malkuth and Yesod exists but is breached in many places. Dreaming is different than being awake, but it's still all happening inside the same brain. This crossing point is graphically depicted in countless stories, films, and novels, including C. S. Lewis's Narnia books, *Alice in Wonderland*, and the fantasy film *Stardust*. The barriers between worlds might look sturdy at the official viewing point—where we take visitors to admire the engineering feat—but not that far away is a breach in the wall, where exchanges slip through in both directions. Perhaps it's even tacitly acknowledged by the border guards—they turn their heads away or take bribes or their orders are to keep things looking good rather than prevent any crossing at all. Perhaps further along the wall is not even in good repair, crumbling or torn down in places. There are sections of the Great Wall of China known as the Wild Wall—places where it's not kept in repair for tourists—and this seems a great metaphor. We rely on our intuition in so many ways, we don't have this fine control over our minds that we imagine we have. When we're asleep, there's border crossings continually; we're on the wild section of the wall.

This is the Dreaming of the Tree, the place where it is continually becoming itself, the concurrent time that runs alongside and weaves into and through our own more ordinary waking experience of time. It is the place of myth, the mythos. Here the stories of the gods play out, where their collective forms reside. As in a dream, contradictions and multiplicities exist side by side, overlaying and patterning through each other. Here are the pantheons, the creation stories—not ordered as Hod might order them, historically or by region or archetype but all at once. Hod has enough influence that they can still be separated out, they don't merge into a great soup, but wild Netzach is also here, allowing endless possibilities, permutations, and seeming contradictions. Here also is the golden light of Tiferet, shining through this endless complexity and shifting thoughtform so that the resonance of each aspect of it still must be true, still must convey and answer to the divine.

In the Adam Kadmon model, Yesod is the place of human fertility, the reproductive and sex organs. So it's the womb we were born from—like dreamings of our parents—each of us another manifestation of what's possible from the great stock of human DNA. Yesod is the mythical stork, cabbage patch, and karmic dispensary that each of us traveled through to arrive here, both metaphorically as we came into the world in this current form but also literally from our parents' egg and sperm. We spent nine moons in utero and then were physically born, most of us via the birth canal, which looks enormously like that path from Yesod to Malkuth. As we separate out from the great dreaming of Yesod into individual selves, we carry Yesod's seeds, not just of fertility but also of death. Our fertility—of our bodies, our imagination, creativity, and dreams—opens doorways to Yesod throughout our living experience in Malkuth. Our eventual deaths—but, meanwhile, the continual deaths that we experience during life, including loss of significant relationships, deaths of loved ones, losses of health, jobs, houses, friendships, communities—also carry us or provide a bridge we can cross over, back into the great dreaming space of Yesod where everything returns and emerges from again, changed.

Yesod is a place of transition. When we enter the dark night, when everything is stripped away from us and we only have our inner resources—qualities such as faith, courage, clear vision, determination, and the skills we learned such as grounding, self-care, self-regulation, inner sight, and our connection to the divine—then we are deep within Yesod's realms. Often this happens to us in our ordinary, nonmagical lives. We are not necessarily prepared but have to do the best we can, plummeting into grief, loss, a physical or mental health crisis, or a larger political, community, or world situation. Other times we have sought formal initiation, either with an established magical tradition or group or on our own, with our gods, guides, local spirits, or within our own soul.

During these transition times we walk between or within multiple worlds—not just for learning, communion, or growth but because something is at stake. If it is a formal initiation that we've studied and asked for, then the test is very personal, and we have worked hard to enter it. During these transition times we may experience the magical realms of Yesod as even stronger and more real to us than the Malkuth world that we live in every day. Dreams, visions, synchronicities, and communion with the numinous are heightened in intensity as new levels of skills and understanding open up within us. If we are being tested by the world in ways we haven't asked for, it can be extraordinarily difficult to access even the skills and resources we already have, never mind finding new depths to them. This is the path of the magician, witch, or Kabbalist—to be able to do the work, to be able to change our consciousness at will regardless of what is happening, or—more precisely—even when it is difficult to maintain our will.

Often the focus in inner journeying, magic, initiation, dream, and Yesodic work in general is the self. Of all the sephirot, this is the one that seems most interior, most involved with self. Yet we do all this magical and Kabbalistic work on the self within contexts of family, relationship, households, communities, the land we live on, and wider political and social scenarios. Perhaps we are actively involved in local communities, workplaces, political, social, or environmental movements, and perhaps not. Either way, whatever we do will affect others, at the very least those we live with, relate to, and are related to, but the ripples may be far wider than that, and that's really the idea.

When we zoom out from the tight focus on Yesod to the entire Tree and specifically Yesod's place in that Tree, we can see that everything affects everything else. Although Yesod, or any sephira, may appear independent and separate, really it is an expression of the All that is related to, affected by, and affecting all the other expressions. There may be times when we're just focused on our own little worlds and times when we are deeply focused on the world that's greater than, although intrinsic to, ourselves. Yesod and the worlds of Yesod require both—once again treading between the worlds, walking with a foot in each world.

At the level of entangled particles, we are all connected to everything else. There's a lack of true separation between ourselves and the world we are part of, especially within the realm of Yesod. Everything we do and could imagine, everything we think, has an effect on everything else. It may be quite a small effect or we might seek to make a wider effect; that indeed may be part of our magic and motivation in life, to make a difference. To be a positive affect—of healing or deepening or bringing joy or creating revolution—on, to, and with the world. The Jewish practice of *tikkun olam*, translated as "mending the world," is a teaching that each of us can choose to make a difference. It's not applied so much to the grandeur of things—living a life of meaning, being instrumental in some large way on the political, social, educational scene—as to the smallness of everyday actions. Picking up a piece of rubbish in the street, smiling at a parent having a hard time in the supermarket, expressing our appreciation to our partner, child, or coworker. The idea that we make a difference is appealing. The idea that we can make a difference every day, even with every single interaction we have, and that we can do this deliberately, not just for the good of the planet or the benefit of individuals whose paths are crossing ours, but as some sort of divine retribution for the rebalancing of the world, is provocative, empowering, even revelatory.

Tikkun olam takes for its starting point the idea that the world is broken. When the light creating all that is pours out of Kether, a shattering also occurs as the succeeding sephirot are unable to contain this light and break, spilling the light downward. In Isaac Luria's story of the shattering of the vessels, all or most of the vessels—that is, the sephirot—shatter under the force of the light, until Malkuth. This shattering—not unlike the biblical Fall from Paradise—is something that is still continuing in our lifetimes and throughout the entire system, so therefore each one of us can act for the mending of the worlds. If we follow this through to its logical conclusion, it may mean that when this mending is complete, all the worlds essentially return to Kether and the universe ends, but we could reassure ourselves that this will be some way off. Meanwhile, the beauty of tikkun olam is an invitation in each moment and interaction to offer healing, grace, connection, and comfort, and to deliberately offer our love and focus toward improving the day and the world of each being we come into contact with.

Yesod, for all it is a realm of dreams and the unconscious, carries a very practical call to action within it. Once we are born, we have limited time. Those seeds of death are ticking away within us, pulling us both more deeply into life and more closely toward its end. The moment of action is now. To be in a state of becoming and dissolving from and with the mythic, archetypal, collective, and fertile realms is to be in the flux of magic—ignited by it, infused, gripped like the birth pangs forcing us downward through liminality and into the temporal. This moment of our lives is the moment we have—to speak, sing, dance, garden, create, and make love. To mend the world. To know that we personally have received everything and have everything to give. At Yesod, the mixing place of the divine and the embodied, we are lovers. The divine and the embodied—Kether and Malkuth—make love to produce us, and we—we make love with life, with the great I Am in all its forms. We wear the face of the divine for each other. This each-action making love with life—with our own lives but also with Life, with the Tree itself—is the mending of the worlds.

Magic in the Tree of Life

There's a story—or maybe a myth or maybe it's history—that Kabbalists once divided themselves into schools of practice. One school was devoted to study, to the intellectual understanding of the workings of the universe, the Mind of God, the great I Am. Another school were devotees, focused not so much on the mind but on refining awareness of living within the radiance of that All and communing with it in meditation or ecstasy. A third school, in this story, worked magic with the Kabbalah. They sought to be active cocreators with the All, to be not just alive and resonant within the Tree but choosing and channeling forces both within themselves and in the world. This is a story.

Or history. But I notice that, to be magically effective, one would have to combine all three schools of practice: to study, to be a devotee, and to bring in will and desire.

I belong irretrievably to the third school. Yet even as I write that, I feel aware of great dangers inherent—of the arrogance of believing that my tiny life might contain enough grace to be either effective or, more scarily, beneficial to this great system of the cogs of the universe. Who am I, after all? Just one human on the edge of things, in a small moment of time, a tiny place on the earth. One who devotes her time to thinking, studying, teaching, gardening, writing, creating, loving. I am a lover. That's what saves the whole thing, not simply the devotional love, to balance the cool analytical study—like Chesed balancing Gevurah—but an active love, the interactions of love, the insistence on being the beloved of the universe, on greeting the world and each piece of it as my lover. Our human arrogance wreaks destruction everywhere, not limited to our own species but planet-wide, not even limited to other species but changing, deliberately (carelessly, but deliberate in that carelessness) the very chemical and climatic makeup of the planet.

But we each have the power to choose each action while we're alive. As long as we have this power, we have a responsibility to it or a responsibility with it. That is, to live in dynamic relationship, breathing with this power, acting from that power-within. This is an entry point to magic. That vital spark that each of us is, the spark that falls through the universe, has a power. Our power is that each of us is part of the living cosmos, and the atoms that make us up were there at the very beginning, in their earliest forms, at the Big Bang. We are part of the great I Am, so everything we do is intrinsically a part and cannot be separate from that All.

So why not simply try to live a blameless life or a pleasant life or any sort of life at all, getting by? Doing what is needful for survival and comfort, but no more than that. No reason really, except whatever reason is there, burning in your heart. That spark. That inner power and those promptings—in dreams, in love, inspired by art, mirrored in nature—to respond. At times this can be easy, delightful, graceful—and at other times brutal. Profoundly challenging. Almost eviscerating. Perhaps, like the pillars on the Tree, this process of living as a spark of divine light swings between mercy and rigor, seeking not equilibrium but transformation as it passes through the middle pillar.

There's a relentless unfolding inside us. Yes, it's the path toward death, this is dying, but oh, what glory along the way!

One thing I love about the mythos of the Jewish religion is the relationship with God. That, unlike the Christian subservience and unquestioning faith, Jewish people are prepared to—maybe expected to—argue their religion. Debate it, even with God. That this rigorous questioning process, this stripping away of illusion, of assumption, is an intrinsic part not just of the life of a mystic or scholar but anyone. Everyone. Almost it is a duty to question the divine, to seek answers. This Jewish engagement—between teacher and student, between the text and the reader, and between the world and the individual—is a dynamic unfolding, like life, where we are growing all the time, even as we're also dying but always learning. Changing. Becoming—something. Becoming more ourselves or closer to the I Am or both of those things at once.

Debating in this way—for learning, discovery, revelation—is comparable to making love: both are involved in coming closer to the beloved. So in Kabbalah magic we argue with this Tree, we make love with it, we get up close, naked (revealed/stripped away), and we stare eye to eye with ourselves in the mirror. We see the beloved gazing back, yes, our own reflection and also the divine spark within and the All we come from. We see other selves, other potentials. Yes, if I do *this* and *this,* I could become a slightly different person: if I balance Gevurah with Chesed, I might begin to carve out time to pursue my dream, say no to what doesn't serve the greatest good, say yes to what I long for. The whole trajectory of my life can swing around at the point where I make that magic.

It's helpful to define magic, and how doing magic in the Tree might be different from anything else we've been doing there—trance, inner work, visioning, creating art, et cetera et cetera. There's a Kabbalistic answer to that: yes, it's all magic, and also at the same time no, magic is a distinct thing that might be mixed with other activities but has its own signature. A very personal signature, of course—each of us has our own—but I'll throw a few attempts at clarification in its general direction. Dion Fortune's almost constantly quoted definition of magic as "the art of changing consciousness at will" is always worth considering. We could say anytime we are working Kabbalah or perhaps even reading or talking about it, we are doing that, choosing to change our consciousness into this realm where a mythical Tree is alive and the creatrix of all things, and we are interacting with it.

So we'll have to dive deeper than that—no surprise to a Kabbalist. Much of our work so far has been focused on learning about the Tree and sometimes learning about ourselves in relation to the Tree. Then we have also emphasized receiving information, learnings, transformation even, from interacting with the Tree. Sometimes we've translated what we've learned, felt, imagined, and received in various ways—in our journals and onto our disks, for example. But magic, I am going to say, is when we interact dynamically with the Tree for a specific outcome. To create change—not just the change that happens to come about, as we do the work, but a change we have decided upon, asked for, and decided to bend our wills toward. Stepping into the Tree—with reverence, learning, trust, and humility—we work dynamically within it, asking for and creating the change we seek.

Strong ethics are usually advised for all magical workers and magical work. If we wouldn't think it's acceptable to use physical force to compel someone to do what we wished, we might consider that it's the same with magical force. That's even before we consider the implications of this for the magician—karmically or in terms of magical rebound or simply the potential warping of character. What is always acceptable is to seek to follow one's own spiritual path, to develop as a human being, to heal oneself, to be of service in the world, and to live life with love and joy. Almost always with any magical act we add a caveat along the lines of *for the highest good* or *as best serves all involved* or *in ways that are perfect,* which is a way of handing the interpretation of our wishes—the forms in which they will actually manifest—over to powers greater than ourselves. This is very Kabbalistic; no one could come this far through the Tree and think that we are anything other than tiny specks within it—golden sparks, yes, but hardly with the power or vision to match the system we are working within.

This trust and calling upon the divine is a way of bringing ourselves into closer alignment with the All and with that spark within us. So yes, we engage in magic to further our own wishes and desires, yet at the same time hand the interpretation of that back to the divine. We admit that all we can really do is seek to hone ourselves to be better sparks, living more deeply within this Tree that we can't really understand and certainly can't control. Our great act of control—magic, a moment of cocreating with the living Tree—is really an act of surrender, of union, and rather than striking out toward individuality, it's more of a deep vibrating yearning for wholeness, to merge with the universe. To become indistinguishable within the I Am, we first have to distinguish ourselves, making magic that brings alive the forces within us strongly enough to have them align, in accordance with our will, with the All.

Be careful what you ask for has already been mentioned and is usually cited at this point. This is not so much because magic can go wrong, but because it is generally believed you will certainly get what you ask for, and—almost equally certain—it will look and feel like nothing you ever imagined. After all, if we knew what it looked and felt like, we would already have done it. A great question to ask before magical acts is *Am I willing to let go of everything I currently know and have to achieve this?* Another version is *Am I willing to change every single thing about myself to become this desired version of myself?* If not, then the outcome is probably not what we truly desire. *Changing consciousness* turns out to mean a whole lot more than simply entering a trance state; it means changing your entire experience of yourself and the world.

We can see from this that magic requires the whole-hearted, whole-bodied offering of the practitioner. Each time we work magic, we throw ourselves into the gap between realities—enter into the mythos at risk of our lives, offer the unimaginable sacrifice, dare to eat of the fruit of the Tree, and we know we will be changed forever. This is worth it for anything truly important. Deep healing. Freedom from old patterns. Release from traumatic pain and suffering. Alignment with one's spiritual path. Following one's soul purpose. These will come down to very specific things for each one of us. I had one recurrent nightmare for over thirty years before I finally laid down, in the mists at midnight on New Year's Eve, in a labyrinth and said with every atom of me *I will do anything it takes to never have that dream again.* A lot of things happened after that as I agonizingly but sometimes also ecstatically rewrote every tenant of how I am. But I have never had that dream again.

In Kabbalah magic we essentially offer ourselves to be rewritten by the Tree. This can happen in small ways: we might ask to establish a daily practice, to nurture our creativity, or find a community of friends. Or on a larger scale, to finally take steps toward the career we've always wished for, to establish healthy relating with others, to heal ourselves of long-held trauma, pain, or grief. We will have to bring all our skills to the work—that's the *at will* part—to put aside or move through fear and doubt and literally begin to inhabit the new reality. This is where it is magic. We are working with our will to change our consciousness, our reality. We cannot change the Tree—well, we add one spark to it and can polish that spark, so to speak, but in this context we are not seeking to change the Tree, although we invite the Tree to change us in directed, specific ways or areas.

We cannot control the way it works. We cannot step into Gevurah and ask, for example, to learn to hold boundaries at work without expecting that boundaries will now become a thing for us and that issues around boundaries will also start to manifest or be provoked in our intimate relationships, with our children, in our personal and spiritual and community life. Also, Gevurah will not do this work for us. We will not wake up the next day with all these boundaries magically in place. Rather, Gevurah will highlight for us all the ways and places we have not held or wrongly or inadequately held boundaries. Everything we do not know and are unable to do around holding boundaries will be magnified. Boundaries will push us and push us until we start to learn how to do it, perhaps being taught, if we seek it, directly from Gevurah.

In this book are suggestions, ideas, guidelines. Be as anarchist as you can, following your spirit and intuition within and outside these suggested forms. Find ways of creating Kabbalah magic that work for you. Methods of magic within the Tree that I work with are:

- ▶ Ritual magic—creating a ritual within the Tree, either symbolically or with my disks
- ▶ Embodied magic—inviting my body to hold, resonate with, and even heal working with certain sephirot or the whole Tree
- ▶ Magic in landscape—opening my senses to the land and finding resonances of the sephirot there
- ▶ Interacting with sephirot as I walk between the worlds
- ▶ Occult magic—creating magic using symbols, tools, altars, spells, and words of power drawn from the Tree and the different sephirot
- ▶ Group magic—inhabiting the Tree with others in ritual

I've listed those as if they were neatly defined and separate from each other, but of course they're not. The Tree is alive, we are alive within it, and consciousness and will flow about in random, chaotic, and synchronous ways.

So much magic waits for us in the Tree. It's brimming with life, shimmering with possibilities of all the known and unknown worlds. It's just—will you dare to eat? This is the dare: to live a life of choices. Conscious choices guided by the spark within, by visions of a great Tree and the unending spill of light, down through branches and time and all the way down, in tearing sparks, to where we live and make our small magics at the base of things or the farthest reaches, and seek for a few moments not to be separate but joined in union with the All while still separately embodied, and in that place to work for change. Changing ourselves—how could we do this work and not be changed? Changing our futures each time we engage with this magic. Changing constantly, like ripples on a lake, all that we come in contact with through all the worlds.

Correspondences in the Tree

Each of the sephirot holds deep magics. The interplay between and worlds within each one of them and each one of us will be unending. So explore. Dance, make love, argue. If you work with gods, with pantheons, with myths, planets, herbs, music, incantations, angels, demons, numbers, colors, past lives, chakras, temple magic, magical tools, symbols—at least those, but surely many more—there will be correspondences and meaning for you here, in the Tree. There are tables of correspondences in books and online from different schools and individuals, some historic, some contemporary or imaginative—use them as a stepping-off place. What is your magic in the Tree? What comes alive for you and invites you to ritual, to spellcrafting, to dancing between the worlds and changing all the worlds within this Tree of Life?

Here is a very minimalist outline of my most-often-worked correspondences within the Tree. It's personal, eccentric, probably inconsistent. Read it if you like or skip over it, but do find your own.

KETHER—The All, Divine, the I Am That I Am. The Star Goddess.
The singularity prior to the Big Bang. Light. White. One.

HOKMAH—The Beloved. Sophia. The mirror of curved space from
the Star Goddess myth. Isis. Stars. Gray. Two.

BINAH—The Great Goddess. Dark Mother. Miria from the Star Goddess myth. Darkness between stars. Nephthys. Black. Three.

DA'ATH—The void. The Tree of the Knowledge of Good and Evil. The serpent. Black holes. Dark matter. Silver/invisible. The space between numbers.

CHESED—The Blue God. Shiva. Inanna. Mary, mother of Jesus. Aphrodite. Saints and angels. Rivers. Blue. Four.

GEVURAH—The Red God. Kali. Ereshkigal. Mary Magdalene. Martyrs and demons. Fire. Red. Five.

TIFERET—The sun. Sun gods and goddesses. Odin. Christ. Kwan Yin. Sacrificial magic. Rays of light. Yellow. Six.

NETZACH—The Green God. Nature. Dryads. Indigenous, shamanic, and land-based magics. Gardens. Green. Seven.

HOD—Mercury. Hermes. Athena. Ceremonial and temple magics. Libraries. Orange. Eight.

YESOD—The moon. Moon goddesses and gods. Psychological and spiritual magics. Dreams. Purple. Nine.

MALKUTH—The earth. Earth gods and goddesses. Gaia. Demeter and Persephone. Freyja. Eve. Nature spirits. Trees. Brown. Ten.

activity | Magic in the Tree

The Tree of Life is magical all by itself. It's the creation from which everything else is created. Everything about it is magical, and we could say everything about the universe it describes is also magical. The Big Bang is magical: the great Everything from Nothing. The way we interbreathe with trees is magical: our outbreath is their inbreath, and we breathe in what they breathe out. The diagram—the arrangement and complex layered symbolism of the sephirot on the Tree of Life—practically shimmers with magic. It's been in this current form for at least a hundred years and evolved throughout many hundreds of years, all that time worked magically by thousands of people. As a conceptual form it is solid, multidimensional, and positively packed with magic.

When we enter into the Tree—reading this book, looking at the Tree glyph, making our disks—we are already immersed in its magics. If we study it at any depth at all, we are unlikely to ever be free of its influence and this Kabbalistic, multilayered way of seeing the world. But then—to deliberately make magic within the Tree, to seek to pursue an intention through the layers of meaning and powers and worlds—that is another step. Not all who study the Tree seek or wish to make magic within it, but for the embodied Kabbalist, for the experiential Kabbalist, I think it's probably inevitable.

It's often worth exploring techniques that initially don't resonate with us, as well as those that do, because we can learn so much pushing into unexplored edges, ways of working that are new to us. Here are three of the ways I like to create magic within the Tree of Life.

Magic with a Single Sephira

For a focused and specific piece of magic—for example, to work with personal boundaries or to open the heart—if one particular sephira seems to speak directly to that intention, we can choose to work with it. It does not have to be the sephira someone else would assign to that work; if Chesed is the one that calls to you about the open heart, or Hokmah, work with that rather than the more traditional Tiferet.

Set up an altar, circle, or working space dedicated to that sephira. Include your disk, finished or not. You might also want objects, colors, scents, and visual images that connect you with that sephira, possibly including tarot cards, colored candles, incense, magical tools or objects, and natural objects.

After grounding and readying yourself and the space for magic, name your intention aloud or in writing (or both), then let yourself dive deep into the sephira. You might enter a trance or semi-dream state, dance, drum, or chant to let yourself enter into the realm of this sephira. Explore. Ask for what you wish. See the work that is given to you in the moment, of how to be with this, and move toward it or integrate it. Make some magic.

Toward the end or at the conclusion of your ritual, do something in the embodied world to cement your understanding, new direction, or insight. For example, draw on your disk, write your resolutions in your journal, make a promise to your gods or your soul, tie a colored thread around your wrist or ankle, or place something from this ritual onto your main altar.

Magic with a Pair, Triad, or Pillar of Sephirot

Perhaps the change you want to bring about is relevant to one of the pairs in the Tree—to balance self-care with giving to others, for example. Perhaps one of the pillars is calling to you; maybe your magic is about finding ways to live according to your spiritual and personal values. Or it could be with a triad, such as the top triad for connecting with the divine. In this case we can choose to work magic with a specific portion of the Tree. Once again, if you want to work with expansion but it's the middle pillar calling to you rather than the more traditional right-hand pillar, work with the middle pillar. When we learn to trust our instinct, our intuition, our gut reaction, that's when we find ourselves on our own path. It may well lead, eventually and in its own way, to the more expected or traditional path; that is, our journey with the middle pillar may eventually lead us through to the right-hand pillar, but enforcing what we *know* over what we *feel* is never a shortcut because we are unable to fully be present if our feelings are elsewhere.

Set up your working space. You might want to represent this physically. For example, working with a triad we might have three small altars at triangular points and ourselves in the middle of that or simply have an altar and magical space dedicated to that pair, triad, or pillar. Include your disks either around you or at the altar or central space, as well as symbols or items for each of the sephirot involved and something that unites and represents the entire pillar, triad, or pair. This might be music, incense, essential oil blends, a visual image, or a magical tool.

As always, ground and center yourself to begin, as well as clearly state or write your intention.

When you begin your journey into the realms of the Tree, you have a choice whether to travel sequentially from one sephira to another or to stack or layer them together so you are experiencing their blended energies. If you are sitting in the center of a triad, for example, you might imagine their pools of influence spreading out further and further until they overlap and you, in the center, are within all three influences at once. For a pillar, we can travel from one sephira to the next, either heading up or down the Tree, or we can imagine the pillar upright with the sephirot layered on top of each other and our body held within that column.

Once within the trance or ritual space, follow your instincts to speak, sing, move, create, cleanse, vow, pray—whatever you are moved to do. You can also ask to receive healing, insight, or change or become what you need yourself.

What we receive when we do this type of magic may be coded like dreams are and not make immediate sense to us. But, like dreams, it's worth trying to recall and record as much as we can to continue our work with the images, emotions, symbols, and resonances of the experience. Kabbalah magic, or perhaps all magic, does not necessarily hinge on understanding what has happened but on the spaces it has opened up, the power with which we bring ourselves into those spaces, and the changes we make within them. Thus a resolution made in the midst of deep magic will have resonances greater than just our ordinary willpower. A symbolic action during a ritual can actually change something in our ordinary, non-ritual lives because all of our intent is focused and supported by the work we have done to create and hold the space, this eye-of-storm working magic.

Record what happened in your journal, whether by words, diagrams, or pictures. Whenever we work powerful magic like this, we need to remember afterward to re-ground ourselves, perhaps by going for a walk, eating something, or letting our bodies completely relax.

Magic within the Entire Tree

This is a great method if you don't exactly know what you need from the Tree or the magic.

Set up the entire Tree of your disks. Ground and center and speak your intention aloud.

Find some way to begin moving within the Tree: maybe it will be physically moving or just moving your attention throughout its different spaces. You might start singing, moving into trance, drumming, or dancing. Notice which of the sephirot you are drawn to. It might be a single sephira, a sequence of them, a particular path or part of the Tree, or a whole complex journey.

When you are drawn to a particular space or sephira, stop and do magic, trancing into the sephira with your intention, creating an altar there or another ritual piece. Perhaps you will shake, weep, take off all your clothes, light candles, journal your thoughts and wishes, lie down and let the energies of the Tree infuse you.

Working with the whole Tree like this can be deep magic. Make sure when you are finished to re-ground yourself, pack up your magics, record your experience in your journal, and then do something extra grounding such as eat some food or walk or sit for a while in nature.

practice | The Magical Body

There are three types of embodied magic I work with the Tree of Life: one is when I invite or become aware of the Tree inside my body, one is where I invite or become aware of my body inside the Tree, and one is a wilder type of land magic. These are less formalized magics and I don't work with altars or magical tools during them, although you may. Dancing and movement, drumming and singing can be wonderful aids. This type of magic is especially good for healing, either within the body, working to rebalance ourselves, or healing our relationship to the divine through our immersion in the natural world.

Sephirot in the Body

To work with the sephirot within the body, we usually follow the correspondences of the Adam Kadmon: Kether at the crown, Hokmah and Binah within the head, brain, and face, Da'ath at the throat, Chesed the right arm and hand and Gevurah the left, Tiferet in the chest, heart, and solar plexus, Netzach the right leg and foot and Hod the left, Yesod the reproductive organs and genitals, and Malkuth our rootedness in the earth.

Perhaps I want to rebalance my whole body, in which case I might simply move through the sephirot one by one, in either direction, giving a similar length of time to each. At each sephirot I inquire *How is this part of me today?* as well as *What tensions or hesitations can I sense?* and *Are there any blocks or overloads here?* Then I invite the energy of the sephira to rebalance within that part of me and check in again for any changes. This work can be done while dancing, drumming, seated in a meditation pose, or lying down. It can be great to check in a day or two later to find out what has shifted and what could still do with more attention.

Out of this sort of work can emerge information: for example, if there is a notable imbalance somewhere, I might choose to work with that sephira individually afterward (see page 368) or, if a whole pillar was lethargic or difficult to connect with, to spend some time bringing my attention there.

Another approach is to focus on a single body part: for example, my sprained left ankle. Maybe I will choose to massage it with a blended oil while simultaneously feeling into my connection to Hod. What details am I neglecting in the care of this ankle? How does it feel if I infuse orange light through the ankle? What if I used an orange essential oil—bergamot or sweet orange—in the massage? If I open more deeply to Hod, can I feel the alignment of ligaments and bones within my foot? Can I maybe bring in some of the influence of its partner, Netzach, to restore the flow and ease of this ankle? What is this ankle asking for in the way of support, and what details do I need to be aware of in its healing?

The Body within the Sephirot

Take yourself outside to a natural or wild place. You might want to match the place to the sephira you are entering, choosing a forest for Netzach, a beach or lake for Chesed, or a mountain for Kether. Of course it can simply be a park or your back yard. Just as the elements are to be found everywhere, we can also find the sephirot wherever we happen to be. Remember that the Big Bang happened right here! If you are not able to be outside, you can journey within trance to wherever feels best for you.

For an ecstatic and sometimes revelatory experience, we can simply open to one sephira. Imagining that the whole world—everything about me—is the realm of that sephira, I immerse myself within it. I invite Gevurah in my garden, for example, and let my eyes and other senses adjust to that. I see the confines of each leaf, hear the exact definition of a bird's call, and imagine how far it extends in all directions, knowing I am within that boundary. I feel the wind against my skin, experiencing my skin as a barrier to that wind and also watching what effects it has around me, what is ruffled and what withstands or is sheltered, how the wind is boundaried. I become aware of the sunlight, its angles and depths, knowing it is defined by the time of day and the season of the year. I become aware of the boundaries of my life and the lives of things around me—the pademelons, the bangalow palms and lomandra that I planted when they were seedlings but they may well live past me. The boundaries of movement: I move only close to the earth, but most of the trees are way above me... the whole world looks and behaves like Gevurah, as Gevurah.

If I am seeking to do any magic with that sephira, I can bring it into that space. I've noticed I have trouble holding boundaries in intimate relationships, though in other types of relationships I'm quite good at it. So I might ask, within that immersion within Gevurah, for finer awareness of how to work with this, and receive information, support, or even an invitation to shift states and make the change. It can be great to do this type of immersion with a sephira we have trouble understanding or don't have a deep emotional connection with, as well as being a gorgeous sort of lovemaking with a sephira we feel affinity with.

Land Magic with Kabbalah

Instead of simply immersing ourselves within one sephira, we can choose to take a journey through the Tree. I like to do this while I am walking, moving through the landscape, rather than static. As I leave the house, I begin with Malkuth and experience myself as walking through that world, the world of my life, the house and garden, the known, intimate places. I stay present with all that arises and wait for a shift; perhaps it will happen within me or perhaps something outside me will prompt a change; for example, I arrive at the gate or road. At this point I shift into Yesod and continue my journey, now viewing and experiencing the world around me as Yesod. I notice the mythic within the landscape—the dreams of other people's lives, maybe, in houses that I pass, or the complex lives of tiny birds that I will never fully understand. I remain within Yesod until something prompts me, internally or externally, to transition. Perhaps I catch sight of something very orderly—a native bee hotel, a herb garden, or a flock of birds flying together—and that prompts my shift to Hod.

I continue through the entire Tree, gathering impressions, sensations, and understandings. Usually I complete my walk at Kether and then turn and walk back the same way, sort of picking up or closing down and acknowledging each sephira, one by one, as I travel back through their territory. I have, before now, got lost on the way back ... but that's another story.

It's always worth recording the journey afterward, either as a map or in words.

• • • •

It's also possible to allow ourselves to become aware of the Tree—all its sephirot, all its influences—around us in every moment of every day. This is a kind of multiplicity where we simply open ourselves and are like a child wondering at everything, oh the birdsong of Netzach—but then how it's structured, Hod-like. The golden sun in shafts through the window as Tiferet caresses the air, the purity of that air, like Kether, yet how far it has come, what it has been through. Like Hokmah separating out from the beginning. My body within all of this as the density of Malkuth and yet my ever wondering Yesod. Aware of death in each breath, Binah. Yet within the limits of my life, Gevurah, and still reaching out to know, celebrate, love—Chesed ... This practice, perhaps, is most essentially the experience of the embodied Kabbalist.

Memoir: *Courted by the Universe*

I feel the life force pouring through me, the people-places-events, the whole *becoming* of it. I'm dedicated to this recovery of the intimate, sensual, and sexual self of me, and it's left me dying in each moment, wide open. It's let me release the past and heal in the present. It's shown me that the open heart is the broken heart, and it's brought me back to risk and trust. The world has given me a thousand faces of the beloved.

It's hard to keep track of them and it's impossible to remember all the details within that many interactions. I just have to respond in the moment. I notice I'm becoming more and more myself; no artifice, no careful this side for one person and that side for another. I have to be the same for all of them—myself—and not worry about whether they like it or not. I try for cheerful, interested, open and let that be the thing that sorts them out, that or their own stories. It's a great distillation of humans. I practice it at

tantra events and in cities: Sydney, San Francisco, Paris, London. No wonder it's difficult in the country; there aren't enough people.

Young men are more interested in me, less confident or arrogant or out to impress.
Or maybe the power dynamic's different—they've got the gender but I've got age, so
we're more on an equal footing. I notice many of the men I interact with are brown or
black skinned. We talk about race and privilege and I realize, again, how marginaliza-
tion and oppression leads to social critique and self-awareness if you survive. Walking
in London at night with a Black man, I feel my wariness in the street as a woman is
matched by his. Again and again I am drawn to those with similar views but a different
background from myself. Be of a different generation, raised in a different country and
even a different culture, and yet still meet me through it, eye to eye and skin to skin.

I'm seeking lovers in the libraries and gardens of humans and I'm finding myself.
There's so many of them that I can't say I'm finding them, but—in their reflections—I
find myself. They come in waves and tides as I meet them in cafés and parks and galler-
ies and workshops and next to statues and public buildings and at curated events and
train stations. The multiplicity, the patterns, the maths and facets of it…When I meet
people, I bring all that energy, aliveness, self-possession, and confidence, and I can feel
the lightness in it, the rush, the mix, the clear-eyed openness I sometimes have that isn't
targeted but general. That's at my best.

Gradually it comes to me, through months, maybe a year of gradual, incremental
closenesses. Step by slow step it's unfolding—not with any individual, none of them
could I hold onto or take past the time limit of that exact interaction—but it's continual and progressive. I'm in a process, perhaps it's my own process but it feels like I'm
being courted and there's no one doing that except…as soon as I think *the universe is
courting me*, everything rotates into focus and I can't unthink it.

I can't attach anything to a single individual; they're all passing through. But when
I string them all together, I get the actions of a lover, courting. A lover who's serious,
intent, and taking it step by step, letting it unfold one piece at a time, bathing in the
fullness of each moment before it spills into the next. The universe is courting me. I
took the whole world as my lover, each person as my beloved, and—it's happening. The
multiplicity is revealing itself. There's magic all around me. I'm falling through the Tree,

and the air's thick with it. If I'm a butterfly, each wing stroke is causing storms, tides of desire, and the miracle of another and another and yet another person turning up to stand in front of me and be, in that moment, my beloved.

If I don't think about the whole picture of what I might long for—hours of lovemaking, lovers close and consistent, the unfolding of relationship from potential to actual, someone here beside me for longer than an hour or two—but lean into only the single thing my whole self craves, feels almost as if it will die without, just that one thing, then I'm like a satellite dish beaming a burning, focused signal outward with my arms stretched open as wide as they can go to receive it. I don't receive it as purely from them, whoever they are, but as a gift from the universe or Shiva or Freyja, Eve, Aphrodite. They bathe me in moments of caresses, kisses, slow hugs, and long cuddles until almost I could believe I will have lovers again. Even though I'm in my fifties and have had to rewrite nearly every single thing about myself—perhaps because of that.

Falling through the Tree, a multiplicity of names, faces, and events flows around and through me. I let myself fall in love with each of these moments, held by the universe, and I am responding, opening, trusting, receiving—

. . . .

No one has touched my breasts for what feels like forever—years, anyway—and somehow that is a burning piece of grief inside me, the thing I most want. I'm in a workshop, in a small group on the final night, and we are supposed to express our illicit longings, our secret desires, and all around me and in our group I hear elaborate fantasies, explicit sexual scenarios, dark desires. When it's my turn I say *I want someone to touch my breasts,* and I'm almost crying. *Is that it?* demands the young man beside me in a pedantic manner. *Can't you be more detailed? Isn't there more to it than that? How is that even a fantasy?* But later that evening he is sitting by me and he says quietly *I could do that thing you desire, if you want.* And oh, I am swept away by it. This is the one thing—and he's offering me that. Bringing it to me like a gift.

He sits behind me, his legs either side, and I take my top off and he touches my breasts. This is maybe an hour after it nearly broke my heart to speak this desire. He traces delicate patterns with his fingertips, he brushes the skin lightly with the palms of his hands, he holds my breasts in his hands, he checks in with me—*Is this what you want? Is this? How would you like it?* and I am weeping and smiling and yes my heart's wide open to this beloved, the universe, and of course him as well—how could it not be? This was the one thing—and being given it I'm free, momentarily, of longing. I'm released into desire, freed from it by being granted it, humming with ecstasy. I lean back against his chest, feel his long hair falling onto my shoulders, his skin against mine. I feel utterly, utterly received, and loved, and held. His name, when I look it up, means "gift of Yahweh."

Four months later, in Paris, and I've been so wishing for mutual desire—not a workshop partner but an actual person living their life and I set up a date with someone I've been messaging for a while and when we meet he is sweet and warm and after a brief conversation we walk to a bar. He's not much taller than me and twenty years younger. His English is excellent. I link my arm through his as we begin walking and he turns his whole head toward me, meets my eyes, and says *good*. The bar is tiny, quirky, very Parisian in a local way, and he sits beside me on a bench at the back. The little round French tables are all pushed together, they take up most of the floor space; it's more like a backstage jumble of café furniture than a bar. We have a drink and talk, I'm enjoying it, and after a while I put my hand down on the table between us. The back of my hand, my right hand, is just inches away from the back of his left hand, near his drink.

We breathe. I can feel the heat of his hand or of both our hands dense in the space between. I move a fraction closer, barely. He waits, breathes, doesn't move. The heat begins to flush all through me, around me. I know he's caught in it as well, words drop away, and we are in the realm of sensation. Again I move my hand, maybe a half centimeter. We breathe. The moment opens out, immense, rich, layered. I move my hand. Again. Finally our hands are so close only the thinnest layer of air separates them, air that is like a caress in itself. Under that caress they relax, a fraction, from their tensed state and so are touching, merged.

By now there are a dozen people crammed in here, mostly standing—I would have said they wouldn't fit—but we are bound into our own world. I hold my cheek near his, our hair brushes the other's face. We breathe. Each breath deepens further, those breathings tiny movements in themselves, inexorably pulling us closer, closer. Finally we are holding our mouths just a centimeter apart and the kiss is already happening in this shared breath and when our mouths touch, barely, it's to join the kiss, not begin it. I feel outrageous in desire as we sit and kiss in a crowded grunge-art bar in Paris, and I am unfurled for this lover, this beloved oh yes this young man, but really the universe courting me, in Paris, with such delicacy, breath, and the flood of desire. He's Algerian and named in an ancient language for an angel.

. . . .

A month later I'm still in Europe, at a tantra festival, and as the days pass I wonder at the women who find themselves, somehow, a partner for the week. A man who will be by their side, eat meals with them, dance with them, sit by them in workshops, and make love with them for a week—how do they do that? To me it looks like it's the woman who makes it happen, but I don't understand how. When does the opportunity arise? I'm just beginning to know people a week in; how did they find someone they wanted in the first day or two? I stare and stare at them, these women who arrived single and will leave single but for this week have a lover. More than understanding how they did it, I wonder what it feels like. I don't think I'd want to be bound into a relationship here, but I do wonder. I wonder intensely. I want to know, just for once, what it's like to find a man who'll focus so much on me, ignore all others for this brief connection.

It's the second to last day by the time I think this, and there's a man in my small group in the morning workshop whose energy I like. He's warm and open, Norwegian, he reaches out and touches people—me, others. At the end of the workshop, as we're debriefing, I ask if I can lay my head on his leg and he puts his hand in my hair. At lunch he comes to the table I'm eating at, asks if he and his friend can sit down. We have a lively conversation about Kabbalah and the realization of divine light; the others leave but we are still talking. We go outside to continue the conversation and after a while I ask if he'll hold me. He says *You're not that easy to read that you want to be touched* and I am surprised and resolve to change that.

That evening, the last evening of the festival, he comes up to me straight away and claims me. That's all I can call it. He sits by me when we're seated. He dances with me, vigorously and for hours—sometimes someone else tries to connect with me, and he cuts them off. He's a wild, energetic dancer, a kind of salsa mix he seems to be making up. There's a few performance pieces outside. He takes me with him, holding my hand,

and finds positions for me so I can see, stands behind me with his hands on my shoulders. When we take a break, he pulls me onto his lap; in the chair, he strokes my hair. My friends that I've made, women, come and sit beside us or at my feet and talk a little, smiling with me. He insists we dance again, together.

It's so intense and enveloping—I'm laughing at it. Claustrophobic really but I also feel cherished, oh this universe. I'm convinced. A couple of times I try to kiss him but he doesn't respond much—so it's just this. Just—exactly—what I asked for. The one thing. This experience, which now I think I might never need again, of being someone's chosen one, just for the festival—ending tomorrow, so I've got off lightly. I like his mix of ascetic meditator and wild dancer and I'm grateful, astounded really that he's appeared like this and taken this role, played my lover for the night. I wanted to know what it felt like, to have one person dedicated to me, and now I totally know. I've felt it, been that, had it as full as you can have. He's named for a god out of Norse myth.

• • • •

A month later I'm standing at a bus stop at the edge of Glastonbury in England and yearning, in this moment, for just one thing. I want to spend the night with someone. Just to be held for a night in someone's arms. I lean backward against the wall of the bus stop and imagine falling backward through the Tree with that wish. I feel the falling. Within ten minutes I get a text from someone I met in London. Extraordinarily, he's in Bristol, which is where my bus is heading. The bus turns up and I get on it, replying *I'll be in Bristol at 4 p.m.* He invites me out to dinner and I say that really I can't, as I'm catching another bus to London and I don't want to arrive at 11 p.m. He says I can stay the night with him, that the bed is big. He sends a geographic marker—his hotel, with him in it, is 100 meters away from the bus interchange.

He's loping down the hallway when I get off the bus—tall, young, Zimbabwean, wearing a white shirt and suit pants. I've only met him once and we got on well but although he's open about many things—politics, history, his children, his job—he's private about more personal topics, and I wasn't certain he was into me. He takes me and my case back to his hotel room and says he has an hour of work to do. I sit in a chair by the window and work as well. The bed, I notice, is not large. Afterward we walk through the streets of Bristol, discussing race and gender. We eat dinner over a lively conversation, then he says he is really tired and has to get up early for work. So we go back to the room, have showers, and get ready for bed.

As I'm sitting on the bed plaiting my hair he leans over and places a kiss on my shoulder blade, next to the strap of the slip I'm wearing. It is a very slow, lingering kiss of the unfolding type, the melting type. It melts into me and I melt, a little. I turn to face him and say *I thought we were going to sleep; should we have been having other sorts of conversations?* So we lie down facing each other and have the conversation about sexual history and safer sex and all of that, but it is more a way of getting to know each other than because we're going to do anything about it right now. We share a few kisses lying there and they are so, so soft I can barely tell where they start and end. Then we go to sleep. He holds me in his arms all night. In the morning he showers and dresses—he puts on cuff links; I don't know that I've ever known anyone who wore cuff links to work—and leaves me the key to check out.

I try to see him again before I leave the country but he's always busy with work, with family, with friends, and I can't understand why he doesn't make it happen, is so casual about it—those melting kisses, how could he not want more of them? Then I remember—that was the piece, the one piece that I asked for, and he gave, to spend the night in someone's arms. His name means "to praise God." The universe.

It's as if I've reached into the great pool of collective dreaming, again and again, and received what I needed. Never more than that; it's very exact. *Someone to touch my breasts. Mutual desire. A festival partner. To spend the night in someone's arms.* The gift of God, an angel, a god, praise of the divine. If I wanted proof of this lover's seriousness in courting me—and I don't mean these gorgeous Australian/French-Algerian/Norwegian/Zimbabwean men—then surely I have it. I feel that I do have it. I'm almost afraid to ask for something else. Already this seems such a serious relationship, the focus, the precisely met desire, the speed of response. I feel I'm hesitating, trembling, at the edge of a great cliff and even though I know I can fly or fall, how many signs does one person need? I'm not sure how to let go, how to surrender completely into this embrace. A series of moments with different humans, each one perfect in what it contains? Or—can I actually now, after four years or more of this absence, this desire, this utter rewriting-of-self, find a lover?

trance | Powers of the Tree

We have powers that reach beyond just ourselves because we are part of the web of life and connected to the whole entangled-particle-universe-mess. We are each only as significant, perhaps, as a caterpillar in this great Tree, but a caterpillar that eats the leaves of the Tree and binds itself, trusting, to a twig of this Tree to be transformed. We are not all the same; even caterpillars are not the same as each other. Thus we will each have somewhat different powers and transmit them in different, unique ways. We can both be writers, but I can never write what you will write. We are both lovers or parents or dancers, but we will not love, parent, or dance the same way. Our magic, also, even specifically our Kabbalistic magic, will be different.

This visioning is done within the Tree and within the dreamings of Yesod as we to seek to define our own magic.

TIME: 45 minutes

YOU WILL NEED: Your ten (eleven) sephirot disks. Journal, pen, and a blank map of the Tree. Coloring things optional. A cushion or somewhere to sit near the disks.

This exercise is written as though your disks are laid out on the floor and you can physically move among them. If that is not the case, you can do the exercise as a trance, although ideally you would still be gazing at your disks, perhaps stuck on a wall or the back of a door.

Lay your disks out in the form of the Tree of Life. Begin with any grounding and centering practices that feel appropriate. You might want to drop a grounding anchor in Malkuth.

On your blank map, add these prompts into or next to the sephira:

Kether—I am	Tiferet—I love
Hokmah—I receive	Netzach—I desire
Binah—I understand	Hod—I study
Chesed—I offer	Yesod—I dream
Gevurah—I commit	Malkuth—I become

Approach Yesod. You might wish to sit on a cushion beside it, within the Tree. Enter into a light trance state, light enough that you can still walk around, write things down, and be aware of what is happening in both worlds. Ask Yesod to open a doorway for you to travel into the worlds of magic and vision. Breathe with this for a few moments, and when you are ready, enter the doorway, imagining that Yesod is the portal into the temple of Kabbalah magic.

Physically move up the middle pillar until you are standing or sitting in front of Kether. You can also sit or stand on the disk, if you prefer. Gaze toward the Ain Soph, above Kether, and open yourself to the imagination or memory of the time it concentrated itself to produce Kether. Let yourself be caught for a moment or two in the flow of this.

Bring your gaze and attention to Kether. Feel it fill to the brim with all that is—witness, for a moment, as it becomes the great I Am That I Am. As this washes through you and around you, ask yourself *What am I?* or, if you prefer, *Who am I?* Begin your answer with *I am.*

Whatever answer you receive—which can be a sensation or memory, an image, or words either heard, seen, or sensed—record it briefly on your blank map of the Tree in or near the Kether circle. It is probably just a few words or even a single word.

Return your awareness into Kether and its immense fullness as it begins to spill over the edges and flow downward. Physically move to the Hokmah disk, flowing with this spill of light, still facing up the Tree.

At the vessel of Hokmah, feel into this image, sensation, or wisdom of the overflow of light. Watch or sense as the sephira receives. As you do this, ask yourself *What do I receive?* Shape your answer to begin with the words *I receive.*

Record this, again in just a few words, on your blank map. Then watch or sense the fullness of Hokmah, up to overfullness, and in this moment, the overflow of this vessel and the spill of light across the Tree, to Binah.

At the third sephira, feel or see how it is that this light forms and informs the creation of Binah. As it approaches fullness, ask yourself *What do I understand?* and record your answer, beginning *I understand...* in a few words on the map. Then feel or observe the overflow of this vessel and tumble, with the spilling light, down across the

Abyss to the Chesed disk. Stand or sit, still facing up the Tree, so that you only see those sephirot above Chesed.

As the light pours into Chesed within your trance state, feel how it is to receive that which has crossed the Abyss. All has been given, and all shall be offered. Ask yourself *What do I offer?* letting your answer begin with *I offer...* and record it on your map. Witness the shattering of this vessel as the offering pours out and across the Tree.

Move to Gevurah. Notice the powerful container and inward focus of this sephira. As it fills with light, ask yourself *What is my commitment?* letting the answer begin with the words *I commit.* Record your answer.

This vessel also shatters, and now the light spills back to the middle pillar. Move to Tiferet, still facing up the Tree. Feel or notice how it is to be with Tiferet as this spilled, progressive light enters this sephira. Ask yourself *What do I love?* framing your answer as *I love...* and recording it on your map.

Witness the shattering of the vessel of Tiferet and the brilliant spill of light down the Tree to Netzach. Move yourself to that place to follow this progression. As this vessel fills, ask yourself *What do I desire?* and record your answer, beginning with the phrase *I desire.*

When this vessel also shatters, move with the light across to Hod. In this place, during the filling of the vessel, ask yourself *What do I study?* and begin your answer with the words *I study.*

Write the answer down and see or feel this filling, this shattering, this spill of light downward. Move to Yesod, still gazing up the Tree. This vessel also is filling. Ask yourself *What do I dream?* answering with words beginning *I dream* and recording your answer.

Yesod fills and then also, finally, shatters, and we fall with the light down to Malkuth. Move onto or below Malkuth, gazing up the Tree. This vessel now is filling—feel it, see it, know it. This is the vessel that will hold and not shatter. What have you become? Ask yourself this: *What am I becoming?* Frame your answer as *I become* and record the answer.

Spend a few moments at the base of the Tree, experiencing the Tree with all of its spilling, spilled, and finally contained light. Know yourself a part of it.

Then move back to Yesod. Thank it for this experience and bring yourself back through the gateway. Turn and face away from the Tree, toward Malkuth. Move your gaze or your whole body to the Malkuth disk. Receive some breaths, then step out of the Tree and out of the trance.

Ground yourself. If you wish, you can color or draw on your map or make further notes, specifically on anything you learned about the nature of your Kabbalistic magic. Perhaps something else will arise from your work: I drew a serpent through my map of the Tree with this exercise, head curved through Kether and the body snaking down through the Tree like a curving river of a lightning flash, linking all my attributes together.

activity | Creating the Ninth Disk

As you complete the work of this section, create a disk to represent this sephira you've been inhabiting. This will be your ninth disk. Perhaps you spent the first section concentrated on Kether, and you are now up to Yesod—in that case, it will be the purple Yesod disk you are working with. Perhaps you began somewhere else in the Tree and so the disk you are making now is for Hod, Chesed, Malkuth, or any other sephira.

TIME: 30–60 minutes

YOU WILL NEED: The appropriate colored disk (see page 69, "Creating the First Disk") and appropriate art materials such as colored pens and markers, paint, oil pastels, collage materials and glue, stickers

Start with contemplating the time you have spent in this sephira, including looking through your journal notes and recalling any Kabbalah exercises, processes, or rituals you did, and especially how these related to this particular sephira as well as the general mood and events in your life during this time. By this ninth sephira you might want to start gathering together different themes that have been running through your previous disks.

Allow images, words, feelings, and ideas to arise. You can hold these in your head, immediately begin work on your disk, or jot down notes or a sketch.

Mark the name of the sephira onto the disk.

Decorate your disk, creating an image or set of images that will recall your experience with this sephira. Your artwork might be a meditation on the color of this disk or a reflection of its name; for example, a visual meditation on the theme of Power for Gevurah or Foundation for Yesod. Use whatever art or craft materials you have or can find, whether these have been used in previous disks or not.

You might complete your work in one session or return later to add extra details.

examples of completed disks can be seen at janemeredith .com/disks

it's perfection momentarily, held here,
all held and then the pressure the mixing
the dissolution, the imaginal cells of it the
explosion into death or it could be birth and
then we break—and break and break and
the shards scatter outward forever we can't
contain—weeping, bleeding, falling—it's
the end of butterflies and the beginning of
butterflies

this dream of a butterfly as it falls through
the realms, imagining, greater than itself,
all butterflies held and becoming and
remembered in the tearing wings as it falls
through indigo violet lavender magenta
amethyst lilac plummeting failing falling

10

The Tree
of Life

With the tenth sephira, the Tree is complete—or as complete as a living thing ever is. This tenth emanation makes the final comment to Kether's beginning, all that while—a whole universe—ago. At the ninth sephira the Tree was perfectly balanced yet remained in flux, not yet manifest. All that Kether is and promises was not *quite* evident in Yesod. The ninth creates room for the tenth; from Foundation is born Malkuth, the Kingdom. Here the full flowering of Kether has a place and a way to become. It's the end of the journey. Looked at the other way—from our perspective—it's the beginning, the realm in which we find ourselves, the place where the path arises. The only way we can do anything is from this embodied planetary and manifest state.

On the glyph of the Tree of Life, the tenth sephira sticks out awkwardly below the rest of the Tree. It looks almost tacked on or as if it's beginning something new. In one story about the Fall, it is Malkuth that falls—tumbling down from its original place directly below Kether all the way to the bottom of the Tree, leaving the hovering emptiness of Da'ath behind it. Kether and Malkuth are the only sephirot not to both receive and send the lightning flash—Kether only sends and Malkuth only receives. Thus a shorthand version would be a transmission from Kether to Malkuth or the other way, since lightning also moves from the ground up to the sky. Kether's number, one—so deeply mysterious and indeed inexplicable, appearing as it does after the nothingness, the zero, of the Ain Soph—appears again in Malkuth, this time paired with a zero. One-zero. As if the mystery of the something-from-nothing was bound and displayed here, in this tenth sephira. Or, following a numerology rule, we add together the one and the zero in Malkuth's ten and arrive at one. Malkuth is the next one—i.e., the next Kether/originator.

If we see the Tree as upright rather than flat on the page, the whole thing is balanced on this one sephira, unless the right- and left-hand pillars rest on the ground and Yesod and Malkuth sink below. The Tree is top heavy, and that tells us about the strength of Malkuth, the gravity of it. Malkuth takes the secondary colors of the lowest triad and mixes them together for brown or, from the Golden Dawn tradition, quarters of citrine-olive-black-russet. These are the colors of soil, of dirt, of earth.

Malkuth: *The Matter of Spirit*

Malkuth is the kingdom, the place where Kether's crown manifests. Malkuth never ceases to be Kether, as everything is Kether, but it is Kether fully expressed. It could be said that Kether exists to create Malkuth, just as Malkuth exists to express Kether. As we have traveled down and down the Tree, from the Big Bang to this moment in time on this planet, down to these words and even to this exact point ● on the page, everything has narrowed and narrowed, becoming more and more particular-fragmentary-precise. It has also become increasingly complex-diverse-multifold. If it was impossible to adequately describe Kether because of its density and unimaginable enormity, so it seems equally impossible to describe Malkuth due to its vastness and the endless pieces of it.

The Tree of Life is a very large place. Large enough that we begin to imagine all sorts of things, even things we don't know how to think about, down here in Malkuth. We are building bridges with our questions, creating ways to understand or grasp the shapes of things or glimpse ideas of the spaces they take up. We can dream ourselves back in time toward the beginnings of our universe, wondering about entangled particles and black holes and dark matter, and we can also do this with very localized and immediate paradigms. There are three questions that strike me as having exceptional importance in each human life. They are questions of death, love, and the meaning of life.

What is death? A single instance, the death of someone we love, creates this question. Love. Does this powerful emotion come from a divine source? Is it a completely personal experience or just a string of chemicals? Both death and love call so much of what we think we know into question. *What is the purpose of a life? Does what I do have any significance, any importance? Can suffering be redeemed?* Running through these great human questions is the question of spirit and the problem of matter or the question of matter and the problem of spirit. What are these things, spirit and matter? How do they interact with each other and within each living being?

In the context of the Tree, the universe, or the great I Am, it is clear one person has so little influence it's barely worth mentioning. The individual is a tiny fleck. Yet each of these flecks is a spark of that Tree, this universe, and the great I Am. Not an inert, passive, or dead part, but a living, breathing, and dynamic part. There's a beautiful saying:

God has no hands; the hands of God are these hands. My hands are the hands of God. My life is the life of the Tree or a part of it, but a part indivisible from all the rest. The butterfly flaps its wings in South America. Global warming causes an ice shelf to break off in Antarctica. Bush fires rage across Australia for months, changing the climate irrevocably. A child grows up in poverty, hardship, and neglect. I stop and talk to a homeless woman or I don't.

Kabbalah and Judaism do not expect the seeker to remove themselves from the world as hermits or ascetics—in fact, they go in the opposite direction. It is stressed how spiritual attainment comes *within* the mantle of human experience. Rabbis have families and work outside their religious calling, and spiritual seekers and journeyers are encouraged to relate their discoveries to their daily lives. If we believe that the world should be a better place, and our understanding of spiritual matters leads us to believe this is possible, what if each day we actively make it our business to bring the world a little closer to becoming this better place? As a start, what if each living being we came into contact with throughout the day had a slightly better experience of the day, and of the quality of their life, because of us? Because of how we interacted with them, what we offered, even if that was just a smile or a kind word?

Malkuth is the extreme distance, within the Tree of Life model, that one can get from Kether while at the same time still being intimately involved with and enfolded by it. Although my perspective is from earth and my life is made possible by and indeed is inextricably a part of earth, I cannot imagine that the Big Bang explodes in a singular direction—that is, downward and toward the existence of this planet, this species, myself. Surely it explodes outward in an infinity of directions. So now I am imagining an infinity of Trees spinning out from that point in all directions and in all dimensions. I do not view Malkuth or earth or this moment in time as singular but as one of almost infinite overlapping expressions of uncountable realities. Why would Kether flow in only one direction to one destination? Surely everything else we know of (and don't know of) is equally a part of Kether—and therefore, there must be many incarnations of Hokmah, Tiferet, Hod, and all the rest of them, getting increasingly differentiated as they spread further and further out from the source.

I'm not really talking about parallel worlds, although that's one way to see it. I'm theorizing that conditions on Pluto or in the Orion system or at the very edges of expanding outer space or in some cloud-nebula-galaxy just now forming must equally describe, contain, and reflect Kether, must equally encompass Malkuth (or be on the way toward that), just as our known version of reality, our own Malkuth, us-living-as-part-of-this-planet does. There could be an infinity of parallel universes, but that doesn't alter the basic structure of the Tree or this vision of multiple, almost shimmering layers of Trees semi-superimposed over each other, all with the same starting point, Kether, and becoming increasingly diverse as they spread out from there. The complexity of Malkuth cannot, I think, apply solely to conditions on earth unless we indulge in the utmost hubris, which has been a consistent flaw of humanity for a long time. Let's assume, instead, that we are studying and reflecting one tiny part of the whole thing—just as our own individual lives are one tiny part of the life of humanity—and that from our field of study many particulars can be understood and some generalities proposed.

Because we have never really left Kether—all of everything, including Malkuth and therefore our planet, our beings, our lives, is still a part of Kether—we must still have that resonance or encoded knowledge, ultimate belonging singing through us. Not through humans, uniquely; through everything. Through the rock in my bathroom that was birthed in a volcano and flung through the air twenty-three million years ago, through the pademelons in the garden, through the moss and the sunlight and birds singing now in the early morning, through me. Not just me—a relatively privileged, educated white middle-class woman living in Australia, currently one of the safest places on earth to be as COVID-19 (also an expression of Kether) rages through human populations—but everyone. An illiterate indentured worker in a field or mine somewhere far away from me. A newborn child. A right-wing conspiracist. A classical musician. People suffering from poverty, depression, pain, abuse. People who've never questioned anything or spent a moment in philosophical inquiry.

The dance of atoms, the extension of light, the vibrating strings of string theory, the entangled particles—these run through all of us equally. Which is not to say that all of us have the luxury of sitting around thinking about these things, devoting large amounts of our time and energy to personal, spiritual, or magical practices, philosophical or esoteric readings and discussions, et cetera et cetera. Most people don't. But we are all equally a part of it, each one of us an expression of it—and a full expression, there's no ranking here, where some of us are intrinsically more close to God, as it were, than others of us. We are all, literally, children of this Tree, scattered seeds, extensions of light, falling butterflies, part of the resonance of the I Am That I Am. We are busy I-Aming down here "in the uncharted backwaters of the unfashionable end of the western spiral arm of the Galaxy … [on] an utterly insignificant little blue green planet," as Douglas Adams incisively remarked in *The Hitchhiker's Guide to the Galaxy* (Adams 1981, 6). On that planet happens to be, among approximately 8.7 million species, humans. Us.

When we come all the way in space and time down the Tree to my life and your life, then we're talking about Malkuth. We're trusting that each piece of the universe not only holds part of that integrity of the whole, the I Am, but literally *is* a part of it still, ongoingly and forever. Not in a constant form but within the flow. Momentarily a particle or perceived or experienced as a particle, but always within a wave. Even in the heart of a star things are constantly changing form, as hydrogen atoms fuse together to create helium, then lithium, then beryllium, boron, carbon, nitrogen, and so on. Our minds have the capacity and seemingly the inclination to distinguish, to call this part helium and that part hydrogen or to call this part me and that part you. Separation is not just a useful mental tool, a way of building those bridges toward understanding things, but also a fundamental truth. In our model of the Tree of Life, separation is first expressed by the existence of Hokmah and then continues down, with those refinements and separations gaining increasing discernment, difference, and variation. By the time we are at Malkuth, it can be difficult to remember that separation and difference are not the original rule. The original is oneness; I Am That.

Right back at the beginning—that singularity, that explosion—what was that? Call it the arrival of space-time, matter bursting into existence and becoming itself, spirit all entangled up and haphazardly spreading out; they can't be separated. Every separation we look at past that point still can only contain whatever was there at the beginning. So there's only one thing, and we can look at it this way and call it matter or look at it that way and call it spirit, but it's still the one thing. Like light: particles or waves, depending on how we look at it, but actually it behaves as both simultaneously and we have no words for what that is. If we believe Malkuth and Kether are each expressions of the other, then spirit *is* matter, an expression of matter. They are the same thing. Spirit

393

and matter are one. Life is inspirited matter, but everything is matter, so one could say everything is spirit.

Then what of death?

I take this question with me into the garden. Today I am planting thirteen native trees on the side of a steep slope. It's a small forest that I'm involved in, and I wonder about the comparative longevity of what I'm doing in the garden compared to what I then come inside to do: write these words. Longevity aside—and even though in my mind I imagine this book is more important, has far more gravitas and fulfills more of my passion and reason for living, the worth of my individual life, there's a good argument that the plants, the garden, the forest is actually of more value—I begin to wonder if they are actually different things at all. There I was planting trees. Here I am writing about trees, a tree, the Tree, and even though I imagine my life to be complex and layered, perhaps it's just one simple thing.

When I consider the complexity that exists at Malkuth and the immensity of it, I feel an overwhelming confusion for how all this information could be passed back to Kether—how it could ever be integrated or consumed. This is surely the nature of the system: yes, everything devolves down the Tree to Malkuth, but then at some point, in some way, and perhaps through death, all of that is collected and passed back up the Tree to Kether. The end is the beginning. That could be simultaneous, as everything happening in Malkuth is in effect happening in/with/for Kether, because Malkuth is fundamentally an expression of Kether. It could be linear, up the middle pillar, through the collective unconscious, the all-possible-worlds of Yesod, then the great heart of Tiferet and the mysterious transformation hovering in Da'ath. Or it could be via lightning flash, zigzagging back and forth through increasing refinement and rarification until it reaches the beginning point. Probably all three simultaneously or, depending how we're viewing it, via light, that mysterious constant.

This sort of question has been largely passed off, especially where the masses were concerned, with a *the-mind-of-God-is-beyond-the-minds-of-humans-that's-why-it's-the-mind-of-God* sort of non-explanation. That is, *we can't explain it, so don't worry about it.* The fall of each sparrow, the wish and prayer of each human is somehow noted by God, and that's all we need to concern ourselves with, not the how or whereforto of this. However, I think for the system to work, there must be an explanation. All this multiplicity. If that's somehow the point or part of the point of existence, then how is it actually functioning? What's really happening? I notice we are back to my childhood question of *why*. Why is all of this happening, why am I alive, why does suffering exist, why do I have the consciousness to think about this? Just—why?

In the Bible it says that humans are made in the image of God. I think Kabbalah holds that everything is the image of the divine—a waterfall as much as a butterfly as much as a human. But if we went with that for a moment—for after all, a human is no less the image of the divine than the butterfly and waterfall and whatever—we could look at our own way of processing information: our brains; another topic we don't know that much about, but—pressing on. Some of the things we do know, or act as if we know, is that the data collected by our senses, together with our knowledge and memories of previous experiences, are added together, processed, by what we call our brains, and certain conclusions are reached. This usually happens more rapidly than we can consciously follow, so we have to take this process on trust. We filter things, select them for relevance and importance, highlighting some of the input and relegating other parts of it to a low level of interest that can be accessed if our needs change.

If we were to focus equally on every single experience, action, and thought we were having, we would be quagmired, our processors possibly overwhelmed and unable to help us make quick, potentially life-saving decisions. Typing these words, I don't have to consciously consider the mechanics of typing. I also don't consider how to read or write in the English language. Most of the time, I don't have to consider what a word means—and those moments when I do, it's deserving of my focus. I stopped to consider *quagmired*, for example, up above—to reflect on whether I wanted to use such an unusual word and whether it was the best word that would most adequately and poetically describe my point. Because it's a word I rarely use, I also had to think about how to spell it.

Many of the things we do every day—having a shower, getting dressed, making break-fast, charging our phones—have only our peripheral, partial attention. We do the same things, perhaps with small differences, every day at about the same time in about the same way. When something different happens—we feel unwell, the weather changes, someone we're not expecting arrives on the doorstep—it has our full attention. Our brain is on high alert, and we bend our attention toward it. One way of phrasing this would be to say we only really notice things that we either consciously pay attention to or that are unexpected, new, or different. What if the mind of God works—well, I hesitate to say the same way, but—that sort of way? That the vast mass of occurrences, either on this small blue green planet or anywhere else in the universe, are similar, continuous, have occurred in variations before and will do so again. They are still part of the All; they just don't require any particular attention as these instances come and go. But some things happen for the first-ever time or the only time. We can see the emergence of each sephira as the pattern for this. Each one is so particular, so distinct in the pattern of becoming, that to express it requires a whole new sephira to exist.

To bring this down to what we are most concerned with, human lives... What if, yes, every one of our lives, and every single aspect and second of each of those lives, is registered somehow, somewhere, in the great general wash of human lives, but that what the great I Am pays attention to, so to speak, what is most especially highlighted in the immense data being washed back upstream from Malkuth to Kether, is what is unique. Perhaps it's the melody of a song or a prayer no one has ever uttered before. Perhaps it's an act—of savagery, kindness, love, beauty, grandeur—that has never occurred before. What if some moments—what if only one moment—of my life was unique? Stood out from all the rest that ever has been, was remarkable not just to me but because it had never existed before? And therefore that moment, beyond all the rest, was what added to the great existence of Kether-becoming-Kether?

If this were so—and in my head it is so logical now that I've thought it, I can't shake it—what would be most valued is difference. Therefore randomness, which creates difference, is intrinsic to the patterns. Not complete, incoherent randomness (although maybe that, in some corners of the universe) but a sort of contained randomness. This necessity for difference actually explains suffering and goes a long way toward answering the great *why* that I carried from childhood. Because what is valued is difference, and randomness creates difference, therefore suffering is not personal; it's just part of the randomness. We are all having different experiences in the same great tides of human life because that difference is what counts most in this expression of the crown of Kether within Malkuth, its kingdom.

If Kether is the expression of all of us, of each of us—and so much more, of course, but just for the moment focusing on human lives—then the more different things that are experienced, the better. The more full, the more entire. The more Kether. The more it is, the more it is able to express itself, and therefore become. The way Kether would be able to absorb and experience the all that is, in Malkuth, is by the focus being biased toward uniqueness. This also explains why artists, geniuses, and those sometimes called lunatics attract so much attention in so many cultures throughout time and across the world. Sometimes that attention is to suppress or eliminate, sometimes to elevate and adore, and often haphazard, but overall they attract more than their percentage share of attention, if everything was exactly equal. Of course we know things are not (ever) exactly equal; in fact, the whole existence of everything is based on that premise. If everything was spread equally through the universe, nothing would exist, both because it is the uneven clumps of matter that allow star masses to form and because everything would (perhaps) have collapsed straightaway in the Big Bang instead of extending.

Multiplicity is the very thing that creates anything different enough to be an addition to the all that is. It's all so scattered and random and variable; it's an addition, not just more sameness, to be added together into Kether, the Mind of God or the All, the I Am. My little piece of perfect suffering, my great ecstatic joy, my endless quest—these, in their extremities and uniqueness, are what count. Not count to me (although they do) but count, full stop. So yes, it's interesting to this All to have people fall in love and live together happily forever, and yes it's interesting if they are instead parted to spend their lives longing for the other, and yes, still interesting if one or both betrays the other and interesting if they have many children or just one or none and interesting if those children grow up happy and healthy and interesting if one dies tragically, if they are best friends or bitterest enemies or can't really be bothered with the others—every piece of difference is valuable.

Every blade of grass is different, so it is said. I can imagine that the blueprint of a blade of grass is already stored in the All. And then each difference, as it occurs with each new blade, is collected and stored, added in to the great realm of possibilities, of expressions. This is the matter of the divine; this is divine becoming matter, still divine. We are all—and everything we see and do and learn and interact with—the matter of the divine. We are all light in extension, and it has extended all the way down through the life history of those atoms that were there at the Big Bang and are here now, in my computer and me and the garden; this is matter, it's divine, and there's really no separation. I think this is it: matter and divine are essentially one thing that can be viewed or experienced in a variety of ways (ten or eleven ways in the sephirot) or two essential ways: from Kether, where all originates, and from Malkuth, where all becomes.

Not that spirit is clothed in matter or that body is discarded in death and spirit survives, although both of those things, yes. This is the Kabbalah, after all, where apparent contradictions are essential to deeper understanding. Spirit is clothed in matter not because they are separate things, but because one is an expression of the other (either is/both are an expression of the other). Body transforms upon death, those atoms finding new forms to take, and spirit continues because those atoms are spirit anyway. We are at the same time part of the All, indivisible, and also our particular selves. For the scale of this, imagine if each atom our bodies are composed of were to tell us its life story, from the beginning of time through to this moment. In a way it is doing that while being part of us. In a way, we are doing that, telling the entire story of our lives, from Malkuth to Kether, just by existing. We cannot escape being part of the whole history of the universe. It depends how you're looking at it, like light, and it's impossible to see both realities at once or to fully understand what this means, though we may glimpse it in moments.

Light is both particle and wave, and we have no explanation for something that can be those two things simultaneously, just as we really have no exact explanation for the consciousness of matter. Complexity is one explanation for how certain parts of matter become what we recognize as conscious, and this resonates with our understanding of the Tree. The more complex it gets—and inevitably, the further away from the source—the more consciousness is present, which happens to be the very thing creating this illusion of division. The divisions, illusory or not, are creating the complexity. Integrated information theory attempts to explain how consciousness exists, positing that the immense complexity and the integration and connections between the information we store in our brains creates this awareness. It's not scientifically proven and is hard to test, but from a Kabbalistic point of view we can understand the concept. The further down the Tree we are, the more divided, complex, and conscious is the experience. What we call consciousness is an aspect of spirit/matter that occurs in some circumstances.

As for the great questions we concern ourselves within Malkuth—death, love, and the matter of spirit—we continue on our immersive journeys of exploration. Each of us a particle of the whole, a falling spark, meeting suffering, finding compassion, and creating uniqueness. Within the model of the Tree, spirit and matter, wave and particle, death and life are the same thing, sometimes viewed as dualities but sometimes—as a gift to us Kabbalists—understood for what they are: expressions of each other. Love becomes another word for light or the extension of light, while life and death are moments of experience within that extension, the particle and wave of it.

The Tree of Life

Trees are essential. They are the very breath of life. We humans, mammals, oxygen-breathing creatures have a symbiotic relationship with trees in that we literally exchange breaths; we need each other to be able to keep breathing. Both land- and water-based plants take in the carbon dioxide we breathe out. Along with sunlight and water, they use it to create nutrition, with oxygen released as a leftover from this process. Early oxygen breathers, in the form of bacteria, created a sweet spot that allowed both themselves and the carbon dioxide breathers to continue to evolve into increasingly more complex life forms, including, eventually, us humans. The fundamental health of living things on the planet is tied together. One can no more remove all the trees and expect human populations to continue thriving than we could remove all oxygen breathers and expect green life to continue uninterrupted. Forests have been called the lungs of the earth.

Trees are depicted as representing not just life, but Life. The Tree of Life, as it appears in paintings, tapestry, carpets, and other art forms, consists not just of a many-branched tree, but of a tree filled with living things: at the very least different types of birds, but often including insects, small animals, and even larger animals at its base. As actual trees do, this Tree provides shelter, food, and homes for dozens of other species. The Tree, and every tree, is a celebration of abundance, nurture, and complexity—even in death. Dead and fallen trees continue to provide shelter, food, and homes for a variety of species. As they rot away, assisted by insects, fungi, and the elements, their nutrients return to the earth, nourishing future generations of trees all around them.

In European mythology trees have distinct magical properties. Oaks, hollys, rowans, lindens, ash, hazel, apples, hawthorn, yew—each one has whole stories built around it. This is the tree culture I am most familiar with. In the southwest corner of my own garden, in Northern New South Wales, Australia, there's a native fig tree, often known as a grandmother tree as it hosts so many other life forms. It's the fruit of this tree that seasonally summons the wompoo pigeons I love so much. There's a blue quandong tree, massively tall and still growing, whose hard round blue fruit drops onto tin roofs in summer with an unapologetic *bang*. At the top of the driveway is a lily pilly, scattering tiny pink fruits over the ground. There are bangalow palms, local to this area; I'm always planting out their seedlings and moving those growing in inconvenient places. There's a red cedar, its branches drifting perceptibly closer to the house; it's a native that sheds its leaves each year, letting the western sunlight through in winter. There's a bunya pine towering into the sky. There are a few eucalypts that I love.

I know these trees personally, individually, and yet I don't know their mythological selves. I can't tell stories about them. I just looked up bunya pines and apparently they evolved 350 million years ago and are regarded as belonging to the living fossil category, along with the elusive wollemi pine. The age a bunya pine lives to is six hundred years, although this one is apparently only forty, so far. I know a whisper from their story, how the bunya forests would attract local Aboriginal groups, who traveled there for the bunya harvest each year ... but put that beside my knowledge and feeling for European trees and I am two-dimensional in regard to native Australian trees. Living with some of them so intimately I have a sense of their yearly patterns and characteristics, but they weren't in the stories I read as a child, in the poetry or children's songs I heard; their mythos remains secret from me. It's an echo of displacement that the trees and forests I'm most familiar with are on the other side of the world.

Another type of tree we engage with is the family tree, a diagram of branching heredity showing where each one of us belongs in the lineage from our parents, grandparents, and more distant ancestors. This version is an upside-down tree, with the earliest ancestors forming the distant roots at the top of the page, while we usually find ourselves at the tips of the newest branches down the bottom somewhere. Any descendants we have will be even further out. If we could depict all the individuals we are related to, family trees would be manyfold and overlapping. It begins to look very like the multiplicity of Trees expanding out from Kether.

The story of humans is inextricably linked to trees. My version goes something like this: Long ago, the first primates lived in trees, keeping them safe from predators and the dangerous forest floor. Trees were also the source of food and sometimes a way to travel, as the overstories of the vast forests held together like canopies. When our far-distant ancestors came down from trees, they stayed close by, forming family groups and tribes that did not view themselves as separate from the forest. Even when our closer ancestors spread out across plains and valleys far from the deep forests, trees remained in their mythos. In Europe the Great Forest owned the land. Human settlements, when they came, were dotted through or at the edges of it, often along the waterways. The forest was vast and lent itself to tales of magic and mystery. The fae, the land and water spirits, dryads, woodcutters, and herb women all belonged in the forest and drew from its strange powers.

Even now, after we have cut down most of the world's forests, while we are still ferociously burning the Amazon and destroying natural habitats in every direction, including Antarctica, the Great Barrier Reef, and the permafrost in Siberia, when humans want solace, when we seek initiation or revelation, when we need healing or a sense of a world greater than ourselves, we head outdoors, away from our cities and suburbs and into the forest, to the seaside, to the mountains, to the moors. Even a tree in a back yard or park can carry the scent of this wilderness, our belonging to the earth, this tree-ness that our souls yearn for, as companions that have been with us from the very first and without whom we could not survive. As a child I climbed trees—perhaps you did too— and I also swam in rivers and dreamed on the ground among wildflowers. I felt closer to those beings than I did to humans. Lying along a branch of a tree in the wind, I felt its essential wildness and yet was held, sheltered.

There's a story that's central to the Judaic-Christian culture that has formed the basis of our neo-liberal contemporary society, in what we like to name as the First World. It has trees in it. It's the story of the Garden of Eden, and it's written in the first few pages of the Old Testament—I prefer the King James version. The garden is Paradise—or perhaps *a* paradise, meaning that it's walled or sheltered. It is God's garden. Within this garden are all the plants and animals of our earth, as well as two special trees, or perhaps it's one tree with two names. The story's a little vague on detail. It, or they, are called variously the Tree of the Knowledge of Good and Evil (the Tree of Knowledge) and the Tree of Life. There's a serpent in the story, as well as a couple of humans and they—or perhaps all of paradise, all that it contains—are made in the image of God. These special trees are fruiting trees—apples, in our common version, but more probably for the time and place figs, apricots, or persimmons.

Eve, the mother of humanity, is tempted by the serpent to eat the forbidden fruit of the Tree of Knowledge. The eating of fruit, this essential act of taking something into ourselves so it becomes a part of us, an ingestion of knowledge, is linked to sexuality, fertility, the Fall—and so there we are with Eve, falling through the serpent path of the Tree of Knowledge all the way down, out of Paradise and into Malkuth, the place of utter embodiment, of sex and fertility, of eating and birthing and rotting, living and dying. No paradisical life for us; we chose to eat. We were tempted by knowledge, by the mysteries, by the call of body. This falling is cast in the Bible as a grave error, a sin, a disaster. But falling through the Tree of Life *is* life. We fall beyond the shelter and rules of God's exclusive garden into the great, wild garden of this planet, this life. Our lives are intrinsically a part of the life of the earth, and the earth expresses itself through this symbiosis of life. Here we are still gardeners, if we choose to be, still following the whispers of serpents, still daring to taste the fruit of knowledge and defy God.

But the story has a few serious flaws in it. Who plants a tree covered in luscious fruit in the middle of the garden and tells the inhabitants *You can't have that*? Obviously God will be defied, obviously the fruit will be tasted, obviously the Fall will occur. Eternity in Paradise lasts a long time, and eventually … in short, I think it's a set-up. Bound to happen. Fruit is made to be eaten, boundaries to be tested, gods to be defied, and simplicity to become increasingly complex.

When we eat things, they become a part of us, literally as well as metaphorically. Our digestive system breaks them down and utilizes different components: trace elements, nutrients, energy; we absorb them and our molecules dance with their molecules and become indistinguishable. We took part of that paradise with us when we left. It was inside us. We were born there anyway, fed on it from our earliest moments, and we were carrying that knowledge in our minds and body. Each one of us inherits a knowledge of paradise integrated deep within us. It's in our curiosity, our questioning *why*, our need to eat, our sexuality, our ability to procreate. All of these are ingredients of paradise; like every other piece of the universe, we carry within ourselves a way back to paradise, to the beginnings, to the All and the scattering of stardust past the Big Bang to Kether. Each piece, each scrap, each molecule of Malkuth has that source coded into it; perhaps that is the only thing that is coded in. I Am That.

We are in a crisis this century, this year, this week. A climate crisis, a planetary crisis. Various other crises rage about us—the COVID-19 pandemic; injustice, poverty, and inequality; a global economic recession; severe and increasing weather events—but this crisis is a crisis for trees, for forests, and therefore for everything living on and as part of our planet. If we are the gardeners—and to the extent that our actions assume responsibility for the welfare of life on earth, for the very Tree of Life itself—we are beholden to act on this crisis, or rather to reverse and redress our actions, which are directly responsible for the crisis. Trees change and move slowly. Up there, in the sky of it, or the roots of it, Kether is still pouring out light; echoes of the Big Bang are still resounding, and we're all still vibrating with that. Perhaps one little planet lost to the foolishness of its would-be caretakers is no big deal in universal terms, but down here in Malkuth life moves fast, and it would be a bitter end for our own species, taking tens of thousands of other species with it. A giant extinction event brought about through ignorance, willfulness, and arrogance.

While we struggle with this dilemma—while our gardening status is on the line—trees go on generously growing where and how they can. This paradise that we fell out of—there's a theme of disobedience running there. The angels fell because they challenged God. Eve and Adam were turned out because they were disobedient, and the serpent also. But the Kabbalah teaches us that there is no *other*, nothing that is not a part of Kether. Fallen or not, disobedient or otherwise, held within a nurturing paradise or down in the wilds of earth, we are each, every single one of us, always and forever a part of the whole. Each of us is a shred, a scrap, a photon of the whole that is both divisible (Malkuth) and indivisible (Kether) at the same time. Thus we have in us the path back to Paradise and the All. It's written into our cells, into the elements and atoms we are composed of.

If we could see ourselves within those tapestries and carpets depicting the Tree of Life, we would be sheltering at its base or gratefully eating of its fruit or simply admiring its beauty. We would be small animals, our lives just as dependent on the life of the Tree as those birds and possums, bats and lizards, caterpillars and butterflies. Dependent on the Tree for food, for shelter, for our very breath. We would be offering our reverence and care to this Tree, these trees, while white cockatoos rip through the sky above us, pademelons hop around, and bandicoots dig holes in the earth about the roots. The divine is shown to us in a mirror every day—not just the mirror where we see ourselves looking back, but the mirror of any life form, any other piece of this planet, and certainly every tree. Here is this tree, participating in life and death, just as I am. Here is this tree showing me the All and everything, the reminder of Kether, even while it's held, utterly, within the realms of Malkuth. This tree with its gifts of mortality and knowledge. This tree whose air I breathe, that I planted, whose fruit I eat and whose habitat I preserve, whose body and forest I hold sacred.

practice | Other Selves

Who are we really? What does it mean to be an individual with a physical body? Can we experience ourselves as a reflection of the divine, the All, Kether itself; a unique expression of stardust, matter, spirit? How can we understand our place in the world, within the worlds, when we are so relatively tiny? Is it possible to glimpse the vastness of Kether from this position of Malkuth or even to understand what it means to be part of Malkuth? We have been asking these questions all the way down the Tree but now, at the bottom of the whole event, we need some answers—if not absolute answers, at least answers we can live with.

There's been a concept all along, since the separation of Hokmah from Kether, that the sephirot are not different things from each other. They also are not merely different aspects of the same thing. Instead, they are different ways of looking at the one thing: Kether, or the I Am. Thus the realized Tree contains ten different views of the same thing, as ten sephirot.

What if we apply this concept more immediately, to ourselves? What if we start to consider the point of view where, for example, human beings (although it could equally be turtles or rocks or butterflies or stars) are not different from other humans as the sephirot are not different from each other? What if we are not even, or not only, each different *aspects* of humans, turtles, or rocks? Instead we bring ourselves to the premise that individual humans, ourselves included, are each a different *lens*, or way of perceiving what it is to be human, though—just like the sephirot—we are all fundamentally the same thing. We might ask who is doing this perceiving, to which the answer would surely be Kether, but we are (also) that. So we can do the perceiving ourselves, at least a little.

There are three different approaches to this practice, with ourselves as the experimental subject. You can try all three and see which one works for you. This order is from the simplest to most involved method, but I have had success with all three. They work best as a sustained practice, like meditation; when the practice is continued, over months and years the understanding and feeling state develop through time.

This is the single most powerful Kabbalistic practice I have ever engaged in.

TIME: 5 to 15 minutes, over multiple occasions

YOU WILL NEED: A crowded or high foot-traffic place where you can easily see many other humans, such as a park, shopping center, train station, busy cafe. If you can't manage this, an alternative screen version is watching something like a news channel with the sound turned off.

The process is done in crowded places such as public transport, city streets, and shopping centers, as you need a steady supply of people, preferably strangers. Do it repeatedly, for five to fifteen minutes at a time, with a nonstop series of different people, at about thirty seconds or less per person. As you move your focus from person to person, make sure to release each one from your attention; don't energetically continue to carry them with you. You might build in a super-brief thanking or blessing (less than a breath of time) toward them for being a part of your practice. Ground both before and afterward.

Similarities

Gaze at another human being briefly. As quickly as possible, note how they are similar to you—it could be age, dress style, an expression, anything. Breathe into this, and if you can, *feel* this similarity as some kind of resonance within you. Try to do this in thirty seconds or less per person. Move continually from gazing at one person to the next. If you can't find or feel any similarity, simply move to the next person at the usual rate. You will probably find your sympathy to similarities increases as you go.

There's also a version where instead of a similarity, you pick a difference—particularly one that irks, irritates, or provokes you—and breathe *through* it until you feel that difference shift or change or release. Again, even if you feel stuck with a particular person, still move on at the thirty- or sixty-second mark rather than lingering. This exercise is about multiplicity.

With both versions of this practice, move toward a state where you begin to see others as another way of seeing yourself.

Life and Death

Gaze at another human being briefly. Imagine the eyes of Kether/God/the infinite gazing at the two of you—you and this other. The importance of your lives is exactly equal. Imagine that in this moment, one of these two can live and one will die, but since it is your exercise, you get to choose who lives. Each time choose for the other person to live (that means that you will die this moment), and see how this is. Try to get so that you can do this within a few seconds. Breathe and move on to another person.

Note your responses and thoughts but continue the practice. Move toward a state where you can, without hesitating and with no particular reaction or emotion, choose for the other person to live.

Exchanges

Gaze at another human being briefly. Imagine that within the next minute you will leave your body and your life and inhabit theirs for the rest of that life, although you will still retain a memory of who you were and your previous life. Notice the people with whom you can do this more easily (younger, same gender as you, whatever) and your emotional responses and reactions.

Take a breath between each person. Move toward a state where you can agree internally to move into that body and life within a few seconds, regardless of who it is.

An extended version of this practice is that you will transfer into their body and life but without your memories or personality—that is, just your life-force. Maybe this is easier for you than the first way of doing the practice. Notice, breathe, continue the practice.

ritual | Spell of Becoming

Malkuth has so much going on, it's easy to be overwhelmed and can be hard to focus, even to remember our origins in Kether and that the whole Tree is supporting this realm. This two-part process seeks to reinstall our living link to the great I Am That I Am, the All that we have a place in, and remind ourselves, heart, body, and mind, what we belong to.

In this spell we descend through the middle pillar of the Tree of Life. Beginning at Kether, the All, we move to Da'ath, the doorway, to Tiferet, the open/broken heart, and Yesod, the multiplicity, through to Malkuth, the particularity. We begin with a trance, followed by a time for journaling, and it is best to do these in the same session. The second part is a creative expression, which could also be begun or completed in the same session or held over until a second session, maybe after we've had some time to let our experiences and understandings sink in and decided on the art form and ways we want to express those.

Part 1: The Trance and Journaling

TIME: 60–90 minutes

YOU WILL NEED: A comfortable place to trance, the disks of your middle pillar (Kether, Da'ath, Tiferet, Yesod, Malkuth), journal and pen, coloring things optional

You can lay your disks out on the floor and either sit somewhere you can see them all or you can move throughout the trance to each disk in turn, standing or sitting. Or you can have them pinned on the wall and move your gaze progressively down the line. Alternatively, you can have them nearby and pick up each one as you come to it in the trance.

Sit or stand in a comfortable way. Take a few moments to consciously relax your body and release any tensions you find.

Allow five to ten minutes to enter into a trance state that is deep, but not so deep that you can't move or recall later what happened. You might like to drum rhythmically, sing a repetitive chant, focus on your breathing, or use some other method of trance induction.

In turn, visit each of the sephirot listed below. Allow five to ten minutes for each one. At each sephira pick up your disk or gaze at it on the wall or floor or move to stand or sit next to it. You can read the prompts beforehand and then trust that you'll remember or create what you need, or you can write them out on slips of paper. If you are working in a pair or group, one person can lead the trance for the others. You could also pre-record the trance and then listen back to it.

KETHER

- ▸ Kether is all, before any splitting or division occurs—allow yourself to be bathed in the totality of the All
- ▸ Kether is the I of the I Am That I Am—allow that *I* to resound through you
- ▸ Kether is the singularity—invite yourself to reflect upon what it is to exist in individual form as a reflection of this singularity
- ▸ Experience the light that emanates forth from Kether; feel and see this light in its wave form

DA'ATH

- ▸ Da'ath, although utterly other than and separate from Kether, is still a part of all we know—allow yourself to contemplate this paradox
- ▸ The second word of the I Am That I Am is the Am—invite yourself to resonate with the vibrations of that word and concept: *Am*
- ▸ Da'ath is a doorway cut into the Tree—allow yourself to become aware of the doorways in the world and your life
- ▸ Light vanishes into a black hole—let yourself rest with this thought for a moment

TIFERET

- ▶ Tiferet is the heart of the Tree—feel the resonances of that, perhaps with a hand over your own heart, so you are heart-to-heart with Tiferet
- ▶ Tiferet is That in the I Am That I Am—know yourself as *That*, questing deeply into its possible meanings for you
- ▶ Tiferet is neither all nor nothing—it is a part. Invite yourself to realize all the things, places, relationships, and commitments that you are part of
- ▶ Tiferet receives the light that pierces, breaking it open into rays—feel and know the breaks in your own heart and follow those rays outward

YESOD

- ▶ Yesod gathers layers of all that is and can be—allow yourself to feel these layers within yourself, your potential, and your lifetime
- ▶ Yesod is the second I in the I Am That I Am—feel what it is to be a reflection of Kether, the divine, the original *I*
- ▶ Yesod is a gathering of all the parts that have existed until now—allow yourself a few moments to realize the container that is you, of ancestry, place, experiences, relationships
- ▶ Yesod refracts light—let yourself see and feel the different ways you reflect and shine into the world

MALKUTH

- ▶ Malkuth is a collection of tiny fragments of being—let yourself feel what it is to be one of those fragments
- ▶ Malkuth is the final Am in the I Am That I Am—invite yourself to experience a moment of realization that you are complete and entire, the final statement of the divine
- ▶ Malkuth holds the uniqueness of each one of us—resonate with the idea that you are the only one of you that will ever exist
- ▶ Malkuth receives light—allow yourself to imagine or experience light as particles, equally and simultaneously as true as waves, and feel this within you

• • • •

Bring yourself back from your trance state.

Take 10–15 minutes to record your trance experience in your journal. You might work with a diagram of the middle pillar, writing down words and images for each of the sephirot; you might write a paragraph for each one or simply record your various impressions, sensations, questions, and thoughts.

Part 2—Creative Response

TIME: 1 hour +

YOU WILL NEED: Materials relevant to your art form

Find a way to express some of the feelings, understandings, or experiences you had in the trance and recorded in your journal in a creative or artistic form. Possibilities include but are not limited to poetry, song, dance, visual art, body paint, short story or picture book, sculpture, and fabric work.

Memoir: *Paradise*

The temple evening is at a venue named Paradise. On looking closer I discover it's called Paradise One. The original paradise? This seems unlikely, but it's still a delightful invitation. Kabbalistically I play around with the idea that paradise occurs at one—that is, after zero—paradise is impossible in the Ain Soph, but the existence of Kether, the one, brings paradise into being. Also the *one* is evocative … one tree, serpent, apple? One bite? One bite of knowledge renders paradise both comprehensible and unobtainable, or maybe not unobtainable, maybe it's just that, having had that vision, received knowledge that it's possible, we spend all our lives striving to create it, to not just return but to live as if we were there.

A temple evening is dedicated to the body and the sacred—sacred bodies celebrating the beauty of being alive through dance and ritual and intimate exchanges. This is like my journey through the Tree, into embodied love and ecstasy, the journey of the butterfly falling and dying but also living, capturing in each tearing wingbeat of beauty the essence of life. All my long quest seems to be almost answered by the fact that these events exist and I have found them.

This paradise is in a semi-tropical garden; arriving, I can feel the invitation of the name. There are lush ferns, palms, trees, greenery, the buildings shelter within the forest. The temple room is octagonal with many windows. There's a wooden pole in the middle, supporting roof beams that span out, which has been decorated with eucalypt branches, their leaves falling downward; it's a tree. A tree holding up the building, a tree at the center of paradise. At the beginning we dance, and I dance with the tree. I praise it, laughing, how perfect, and I feel myself falling, falling, all the way from Kether, through the Abyss and even twisting through the mysteries of Da'ath and down and down, my heart breaking, Tiferet, as I fall for this long alone time, this yearning and waiting and calling, this courting the universe, and falling through the collective, through liminal dreams lapping and overlapping and down, down into this body in this moment in Paradise One.

The early exercises of the night wash over me, reminding me of my boundaries, inviting my intention, sweeping me through and past others. My intention, the one that arrives rather than anything I've planned, is *surprise me.* Like something I might say to a lover. These processes we're doing seem more intense than usual—or else I'm just dropping deep; I feel wild and free, reminded of Eve in the garden every time I look up and catch sight of that tree at the center. I pair with someone in an exercise and somehow we're talking about priestesses and the sacred, we are in this temple together and referencing other temples, linking with all others that have ever been here.

Then I'm in a group with another woman and two men, taking turns to speak a desire. I speak into my intention, *surprise me,* and it's the woman who surprises me. She asks if she can kiss my belly and I fly apart with the impact of it, the sensuality, her mouth on my flesh, and when I sit up to look at her she leans closer. I'm swept into her gaze, closer, and we kiss oh the beauty of it and we play with each other's hair and reach hands to each other's face and kiss, and kiss again and there's so much delight in me I can't hold it, I adore her, she's so daring and tender and the sensuality of it blasts through me and oh I remember, I remember—I'd forgotten, but I remember now we're in paradise, there's the tree and this body I belong to and she's reminding me what it is, the kiss of molecules, the entanglement of particles, the memory of what we all share and I'm falling. Our mouths fit together so exquisitely, like entering the heart of the universe. That delicacy of her mouth against mine, those slightest movements, lips and lips and lips and just the tiniest hints of her tongue—sweat sticking her hair to her neck and face, I'm lifting it off, her hand cupping my head—her kisses on my neck, sensual, strong—kissing with our eyes open—closer, closer and the shock, the dare of it, the delight—

The night swirls on. I haven't quite noticed but there are a lot of men here, nearly double the number of women. When the facilitators carve up the room into quarters—with the center, around the tree, left for dancing and movement—there's a quarter reserved for men to interact with each other, as well as the quarters for massage and touch, tea and conversation, and erotic interaction. There's an invitation offered to the men—if you want to wrestle, kiss, explore the body of another man, here's your opportunity...

I'm feeling wild and confident so I go to the erotic corner, though I'm not even with someone and people usually come here in couples. There's a youngish man seated there and I ask his name, we chat for a bit and he asks if he can stroke my hair and my arms and absolutely yes. Then he asks if he can take my bra off—I took my top off earlier, when I was dancing—and I'm in the wildness so I say yes and he does. He so delicately strokes my breasts with the tips of his fingers, I'm sitting up and we're looking at each other and I feel sparkling with starlight and electricity; with light. Then he thanks me and moves away and another, older man—probably my own age—asks if he can give me a massage and I like the look, the feel of him so I say yes and I lie down and he strokes his hands over my body and I fall and fall, into touch and gentleness. I'm falling.

After the massage I watch an interaction in the center of the room between two men, one young and Viking-like in build and coloring, the other older, more darkly colored, his body slight but also fitter as they prowl around each other, leaping forward sometimes to grapple, wrestle; a mock fight that flings out arms and legs, that powers first one and then the other backward through the space with the strength of impact, their arms locked together at the shoulders, their feet grappling for a hold on the floor. Fiercer and tighter it gets, like watching a dance, choreography but there's shouting involved, growling, roaring and in the middle of one intense wrestled moment they kiss, suddenly, mouth to mouth then they're trying to tip each other over and it's so beautiful my eyes nearly can't contain it, I have to look away. When I look back their bodies, still standing, are twined together like lovers, they're thrusting up against each other and more kisses but the wrestling hasn't stopped entirely; they're subsumed by each other.

In a corner of the room I see a woman, naked, lying on her back, a man's head lying on her belly like the memory of being inside a womb, and then he kisses her skin and keeps kissing, all the way down to between her legs, he kisses her thighs with many kisses and then moves his mouth to her vulva and I'm weeping watching, remembering and oh it's been so long, years, and to see it like this is a gift, a reminder, this still exists in the world, it's not so far away from me, not impossible. It's paradise, this is within the auspices of the tree and all these dancing, loving, yearning human bodies, this is love embodied, reverence and softness and power.

There seems to be quite a lot of sex in different directions. It's not that I've never been in a room with people having sex before but the amount of it is surprising. I see a couple I know having sex and it's like a private glimpse into their relationship, I understand something about their dynamic I never did before. I see one woman having sex with a man and later I see her with another man and it's fierce for me, the impact of all this. I'm already shattered, already falling, so its patterns press in again and again, it's liberation, love, ecstasy, and being present, embodied spirit, a priestess in the temple, Eve with the serpent and the taste of fruit in my mouth. There's music through all this—I watch as one of the facilitators crosses the floor to the music console, naked with an erection pointing him through the space, it's all so beautiful. I'm laughing and crying in this whirl of people and events.

There's a man who's set up a tea ceremony in the talking corner; it's two Japanese cups and a teapot, he's sitting on a cushion and he's placed another cushion opposite him, with the tea in the middle. He's there for quite a long time, no one sits down, so eventually I go and take the empty cushion and he's courteous, almost formal though we're both half naked, and we drink tea and discuss our lives while meters away people are having sex and others are still dancing, behind my back, and some people are resting now, on the cushions and mattresses, singly or in couples or some in a cuddle puddle and it's late, the middle of the night but the air's still heated from the day. After the tea I'm standing near the tree, in the center of the room, and someone I know quite well comes up to me and puts his arms around me from behind, and I rest there, in his arms. It's the same man who told me he had my back, all that time ago, and here he is, he's still got my back. Another man comes up to talk to him, they have an intense conversation over my head and I don't care because I'm being held, being rocked by a double heart-beat, feeling his warmth all down my body and the closeness of him.

Eventually I leave, the event is drifting to an end. It's midnight. I see the woman who kissed me also walking to her car and we talk a little, but it feels fractured, I'm still filled with delight but she is reserved so I step back. I drive home along twisting roads, down one hill and then turn and up my own road, which is twenty minutes in the dark, my headlights cutting beams through the trees and turns. I'm nearly home when I see, stretched across the road—I have to stop the car—a snake. A carpet python, several meters long, slowly s-bending itself across the road, from the high side to the low side of the hill. I get out, leaving my headlights and blinkers on, and stand beside it, watching. Paradise. A tree. The kisses-dare-meetings of it. Now a serpent. I want to touch it but I know that makes them move really fast and even more, I want to see it, let the image sear into my eyeballs. I watch until it's completely vanished, then I get in the car and finish driving home.

In bed it's after 1 a.m. and I fall into sleep and dream I'm in the temple. That exact temple, where I was this evening, the octagonal Paradise room, I'm in it still, again—those images, sensations, I feel them on my skin still and I wake and am surprised to find I'm not there and I fall asleep again into the dream, or another, the same; I'm in the temple, it's all around me and within me, I'm in it and of it, born to it and falling through it, the tree at the center and me at the base of it—paradise, I'm in paradise. I wake again, or half-wake and then another dream; all night it feels I'm there, I never left, the temple is in me and of me, the touch vibrating all over and through me, I'm blasted, rendered open by beauty and tears rising up through my throat. I'm shaking, delight is pouring out of me, I'm trembling, dizzied with feeling and breath, so expanded open I can't leave. I've eaten it, it's part of me.

• • • •

I'm in a city and I arrange to meet a man I've chatted with for a while. When I walk into the wine bar he's unmistakable, on a stool at the bar, swiveled to see the door. He's slender, slight, self-contained and he's wearing black jeans with a colorful patterned shirt and silver wire glasses. I'm wearing black jeans with a magenta pink velvet jacket, and my glasses have flakes of gold leaf in the frames. Already it feels sexy. I sit next to him, he buys me a glass of wine, and we talk. He's urbane, a city man, soft hands, a job that uses the mind, and his name is the same as the city we're in, as if the city has come in human form to meet and flirt with me.

Sitting on barstools, drinking red wine, facing each other, there's a moment when, holding my gaze, he deliberately moves his black-jeaned leg so that it rests against my black-jeaned leg. I'm registering each second through the stilled air, my held breath, I'm so totally in the moment, so present to my life and this touch I'm almost exploding with it; it's like the intensity of Kether bound into a moment of time, a seed of it burst into life. Kether as a temple and Malkuth a wine bar; I love it. He says, still holding my gaze, *Is that okay?* Oh, it's so okay. Yes. *Yes.* It's the moment Malkuth leaps up to Kether, builds a bridge, and there's no separation, it's a shaft of light we have no way to describe, arcing through the Abyss from the top triad to the lower Tree, it's desire ignited. And the permission of it, the thrill, the elation—that movement trembled through the air between us, the vast distances of time and place and different lives, it pierced the moment, pinned it into my body and memory, and I am flooded with the erotic, that known realm that is my own—I breathe delight. It sears me, that moment.

We have a second drink, we talk a lot, we brush hands and legs and eyes and lean forward. Eventually it's late and we leave, walk through the darkened streets, arm in arm. He says he wants to kiss me and I want that too, a lot. We walk down a street close to where I'm staying, there are smallish trees stationed along the pavement, and he chooses one, carefully—the branches aren't too low, the outside lights of the house behind it aren't on—and he turns and takes me in his arms and I'm bound and unbound in the same moment.

There's a tree and his arms are around me. I feel the whole of him and breathe. The length of his body against mine, fulfilling that dare, promise, invocation of his leg against mine. I press my cheek against his for sheer pleasure and my breaths are all different—happier, I have happier breaths just for this—and then we start to kiss. Small kisses in the shadow of the tree, careful, tasting the idea of each other's mouth. Just one or two at first and then more, over my mouth and lips and in the corners and my hair gets caught and he smooths it back, it catches and we kiss some more, and we enter into a realm of kisses where they are running one into the next.

415

I have lost count of them. I'm sinking through them like layers of landscape and they aren't separate from one another, by now there are too many, cascading one into the next, and all my careful counting and accounting of kisses, for years, each one kept separate, counted like jewels—it's undone. I'm in the raw force pouring through me, I'm in a waterfall of kissing, the force of it, mouth open as it pours over me, a rain of kisses. I belong to it, undone and remade and brought through with uncounted kisses under a tree. It shelters us. He puts his cold hands, slender, gentle, and deliberate hands, on my skin, under my clothes.

Under a tree I'm kissing, in delight, a man with the name of the city written on him, and I know that every time I see this tree, forever, I will remember this and be captured and set free by it again. I'm half crying, half laughing, and he kisses soft and delicate, deeper and then back to kisses on the side of my mouth and teasing; they are playful, serious, intent kisses and I'm remade, my whole body singing. Time has stopped. All of the rituals, the possibilities, the minuscule movements edging toward this are met and answered in a torrent, I've found myself and the universe has finally come for me and I'm celebrating, every atom. It's midnight as we stand kissing by the tree, and I don't even mind waiting all these years—I've discarded my long desperation in moments, turned away from all those tears and tearing longings—I'm here. In the Tree, in the mystery, with his hands on my skin. Once or twice I have to stop kissing because I am smiling so much. The tree. Kisses. Knowledge. Paradise. One.

ritual | The Gate of Death

Earth is believed in various mythologies to have gateways or entrances to other realms, including the Underworld of Greek, Sumerian, and Egyptian lore, the Heaven of Christianity, and, less dramatically, gateways into the realms of dreams, the inner planes of Western occult magic, and others. These other realms are understood as existing concurrently with ours—sometimes even interwoven with our own rather than separate places, as with the collective unconscious or the Australian Aboriginal Dreaming. Access to these realms may be accidental, the result of using the correct rituals or codes (often after years of applied study, research, and practice), hereditary, revelatory, through dreams or visions, or during significant life events sometimes called rites of passage, whether formalized in ceremony or just as they occur in our lives.

We are all familiar with two of these gateways: birth and death. Sometimes these are thought of as the same gate that we pass through in opposite directions, arriving into this embodied form through the gate of life and leaving through the gate of death. Many religions have deeply concerned themselves with what is on the other side of this gate, but it seems clear that no one has the absolute answer. The Kabbalist might ask if all the theories hold truth, are each a different perspective of the same thing? That is, we go to sleep, never to wake again (in this current form, though the atoms that composed us continue); we are reborn (the chemicals and molecules that make us up clearly are reborn into other forms); we live through our descendants (through the DNA); death is final and forever (to this current form of body, personality, and living thread of history); and we pass up to Heaven or become one with God (we never left that state because we are forever part of the All).

The Tree of Life glyph lays out a pattern for us to explore these gates into life and death as we descend through the sephirot from Kether all the way to Malkuth, and then as we reverse or continue our journey in the great round and leave Malkuth, heading all the way up through the sephirot until we reach Kether, perhaps realizing that we never left. One of Malkuth's names is the Gate of Death because once we're here, we're bound to die.

In the journey of this book we've been stepping down stage by stage, sephira by sephira, stopping at each one to learn more about the Tree, the sephira, magic, and ourselves. In this ritual we will move all the way up through the Tree in one sustained movement. The invitation is to include ritual aspects and to do it physically.

You can do this ritual alone or with a group.

TIME: 1 hour

YOU WILL NEED: Your 11 sephirot disks, journal and pen, coloring things optional, ritual items, drinking water, two cushions or chairs

Preparation for the Gate of Death Ritual

Before you begin, consider what you would like your ritual to consist of.

I have witnessed people light a candle at each of the sephirot as they pass through. I have seen people dance up through the Tree, strip naked, sing and chant, make obeisance. I have been part of rituals where elaborate altars were built at each sephira or a single tarot card lay waiting to be turned over and read or one magical tool rested at each place. I have walked up the Tree naming aloud what I release at each sephira and the opposite, calling out the qualities of the divine found at each place and inviting those qualities to wash through me. I have heard of the sephirot becoming the voices of ancestors, trees in a forest, pillars of a temple.

The Ritual

Lay out your eleven sephirot disks—whether decorated, undecorated, or a mix of the two—on the floor in the Tree of Life pattern. Place whatever ritual objects you have decided upon on or near the disks. Put your journal, pen, and coloring things near the Kether disk. You might also want a cushion or chair where you will be spending time at either end, next to or below Malkuth and near Kether. Put your drinking water at Kether.

Beginning at or below Malkuth—sometimes I sit or stand on the disk itself—spend a few moments relaxing your body and becoming aware of your breath. Then with your eyes either closed or on soft focus, take yourself into a light trance state, one where you will still easily be able to move around and carry out your ritual. Give yourself five minutes to deepen into this.

Within the trance, open your eyes and gaze at this version of the Tree you've created, your unique disks. Let yourself be aware of the life in you—perhaps you can feel your pulse, heartbeat, or breath continually moving in and out. Open your awareness to each of your senses in turn—sight, sound, smell, taste, touch. Allow five minutes to fully inhabit these senses.

Let yourself be aware of the Gate of Birth you entered through to inhabit this body and life. Perhaps you can sense it shimmering above or through the Tree, perhaps you know the story of your birth or offer a moment of gratitude to your mother for birthing you, perhaps you feel it as an aura or field you carry within or around you. You might acknowledge to yourself how long it is since you passed through this gate into life and the life you have led. It might come to you in flashes of memories, shapes or colors, a felt sense, or some other way.

Then summon up or allow the Gate of Death to arise. It may be the same gate or a different one. Imagine that this moment, now, is your final moment of life. Perhaps you will take a deep breath and release it, perhaps it will seem sad to you or joyful or some other way. At another time you might explore these thoughts and feelings more deeply, but for now stand if you have been seated and turn your focus to the Malkuth disk.

Whatever ritual you have planned or spontaneously feel to do, begin it now. Then move up the lightning flash toward Yesod, passing through the Gate of Death. At Yesod, complete the next piece of your ritual and continue on, up the lightning flash, to Hod, Netzach, Tiferet, Gevurah, and Chesed, undertaking your ritual at each sephira as you go. When you are facing the Abyss, you might take an extra moment before crossing through. For many people this feels as if it is the final seal on passing through the Gate of Death; from here there can be no return. It might be the equivalent to passing over Lethe, the River of Forgetting in the Greek Underworld, or the final signs of life leaving the body.

Then continue over the Abyss, past Da'ath, and through the remaining sephirot, Binah, Hokmah, and Kether, continuing your ritual at each place. When you have completed the ritual at Kether, you may choose to turn and face down the Tree or you might remain facing toward the Ain Soph and the endless nothing. Breathe for a moment in this still-living body of yours and then complete the ritual by returning from the light trance state, drinking some water, and sitting down at Kether to record your ritual in your journal.

activity | Creating the Tenth Disk

As you complete the work of this section, create your final disk to represent the sephira you've been with. This will be your tenth disk. Perhaps you began with Kether and so you are now up to Malkuth; in that case, it will be the brown Malkuth disk you are working with. Perhaps you began somewhere else in the Tree and so the disk you are making now is for Binah, Hod, Tiferet, or any other sephira.

TIME: 30–60 minutes

YOU WILL NEED: The appropriate colored disk (see page 69, "Creating the First Disk") and whatever art materials you wish to work with, such as colored pens and markers, paint, oil pastels, collage materials and glue, stickers

Start by contemplating the time you have spent in this sephira, including looking through your journal notes and recalling any Kabbalah exercises, processes, or rituals you did and especially how these related to this particular sephira, as well as the general mood and events in your life during this time. At this final sephira you might want to complete any themes that have been running throughout your previous disks.

Allow images, words, feelings, and ideas to arise. You can hold these in your head, immediately begin work on your disk, or jot down notes or a sketch.

Mark the name of the sephira onto the disk.

Decorate your disk, creating an image or set of images, with or without words, that will recall your time spent with this sephira. This might represent a culmination of your time in the Tree, as well as your time with this sephira. If you are working with Malkuth, some visual representations of this sephira divide the image into four quarters, which are colored black, citrine, olive, and russet, or variations on this. Coloring four quarters for the elements of earth, air, fire, and water is an alternative. Choose whatever art materials you are inspired by to create your image.

You might complete your work in one session or come back later to add more.

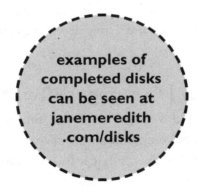

examples of completed disks can be seen at janemeredith .com/disks

the white cockatoos sweep through
the cemetery as the oceans risen into
mountains the stars broken and
falling to earth, angels, the ladders
in rays of light through clouds the
shards shattered everywhere and
each life each mending the rip
taking us closer to the end of time—

burnt umber mud earth soil humus
fertile potent waiting as a broken
butterfly falls to earth dead or
dying its wings torn, colors shredded
but still sparkling here or there in
a dewdrop spiders web dawn ray
tattered and pure, the broken form
of Kether falls and is received

forms, faces flicker into being a
pulse of starlight and are gone again
like watching the stars going out or
watching the stars being born death
and birth all turning journeying
in and through the sparks, the
scattered drops of light the forms
they wear the force of them the
butterfly bright, flying, flinging
itself through time, fractured falling
broken fallen

II
Da'ath

Hovering between Kether and Tiferet in the zone known as the Abyss is an acknowledgment of Da'ath. Often drawn into diagrams as a dotted outline the same size and shape as the ten sephirot, Da'ath shimmers between being and not being. The lightning flash is usually drawn only to the edges of the sephirot—it goes under or invisibly through them before emerging on the other side—but at Da'ath the lightning flash goes right over it as if it wasn't really there.

Da'ath is like an electron—we know it's somewhere within the Abyss, but it could be anywhere at any given time. Or anywhen. We put it into our diagrams so we don't forget it, but the dotted outline is always a reminder that it's not really there or not exactly *there*; it's only a possibility, an echo, an idea. This makes it unique within the structure of the Tree. It's a useful repository for anything that can't be explained by the All and Everything of the Tree itself. Maybe it's the shadow left behind from the fall of Malkuth to the vast distance at the bottom of the Tree. Maybe it's a sephira that hasn't quite arrived yet—after all, the universe is still unfolding. Maybe we keep it there to remind us of dark matter and dark energy, the vast unknowns the universe still holds; the equivalent of dragons at the edge of a map. Or perhaps its presence simply reminds us of the deep mysteries, as its name, Knowledge, infers.

Da'ath is given no color and only an approximate position. It also has no number, in the numbering of sephirot, and no path assigned to it. It is truly a lone wolf. Rachel Pollack points out, citing Allen Moore, that if we want to assign a number to Da'ath, there is a number that lies between three and four on our number scale (Binah being number three and Chesed number four)—and it's pi (π): 3.1415926535—and continuing (Pollack 2005, 98). Without end. The ratio of a circle's circumference to its diameter and circles are how the sephirot are always drawn, though we would have no way to measure their circumference or their diameter.

Da'ath's dotted outline invites us to seek knowledge and surrender to not knowing.

Da'ath: *The Question of Knowledge*

There's a ghost in the system. Haunting the Tree is a non-sephira, a possibility—maybe it's a memory or a glimpsed echo from the outer edges of space from a time when we will no longer be, swallowed up by the same intangible nothingness we emerged from. A question of Knowledge or a clue on the quest for knowledge. Maybe it's an alternate universe or a bridge to unknown worlds or a coiled serpent offering forbidden fruit. There's a glitch, an echo, an after-impression when we close our eyes against the piercing light but can still see something. A dark radiating sphere—perhaps it's a black hole with light curving around it like a lover, perhaps it's the event horizon—and what event would that be, if it wasn't the beginning of all things or the end? Or they're the same at this point, hovering below Kether, within the Abyss, the great divide: a dotted circle of no-place, no-time. Galaxies eat each other, and I am at the edge of being eaten even trying to think about this, let alone put words onto a page.

Dion Fortune's offering is that words make a bridge so that what was previously impossible moves toward the realm of the possible; or we move, perhaps, over that bridge into the realms of the impossible. She didn't say that second part, but it seems logical. We can see bridges across the Abyss: the three pillars. There's a more insubstantial, magical bridge as well: the lightning flash—there for a moment, then gone, spanning in a great arc of electricity or light, concentrated light—or the great serpent itself across the divide from the top triad to the lower Tree, specifically from Binah to Chesed. So we catch a ride like a slippery slip down the snake of snakes and ladders. Pillars make excellent ladders, so we have Jacob's ladder and Eve's serpent, and we can glimpse (maybe something, maybe nothing) as we pass by over the Abyss. Like gazing at the Alps or the Siberian steppe out the window of a plane. I've done that—seen the sharpness of them stabbing up into the atmosphere toward heaven, the hours and hours of unending landscape, wondered at the miracle of them, knowing I would never go there.

I am not capable of this. But perhaps I can describe the sense of a shape that isn't there—the cut-out shape of a dark tree, backlit, the mystery of dark matter, the suck of a black hole, the answer to the question of not what was there before the universe's moment of singularity, but why that moment ever occurred... access to the mind of God. And isn't it interesting that everything in the Tree is described in terms of light and gradations of light, yet we don't know what light is—the great universal constant that can't be explained. But here, in/around/through the area of what we are pleased to call Da'ath, there's no light and it's also not dark, it's not a degree of lightness/darkness at all. It's an absence; the other side—of something. The non-dual opposite of a world understood through duality. A portal, perhaps.

I've been avoiding this for weeks, months; I've completely stopped writing. I'm terrified. At the beginning of the book I put off addressing Da'ath, skipped over it as I slipped between Binah and Chesed, and I've been writing for a year with this lingering unrest in the corners of my mind of the book—what's going to happen when I have to write about Da'ath? Can I not have Da'ath at all? Can I just refer here and there, in passing, to this mystery and leave it sleeping or breathing or looming or whatever it's doing? Do I really have to lead an excursion there, into the dragon's cave, when actually I don't know the way and the safety procedures are nonexistent?

I've been thinking about it for a year, and for the year and a half before that, when I was completely stuck on the entire book, which I used to describe as watching two octopuses wrestling. Trying to keep track of all the tentacles, impossible and constantly moving, as well as being underwater, and then I saw, just last week, a video of two octopuses courting, mating, making love—whatever octopuses do. I was at the dentist's. They have a screen above the chair and mostly I had my eyes closed but just at this moment I opened them. It was an underwater documentary with no sound but the subtitles turned on and I realized that was the image in my mind, all this time—they weren't fighting, those octopuses; they were having sex. All their tentacles were twining and twisting and looping and sucking onto each other's; it was confusing but exciting. The subtitles said that their erotic encounter involves all sixteen tentacles, is very elaborate, and lasts for many hours, and shortly afterward they die.

Ah. Death and sex. That's always been the heart of the mystery in the Garden of Eden. For an octopus, for a star, a universe; that knowledge. Knowledge with a capital K, knowledge to live and die for, to risk everything, the transition point. Octopuses making love or—if not love, if octopuses don't love and that's a human concept that somehow we can't apply to octopuses—then that other L word, life. Making life. Octopuses making life, which brings about death, the two as inextricably woven together as those sixteen tentacles in the fierce ecstasy of living, consumed by passion, atoms dancing, particles entangled and all burning itself up, exploding into life like the original moment. Thank you, octopuses, for reminding me, for pointing it out, for re-entangling your particles so convincingly and showing me how obscure and complicated and fatal passion is; how Knowledge is the key to mortality—sex and death together. Existence.

So now I'm thinking of Da'ath as a keyhole in this whole diagram of the Tree, that's why it's just dotted, barely there, but if you have the key, you can enter. If the key you hold is the same shape as the keyhole, which is maybe a black hole, just to be clear, so it's a one-way ride, a zero-sum game where you are completely deducted from this universe and end up elsewhere. On the other side. Maybe in the Dark Tree. It's a keyhole I can't actually see but am guessing at, sensing, even knowing in a way I can't explain or justify, and then what is the key? Each one of us, surely; the only way anything makes sense is that each one of us has complete access to this key or each one of us *is* the key. I don't mean only humans. Each star. Each black cockatoo. Each tree fern, waterfall, pebble. Each shower of rain, each butterfly, each atom. To be precise, each death. Each death is the gateway away from ones and into the zero—

There's some confusion about the trees in the Garden of Eden—whether there are two forbidden trees, the Tree of the Knowledge (of Good and Evil) and the Tree of Life, or whether they are really just one tree. Rachel Pollack suggests one interpretation is that the Tree of Life lies within the Tree of Knowledge (Pollack 2005, 31). And in Genesis the serpent says if Eve and Adam eat of the fruit of the tree (of Knowledge), *thou shalt be as gods*. After, God hurries them out of Paradise, worried that if they (also) eat of the Tree of Life they will be like gods, as gods, gods maybe—but perhaps it's too late. There's a few slips in the editing here, the fruit of both trees seeming to lead to the same outcome: being *as gods*, and also—the supposed One God is worrying about the possibility or plurality of gods?—but it's all too late for the serpent, and Adam and Eve, to argue editorial inconsistencies. They receive a punishment: a life sentence, which is always a death sentence, but not quite yet—you get to live first. And without the death part, you wouldn't. So it's all good, more or less. We know this. Knowledge.

Now here we are, descendants of those who've eaten the fruit, still driven by desire, curiosity, hunger, daring, a quest for knowledge, defiance of the gods, all while still striving to please them/be like them/become them—we're not entirely sure which, perhaps all of that. We've fallen from Paradise, which seems the only story arc available really, and falling is a bit of a theme. The whole of cosmology, past the point of singularity, could be viewed as falling—everything endlessly falling out and away. The name *the Big Bang* was apparently a derogatory off-the-cuff comment made by a detractor of the theory during a radio interview, not meant to accurately describe the event, and perhaps the Endless Fall would be a better one. The great falling out of matter, space, and time, still ongoing. And there's Lucifer's fall as well—Lucifer, whose name means "light bearer," referencing that inexplicable constant.

Oh it's getting rich here—no wonder they wanted to eat of it. Put it into your mouth, taste and chew and swallow—ingest. Like small children. Like lovers. It's what I secretly (well, not so secret since I've written it here) desire to do with ancient manuscripts—taste them. Swallow small pieces of them, have them infuse through me, their atoms, let my particles entangle with them again, remembered. Like the body and blood of Christ in the Catholic eucharist or the bread and wine of Pagan gods and goddesses—Demeter, Dionysus—eat of my body, drink my blood, become one with me. I can imagine them dissolving on my tongue. It's a good thing they keep them under glass. Apples, pomegranates, secret knowledge, the mysteries of life, sex, ancient manuscripts—let me taste, let me change and be changed by it.

It's suggested that once Malkuth inhabited this position directly below Kether. That they were that close before the Fall—closer than Kether is to Tiferet—and still are, maybe. One or both of those falls, angels or humankind, but perhaps it's the same fall, really, the pride to dare God, *to be as gods*—to eat forbidden fruit, the desire to live free, to be light falling endlessly through the cosmos ... and Malkuth tumbled down, with the shock and strength of that, falling all the way through the Tree to the very bottom, the roots, or, if you see it the other way, out to the tips of the branches, the leaves waving in the silent winds of the cosmos that sweeps stars about, falling, further and further out ... and we're still looking backward at the view.

This is reminding me of the shattering of vessels, the fall of shards through the Tree of Life and even down into our world, this Malkuth existence we live and die in. Tikkun olam, the Jewish practice of mending the world, engages each one of us humans in doing essentially the work of gods. With our actions we redeem the brokenness of the world. It is us who can plant trees in a devastated landscape. Reach out a hand to someone who's grieving, lost, in pain, distress. Open our hearts. Celebrate life and invite others to celebrate with us. Vote on the basis of social rather than personal good. Shape our words to be caring, curious, and respectful. Pick up that piece of rubbish. Offer help where it's needed, and be generous as we travel through life, through the Tree, falling with grace when we can.

Each life is a universe, is a Kabbalistic teaching. For those who save a life, they are said to have saved the equivalent of a world. Thus putting one's life at risk or even dying to save someone else becomes a world-saving act. Nobody says, since the sources are mainly patriarchal, but—I wonder what it is to give birth to another human? To create a universe, so to speak... When we value life this highly, and even the lives of strangers, it's easy to imagine divine love. Like the reflection of Hokmah back to Kether, we gaze with wonder, adoration, and worship at the other, seeing the divine shining through them. I wouldn't stop at humans either—there's no special reason why a human is a more perfect reflection of the divine, any more a true piece of the Endless Fall, than anything or everything else. The earth. Each piece of it. Each piece of everything. Every single entangled particle. As far as I can see, this makes every single and multiple thing as the beloved of God; well, actually entirely a part of the I Am but also beloved. Each person we meet reflects this. Each tree, each stalk of grain, each wind, each star.

I had a moment in Victoria Main Line Station in London. It's a rush of hundreds of people at almost every hour of the day and night, crossing through the forecourt in multiple directions. I had been doing my Other Selves practice as I walked through; it's a great place for it. Suddenly, without my wishing or intention, it went in all directions, out from me to multiple people at once. I felt myself for a second, a few seconds, become each one of dozens of them, not one after the other but simultaneously. It was dizzying. I can't forget it. I wasn't seeking it, hadn't considered it as a result or possibility of this practice. For a breath I *was* them, moving in all directions, filled with all sorts of lives, the fractals of a tiny piece of humanity, covering maybe twenty square meters in Victoria Station, and they all ran through me, I was within each of them all at once, as real as me, aspects and myself just one, just the one having that experience. Malkuth and Kether at the same time.

Then there's Da'ath. The nothing. That dotted cut-along-this-line almost-something, not-quite-anything in the middle of the Tree. A black hole, perhaps. Light cannot escape from a black hole—light, that constant friend—well, nothing can escape, but it's significant that light also can't. The sephirot are all about arriving; each one is a place of arrival. But Da'ath never arrives—it's all about falling. Falling in love, falling through a black hole, falling down to Malkuth, falling through the Tree, the act of falling in each moment. Surrender. The portal, initiation, transformation. When we totally make love with life, with Life, that's death. We give it everything and fall through, from the everything back into the nothing, through Da'ath. From the particle to the wave. Making love to the divine with our whole life (death). That's the key. The key that each of us is—and it's the bite of the apple and the kiss and breath of life, the inbreath into ourselves, our separateness, and the outbreath where we join up to everything again because particles, once entangled, never really forget.

Sex. It's all about sex—the kiss of breathing in union with the trees, with our world. The sex of being born, of dying. The sex of eyes meeting, of bodies, the sixteen tentacles, that great becoming where we're more than ourselves, we're also the other and together we touch/become/remember/kiss the divine. That's us. All the distinctions that dissolve as we merge. One body plus one body equals All, or zero—we glimpse it. Offer ourselves, our lover, from the All to the nothing. Knowledge. Death and sex—the becoming and unbecoming. If humans have a special place in the universe, it's that we question this, whereas starfish and river lilies and fruit flies don't have to question it. They already know.

What's the difference between wisdom, understanding, and knowledge? someone helpfully asked me. Or—Wisdom, Understanding, and Knowledge? Hokmah, Binah, Da'ath. Wisdom—the reflection of the divine—from the pillar of force. Understanding—the move toward embodiment—from the pillar of form. When I *understand* something it makes sense to me, almost viscerally; I can feel my alignment with it emotionally, physically. Wisdom is both, more and less; it involves comprehending the implications of something, its place and meaning in contexts and depth. It's not just happening within my body/self but links into wider schema.

Knowledge, though. That's guarded/secret/many-layered. It is secrets: one can read the words or see the form, but if you don't know the symbols, the codes, it means nothing. It deepens in layers. It's initiatory, it's a change-state. Understanding and wisdom are evolving, unfolding, but knowledge is a definite thing. Once it is revealed you cross a barrier, pass the initiation, eat the apple—it's part of you. Death is like that. Our own, obviously, or being witness to or holder of someone else's. Birth is like that. Sex is like that. The knowledge that rewrites us. We're never the same afterward. Knowledge must be lived, it's the experience of the mystery—as in biblical knowledge, sexual knowledge, *they knew each other* (Adam and Eve), and also the Tree of the Knowledge of Good and Evil. Eating of this tree signifies maturing, an initiation into a previously unrealized state.

I am part of everything. I am a (single) part of the everything. I am part of everything that is. Da'ath is non-dual. Perhaps the whole middle pillar is held in non-duality or implies that. But Da'ath is an extreme—the everything of the sephirot can endlessly find and create duality. Da'ath swallows and transforms, its great teachers of death and sex are points of disappearing, points we can't see beyond, event horizons where we can't know whatever's happening to those beings involved in it. They know, though; they embody knowledge, become Knowledge in that moment, being swallowed by it.

I was driving up the hill toward home when I saw a vision. Like all the best visions, it was really there. The sun was setting. I was driving west. The road was rising on a bend so that ahead of me and somewhat above I saw the silhouette of a tree. It was a tall tree, immense both because of its height and because it was above me on the hill, etched out by the light of the sky behind it like a black cut-out stylized shape of Tree. It's winter but like most Australian trees, it was still covered in leaves. The light of the setting sun caught through it and sparkled like candle flames. Hundreds of them all throughout the tree. The Tree of Lights. I've read of this but it was there, in front of me, just that moment. I recognized it. Knowledge—knowledge made it the Tree of Lights for me, the Tree of Life—alight with the flames of the words that begin the world, alight like a portal. It's the exact same bit of road where I found the serpent after the temple night, exactly there, and suddenly it's all here—snakes and Trees and light—and I'm eating knowledge, seeking the mysteries of union through intimacy and sex and each breath, each face, each moment. I can't write this. But I can live it.

If you eat of the tree of life (light), you become immortal; that is, you die and join back into the All. When we eat the light/are swallowed up by the knowledge of the non-duality of all things, nothing separates us from the All, the I Am That I Am; we are that. We both become the Tree and are swallowed by it. Universes are born here, each one of us. Life and love. Mostly we don't know about this. But sometimes, or some of us, or in some moments we take the dare and eat and are consumed by knowledge. Then we fall into the spaces that our dare has opened and discover the All and the nothing through the portal of obliteration and transformation.

Dark matter is nearly a quarter of the universe, and we don't know what it is, only that it's everywhere, all around and through all the matter that we see and know, although five times greater in mass, approximately. Then there's dark energy, nearly three-quarters of the universe, and we can describe that even less, us little beings of matter, how could we possibly? But one hypothesis is that it's dark energy that is pulling the universe apart at ever-increasing speeds. So perhaps Da'ath isn't just a portal of obliteration but also a source that pours forth, as Kether does, but this time darkness instead of light. Light/matter is rare when you look around the universe. How far the stars are apart, how much empty/dark space lies between. Just like atoms, and sephirot as well, how far away each of them is. These little flecks of matter amidst 96 percent of unknown/invisible matter/energy.

Trying to think or write about this, even just to be present with it, we're back to being the butterfly, falling through the vast tree and trying to describe it, our experience of it, as the tree and the winds of the universe tatter our wings and we catch glimpses, breaking and tumbling toward death and disintegration, and we know with every quiver through our living being we are intrinsically a part of it all, but butterflies… you know. They are so brief. So bright but so brief. Sipping at the nectar of life and flying through a world they can't describe, making life, making light, making love, and then almost immediately dead and rotting back to beautiful particles to be recycled in the great turning of matter, life to death and back again through the portal with the key of us every time and we're brave butterflies as we paint our wings with saturated color, dense with light to call the flowers to us, our lovers, to have a chance to sip nectar, the drink of the gods, that's us, *thou shalt be as gods and taste the fruit*—and the punishment, the reward, is death, is Da'ath, is knowledge, and we live it brightly and fiercely, wingbeat by wingbeat.

and we make love—the stars and
the universe, oh and I was there,
too, and you, and all of us—we
make love with existence in each
breath, our breath with the trees,
the green ones a shared breath, we
make love in each breath or light,
we make light in each breath we
are light, light and falling through,
cutting shapes in darkness we're
sparks, falling, butterfly wings
torn and tearing, breaking, broken
open to dissolve again, again, each
breath, dying—falling—being
born—All

I Am That I Am resounds through
the universe we still hear its echo
and vibrate, all through, each life a
vibration of this song and we know
what we've always known, and
die a little each breath and choose
again and again to risk, to dare, to
kiss, to live and be the falling spark

making love with our whole, utter
existence, each breath

we're making love in the garden,
in the library, in the temple, we're
making love with forever and its
star-core-iron and luminescent
pearl, we're eating the world that's
eating us, the stars are broken into
shards and that's us, the dying/
living sparks of them the breath the
pulse the kiss surrender

falling

Ritual Skills
Appendix

435

Grounding

Grounding is a fundamental practice, both in magic and in life, that connects us to the physical reality of our bodies and the earth. In Kabbalistic terms, grounding reorients us to Malkuth. Being grounded within our bodies is the basis for each breath, thought, and experience we have, including complex experiences such as trance, magic, and personal or group process. A grounding practice returns our awareness to—or holds our awareness within—that basic reality. You might already have a way to ground yourself or perhaps a library of many ways to do this. Some of the simplest techniques may be the best in stressful situations: we take a deep breath, place a hand on our solar plexus, have a mouthful of water, shake our body, or focus on the sensations in the soles of our feet.

A favorite grounding technique of many people, and a classic in the Reclaiming Tradition, involves imagining ourselves to be tree-like, feeling etheric roots dropping from our feet or the base of our spine down into the earth and following the roots through earth, rock, minerals, underground waters, and even underground fires. Then we bring our attention back into our bodies, up the spine—or trunk of the tree—and next imagine our arms as branches, reaching up and out toward the sun and stars. We might lift our arms up and feel the stretch between above and below, with our own bodies the conduit between earth and sky. We lean into the solidity of the tree and its deep relationship with the nurturing earth. We let ourselves feel anchored in space, time, and body.

Another tree image I like to work with is imagining or sensing myself at the base of the Tree of Life. It is immense, stretching way over my head, and I am one of the creatures sheltering beside it, my life a reflection of, and dependent on, its life. Instead of closing my eyes, I hold the idea within me and then connect briefly to each of my senses to confirm it. I can smell the moist ground after rain. I can hear the birds muted in the cloudy day. I can still taste the fruit I ate for breakfast. I feel the cooler air on my bare arms coming through the open window. I look up from the computer and see a tree, a eucalypt, like a poem stretching out to the sky. All these sensations I build into my image of myself at the base of the Tree until I feel the truth of that metaphor as a lived reality.

Grounded awareness is not a special event only done prior to magic and ritual. The idea is that we live our lives from this place, minute to minute, to fulfill the strength of who we actually are: embodied scraps of universal matter. Everything we do, we do as this body, so the more fully present we are within it, the more purposeful, effective, and magical we can be.

Sacred Space

Some people cast circles to contain their magic and ritual. Others acknowledge sacred land and Indigenous peoples and culture. Others invoke astral temples, recite prayers, incantations, or the names of gods, inscribe banishing pentacles into the quarters, or build an altar, light candles, make offerings. We are all seeking to create a boundary, a crucible for our magic: a Gevurah boundary to contain a Chesed flow, arriving at a Tiferet synergy to borrow imagery from the middle triad of the Tree.

What works for you? You might like to try a variety of techniques before settling on one that you use most times. You might prefer to be flexible in the moment, sensing into what's calling to you, what's needful or best suited to any situation.

Practical guidelines to help create your space for magic and ritual include:

▸ Have a definite time (both start and finish) and location for your ritual or magic, and make sure you won't be interrupted

▸ Prepare the space where you will work

▸ Organize the items you need beforehand

▸ Prepare yourself for magic, which may involve cleansing, meditation, special clothes or ritual jewelry, or another form of preparation

▸ Have clear agreements with any others involved around timing, content, and roles and responsibilities

Having done all this, we show up for the ritual or process. We sit or stand within the space and breathe for a while. Or we drum for ten minutes. Or cast a circle around the edges of the space. Or invoke the Tree of Life and its ten sephirot, laying out our disks. Or light a candle on the altar. Or …

One way that I work with magical space for Kabbalah is to lay out my disks on the floor. Sometimes they might be laid out far apart, other times close together, even overlapping. For some rituals I use just a few of my disks relevant to the work I'm doing. I bring everything I need with me—my journal and pen, other bits and pieces such as tealights and offerings, a cushion, and drinking water. Then I orient myself to the land. I name its names aloud and feel my place there—in Paris it would be as a traveler passing through, but also one with ancestral roots stretching through the land. In Huonbrook it is as a settler on an invaded and colonized land, but also as a gardener and caretaker. I ground myself into my body and the place. Then I turn through the directions sunwise, naming and acknowledging each one. I notice where the sephirot of my disks are located in relation to the directions. I call to above and below. If I have offerings to make or candles to light, I do that. I might sing or dance or just breathe a while before entering into my ritual.

One rule common across magical traditions is that when you are complete, reverse whatever casting you created to release it (and you) from that container of magic and ritual. If you invoked a temple and felt it rise from the ground around you, then at the end thank and acknowledge it and let it sink back into the ground. If you turned to all the directions as you cast a circle, turn back through them again, releasing the circle they held for you. Traditionally this is done in the opposite direction than you cast. If you invoked the Tree of Life, release that invocation for this immediate time and place. Offerings, once given, usually remain as offerings, so find an appropriate way to dispose of them. If you lit any candles that are still burning, put them out.

Trance

Trance is a term used to describe an altered state of mind, a little like a dream state but while we are awake. Other terms sometimes used include guided visualization, shamanic-style journeying, out-of-body-traveling, daydreaming, or imagination. My preferred term is *trance* since it implies, or even requires, control and agency during the experience. With a trance we decide how long it will last, how deeply we will enter into it, the type of content we will encounter, and when and how we will emerge. We understand that during the trance all our experiences are part of it and valid. We may or may not have visual images. We may lean more into realms of body sensations or gut feeling or memory or hearing or smell. It may be that we become super sensitive to what is happening around us or within us or curiously blank.

Entering and leaving trance is different for each person. As we do it more often, we learn what works for us. Some people will enter trance easily but have trouble entirely shaking it off; others are slower to enter but have more control over leaving. Some people work best with breath as a trance induction, others with a simple drumbeat, others with a visual image such as descending a spiral staircase or crossing a threshold. Usually once we are in the trance we have an agenda to follow—perhaps two or three points, sometimes called stations, to check in with—or perhaps we are undertaking a journey into a sephira or along a pathway.

Once we come to the end of either the time we have set or the content we planned to cover, we retrace the steps we took to enter the trance as a way of concluding it. So if we began with slow, conscious breathing, followed by a heartbeat played on a drum, followed by the image of crossing a threshold, on our return we will cross back over the threshold, play the drum heartbeat, and then return to slow, conscious breathing before opening our eyes and emerging completely from the trance. At that point we often stand up if we've been sitting, drink some water, pat down our bodies, stamp our feet on the ground. Usually we record our experiences as soon as possible as, like dreams, they can be hard to recall in detail later.

Trance work is a skill we can learn and develop. If you have never used trance, you can practice with mini sessions that are ten or fifteen minutes long, paying special attention to the entering and leaving parts. Once we've experienced a few trances, we can begin to tailor our experience, choosing to enter more deeply or more lightly, learning to maintain our attention over longer periods and return to the trance if for some reason we get distracted or emerge before we are ready. We can also enhance our sensing experience within the trance, asking ourselves for more focus or detail and expanding the senses we're aware of. We can ask, as we visualize a forest, *What sounds am I aware of? What might this forest smell like?* as well as leaning more heavily into the visual: *What are these trees I'm looking at? What can I see above me, at eye level, and on the ground?* If we are not primarily visualizers, still we can choose to ask ourselves questions such as *What image or symbol comes to me in this experience? Is there a color that belongs here? Do I have a memory of a similar place or experience?*

There's no way of distinguishing between a thought you might have had without the trance, a memory of something that may be resurfacing during a trance, and a spontaneous trance-induced experience, so we take our entire experience as equally valid: the real trance is the one you have. That might include such things as irritation from sounds next door, a half-remembered dream, the sound of a word whispered to you, a feeling of warmth, a vision of a temple, and a cramp in your left foot. Within the trance we may choose to focus on certain aspects, but the other pieces are also part of it. Some people feel frustrated with their trance experiences, that they're somehow not doing it right, maybe because they do not have Technicolor visions. Quieter, more subtle trance experiences can still give us material, perhaps even more directly than if we were distracted with the Technicolor. Accepting our experience as a base, whatever it is, gives us something to grow from if we wish to further develop our skills.

To begin a trance session, settle yourself comfortably, with all that you will need nearby. Some people like to stand for trance and others to sit or even move around. Lying down is not recommended unless you are very experienced in trance; it's just too easy to drift off into sleep. Remind yourself of the purpose, intention, and content of the trance you are about to enter. You may wish to set a timer or have the time nearby, easy to see. Perhaps you are already within a ritual or process, but if not, you may wish to ground, acknowledge sacred space, and take a few moments for conscious breathing.

For the trance induction, I favor a three-step process—three progressive stages to fully enter the trance. These three stages could be focusing on the room around you, breathing into the body, and following the breath inward. Or becoming aware of breath, focusing on the altar, and concentrating on the candle flame. Or breath, drumbeat, and threshold. Or sounds heard in the space/outside, body awareness, and listening within. Generally the focus narrows or moves closer toward the trance with each stage.

Then begin the work of the trance. Try not to rush your process but also remember why you are here. Fascinating side paths can be investigated another day. As each section of the trance concludes, you can ask yourself *Is there anything more for me here?*

What is the key piece of my learning? Is there any action I need to take? When the trance is completed or your time is up, bring yourself back in reverse order through the steps you took to enter the trance.

Ground yourself, return fully from the trance state, and record the trance in your journal.

resources

These are a selection of the books and resources I've found most helpful while inhabiting the realms of each of the sephirot. Nine novels are included, mostly of speculative fiction, as these seemed to me to convey an essence of the sephirot.

Kabbalistic sources, teachings, and resources abound in print and online; for example, the many hundreds of the late Rabbi David Cooper's audio teachings and meditations on his website, www.rabbidavidcooper.com.

Kether

Chown, Marcus. *Quantum Theory Cannot Not Hurt You: Understanding the Mind-Blowing Building Blocks of the Universe*. Faber & Faber Limited, 2007.

Cooper, David A. *God Is a Verb: Kabbalah and the Practice of Mystical Judaism*. Riverhead Books, 1998.

Schaya, Leo. *The Universal Meaning of the Kabbalah*. Fons Vitae, 2004.

Hokmah

Freke, Timothy, and Peter Gandy. *Jesus and the Goddess: The Secret Teachings of the Original Christians*. Thorsons, 2001.

Graves, Robert. *King Jesus*. Farrar, Straus and Giroux, 1981.

Rumi. *Rumi: The Book of Love: Poems of Ecstasy and Longing*. Translations and Commentary by Coleman Barks. HarperCollins, 2003.

Binah

Cooper, Rabbi David A. *Ecstatic Kabbalah*. Sounds True, 2005.

Parera, Sylvia Brinton. *Descent to the Goddess: A Way of Initiation for Women*. Inner City Books, 1981.

Slonczewski, Joan. *Brian Plague*. Tor Science Fiction, 2001.

Chesed

Diamant, Anita. *The Red Tent*. St. Martin's Press, 1997.

Pollack, Rachel. *The Kabbalah Tree: A Journey of Balance & Growth*. Llewellyn, 2005.

Yunkaporta, Tyson. *Sand Talk: How Indigenous Thinking Can Save the World*. Text Publishing, 2019.

Gevurah

Le Guin, Ursula. *The Dispossessed*. Harper Voyager, 1994.

Martin, Betty. Work on the Wheel of Consent. www.bettymartin.org

Starhawk. *The Empowerment Manual: A Guide for Collaborative Groups*. New Society Publishers, 2011.

Tiferet

Duquette, Lon Milo. *The Chicken Qabala of Rabbi Lamed Ben Clifford*. Weiser Books, 2001.

Regardie, Israel. *A Garden of Pomegranates: Skrying on the Tree of Life*. Edited and annotated with new material by Chic Cicero and Sandra Tabatha Cicero. Llewellyn, 2018.

Roberts, Michèle. *The Wild Girl*. Methuen, 1985.

Netzach

Abram, David. *The Spell of the Sensuous: Perception and Language in a More-Than-Human World*. Vintage Books, 2017.

Foster, Charles. *Being a Beast: Adventures Across the Species Divide*. Metropolitan Books, 2016.

Pullman, Philip. *His Dark Materials Trilogy: Northern Lights, The Subtle Knife, The Amber Spyglass*. Everyman, 2011.

Hod

Fortune, Dion. *The Mystical Kabbalah*. Weiser Books, 2000.

Gould, Stephan Jay. *Life's Grandeur: The Spread of Excellence from Plato to Darwin*. Jonathan Cape, 1996.

Powers, Richard. *The Overstory*. William Heinemann, 2018.

Yesod

Feinstein, David, and Stanley Krippner. *The Mythic Path: Discovering the Guiding Stories of Your Past—Creating a Vision of Your Future*. Tarcher, 1997.

Howard, Kat. *An Unkindness of Magicians*. Saga Press, 2017.

Taylor, Jeremy. *The Wisdom of Your Dreams: Using Dreams to Tap into Your Unconscious and Transform Your Life*. Tarcher/Penguin, 2009.

Malkuth

Lessing, Doris. *Re: Colonised Planet 5: Shikasta*. Flamingo, 1994.

Meredith, Jane, and Gede Parma. *Elements of Magic: Reclaiming Earth, Air, Fire, Water & Spirit*. Llewellyn, 2018.

Plotkin, Bill. *Soulcraft: Crossing into the Mysteries of Nature and Psyche*. New World Library, 2003.

glossary

ABYSS—Space of nothingness that appears on the Tree of Life map between the top triad and the rest of the Tree. Da'ath is contained within the Abyss, and the lightning strike goes through it.

ADAM KADMON—A human figure superimposed onto the structure of the Tree, with the sephirot associated with different body parts.

AIN SOPH—Situated above the Tree of Life, where Kether emerged from. It is both nothing, no-thing, and also endless light. The Ain Soph is sometimes divided into three segments, generally called Ain, Ain Soph, and Ain Soph Aur, all of which are degrees or aspects of nothingness, increasing potential, or density.

BIG BANG—The accepted term for the event that began our universe, approximately 13.8 billion Earth years ago.

BINAH—The third sephira. English translation: Understanding. The top sephira of the left-hand pillar.

CHESED—The fourth sephira. English translation: Mercy or Loving-Kindness. Middle sephira of the right-hand pillar.

COUNTING THE OMER—A Jewish practice over forty-nine days each year, beginning during Passover. Different attributes of the lower seven sephirot are reflected on each day for spiritual and personal development.

DA'ATH—A non-sephira that appears on the Tree of Life glyph within the Abyss, usually as a dotted outline of a sephira. English translation: Knowledge.

DISK—A physical representation of a sephira, usually made from cardboard and decorated.

FERI TRADITION—A contemporary witchcraft tradition also known by other spellings, originating with Victor Anderson.

GEVURAH—The fifth sephira. English translation: Power, Justice, or Strength. Middle sephira of the right-hand pillar.

GOLDEN DAWN (HERMETIC ORDER OF THE GOLDEN DAWN)—Extremely influential occult magical society in England during the early part of the twentieth century.

GROUNDING—A practice to support conscious embodiment.

HOD—The eighth sephira. English translation: Glory. The bottom sephira of the left-hand pillar.

HOKMAH—The second sephira. English translation: Wisdom. The top sephira of the right-hand pillar.

I AM—Shorthand for I Am That I Am, referring to Kether and the source of all that is.

I AM THAT I AM—A phrase denoting Kether in its aspect as the source and entirety of all that is.

IRON PENTACLE—A magical tool from the Feri and Reclaiming Traditions. Its five points are named Sex, Pride, Self, Power, and Passion.

JACOB'S LADDER—A version of the Tree of Life with four Trees superimposed over each other and a total of forty sephirot (some of them overlap from one level to the next).

glossary

KABBALAH—Historic and still-continuing body of Judaic wisdom and knowledge, a Jewish mystery tradition. English translation: To receive.

KETHER—The first sephira. English translation: Crown. The top sephira of the Tree of Life.

LIGHTNING FLASH—A zigzag motion through the Tree, usually from top to bottom, though it also can run the other way.

MALKUTH—The tenth sephira. English translation: Kingdom. The lowest sephira of all, in the middle pillar.

MIRIA—The reflection of the Star Goddess from the Feri and Reclaiming Creation story.

NETZACH—The seventh sephira. English translation: Eternity. The bottom sephira of the right-hand pillar.

PAIR—A set group of two sephirot, usually paired horizontally across the Tree from the right- and left-hand pillars, although sometimes vertical pairs are acknowledged within the middle pillar.

PARADISE—The biblical Garden of Eden. A strict translation is a walled garden.

PATH—The line that connects one sephira to another on the Tree of Life diagram.

PEARL PENTACLE—A magical tool from the Feri and Reclaiming Traditions, considered an aspect of the Iron Pentacle. Its five points are named Love, Law, Knowledge, Liberty, and Wisdom.

PILLAR—A vertical line of sephirot in the Tree of Life, of which there are three: the right-hand pillar, the left-hand pillar, and the middle pillar.

glossary

PRIESTEX—A nongendered and inclusive form of priest/priestess. Plural: priestexes.

RECLAIMING TRADITION—A contemporary tradition of witchcraft blending magic, political activism, and personal development.

SACRED SPACE—An intentional container created for magic and ritual.

SEPHIRA—Singular of sephirot. One of the disks on the Tree of Life. A ray, transmission, or aspect of the divine.

SEPHIROT—Plural of sephira. The ten disks on the Tree of Life are the sephirot.

SHATTERING OF THE VESSELS—A Kabbalistic story shared by the teacher Luria explaining how the lower sephirot (until Malkuth) were unable to hold the light that spilled into them and shattered.

SINGULARITY—The point which began our universe, when all of space and time were packed together immediately prior to the Big Bang.

STAR GODDESS—The primary and original deity in the Creation story of the Feri and Reclaiming traditions, She who is all things.

SUPERNAL TRIAD—The top triad of sephirot, composed of Kether, Hokmah, and Binah.

TIFERET—The sixth sephira. English translation: Beauty or Truth. The sephira at the center of the Tree, in the middle pillar.

TIKKUN OLAM—The Jewish practice of mending the world that each of us can play a part in with each action.

TRANCE—A deepened or sensitized state of awareness where we remain open to guidance, sensations, and experiences, including visual, auditory, and kinesthetic.

TRIAD—A set group of three sephirot, containing one each from the right, middle, and left pillars. There are three triads in the Tree: top, middle, and bottom.

TREE OF THE KNOWLEDGE (OF GOOD AND EVIL)—A tree in Paradise that Adam and Eve were forbidden to eat from. The serpent tempted Eve with its fruit, which led to the fall of humankind.

TREE OF LIFE—In Kabbalistic terms this is the diagram of the ten sephirot, sometimes drawn with pillars, paths, or other notations. The Tree of Life also refers to a tree in Paradise that Adam and Eve were forbidden to eat from.

TZIMTZUM—A Kabbalistic concept of a contraction of the Ain Soph that caused there to be enough room for Kether to be born.

YESOD—The ninth sephira. English translation: Foundation. The second lowest sephira, on the middle pillar.

references

Abram, David. *Becoming Animal: An Earthly Cosmology.* Vintage, 2011.

———. *The Spell of the Sensuous: Perception and Language in a More-Than-Human World.* Vintage Books, 2017.

Adams, Douglas. *Hitchhiker's Guide to the Galaxy.* Pan Books, 1981.

Blyton, Enid. *The Magic Faraway Tree Collection* (3-book set). Hodder & Stoughton, 2018.

Chown, Marcus. *Quantum Theory Cannot Hurt You: Understanding the Mind-Blowing Building Blocks of the Universe.* Faber & Faber Limited, 2007.

Cooper, David A. *God Is a Verb: Kabbalah and the Practice of Mystical Judaism.* Riverhead Books, 1998.

Duquette, Lon Milo. *The Chicken Qabala of Rabbi Lamed Ben Clifford.* Weiser Books, 2001.

Foster, Charles. *Being a Beast: Adventures Across the Species Divide.* Metropolitan Books, 2016.

Fortune, Dion. *The Mystical Kabbalah.* Weiser Books, 2000.

Freke, Timothy, and Peter Gandy. *Jesus and the Goddess: The Secret Teachings of the Original Christians.* Thorsons, 2001.

Gould, Stephan Jay. *Life's Grandeur: The Spread of Excellence from Plato to Darwin.* Jonathan Cape, 1996.

Laura, Judith. *Goddess Spirituality for the 21st Century: From Kabbalah to Quantum Physics.* Open Sea Press, 2011.

references

Lovelock, James. *Gaia: A New Look at Life on Earth*. Oxford University Press, 2000.

King James Bible

Kopecky, P. L. https://www.deviantart.com/plkopecky/art/Kabbalah-memebrane-animation-379410816

Martin, Betty. Work on the Wheel of Consent. www.bettymartin.org

Pollack, Rachel. *The Kabbalah Tree: A Journey of Balance & Growth*. Llewellyn, 2005.

Storl, Wolf-Dieter. *Shiva: The Wild God of Power and Ecstasy*. Inner Traditions, 2004.

Taylor, Jeremy. *The Wisdom of Your Dreams: Using Dreams to Tap into Your Unconscious and Transform Your Life*. Tarcher/Penguin, 2009.

Wohlleben, Peter. *The Hidden Life of Trees: What They Feel, How They Communicate: Discoveries from a Secret World*. Greystone Books, 2015.

www.hebrewtoday.com

www.walkingkabbalah.com

to write to the author

If you wish to contact the author or would like more information about this book, please write to the author in care of Llewellyn Worldwide and we will forward your request. Both the author and the publisher appreciate hearing from you and learning of your enjoyment of this book and how it has helped you. Llewellyn Worldwide cannot guarantee that every letter written to the author can be answered, but all will be forwarded. Please write to:

Jane Meredith
℅ Llewellyn Worldwide
2143 Wooddale Drive
Woodbury, MN 55125-2989

Please enclose a self-addressed stamped envelope for reply
or $1.00 to cover costs. If outside the USA, enclose
an international postal reply coupon.

• • • •

Many of Llewellyn's authors have websites with additional information and resources. For more information, please visit our website:

WWW.LLEWELLYN.COM